# The Transformation of Southeast Asia

D0148830

# The Transformation of Southeast Asia

International Perspectives on Decolonization

Marc Frey, Ronald W. Pruessen, and Tan Tai Yong, editors

An East Gate Book

*M.E.Sharpe*
Armonk, New York
London, England

An East Gate Book

Copyright © 2003 by M. E. Sharpe, Inc.

All rights reserved. No part of this book may be reproduced in any form
without written permission from the publisher, M. E. Sharpe, Inc.,
80 Business Park Drive, Armonk, New York 10504.

**Library of Congress Cataloging-in-Publication Data**

The transformation of Southeast Asia : international perspectives on decolonization / edited
by Marc Frey, Ronald Pruessen, and TAN Tai Yong.
    p. cm.
"An East gate book."
Includes bibliographical references and index.
ISBN 0-7656-1139-2 (cloth: alk. paper) — ISBN 0-7656-1140-6 (pbk.: alk. paper)
    1. Asia, Southeastern—History—1945– 2. Decolonization—Asia, Southeastern, History.
I. Frey, Marc, 1963– II. Pruessen, Ronald W. III. TAN, Tai Yong.

DS526.7.T7 2003
325.59′09′045—dc21                                    2003042382

Printed in the United States of America

The paper used in this publication meets the minimum requirements of
American National Standard for Information Sciences
Permanence of Paper for Printed Library Materials,
ANSI Z 39.48-1984.

BM (c)  10  9  8  7  6  5  4  3  2  1
BM (p)  10  9  8  7  6  5  4  3  2  1

# Contents

# Introduction

## Marc Frey, Ronald W. Pruessen, and Tan Tai Yong

This is a book based on two somewhat ironically linked premises: The dawn of the twenty-first century sees widespread appreciation for the significance of Southeast Asia in global affairs, yet has quite a shallow understanding of the region's dynamics and history. Headlines and sound bites constantly highlight Southeast Asia's importance, even if they prod a fairly wild counterpoint of glowing forecasts and alarmist warnings. On the one hand, few would doubt that this region has been (and will remain) a notable frontier in the evolution of "modernization" and "democratization"—as well as a key laboratory for the experiments of "globalization." On the other hand, equally few can ignore the region's volatility or problematic portents: the 1997 "Asian meltdown," the ethnic violence of Indonesia, the contested waters of the South China Sea, or the smog and traffic jams of Bangkok. Yet, how well do today's more appreciative observers *understand* this significant and tumultuous terrain? Do political and business leaders get beyond the sound bites? Have scholars, for their part, remained too wedded to older questions and perspectives, thus making themselves unable, as a result, to fully delineate the complex overall trajectory of Southeast Asia's modern history?

At the beginning of a new century, for example, it is well past time to shift analysis of a key historical process like "decolonization" to a mode befitting a "post–Cold War era." In the most elementary sense, certainly, the chronological boundaries of the Southeast Asian chapters in this story need to be broadened. Attention should be made to range both backward and forward from the early Cold War years that are too often seen as the single crucial timeframe: The varied evolutionary patterns of Europe's empires (and Japan's) —from the late nineteenth century through World War II—yield important insights into the specific events of the 1940s, 1950s, and 1960s. In turn, the political, economic, and cultural currents of the "postcolonial" era (very much including Southeast Asia's gradual adjustment to globalizing forces) also offer clues to an understanding of the dynamics of decolonization—hints regarding earlier motivations, for instance, or tests by which to evaluate previous judgments and predictions.

Analytical approaches to decolonization need to be stretched even more than timeframes. Two key examples: (a) There should be greater appreciation for the multifaceted nature of the decolonization process. Ample reasons remain to continue serious study of the more formal political and strategic dimensions that figure prominently in traditional studies. At the same time, sensitivity to postcolonial and contemporary issues encourages greater attention to economic and cultural developments. (b) Some emphasis should be placed on comparative analysis as well, with respect to both research foci and style. The relatively distinct nature of British, French, and Dutch approaches to decolonization suggests the logic of a careful mapping of alternatives. So, too, do the differences between European and U.S. policies—and, in particular, the differences between Asian experiences with any and all of these. Such a comparative agenda, in turn, underlines the potential value of collaborative efforts: bringing together European, American, and Asian scholars for the sharing of perspectives and insights. This volume is designed to both chart a path toward a reconceptualization of key features of Southeast Asia's history and to highlight some of the insights that can be gained when new questions are asked and new perspectives applied.

Decolonization is an especially critical facet of Southeast Asia's history, and, as a result, one especially in need of new analytical approaches. Where previous scholarly work has often focused on imperial history or the experiences of individual colonies, for example, the story will be conceived and told differently here. The chapters in this volume emerge from new and wide-ranging research, blending up-to-date archival findings with sensitivity to cutting-edge theories in relevant fields like international relations, economics, anthropology, and cultural studies. The seventeen contributors have also made a conscious effort to think along comparative and international lines to build a whole that is distinctly greater than the sum of its parts.

Several key themes become common threads in this collaborative, comparative undertaking: First, decolonization in Southeast Asia is best regarded as a process that began in the late nineteenth and early twentieth centuries. It was often, ironically, a process that was either twinned with or even prodded by the consolidation efforts of imperial powers in the late colonial period. Second, decolonization is also best understood as a process that did not end with transfers of formal power in the 1940s, 1950s, and 1960s. Cultural emancipation and economic developments, for instance, should be seen as integral parts of a transition to postcolonial orders—and steps in these directions have had complex and open-ended timelines. Third, both endogenous and exogenous factors influenced the course of decolonization. Nationalism and the desire for political, economic, and cultural self-determination clashed with—and were profoundly affected by—the determination of colonial powers to maintain the kind of asymmetrical relations that brought prestige and economic rewards. Fourth, the strength of nationalist movements in Southeast Asia combined with the military-economic weakness of the European colonial states to yield a rapid transfer of power in Burma, Indonesia, and Vietnam. Only in Malaya was Britain able to exert enough control to produce the gradual process that the colonial powers would have preferred to implement throughout the region. Fifth, the United States must be seen as a major actor in the story of Southeast Asian decolonization, in spite of its limited previous involvement in the region. The American role was a complicated one, however, whatever earlier assumptions may have been concerning its seemingly simplistic Cold War sources. U.S. leaders did regularly see the post-1945 world through anticommunist lenses and this generated clear suspicion of left-wing nationalist movements in Southeast Asia. But Washington views were also shaped by deeply held beliefs about race, democracy, and the American mission in the global arena. Resulting U.S. policies were always multifaceted, with emphasis veering from the encouragement of gradual emancipation and continued cooperation between Europe and Southeast Asia to grander plans for regional integration, development, and "state-building."

The first chapter by Paul H. Kratoska introduces some of these major themes. Taking the perspective of the longue durée, he demonstrates that well before World War II there was a lively debate about colonialism and colonial reforms within metropolitan societies. To varying degrees, Great Britain, France, and the Netherlands responded to a rising critique against colonial rule, both in the metropoles and in Southeast Asia, where nationalists—intellectuals working for independence—asserted the right of the people to govern themselves. During the crisis of the capitalist system in the 1930s, however, the colonial powers suspended all projects of imperial reform because the colonies were regarded as indispensable for the stabilization of the European economies. The mental maps of most decision makers in Paris, London, or The Hague did not change much during World War II. In fact, all three colonial powers returned to Southeast Asia in 1945 with the intention of regaining their respective territories. With the exception of Malaya, however, where communalism retarded the development of nationalism, the colonial powers were confronted with broadly based independence movements. Ultimately, European strategies to cope with this challenge proved insufficient. The costs of winning independence, though, were high. In Indonesia, low-intensity warfare and two Dutch offensives left tens of thousands dead, and in Vietnam a terrible colonial war was only the prelude to an even deadlier contest.

World War II can truly be regarded as a watershed in the history of colonialism. As Jost Dülffer explains in chapter 2, colonial rule was not simply shattered by Japan. Both Germany and Japan pursued grand colonial projects during the war in an even more aggressive way than had other European powers in the past. Economic exploitation and terror reached unprecedented levels. Mass murder was an integral component of Japanese occupation policies in China and Southeast Asia. In Europe, German colonialism in the East and harsh occupation policies in the West made possible the extermination of millions of European Jews. Nationalists in Southeast Asia profited from the transition of colonial rule from the Europeans to the Japanese. Whether they cooperated with the Japanese (e.g., as did Aung San and Sukarno) or opposed all forms of colonialism (as did Hồ Chí Minh or Sutan Sjahrir), both groups fought for eventual independence. When, at the end of the war, Japanese power receded and European influence was still negligible (with the exception of the British), nationalists seized the moment and filled a power vacuum.

That decolonization needs to be conceived as a process that did not necessarily end with a formal transfer of power is highlighted by J. Thomas Lindblad in his chapter on the economic impact of decolonization. Filling a power vacuum to effect independence entailed the channeling of revolutionary energies and ideas. Ruling elites regarded economic progress and modernization as a key prerequisite for the stabilization and orderly development of the newly independent nation-states. Chapter 3 analyses four aspects that are vital for an understanding of the economic development of Indonesia, Malaysia, and the Philippines in the early years of independence: economic challenges, economic policies, the investment climate, and the actual development of foreign capital commitments. As Lindblad suggests, there was no preferred path to economic progress. Instead, three different approaches yielded only mixed results.

Chapters 4 and 5 are devoted to the decolonization of the French empire in Southeast Asia. Bruce M. Lockhart focuses on the widely neglected but important theme of the role of the monarchies in Cambodia, Laos, and Vietnam. The returning colonial power regarded all three as linchpins of French power in the Far East. Against the backdrop of events between 1945 and 1955, Lockhart's chapter analyses the role of the monarchy within the three respective societies, as well as within the context of imperial designs. By utilizing French, Cambodian, Laotian, and Vietnamese sources, he sheds new light on the development of nationalism, changes in culture and identity, and power structures in what was then known as Indochina. As a traditional loci of power, the French anchored their policies of recolonization and decolonization to the monarchy. But French designs also necessitated the formation of new institutions through which influence could be exerted.

As Hugues Tertrais explains in chapter 5, post-1945 circumstances dictated a new approach to the administration of the French territories in Southeast Asia. The French decided to create a federation of autonomous states as part of a reformed empire called the French Union. The federalist model drew on earlier French experiences in Indochina and it seemed suited for a world transformed by the war. But the Việt Minh and the Vietnamese communists under Hồ challenged the Associated States of Indochina. Moreover, these groups were not the only ones who called for independence. Nationalist sentiments within the French-dominated autonomous governments of Cambodia, Laos, and Vietnam greatly complicated cooperation among the three countries. This in turn destroyed French expectations to retain power over territories held together by a combination of federal and central institutions.

As in Indochina, federalism also assumed central importance in the struggle between the Indonesian Republic and the Netherlands in the period between 1945 and 1949. Marc Frey's chapter on decolonization in Indonesia identifies the major actors and explores the options and strategies of the protagonists. The outcome of the struggle, the transfer of power, and the adoption of a unitary model of political organization was the result of endogenous and exogenous factors. Instrumental for the success of the republic, however, was a unique blend of diplomacy and armed struggle. The strength of the Indonesian nationalist movement, Frey argues, derived from the fact that it was the sole political agent that was able to represent a common Indonesian identity, an identity that had evolved prior to World War II and that had captured the imagination of the vast majority of the Indonesian population during and after the Japanese occupation.

Chapter 7, written by Karl Hack, is a meditation on approaches and theories toward decolonization. While the particular emphasis is on the end of the British Empire in Southeast Asia, Hack raises issues that are of equal relevance for the study of decolonization in Indochina, Indonesia, and beyond the region. The problems the chapter addresses are based on a series of questions: What are the appropriate geographical structures for decolonization in this "region"? What is the appropriate temporal structure for decolonization? What can be done about the "plural society" that exists in the academic world of decolonization, where colonial, diplomatic, radical, nationalist, and subnational accounts meet in the seminar room, but rarely mingle? How far does the notion of a sharp division between European-dominated colonial and Asian-controlled postcolonial periods impose an artificial periodization? While chapter 7 offers no final answers to such questions, it invites us to rethink the connection between event, structure, and time, three central categories of historical inquiry. Hack shows the complexity of issues that are involved in the study of decolonization, and he illuminates the variables with which the authors of this volume grappled.

Chapters 8 to 11 deal with the decolonization of the British Empire in Southeast Asia after 1945 from four different perspectives. In his overview of British policies in Southeast Asia, Nicholas Tarling argues that Britain did have a coherent regional strategy after World War II. It envisaged decolonization and hoped for continued cooperation between the former colonial powers and the newly independent countries. Dutch military actions against the Indonesian Republic and the war in Indochina excluded cooperative approaches to decolonization. They also greatly complicated Britain's regional design. But with regard to its own territories in Southeast Asia, Britain was able to realize its aims. The unification of the various British dependencies in the Federation of Malaysia stood at the heart of the "Grand Design." As Tan Tai Yong explains, however, this design depended to a large degree on the cooperation of nationalist leaders in Malaya and Singapore. The eventual failure of the Grand Design in 1965 was not the result of British weakness, but of ethnic confrontation and particularist interests. Moving back in time a little bit, Kumar Ramakrishna examines the preconditions for realizing British decolonization in the framework of the Grand Design, namely, the suppression of the communist insurgency in Malaya. In his chapter on the Malayan Emergency, Ramakrishna concentrates on the operational dimension of the conflict, a neglected but critical aspect of the war against the insurgents. Ramakrishna demonstrates that the British were eventually successful because by the mid-1950s the Malayan Communist Party had alienated the strategic rural Chinese community through its ill-conceived terror campaign. In contrast, the British succeeded in the war for the "hearts and minds" because they were able to win over the rural Chinese. Malaya's decolonization was thus carefully prepared and executed, and the British were very much able to make their imprint on the process. A similar picture emerges with regard to Singapore. In his chapter on the role of nationalism in the decolonization of Singapore, Albert Lau asserts that Singaporean nationalism was not very well developed and that the British were in control of decolonization. While nationalism was the driving force of decolonization in Burma, Vietnam, and Indonesia, in Malaya and Singapore it was the British Grand Design that shaped the developments leading up to independence. A major reason for the strength and persistence of the colonial power was the multiethnic and multicultural character of the British colonies.

During the 1950s, the United States emerged as the most influential outside actor in Southeast Asia. The roots of American involvement date back to World War II, when Washington first developed an interest in the Japanese-occupied European colonies. In his chapter on the United States and Vietnam, Mark Philip Bradley takes issue with those who argue that while Franklin

D. Roosevelt pursued a policy of freedom and liberation for the colonized world, the administration of Harry S. Truman opted for a security-centered approach that consistently favored the European powers. In contrast, Bradley emphasizes the continuities of American perceptions of the non-European world. He shows that American ideas about "the other" shaped policies toward Vietnam during and after World War II. The importance of ideas and the role of ideology in foreign policy is discussed by Robert J. McMahon in his overview on American relations toward Southeast Asia in the era of decolonization. McMahon argues that the condescension and paternalism so frequently displayed by Americans in their dealings with Southeast Asians not only made genuine cooperation and mutuality exceedingly difficult to establish, but also bred resentment among those on the receiving end of such attitudes. This problem was exacerbated by tremendous power disparities. The preoccupation of American policy makers with credibility pushed Washington to assume greater obligations in Southeast Asia. But as Ronald W. Pruessen points out in his chapter on John Foster Dulles, the process of assuming responsibilities and exercising power was complex. Dulles's policies toward Southeast Asia in the 1950s—like American policies in general—could appear erratic or even muddled. This resulted from conflicted sentiments concerning decolonization. On the one hand, Dulles and others saw themselves as worthy standard bearers of their country's historical anticolonialism. On the other hand, they were regularly reluctant to follow ideals to their logical conclusions. Nationalist movements in Southeast Asia were viewed with suspicions that translated into opposition, because they threatened the health of the European powers the United States wanted to keep as potent allies or because they directly challenged American visions and ambitions.

Regional cooperation was one tool of special interest to Washington, especially in the years following Điện Biên Phủ and the Geneva Conference. Kai Dreisbach, in chapter 15, makes clear that this American interest was motivated by strategic and economic concerns. Moreover, regional cooperation was, to a certain degree, Washington's answer to political developments in the aftermath of decolonization. Its strong anticommunist position and its disapproval of political neutralism, however, prevented a truly regional cooperation in the 1950s. The Association of Southeast Asian Nations (ASEAN), founded in 1967, came into being without American involvement. Moreover, Dreisbach maintains, ASEAN was established in part to reduce tensions caused by the American involvement in Vietnam. Close bilateral relations with the noncommunist countries, regional cooperation, and economic development were the pillars on which American policies toward Southeast Asia rested. While McMahon shows how the discourse on development integrated older, more racialized notions about the non-European world, Nick Cullather, in chapter 16, identifies some of the instruments of development. The aim of development was to transform Southeast Asian countries, whose economies and societies were perceived as "backward," into "modern," stable, and prospering nation-states. Increased food production played an important role in the peaceful transformation of the region. But, as Cullather explains, the "Green Revolution" was not invented for the region by Americans, but developed as a multinational project that involved actors from Southeast Asia as well.

In chapter 17, Wang Gungwu ranges over the varied issues addressed in the book and seeks to map multiple levels of analysis. He also charts directions for future research.

Words of thanks should conclude this introduction. This book would not have been possible without the willingness of the contributors to cooperate in such a joint project. Earlier versions of the chapters were presented to a workshop held in February 2001 in Singapore. Sponsored by the Fritz-Thyssen Foundation, the University of Toronto, and the National University of Singapore, the workshop provided opportunities to both test ideas and discuss draft chapters. We thank the sponsoring institutions for their generous support. We also thank Wibke Becker, Philipp Janssen, and Kelly Lau for invaluable assistance in preparing the workshop and the book.

# The
# Transformation of
# Southeast Asia

# 1

# Dimensions of Decolonization

## Paul H. Kratoska

The story of Southeast Asian decolonization—as with decolonization else-where—is multifaceted. Hindsight allows clearer delineation of at least some of the complexities.

The long timeline of the story has become increasingly evident. Well before World War II, the powers that governed colonial territories in Southeast Asia were contemplating changes in colonial policies—changes that envisioned a systematic and orderly transition to self-government and eventual independence under international control. After 1945, of course, these powers lost control of the process, for nationalist leaders preferred a future of their own choosing to one determined by the colonial powers, and treated the argument that a gradual transition was needed to develop institutions and train personnel as a ploy to prolong colonial control. In the absence of a planned transition, the disparate collections of regions that made up British, French, and Dutch colonial territories in Southeast Asia were forced into the mold of the democratic nation-state, with lasting and not always positive results.

If Southeast Asian decolonization unfolded over a long period of time, the relinquishment of European power also resulted from multiple factors. In his primer on the decolonization process in the British Empire, W. David McIntyre outlines three aspects of historians' explanations for the fall of empire: the metropolitan dimension ("politics and society, trade and finance, and government policy"), the global dimension ("the changing international environment"), and the colonial dimension ("what is called colonial 'nationalism,' but which in many cases should perhaps be described as the independence-seeking coalitions"). Historians, he says, "are agreed" on these basic divisions, although they "differ widely in the emphasis which should be given to each."[1] Charles-Robert Ageron takes a similar viewpoint on French decolonization and offers the same range of explanations: domestic politics (the "colonial party," religious opinion, and the views of intellectuals), international opinion (the League of Nations, communist anticolonialism, American anticolonialism, and the United Nations), and nationalism in the colonies.[2] Dutch decolonization, recently summarized by H. W. van den Doel, was largely the story of the Indonesian war of independence but involved the same combination of forces.[3]

It seems appropriate to begin this volume on Southeast Asian decolonization with an overview of some of these chronological complexities and multifaceted dynamics.

## Background

World War I (1914–1918) brought an end to a long period of colonial expansion that left large parts of Asia and Africa under Western rule. Colonial policy and the administration of colonial territories caused a great deal of dissatisfaction in the West, both among proponents and critics of empire. The former urged governments to bring greater unity to their empires, turning them into effective economic and political units, rather than loose alliances of "practically independent states."[4] Critics saw colonies as a source of substantial risk and limited tangible benefits, and found the morality of the imperial relationship objectionable in that it involved economic exploitation and an unsavory racism. The build up to World War I highlighted yet another objection to colonialism: the potential it created for generating conflicts between the European powers. The solution appeared to lie in moving colonial territories in the direction of self-government and independence.

During the forty years preceding the war, Southeast Asia experienced considerable economic development within fairly open economies. Companies financed by the sale of shares in Europe located marketable natural resources and opened plantations and other enterprises to exploit these resources in Sumatra and Borneo, British Burma, British Malaya, and French Indochina. There were lean periods as lands were cleared and commercial crops established, and colonial administrations faced strains as they searched for revenues to develop basic infrastructure, but by the early 1900s these efforts were bearing fruit. Paul Doumer, with his policy of *mise en valeur* (expressed somewhat inadequately by the English word "development"), made French Indochina both efficient and prosperous.[5] At the same time, the export of primary products brought prosperity to British territories in the region and to Sumatra and Borneo.

The 1920s and 1930s produced a number of proposals for reforming colonial rule, but in Southeast Asia these discussions were overtaken by events when the Japanese put an end to Western control in the region at the end of 1941. During the Japanese occupation, the colonial powers developed plans for postwar initiatives, seeking to remedy the inefficiencies of prewar colonial administration and to justify the resumption of imperial control. There was now talk of self-government and even of eventual independence. After the war, however, nationalist leaders would spurn these initiatives—which they saw as thinly disguised attempts to perpetuate colonial rule—and press for immediate independence. The efforts of wartime planners led to peaceful handovers in some instances, and revolutionary war in others. Either way, the speed with which changes had to be made, and the lack of a systematic and orderly adaptation of colonial institutions, complicated an already difficult process. Dutch proposals to create a commonwealth were stillborn, but schemes to turn colonial relationships into partnerships of equals survived in the British Commonwealth and for a time in the French Union, although both were loose associations rather than focused political groupings.

## The 1920s and 1930s

The 1920s brought a new emphasis on imperial trusteeship and along with it a concern for social welfare in colonial territories. The 1930s were dominated by efforts to deal with the Great Depression and the threat of war and attempts to create more tightly integrated colonial empires.

The settlement that followed World War I placed colonialism on a new foundation. Hitherto, the Western powers had acknowledged rights gained over colonies and protectorates either by conquest or by voluntary cession. The countries that ratified the Treaty of Versailles eschewed conquest as a legal basis for acquiring colonial territories, leaving voluntary cession as the only legitimate means of establishing colonial control. Holders of existing colonial empires added little or no additional territory after 1918, but Germany, Italy, and Japan all sought to acquire territories in defiance of this new principle, pleading the need to secure sources of raw materials and food, outlets for surplus population, and a market for manufactured goods; they also desired equal standing with existing colonial powers to satisfy the claims of national prestige.[6]

The "mandate system," which was created to administer colonial territories formerly held by Germany, offered a possible model for setting up a system of international control over colonized areas. Each mandate became the responsibility of a single power, subject to supervision by the League of Nations, and countries holding mandates adhered to a code that committed them to offer all members of the League of Nations equal opportunities for trade and commerce, to safeguard the rights and protect the welfare of the populations, and to prepare the mandated territory for independence. Influential critics of colonialism, among them Arnold Toynbee and J. L. Hammond, saw the mandate system as an arrangement that could be extended to all colonial territories. Hammond wrote, "So far as the government of backward races is concerned, there should ideally be only one Great Power, and that

Power the League of Nations. If such a revolution were possible we should see men of all countries administering the African territories not under a national flag, but under the flag of the League, men differing in blood, race and other respects but united in accepting a common standard, and certain common ideas of justice and duty."[7]

The Versailles peace conference had discussed a proposal along these lines, but concluded that such an arrangement would be unworkable and was likely to provoke international jealousies. The Covenant of the League of Nations injected a new emphasis on social and humanitarian issues into international affairs. The idea of colonies as possessions began to give way to a concept of colonies as territories held in trust—for their own inhabitants and for the world at large—and colonial administrations faced pressure to devote substantial resources to the welfare of the people under their control, paying attention to refugee matters, health, slavery, the opium trade, suppression of the traffic in women and children, education, housing, and sanitation.[8]

The Netherlands pioneered an "ethical" colonialism that dealt with issues of social welfare. As early as 1901, the Dutch began to base their colonial policy on the idea that it should provide material and other benefits to the people of the Indies, concentrating on irrigation, immigration of people from more to less crowded areas of the archipelago, agricultural credit, promotion of industry, and improvement of transportation.[9] This ethical policy gave the government a degree of regulatory control over the activities of the private sector and set in motion a range of social and cultural initiatives intended to benefit the local population. Even critics of colonialism shared these ambitions. The social democratic leader H. H. van Kol, for example, wrote in 1901 that colonial administration should hasten "material, moral and spiritual evolution" in preparation for the independence that lay inevitably in the future.[10]

During the 1920s, other colonial administrations adopted policies that resembled those of the Dutch, although in the Netherlands Indies itself the ethical impulse was by this time beginning to fade. Leading figures in the British Colonial Office, including Sir Alfred Milner and Leopold Amery, emphasized the need for both economic and social development. Amery told the House of Commons in July 1919 that the task of the Colonial Office was to set up "a new and more positive standard of our duty and obligation towards the peoples to whom this house is in the position of trustee."[11] Sir Frederick John Dealtry Lugard argued that the colonial powers had a "dual mandate" to serve the interests of both rulers and ruled. Britain's imperialism, he said, operated for the "mutual benefit of her own industrial classes, and of the native races in their progress to a higher plane."[12] Sir Herbert Samuel, discussing a colonial development bill passed by Parliament in 1929, similarly asserted that "[t]he nation now recognizes in colonial development both its duty and its interest."[13]

French officials also claimed that colonial rule promoted the welfare of people in the colonies while offering benefits to the international community. Albert Sarraut, the minister for colonies, announced a policy of economic development in a speech before the Senate in February 1920 and the following year created an ambitious program of public works for the colonies and protectorates under his ministry.[14] Anticipating Sir Lugard, he explained his philosophy in a book published in 1923, "The France that colonizes does not do so for itself: its advantage is joined with that of the world; its effort, more than for itself, must be of benefit to the colonies whose economic growth and human development it must assure."[15] His plan had largely been abandoned by the time the book appeared, but succeeding governments continued to emphasize the need for the metropole to promote colonial development.

## The Impact of the Great Depression

Until the end of the 1920s, the development of the material resources of colonial territories took place within a context of free trade—"for the benefit of the world at large," to quote Sir Lugard[16]—but the colonial powers responded to the depression by adopting tariffs and quotas designed to contain economic activity as much as possible within their respective empires. The British author Norman Angell wrote in 1931, "We are engaged in the discussion of projects for the economic unification of the Empire; for rendering it economically self-sufficient; for keeping its trade for its people."[17] Protection was a significant departure from the open door policies that had prevailed earlier in the century, and in the words of Sir Samuel Hoare, speaking before the Assembly of the League of Nations, created a natural "fear lest exclusive monopolies should be set up at the expense of the countries not possessing Colonial Empires."[18] Moreover, duties and quotas benefited manufacturers in Europe but increased the cost of living in the colonies; in Southeast Asia, for example, Japan offered cloth and other everyday goods at prices substantially below those charged for comparable European goods. Denying people access to cheap imports at a time when export economies faced falling prices and low demand caused anger within the colonies and seemed to belie claims that colonial states promoted local welfare.

In 1932, the Ottawa Conference brought together representatives of Britain's dominions and colonial territories, and the delegates forged a policy of imperial preference. Although this move was welcomed by groups favoring a more closely integrated "united empire,"[19] Sir Lugard told the Royal Institute of International Affairs in 1936 that while the abandonment of free trade by the

United Kingdom "in the face of hostile tariffs imposed by foreign nations" had been justified by results, the move had given rise to complaints that countries with colonial territories were using them to deny others access to crucial raw materials. He called for a reversion to traditional free trade policies on the part of all powers.[20] Elsewhere on the political spectrum, the Labour Party in the mid-1930s adopted an election manifesto with a similar agenda, calling for "international control of sources of supply of raw materials, and for the extension of the mandate system for colonial territories."[21]

Like Britain, France responded to the economic crisis by strengthening ties with its colonies. During the depression, French financial assistance to the colonies increased substantially (averaging four times more in constant francs in the period 1931–1939 than in the period 1914–1930), and owing to tariffs that favored colonial products, the colonies also played an expanded role in the trade of France, accounting for less than 15 percent of French imports and exports in 1927 but 34 percent in 1936. The Méline tariff of 1892 had brought Indochina within the system of metropolitan tariffs, and changes in 1928 fully assimilated it and other colonial territories into the tariff system. In Indochina, imports from China and from Singapore fell sharply while the proportion of imports of French origin increased. However, Indochina exported relatively little to France or to other French colonies, and its economic well-being rested on the existence of a complementary trade with China, which purchased far more from Indochina than it sold there. Colonial officials criticized the new system of tariffs, pointing out that Indochina was and would remain dependent on the region for a significant share of its trade.[22]

Since 1883, all French colonies had been represented on a colonial council (the Conseil supérieur des colonies), but this body functioned only in a consultative capacity. The 1930s brought efforts to tighten the political integration of the empire, including a short-lived project to create an empire ministry in 1934, but these initiatives produced no lasting institutional change.[23] The advent of the leftist Popular Front government in 1936 seemed to herald a new departure in colonial politics. Marius Moutet, Léon Blum's minister for colonies, was on record as favoring radical changes in Indochina, including political rights, a constitution, and self-government, although he envisaged a very long period of transition to overcome negative influences obstructing the development of a socialist state and society and to build an edifice that could withstand both foreign imperialism and indigenous feudal forces.[24] The Popular Front government eased the politics of force and repression in colonial territories and created a commission to carry out an ambitious study of conditions in the colonies, with particular emphasis on social and welfare issues. It also introduced an economic plan designed to achieve modernization and to promote social welfare though improved labor codes, better health care, and safeguards against famine. However, Blum fell from power long before these measures could have much effect, and his successors concentrated on the defense of the empire rather than on welfare issues.[25]

The Dutch had little interest in questions of imperial integration, for unlike France and Britain through their respective empires, the Netherlands was too small a market to absorb the produce of the Indies. The colony faced a serious imbalance in trade with Japan, which exported substantial quantities of goods to the Netherlands Indies but imported very little, and the administration introduced protective measures against Japanese trade that largely took the form of quotas. The government also imposed restrictions on imports of rice from other parts of Southeast Asia and encouraged local production of needed goods.[26]

The general trend in the 1930s toward closer imperial ties is clear enough, but during the same period individual colonies adopted policies that shifted them in the direction of greater autonomy. Exercises designed to cut costs through decentralization and devolution of power brought greater numbers of local people into colonial administration. Moreover, individual colonial governors continued to be responsible for meeting their financial obligations from domestic sources and responded to the depression by attempting to build up local production to replace imported goods and become more self-sufficient. These policies largely negated efforts to achieve imperial unity.

## War and the Future of Empire

The Atlantic Charter, announced in August 1941, proclaimed the "right of all peoples to choose the form of government under which they shall live." The statement was drafted as a basis for a future political settlement in Europe, but it provided a clear platform for nationalist self-assertion in other parts of the world.

In 1942, the Institute of Pacific Relations convened a conference at Mont Tremblant, Quebec, which was attended in an unofficial capacity by many officials closely involved in the formulation of colonial policy. According to George H. C. Hart, all those who took part "accepted the implications" of the Atlantic Charter, but there was considerable controversy over when and how changes were to be made, with some members "inclined to brush aside with impatience the alleged problems of execution as dilatory obstacles put up *pour besoin de cause* by rank imperialists or by unimaginative conservatives." A consensus gradually took shape on two points. One was that "representative and responsible government cannot be established by the stroke of a pen . . . and that, although one may criticize and even condemn with more or less justification some of the colonial powers for not having been more progressive in the past, one cannot remedy that shortcoming by decree." On the other hand, it had become evident that "the world at large was not going to accept vague ideals and promises at their face value; that every government involved would be expected to endeavor to make known its practical intentions, and that the carrying out of pledges embodied in the widely criticized but nevertheless generally acclaimed Charter was not the concern of the colonial powers and the subject peoples alone."[27]

There was also agreement that "generally speaking, the hitherto responsible power would be technically and psychologically best fitted to pave the way for well-prepared independence." The need was to prevent "prudence as an incentive to true progress from becoming a pretext for procrastination." The idea of creating either an international or one-power mandate aroused little enthusiasm, but there was a general feeling that some sort of postwar cooperation was required. This cooperation would be best achieved through regional councils wielding certain sovereign powers and operating within the context of a larger international organization, while working in concert with each other.[28]

With the Japanese invasion, Britain lost a small but significant portion of its empire, and what remained would prove vital to the war effort; South Asia in particular provided manpower and crucial military facilities for the fight against Japan. Britain's war objectives focused on recovery of lost colonial territories, and the government made clear its intentions to maintain the British Empire after the war. The War Cabinet declared that the Atlantic Charter was "directed to the nations of Europe whom we hoped to free from Nazi tyranny, and was not intended to deal with the internal affairs of the British Empire."[29] Concerning "the progressive evolution of self-governing institutions in the regions and peoples which owe allegiance to the British Crown," Winston Churchill told Parliament that it would be a mistake to formulate future colonial policy before the war was over. In any case, he said, "[w]e have made declarations on these matters which are complete in themselves, free from a[m]biguity and related to the conditions and circumstances of territories and people affected. They will be found to be entirely in harmony with the high conception of freedom and justice which inspired the Joint Declaration [the Atlantic Charter]."[30]

In reality, they were scarcely to be found at all. Harold Macmillan observed that the prime minister could hardly have "realised the true nakedness of the land when he made the statement: 'The declarations are not complete in themselves, nor are they free from ambiguity. They are scrappy, obscure and jejune.'"[31] When pressed to publish these declarations, the government was forced to temporize and fell back on a concept of colonialism as "partnership." This idea helped to deflect further attacks, and a new concept of "colonial mission" gradually took shape "which sought to reshape the Imperial system on the basis of equal relationships and common economic and social benefits."[32] The tide was running strongly against imperialism, however. Pressure from anti-imperialist quarters and particularly from the United States forced the British Foreign and Colonial Offices to accept the principle that after recovering dependent territories at the end of the war, Britain "should develop their resources, ensure their security and prepare them for eventual self-government, in accordance with the principles of the Atlantic Charter and within the framework of some Pacific Regional Council."[33]

In France, a country invaded and partly occupied, preservation of its empire provided a justification for accepting the armistice with Germany. The French empire, according to Ageron, was "the supreme hope of a vanquished France," and officials of the Vichy regime promoted the idea that because of the empire, France, although defeated in Europe, was "not a people without territory, not a nation without people, not a State without resources," and "remained one of the Great Powers that would decide the organization of the world."[34] In June 1943, Charles de Gaulle created a government-in-exile and designated it the French Committee of National Liberation (in June 1944 it was called the Provisional Government of the French Republic). The committee announced its policy toward Indochina in a statement issued on December 8, 1943:

> France intends to give them [the peoples of French Indochina] in the bosom of the French community a new political status, in which the liberties of the different countries composing French Indo-China will be extended and consecrated in the framework of a federal organization; in which the liberal character of the ways of living will be accentuated, without losing the original stamp of the Indo-Chinese civilization and traditions; in which, lastly, the Indo-Chinese will be able to occupy all ranks and functions in the government offices.[35]

René Pleven, de Gaulle's commissioner for colonies, declared that his ultimate goal was to achieve self-government for Indochina:

> An Imperial Conference held at Brazzaville early in 1944 anticipated colonial representation in a future French constituent assembly, as well as the creation of a colonial parliament, but did not entertain the possibility that territories might become independent.
>
> The aims of France in her civilizing work in the colonies exclude any idea of self-government, any possibility of development outside the French Empire; the formation of independent Governments in the colonies, however distant, cannot be contemplated.[36]

However, Pierre-Olivier Lapie asserted that both Pleven and Henri Laurentie, the director of political affairs in the Colonial Commissariat, had "a clearer realization than ever before that the colonizing nation's sole aim is to transform the colonized areas into states which will some day be its own equals," and ultimately might be "freed from their link to France, if such is their wish."[37] De Gaulle himself did not go quite so far, but he announced in 1944 that the objective of French colonial policy was self-government.[38]

In the Netherlands Indies, the opposition to Dutch rule included many people with socialist leanings, and the rise of an expansionist fascist and totalitarian government in Japan caused considerable alarm. Indonesian leaders made overtures to the Dutch in the late 1930s, offering cooperation against Japan in return for political concessions, but the government rebuffed these offers. Dutch officials said that discussions of political change could not be pursued until the war was over, and many of them viewed the Indonesian initiatives as a disgraceful attempt to exploit momentary Dutch weakness. It was in the context of such discussions that Governor-General B. C. de Jonge made a statement that inflamed nationalist opinion, asserting that the Dutch had been in the Indies for three hundred years and would need to remain for a further three hundred years before the colony would be ready for any form of self-government.[39] Dutch socialists, despite their critical stance toward imperialism, concurred with this analysis, arguing that independence to the Indies without adequate preparation would cause internal chaos and would likely result in annexation of the territory by rival colonial powers.[40]

The Dutch did appoint an official Commission for the Study of Political Reforms, chaired by F. H. Visman. Few historians give this initiative more than passing mention, and an authoritative Indonesian school textbook dismisses it in a single sentence, stating that the commission was convened to determine the wishes of the people but did not fulfil its mission.[41] At the time of its publication, however, the Visman report seemed to mark a significant step in reshaping the colonial relationship. The commission was appointed in September 1940, after the fall of the Netherlands had made the Netherlands Indies practically if not legally autonomous, and assigned the task of investigating "the wishes, aspirations, and attitudes of the various peoples, social-economic classes and groups in regard to the political development of the Indies." Testimony focused on possible administrative reforms in the Indies rather than changes in the relationship with the Netherlands, and produced calls for greater provincial autonomy and a federation of Indonesian states. The commission claimed to have found no sentiment in favor of independence: Indonesians wanted changes in the structure of the kingdom, but "another wish existed without exception by all those heard, namely the wish not to break the bond which had been forged in the course of centuries between the Indies and the Netherlands."[42]

An amendment to the Dutch constitution in 1922 had replaced references to the Netherlands and its "colonies" with a formulation that read, "The Kingdom of the Netherlands consists of the territories of the Netherlands, the Netherlands Indies, Surinam and Curaçao." The change had little immediate effect, but in December 1942 Queen Wilhelmina promised in a radio broadcast that after the war the kingdom would be reconstructed on "a solid foundation of complete partnership." Her talk envisaged

> a Commonwealth in which the Netherlands, Indonesia, Surinam and Curaçao will participate, with complete self-reliance and freedom of conduct for each part regarding its internal affairs but with readiness to render mutual assistance. . . . [Such] a combination of independence and collaboration can give the Kingdom and its parts strength to carry fully their responsibility both internally and externally. This would leave no room for discrimination according to race or nationality; only ability of individual citizens and needs of various groups of the population will determine policy of government.[43]

Jan Otto Marius Broek argued that this broadcast statement undercut the suggestions of some commentators that the new colonial policy of the Netherlands was simply a response to current events—"the expression of a sudden change of heart, forced on the Dutch by the misfortunes of war," as one put it. The new policy was rather the product of a long evolutionary process.

> The error is serious because it hinders effective cooperation between progressive elements in the colonial empires and those in the United States; the latter are apt to proceed on the assumption that British and Dutch colonial liberal policies are insincere makeshift proposals based on wartime necessities, while the former, put on the defensive, feel that they need to stress the accomplishments of the past and the difficulties in the way of more rapid progress. This bickering threatens to destroy the common front which all progressives, regardless of nationality, should form against the reactionary forces which, after the war, will attempt to re-establish the colonial status quo.[44]

Such an understanding was important for the Netherlands, because the queen's statement—seen in this light—appeared to satisfy American demands that colonial territories move in the direction of self-government in a way that would blunt pressure for further concessions.[45]

The Japanese gave at least a nominal independence to the Philippines and

Burma in 1943, and in the final months of the occupation allowed Indonesia to move in the same direction. Local wartime governments in these countries inherited colonial systems that separated the territory under their control into a number of administrative areas based on local social or cultural conditions, and each adopted policies directed toward unifying the population to form a single nationality under a central administration. In Burma, Ba Maw introduced a "New Order Plan" that called for "absorbing the Shan and Karenni States into the new State of Burma" and ending the special status enjoyed by residents of these areas.[46] A 1944 radio broadcast from Rangoon announced that because all people in Burma (Burmese, Shans, Kachins, Karens, and so on) were part of a single Burmese people, "Mahabama," they had been "consolidated into one unit under the organisation of the Mahabama Asiayone," the government's political organization.[47] In the Philippines, President Manuel Quezon had said before the war, in a speech to the Moros of Lanao in 1936, "You, the Mohammedans and you, the Christians, constitute one people."[48] Sukarno similarly supported the idea of a single "bangsa Indonesia" or Indonesian nation. Discussing the first of the republic's five guiding principles (the Pancasila)—"nationalism"—Sukarno said it referred to "neither Javanese nationalism nor Sumatran nationalism nor the nationalism of Borneo, or Celebes, Bali or any other, but the Indonesian nationalism which at one and the same time becomes the principle of one national state."[49] This predilection on the part of Southeast Asian nationalists set the stage for a last confrontation with the imperial powers, which attempted after the war to promote federal systems of administration within the colonial territories by using states based on local nationalisms.

## The Postwar Era

### *The United Nations*

The UN Charter devoted more attention to colonial issues than did the Covenant of the League of Nations, as it included an explicit statement of the principle of self-determination—although the charter held up self-government rather than independence as its objective. The charter's Declaration Regarding Non-self-governing Territories placed colonial issues squarely within the international public domain and established the right of the organized international community to monitor and evaluate the activities of colonial administrations.[50]

Trusteeship explicitly directed toward self-determination replaced the system of mandates, and the General Assembly took steps to apply the principles used in existing Trust territories more widely to all dependencies.

Secretary-General Trygve Lie said the Trusteeship System would provide "a reassuring demonstration that there is a peaceful and orderly means of achieving the difficult transition from backward and subject status to self-government or independence."[51]

Nonetheless, there remained a great deal of ambiguity associated with the issue: a committee report stated that the charter "implied the right of self-government of peoples and not the right of secession." Article 2.7 of the charter stated that the United Nations was not to interfere in the domestic affairs of member states, although it was by no means clear what constituted a domestic matter. The Indonesian revolution highlighted these complexities: The leaders of the Indonesian Republic, seeking self-determination but also independence, turned to the United Nations for assistance in overcoming what they portrayed as a violation of their sovereignty by a foreign power; the Dutch presented the conflict as an internal matter and therefore outside the remit of the United Nations. Broek's "progressive elements" revived proposals calling for the internationalization of colonial affairs as a way of reshaping the postwar world. Raymond Kennedy, an academic who worked with the United States' Office of Strategic Services during the war, published this summary of the argument for internationalization in 1946:

> If we are to plan courageously for a brave new colonial world, we may well consider the possibility of a real departure in policy all over the so-called "backward" regions of the earth. Assuming the existence of a powerful international body, each formerly colonial area could be "internationalized," in the sense that no one state would be its owner or solely responsible for it. The goal in each case would be complete self-government, independence within the framework of the international body, as soon as possible. Each former colony would be administered, or rather prepared for independent statehood, by the nation which had owned it before the war, the reason for this provision being that such nations are already experienced in governing their particular possessions and know local conditions and requirements.
>
> To ensure that the nation in charge of each mandated colony would really set about fostering democratisation with a view to the earliest possible emancipation, the international body might be represented in each colonial capital by a committee of representatives of several member states. . . . In this way, a guaranteed "timetable" for independence could be achieved.[52]

With regard to Southeast Asia, Kennedy argued for a possible union of the Philippines, the Netherlands Indies, and Malaya on grounds that they constituted a distinct "culture area," with differences in religion, language, and culture that were "no greater, in sum, than those existing among the various parts of the Indies themselves."[53] Other proposals went further, calling for the creation of a single state embracing all, or nearly all, of Southeast Asia, on the grounds that there were underlying commonalities across the region, and the artificial barriers introduced by the colonial powers should be broken down. Opponents of this approach emphasized the differences found among peoples living in the region and favored keeping the colonial territories intact. Hart wrote in 1943:

> Fundamentally, there is little in common between the Netherlands Indies and any of the other parts of Southeast Asia. Such meagre affinities as do exist are with the Philippines and Malaya, the only countries with an original Indonesian population. In Malaya, large-scale Chinese and Indian immigration has diluted the aboriginal Indonesian population to a bare 45 per cent of the total inhabitants—as compared with 98 per cent in the Netherlands Indies. . . . In the Philippines, the Spaniards . . . imposed upon the inhabitants their religion and culture and, in the higher classes, even their language. . . . Consequently, there is between the Netherlands Indies, Malaya and the Philippines only a certain affinity of race; but there the connections end. . . .
>
> With the other territories which are sometimes included in such amalgamation schemes, there are neither racial, religious, nor cultural ties. . . .
>
> The fact that there are no historical, political, cultural or religious ties which might justify the unification of the countries of Southeast Asia, and that there is no inclination of the peoples in that part of the world to be incorporated in a political unit and, still less, to be placed under some joint outside authority, appears to afford ample reason to abandon the idea altogether.[54]

Hart considered the economic implications of unification, and here, too, saw no justification for union, "The most conspicuous point about most of these countries, viewed from the economic angle, is that they are all exporters of, to a great extent, identical raw materials and other primary products to the temperate zone and to industrial centers of Europe, America, Australia, China and Japan. The interregional trade between them, compared with this export trade and with a fairly large import trade from the same industrial centers, is almost negligible." He also dismissed the idea that a unified Southeast Asia might make a military and strategic contribution to regional security, arguing that an improved defensive system for the Pacific region could only be achieved by "a world-wide and powerful organization," and for this purpose it was preferable that "existing connections with major world powers, revised and fitted into a world organization, should be maintained and strengthened, not severed."[55]

As their colonial territories moved toward independence, the British and the Americans, who oversaw peaceful transitions, sought to put regimes in place "with which they could hope to live subsequently."[56] Both left behind administrations with which they had much in common and could expect to maintain cordial relations. To some extent, the Dutch and French also pursued this strategy, but with much less success. French efforts to reinstate the former Vietnamese emperor Bảo Đài and displace Hồ Chí Minh are one example. In Indonesia, the Dutch had no realistic alternative to offer in place of Sukarno, but Lieutenant Governor-General Hubertus van Mook, the senior Dutch official in Indonesia, cultivated local leaders (such as Anak Agung, the leader of the Dutch-sponsored state of East Indonesia, the Negara Indonesia Timor) to counterbalance the Javanese-dominated nationalism of the Indonesian Republic.[57] Ultimately, both France and the Netherlands made unsuccessful attempts to control the process of change through military force. They left behind successor regimes that were hostile to their former rulers, although still cast in some ways in the same image.[58]

Growing concern for security in the context of the Cold War intensified pressures for independence, because the Americans anticipated that efforts to sustain colonial rule would generate instability and provide fertile ground for communist agitation, while independent governments would align themselves with the Western powers. "The repercussions of the cold war worked in favour of a swift transfer of power."[59]

Wartime planning for Burma and Malaya contemplated a number of far-reaching changes, but Britain lacked both the military force and the political will to implement these arrangements. The Viceroy of India, Lord Wavell, writing about India but making a point that applied to the entire British Empire, commented in 1947 that "the really fatal thing for us would be to hang on to responsibility when we had lost the power to exercise it." The Allies had drawn heavily on India for manpower and resources in fighting the war against Japan, and any further military activity in the colonial territories would also have required the use of Indian forces. However, India was unwilling to defend imperialism, and Britain's position there was rapidly deteriorating in any case; by 1946, the War Cabinet considered the Indian army unreliable.[60]

"Burma Proper" had been given self-government in 1935, with a parliament and prime minister responsible for domestic affairs, but this arrangement did not apply to the hill regions of British Burma, which became known as the "excluded areas." During the war, Burma was the scene of extensive fighting, and British planners felt that it would be necessary to roll back the clock, restoring full colonial rule to facilitate economic recovery and cultivate a new political elite less tainted by association with the Japanese than the group of men around Aung San, the nationalist leader. However, when

Burmese leaders rejected this approach and demanded an early end to British rule, Britain had no way of resisting them and no real desire to do so. The transition to independence was peaceful and reasonably amicable, although the new government opted not to join the British Commonwealth. Under the leadership of Aung San, the Burmans held meetings with representatives of minority communities to work out an internal federation, and after Aung San was assassinated the new government pursued a similar line, but with less success.[61] The government of independent Burma almost immediately faced severe opposition and within two years was in the midst of a civil war, with armies raised by communists and by minority groups ranged against it.

In the Malay Peninsula, Britain introduced a scheme for a Malayan Union that brought the states of the peninsula under a single administration. This arrangement aroused vigorous opposition on the part of the Malays, who insisted on maintaining the separate identity of the individual states and in the end forced the British to replace it with a federal system in 1948. The Malays did not press for early independence, fearing the political influence of the Chinese, who constituted a majority in some states. Independence came in 1957, delayed by this issue and by the Malayan Emergency, a war fought against an opposition that was mainly Chinese and communist. The constitution worked out for independent Malaya included safeguards for the political and economic position of the Malay population.

On March 27, 1945, France announced the creation of a French Union made up of "the Indochinese federation together with France and other parts of the community." The prewar emphasis on social and economic development was maintained, and a law passed on April 30, 1946, gave priority to satisfying the needs and the social progress of autochthonous peoples, as well as cooperating in programs for economic recovery.[62] The postwar Constituent Assembly included provisions for the French Union in the draft constitution for the Fourth Republic. According to Charles André Julien, delegates trying to reconcile federalism and assimilation "threw together clauses inspired by opposing and sometimes contradictory schools of thought."[63]

The formula of a union based on free consent was used, but it was also stated that the overseas territories were part of France and came under French law. There was complete contradiction between the Jacobin principle of the "French Republic one and indivisible," quoted in Article 114, and the "Union based on free consent," referred to in Article 41.[64] The new constitution established important principles for inhabitants of French colonies, including the granting of human rights and citizenship and the creation of local assemblies.

By 1947, the French Union was facing armed challenges in Indochina and Madagascar, and a survey of public opinion taken in that year indicated that just 37 percent of the French population believed in its durability.[65] Within a decade, the union was effectively dead. It had operated on the principle of voluntary participation by associated states, and many states had shown clearly that they had no wish to remain tied to France.[66] In Indochina, the conflict began with an effort by France to recover its lost colonial territories. Because Vichy France and Japan were allies, the Japanese left Indochina in French hands until March 9, 1945, when the changed situation in Europe caused them to take control of the territory and intern the French population living there. The Japanese installed an indigenous regime headed by the emperor Bảo Đại, an arrangement the Việt Minh resistance immediately challenged.

On March 24, 1945, the French government announced a new constitutional status for Indochina, which would no longer be a colony but rather a state known as the Indochinese Federation, made up of five parts (Cochin China, Annam, Tonkin, Cambodia, and Laos). In making this announcement, France sought to forestall objections from the United States and other anti-imperialist powers to resumption of French rule and at the same time to reach out to public opinion within Indochina by introducing political reforms. With regard to the latter objective, the announcement was counterproductive, for many Vietnamese wanted to unite Tonkin, Annam, and Cochin China into a single state, and saw the French gesture as a scheme to keep Vietnam divided and weak. International opinion would remain hostile to imperial adventures, but when de Gaulle sent an expeditionary force to Indochina in October 1945 it was clear that, whatever other powers might think of such a move, none of them was going to offer significant opposition. The British, seeking to strengthen France in Europe and concerned about stability and undesirable precedents in the Far East, voiced open support, and at the San Francisco Conference the United States assured the French that it had never questioned French sovereignty in Indochina. When de Gaulle acted, Acting Secretary of State Dean Acheson said the United States had "no thought of opposing the reestablishment of French control."[67]

On March 6, 1946, the French signed an agreement recognizing the Democratic Republic of Vietnam (DRV) as a free state within the Indochinese Federation and the French Union. However, Cochin China, the only part of Vietnam that had been a true colony rather than a protectorate, remained outside the DRV. Citing Cochin China's distinctive history and peculiar economic and administrative patterns, France proposed to maintain its separate status, and on June 1 recognized a free Republic of Cochin China. The DRV, for which Cochin China represented a source of rice and export earnings as well as an outlet for surplus population, strongly opposed French pretensions in the south, and this issue among others sustained the conflict between the two sides.

In 1949, China, now under a communist government, threw its weight behind the DRV, changing the entire complexion of the conflict. What had been an effort by an imperial power to regain control over its former colony was now firmly established as part of the Cold War, and the conflict quickly became internationalized. France's 1954 defeat at Điện Biên Phủ marked the end of French involvement in Indochina, but outside forces shaped the settlement that followed. Hồ accepted a division of Vietnam at the seventeenth parallel during the negotiations at Geneva under pressure from China, which hoped to forestall American intervention.[68] The Americans, unhappy about a capitulation to a communist regime, wanted France to fight on, but the French lacked both military capacity and political support at home and saw no alternative to a transfer of power. Marilyn Young observes that local realities counted for little in the negotiations, "Each of the major powers—China, the Soviet Union, the United States, and France—had its own agenda, and a united, sovereign Vietnam was not on anyone's list."[69]

Like France, the Netherlands hoped to overcome international opposition by means of a fait accompli in Indonesia. In February 1946, the Dutch government issued a policy statement on the future of Indonesia that took the unprecedented step of discussing possible independence: The people of Indonesia, it said, "should, after a given preparatory period, be enabled freely to decide their political destiny," and the Dutch government was "to create and to fulfil as soon as possible the conditions which will permit such a free decision to be taken and which will assure its international recognition." Then came a crucial detail: Indonesia was to become a commonwealth made up of "territories possessing different degrees of autonomy," although a single citizenship extending across these territories would embrace people of all ethnic and racial groups.[70] This statement represented an enormous departure from Dutch policy before the war, but failed to satisfy the nationalist aspirations of Indonesia's postwar leadership, which favored a single state embracing the entire territory formerly controlled by the Netherlands Indies or possibly a greater Indonesia that would include the Philippines and the Malay Peninsula. Beyond this issue, however, lay a broader concern, for the new leadership flatly rejected Dutch pretensions in claiming a right to determine Indonesia's future.

Until the final phase of the conflict between the Dutch and the republic, the United States sided with the Netherlands, and American support was, in the words of Robert J. McMahon, "a sine qua non for the continuance of The Hague's presence in the archipelago." However, when the republic suppressed a communist uprising at Madiun in 1948, the Americans began to see Indonesia as a possible Cold War ally, and after the Dutch launched their second police action in December 1948, the Americans threw their support behind the republic, motivated by "the weight of domestic and international opinion, concern for the viability of the United Nations, and the strength of a vigorous Indonesian guerrilla movement that thwarted all Dutch efforts to pacify the islands and exposed The Hague's policy as an abject failure." At this point, "the Dutch position became untenable."[71]

The colonial powers faced questions about military power and political will in evaluating their postwar position vis-à-vis their colonial territories. However, in each country there was also a crucial question of public support for imperialism, and despite efforts over the years to inculcate a sense of pride in empire, it became clear after the war that popular support for colonial adventures was lacking. Neither the British nor the Americans attached importance to empire as a necessary condition of their own continued economic prosperity and political strength. In contrast, the Dutch considered that the loss of Indonesia would devastate their national economy, while the French, with their assimilationist traditions, viewed the loss of empire as in some respects a dismemberment of France itself.[72] However, public opinion surveys carried out in France and Britain suggested that people had little interest in imperialism. In France, the concept of the French Union was poorly understood, and many people considered it to be simply the old empire with a new name, rather than a new form of partnership. This lack of understanding extended to basic knowledge of colonial affairs: A survey conducted in 1949 revealed that 19 percent of the French people did not know the name of a single overseas territory held by France, and just 28 percent could name five or more. Some 32 percent of those surveyed said they knew nothing about colonial matters, and 52 percent declared themselves indifferent to colonial issues; roughly the same proportion could not give a reasonably accurate definition of the French Union.[73]

In Britain, a survey conducted in May 1948 revealed a similar ignorance of colonial affairs.[74] Moreover, popular feeling had turned against the British Empire. The well-known historian A. J. P. Taylor summed up the British situation in the following way, "The archives now reveal that Great Britain was fighting the Second World War in order to recover the British Empire and even (as with Libya) to add to it. Those who did the actual fighting had simpler aims. They fought to liberate the peoples of Europe from Germany and those of the Far East from Japan. That spirit dominated after the war. The British did not relinquish their Empire by accident. They ceased to believe in it."[75]

## Conclusion

"Colonialism" was a set of complex and shifting phenomena, shaped by political and economic pressures in the countries that held overseas territories, in the colonial areas, and in the broader world environment. The penultimate phase of colonialism in Southeast Asia, preceding the transition to independence, featured radical proposals designed to restructure the territories held by the colonial powers and to create new mechanisms of government and administration. When the Japanese occupation temporarily put an end to Western rule in Southeast Asia, the elimination of many vested interests seemed to create an environment conducive to change. The Western powers fought the war with a determination to restore the prewar status quo, however, while reformers within the colonies, who would become a dominant force after the conflict, wanted to take over the colonial territories and their tools of administration intact rather than explore new forms of organization that threatened to curtail their autonomy. When the colonial powers promoted local nationalism and federal schemes, these reformers countered with a form of nationalism that embraced the disparate peoples who lived within their respective territories and with centralized administrations that drew together the somewhat ramshackle structures of the colonial state.

Western proposals for internationalizing colonial territories came to naught, and in the aftermath of the transition to independence the former colonial powers faced new states driven by an aggressive nationalism and an urgent need to create self-supporting economic and political structures. At the same time, they found varying degrees of good and ill will arising from shared experiences in the past and cautious interest in reshaping old colonial linkages to serve new national agendas. Ahead lay a tortuous process of negotiation to create a new order.

# 2

# The Impact of World War II on Decolonization

## *Jost Dülffer*

In 1933, the British Defense Requirement Committee, a subcommittee of the Committee of Imperial Defense, debated the possibilities of a future war. Germany, Japan, and Italy were seen as the most probable potential enemies. The threat potential of each, however, was perceived differently.[1] While Admiral Ernle Chatfield regarded Japan as the most dangerous threat to the British Empire, Sir Robert Vansittart, the permanent undersecretary of state, argued that it was Germany. The compromise formula of the committee, proposed by Sir Maurice Hankey, saw Japan as the greater immediate danger, but Germany as "the ultimate potential enemy." There was unanimity that the most difficult constellation for the British Empire would arise if all the three powers were expanding simultaneously. To avoid such a crisis scenario, an appeasement policy was devised—designed to use compromise as a means of reducing the tensions of one or two potential enemies. France and the United States followed Britain's lead in this: each also tried to avoid a war that was seen as a threat to the world economy and to domestic welfare.

World War II turned the worst-case scenario into reality, with cumulative effects on the status quo powers. By 1942, Germany had occupied large parts of Europe and directly or indirectly dominated the territories from France, Belgium, and the Netherlands in the West to Norway and Denmark in the North. Large parts of Eastern Europe passed into the German orbit while the Wehrmacht fought Soviet Russia from Murmansk to the Caucasus. In the South, the German empire shared its dominance with Italy in the Balkans up to Crete and the Aegean Sea. In North Africa, the Axis powers invaded Tunisia and reached parts of Egypt on their way to the West, while Italy held Ethiopia and Somalia in East Africa. Japan, on the other hand, controlled large parts of the western Pacific Ocean and parts of China (especially Manchuria and most of the coast). Southeast Asia from Burma to portions of New Guinea also came under Japanese domination.

The three expansionist efforts together created the basis for a gigantic new phase of empire building. Although brought to a halt by a worldwide coalition in 1945, the Axis push seemed like the wave of the future in the late 1930s and early 1940s. As such, German, Italian, and Japanese impulses toward empire have an often-unappreciated relevance to the study of post-1945 decolonization, a relevance that can be gauged by considering four issues:

1. Program and intentions of the Axis powers
2. Implications for the dependent or colonized countries
3. Impact on the colonial powers
4. Overall significance for the international system

Nazi Germany was determined to secure *Lebensraum* (living space) in the East, with eyes essentially set on expansion as far as possible to the Ural Mountains. Racial and ideological calculations were key motivating forces, for example, the perceived superiority of the German and Aryan race over Jewish bolshevism. Economic motives were also relevant, as territorial expansion would facilitate economic expansion in the future. The General Plan East of the years 1942–1944 envisioned a German settlement campaign that would bring a "racial nucleus" of approximately 110 million men to the East through the resettlement of up to 25 million people. Germans from all over the world would be the beneficiaries, while Jews and segments of the Slavic population would be eliminated or resettled in ways that would make them slaves of their new masters. It was a murderous new brand of colonialism.[2]

There were also plans for the acquisition of other colonies in a more traditionalist style. Forced to renounce its former colonies in the Versailles Treaty of 1919, Germany came to advocate the integral restitution of all these territories in the 1930s. The government secretly approached Japan in 1937–1938 with a view to abdicating all rights in the Pacific, but remained convinced that former African colonies (Southwest Africa [Namibia], Togo, Cameroon, and German East Africa [Tanzania]) should be restored. Internal plans spoke about the "colonial mission of the white man" and envisioned a "White brain, black arm" division of labor.[3] Following the German victory over western Europe in 1940—which brought the colonial powers France, Belgium, and the Netherlands into the German orbit—colonialist claims and internal plans were expanded. While these continued to be seen as secondary to expansion in the East, economic interest groups, the German navy, and sectors of the Foreign Office envisaged a colonial empire in Central Africa.[4] Apart from naval bases around the continent, Madagascar was regarded as a possible site for the relocation of European Jews.[5] Africa as a whole would form a "supplementary space" for the German economy. A June 1940 plan from the Naval High Command envisioned a German Central Africa composed of the Belgian Congo, French Equatorial Africa, and the whole territory of French West

Africa south of the Senegal River (French Guinea, the Ivory Coast, and Dahomey, as well as parts of the French Sudan and Niger). Because South Africa, a potential partner, might acquire former German Southwest Africa, Germany might also acquire parts of the territories north of that region—and eventually Portuguese possessions as well. German plans through 1942 saw the western part of North Africa as a region of competition and conflict between Vichy France, Spain, and Italy and assumed that this region would have to be dealt with according to tactical expediencies while war continued.

In principle, the Third Reich did not challenge the long-term aims of fascist Italy in North Africa, which somewhat vaguely envisioned the restoration of the former Roman Empire. Besides Ethiopia and Somalia (conquered after 1936) and Libya, the whole Mediterranean area lay in this realm, as did parts of southeastern Europe (the Balkans) and the Middle East. Because of Italy's defeats from 1940 on, German troops supplemented or replaced Italian military in North Africa as well as in the Balkans, where the two fascist regimes split their responsibility for the occupation of Yugoslavia and Greece. Together, the Axis partners planned to eliminate the influence of the European colonial empires by a new partition of Africa and the liberation of the Arab world, especially in the Middle East.

This vision opened up fields of potential cooperation with Japan. The most basic agreement in this direction, however, was the joint military agreement of January 18, 1942, which in the final analysis amounted more to a separation of operations and the possible delineation of distinct spheres of influence.

As with the Third Reich, Japan's expansionist plans grew from racial, ideological, and economic roots. The concept of a superior "Yamato" race, for example, provided one springboard. The problems of the Great Depression were intensified by early wartime needs for energy and raw materials, leading to the burgeoning imperial vision captured by the term "Greater East Asia Co-prosperity Sphere."[6] During 1942–1943, the Japanese Ministry of Health and Welfare developed plans to "establish the superiority of East Asia in a new global economy." The war had to continue "until Anglo-American imperialistic democracy had been completely vanquished and a new world order erected in the place," it was argued.[7] Plans envisioned four stages of enlargement. While the first stage roughly comprised the then occupied countries on the mainland, stages two and three targeted large areas of Southeast Asia as well as Australia, New Zealand, and the remainder of China. Stage four envisaged the incorporation of India and the Soviet territories east of Lake Baikal.

Japan's expansionist actions were complicated in nature, but significant in impact. On the one hand, it would be tempting to dismiss performance as a sham. Although direct conquest was not propagated, a Japanese "New Deal" for Asia actually came to involve suppression, exploitation, and sometimes murderous warfare in the occupied countries. On the other hand, continual emphasis on Asian interests and Asia's future had powerful long-term implications. At the Great East Asian Conference held in Tokyo in November 1943, for example, Prime Minister Tojo Hideki claimed, "Japan is grateful to the nations of Greater East Asia for the whole-hearted cooperation which they are rendering in this war. Japan is firmly determined, by cooperating with them and by strengthening her collaboration with her allies in Europe, to carry on." A joint declaration stressed mutual cooperation, fraternity, common economic development, and regional cooperation, "The countries of Greater East Asia by respecting one another's traditions and developing the creative faculties of each race, will enhance the culture and civilization of Greater East Asia."[8] Even if this well-orchestrated conference had not much to do with actual occupation policies, a platform was created in which an anticolonial discourse could become dominant. As Peter Duus, Ramon H. Myers, and Marc R. Peattie state, "By liberating the colonial peoples, not only would Japan lay the foundation for their national independence, it would also create a regional economic block that would benefit its inhabitants rather than outsiders."[9]

German rule never had more than limited anticolonial appeal. The concept of *Lebensraum* in the East was not likely to be a useful tool for dissolving the multiethnic Soviet empire, for example. Suppression and exploitation of all Slavs was too blatantly obvious and controlling. Only chief party ideologist Alfred Rosenberg, who became minister of the occupied Eastern territories, tried appealing to the different peoples of the Soviet Union to unite against the "Great Russians." This policy of a potential national and anticolonial breakup of the Russian empire had no chance of implementation within the framework of the actual occupation policy, however. The "European crusade against Bolshevism" was only a propaganda device, and post-1943 efforts to unite the industrialized regions of Europe in a kind of economic community also failed because the clear preponderance of German interests and warfare was obvious.

Nor were anticolonial appeals of any importance in Africa. Even anti-British appeals to South African politicians and the Boers in particular were of little use because the Axis powers had no real power with which to support the possibility of realignment in the area. Moreover, apart from the French colonies, which were controlled by "Free France" under Charles de Gaulle in London, Vichy France derived part of its remaining domestic as well as international authority through its overseas possessions, especially in Africa. Any German attempt to exert a direct influence in these territories would have driven them into the Allied camp while simultaneously weakening Vichy authorities.

Somewhat different was the situation in the Balkans. Although Germany and Italy split up former Yugoslavia by creating a dependent fascist Ustascha state in Croatia, this amounted to something like a nation-building effort within a multinational state, rather than decolonization.[10] In the Middle East, on the other hand, German warfare did open up certain anticolonial possibilities in 1941–1942. German troops planned to unite their forces in the Middle East by moving southward from the Caucasus, eastward from Libya to Egypt, and possibly also from the Balkans (with the assumption that Turkey would eventually join the Axis powers). Anti-British propaganda by the Germans was popular in Egyptian nationalist circles—particularly with the Wafd Party that included the young officers Gamal Abdel Nasser and Anwar el-Sadat. Amin el-Husseini, the grandmufti of Jerusalem, was regarded as a potential alternative to the British mandates system. More important, however, was the idea of a nationalist revolt in Iraq: this actually took place in 1942 but failed because German military support did not materialize as expected. A culmination of projected maneuvers in the region came with a joint German–Italian–Japanese declaration on the liberation of India and Arabia, on April 13, 1942, "Japan, Germany and Italy do not have second thoughts to replace Great Britain in India or Arabia. What the three powers actually want is the immediate realization of the idea 'India to the Indians' and 'Arabia to the Arabians' and the earliest possible rise of the day when these people as free nations will contribute essentially to progress of culture and civilization of the world."[11] The declaration was never published, however, because the overall strategic situation never brought the Axis powers into a position where they could combine an appeal to revolt with appropriate military action.

Asian reactions to Japanese expansion were thus different in many respects from European responses to German conquest and nation-building. Germany and Italy only made minor moves toward conquering colonial territories of Africa, whereas Japan overran great parts of European-ruled Southeast Asia in only a few months. Japan's military success exerted great influence on indigenous elites. What these elites had not envisaged or dared was now achieved by an Asian power: the breakdown of colonial rule.

Thailand's role was singular in the Japanese sphere because it remained formally independent.[12] Although Prime Minister Phibun Songkhram concluded a formal alliance on December 21, 1941, and declared war on the United States and Great Britain, Thai policies consistently tried to steer a cautious course between distance and collaboration. Initially, Japan respected Bangkok's policy of refraining from a close alliance. Later in the war, however, Tokyo's approach to Thailand evolved into a thinly veiled effort to dominate the country. Somewhat comparable to the Thai situation was that in the

Philippines. This U.S.-held territory had been promised independence well before the Pacific war and its political elite was more or less satisfied with that prospect.[13] José P. Laurel, who functioned as a placeholder for President Manuel Quezon, who was in exile in Australia, initially did no more than necessary to accommodate Japanese wishes as a typical collaborator.

The case of Indochina was different. The Japanese exerted the authority of an occupational regime, but in this case it was essentially over another colonial regime—given the fact that Vichy France retained formal autonomy in the ruling of Indochina. Thus emerged a kind of double colonialism, with Japanese predominance forcing France into a kind of *sub*domination. All left-wing national forces and their propaganda were energetically suppressed as a result.[14]

Burma and Indonesia belonged to a similar category of nationalist hopes during the Japanese occupation. Japanese troops were greeted as liberators in Burma as well as in Indonesia.[15] At first, Japanese anticolonial propaganda was widely accepted, but after half a year of occupation, disillusionment spread and tendencies to resist increased. Still, nationalist leaders in both countries found it useful to comply to Japan's hegemonic position in order to achieve national independence. In Burma, Prime Minister Ba Maw, in an endeavor to keep his anti-British profile, sought close cooperation with the Japanese leadership, a tendency that he had developed even before the Japanese invasion.[16] He used his relations with the Japanese in order to modify the hardships of occupation. At the Greater East Asia Conference, he voiced opinions that were bound to flatter Japanese ears. He kept his loyalty to Japan until the end of the war, and he favored fighting the British even after the Japanese retreat. Eventually, Defense Minister Aung Sang realistically assessed Japan's diminishing military potential and shifted the loyalties of his Burma liberation army.[17] This shift became the basis for negotiating independence.

In the Indonesia case, important national leaders like Sukarno and Mohammed Hatta had been imprisoned by the Dutch authorities for eight years. Both had reason to seek Japanese assistance for liberation from European dominance. Sukarno was ready to accept any means for the liberation of his country, but also seemed to be positively impressed by Japan's East Asian ideology as well as by its modernization efforts. Hatta, in contrast, probably kept a greater distance from Japan and paid only lip service to the occupier's Asian intentions. Both, nevertheless, stressed the need for discipline and compliance during the war. Their ultimate objective was to gain independence by 1947.

The situations in China and India were more complicated. China remained an independent state, but Japanese attempts to create an alternative government by promoting Wang Ching-wei failed. This puppet regime, formally allied with Japan, never became a popular alternative to either the Kuomintang government or the communist forces.[18] The Indian case was especially important. India became a cornerstone for the decolonization process after the spring of 1942, when it was threatened with direct Japanese attack. (Like the Soviet Union, India could have been the focus of a German-Japanese combined military operation.) Because it was indispensable to British war production and because it became the central geographical link for the support of China by the Western powers after the fall of Burma, the threat of a Japanese inroad was used as a tool for the promotion of Indian independence. At moments in 1942 and again in 1944, sectors of the Indian population in the East developed a sympathetic orientation toward Japan.[19] The culmination of this phenomenon was the Congress Party's "Quit India" resolution of August 1942. Though Jawaharlal Nehru was clearly oriented toward the Western political model, he nevertheless thought it expedient to push for an Anglo-American withdrawal in order to deprive Japan of all pretexts for an assault on India. Nehru was anxious to steer a moderate course that would prevent driving Indian policies during the war toward the Axis powers by rousing too much anti-British feeling, but the British cracked down on the Congress Party, imprisoned many party leaders, and suppressed the uprising of August 1942. The June 1942 conference of Southeast Asian Indians in Bangkok increased pressure for immediate Indian independence from abroad added to the national conflict.[20] An Indian Independence League and the nucleus of an Indian National Army, formed outside the country, were the most significant signs. After the British had consolidated the military position in India, toward the end of 1942, pressures for Indian independence declined. But the possibilities of the double effect of external warfare and internal opposition remained a threat to British rule.

In July 1943, Subhas Chandra Bose, who in exile had developed sympathy for the German model of national socialism as well as for Soviet communism, took over the coordination of the Southeast Asian Indian forces in Singapore. In coordination with Tokyo, he proclaimed a "Provisional Government of Free India" on October 10, 1943.[21] At the same time, "Free India" declared war on Great Britain and the United States (though not on China). Bose was able to hoist the Indian flag of the Congress Party on the Andaman Islands on Indian territory, while proclaiming the liberation of his motherland as a goal for the following year. Bose remained politically dependent on Japan, and with the failed Japanese (and "Free Indian") attack on Imphal in March 1944 a "March on Delhi" project was doomed. Bose's public appeal to Mahatma Gandhi in July 1944 thus had no political effect. As a manifestation of Indian nationalism, however, Bose's appeal carried a meaning well understood by many, "India's last war of independence has begun. Troops of the Ashad Hind Fouj are now fighting bravely on the soil of India and in spite of difficulty and hardship they are pushing forward, slowly but steadily. This armed struggle will go on until the last Britisher is thrown out of India and until our Tricolour National Flag proudly floats over the viceroy's house in New Delhi."[22]

To sum up: National independence in Japanese-dominated Asia was declared only after the military successes had passed their zenith. While Thailand remained independent, Burma and the Philippines declared their national sovereignty in 1943. Indonesia and Malaya remained "imperial territories," but the former was promised independence after the war in November 1944.[23] The Greater East Asia Conference of November 5, 1943, thus represented a meeting of six only superficially independent allies of Japan: Burma, Manchukuo, (Nanking-)China, Thailand, the Philippines, and Free India. Although in political reality this did not change the character of suppression and exploitation, the status of international independence could not easily be revoked after the Japanese defeat in 1945.

According to a memorandum written by Bose for the German government, the Indian leader expected "the collapse of the British Empire" following the fall of India. And, he continued,

> Canada, Australia and New Zealand will gravitate towards the United States of America. Ireland, South-Africa, India, Palestine, Egypt, Iraq etc. will throw off the British yoke and attain full-fledged independence. And the African colonies of England will be divided among the other powers. Great Britain will remain as a third class power in Europe, with no influence on the Continent. . . . It is hardly necessary to add that we in India want to see the complete dismemberment of this Empire, for we regard it as the greatest curse in modern history.[24]

The realization of such a vision depended on the outcome of the war, which at some points was not so clear as the later Anglo-American victory suggested in hindsight.[25] Nevertheless, there was unanimity in the British War Cabinet that Britain's position in Asia had to be restored once victory was achieved.[26] As Winston Churchill put it in 1942, a British dominion could not be "overwhelmed by a yellow race"—and in the British perception indigenous people were rather looking forward to the "liberation" by white peoples instead of a continuation of Japanese rule. Soon after the war, the Labour government expressed itself proud of the fact that "no British Colony was permanently lost as a result of foreign conquest."[27] But the shock of the Japanese conquest and in particular the speedy conquest of Singapore went deep. It was seen as the greatest defeat in British military history:

For the time, the curtain has rung down on Britain's colonial holding in the Far East, and whenever it is rung up again it will certainly be on a radically different scene. There can be no return to the old system once Japan has been defeated. . . . The need is for entirely new principles, or rather, the consistent application of principles to which lip service has long been paid. For the Colonies—Malaya, Indochina and Netherlands-India—there can be only one goal, the creation of independent nations linked economically, socially and culturally with the old mother country, but leaving to stand firmly on their own feet.[28]

Decolonization had been a vague concept in British political discourse for decades prior to the 1940s. World War II now accelerated this tendency considerably. On the one hand, it became more generally recognized that indirect rule had often only helped to stabilize the position of indigenous leaders or chiefs rather than make it possible to "socially upgrade" the rest of the population. A new and dominating elite had developed rather than responsible self-government. The war years turned representation and self-government into the new catchwords for the future. Even if no clear timetable was evident, it was assumed that movement in this direction would begin immediately after the war. On the other hand, there was ongoing skepticism about the future possibility of a new Commonwealth that incorporated different ethnicities. Politicians of all parties envisaged Britain continuing to conduct the external affairs as well as the foreign trade of the former colonies. The debate about the status of these territories during the war—whether they would belong to the Commonwealth or get Dominion status—inclined more and more to greater independence within the British Empire. As early as 1942, India and Ceylon were promised to get eventual independence, while for Burma the status of domestic self-determination and possible independence was envisaged for five or eight years after the end of the war.

World War II acted as a catalyst in both Labour and Conservative circles. In 1940, a Colonial Development and Welfare Act foresaw large expenditures for social and educational purposes, especially in the African colonies and the West Indies. Pressing war needs limited immediate spending, however.[29] With a view to developing the colonies after the war, a new Colonial Development and Welfare Fund was established in February 1945. Clement Attlee's Labour government then proceeded to test the limits and opportunities of this kind of benevolent paternalism after July 1945.

French colonial rule was even more shattered than the British Empire. The greater part of the African colonies as well as Indochina (under Japanese domination) remained loyal to the Vichy government. While being unable to contribute materially to the declining power of the government in Europe, the French colonial administrators were more or less forced to accept a greater degree of indigenous cooperation. This encompassed a tendency toward greater autonomy. How far the catchword of patriotism was understood in terms of African nationalism is a difficult question to answer.[30]

Racial discrimination apparently played a role in Vichy colonial thought and practice as well. For tactical reasons, Vichy officials promised independence for the mandated states of Syria (in 1941) and Lebanon (in 1944). This had repercussions for immediate postwar reoccupation by French forces of the Comité National Française de la Liberation Nationale (CFLN). Free France, on the other hand, tried to strengthen its image as a great power with colonial possessions—even at the price of an attack on Vichy troops in the failed attempt to reconquer Dakar. In terms of politics as well as transport, however, de Gaulle's forces were dependent on British capabilities and also on U.S. support (after 1942–1943 in North Africa). Neither country wanted to contribute directly to the restoration of French colonial authority. But as with Vichy France, Free France colonial administrators had to rely on local "Évoluées" to a greater extent than before. This had a tendency to strengthen new elites and to form the nucleus of a future national class.[31]

The founding of the CFLN in Algiers in June 1943 highlighted the perception of a new kind of relationship between colonies and the metropole.[32] At the colonial conference in Brazzaville, de Gaulle sought a solution through "integration into the French community." This community, it was argued—or Union Française, as it was subsequently named—should create French citizens in "plus grande France." The intention was to provide the status of French citizenship for an elite of indigenous people with full rights accruing via assimilation—but without running the risk of a future *reverse* colonization of France by a majority of extra-European citizens. Only in vague notions of "federalism" were concessions envisaged involving some forms of local self-determination. In comparison to the British model, the Union Française would lead to a very different kind of connection, "Colonialism should be surmounted by elevating the vassals to full citizens and by creating political units anchored firmly in the new French constitution."[33]

This finally happened in 1946, with a differentiated model of territories, all belonging to the new Union Française. But from Algeria to Syria to Vietnam, military conflict with nationalist forces demonstrated the limited attractiveness of this model.

The case of the Belgian Congo was different from both the British and French examples. The Belgian government in exile kept formal authority over its colony, but U.S. interests penetrated the Congo in a much stronger way than in any other country. It was uranium that most aroused American interest from 1942 on, thanks to the Manhattan Project. In a tripartite agreement with the United States and Great Britain, the London-based Belgian government committed much of its uranium to the United States. It was economic exploitation as well as transit routes that made Africa (especially the Congo) increasingly important for U.S. military strategy during World War II. On one occasion in 1943, Undersecretary of State Sumner Welles even argued "that in the case of the Congo and many other areas, it would certainly take more than a hundred years [to achieve self-government]." Meanwhile, Belgian authorities in the Congo worried about the problematic impact of American troops with black soldiers, "American blacks and Congo blacks have only color in common. American Negroes are a civilized people. Their presence would have a bad effect on the Congo natives, especially on the detribalized native clerks. The latter could immediately think, they should earn the same wage as American black troops." As a consequence, U.S. penetration in the Congo was administered by Belgian authorities following the liberation of Belgium in 1944–1945.[34]

The Netherlands experiences provide yet another example. While Dutch colonial rule in Surinam was never threatened during the war, the Japanese occupation of Indonesia brought about a complete breakdown of communications between center and periphery. To regain the initiative, Queen Wilhelmina declared in December 1942 that after the war the old colonial order would be replaced by a Dutch-Indonesian union based on equality and freedom. However, as Dutch strategic planning during the war made clear, the reoccupation of Indonesia and the establishment of a position of strength had to precede all efforts at creating the union. By 1945, the Dutch position was probably the weakest of all colonial powers: due to the German occupation, its economy lay in ruins; to regain a foothold in Indonesia, it was dependent on the Allies; and it faced a determined and relatively well-organized nationalist movement. The idea of a union survived World War II, however, and even independence day. It envisaged a common foreign policy and a common trade policy, with the Dutch queen as head of the union. However, due to the relative strength of the nationalist movement and the overall weakness of the Dutch, it was a stillborn creature from its inception. In contrast to Indonesia, the Dutch position in Surinam and Curaçao remained secure. Continued colonial rule during the war, ethnic heterogeneity, and the absence of any kind of indigenous nationalism made continued Dutch colonial rule self-evident.[35]

The expansionist policies of the "fascist" states translated into some of the greatest colonial experiments in history. Although the experiments' exploitative, terroristic, and racist impulses failed, they had a significant impact on the international system of the twentieth century—very much including the future of colonialism. Multiple forces affecting both imperial powers and colonial populations—in Southeast Asia and beyond—can be seen as gestating during the war to defeat the Axis.

John Darwin, for example, cites World War II's impact on the imperial will of once powerful states in what he describes as the "metropolitan theory" of decolonization.[36] Although Britain and France had been reexamining relationships and structures prior to 1939, the speed of movement and the nature of policies was clearly accelerated by the war. In particular, more attention was paid to devising means of maintaining imperial greatness by working with colonies on a process of social, economic, and political development.[37]

Darwin also cites an "international theory" that emphasizes the decline of the European colonial powers within the context of the global arena. France had lost its great power status during the Vichy period of occupation and collaboration and was then only reinstalled as a great power because of Britain's desire to concentrate more on its empire and less on the European continent. In the British case, "imperial overstretch" was based on international debts and growing dependence on the United States. It found an important early expression in the U.S. loan to Britain in 1945.

The course of World War II also saw the emergence of major *local* difficulties for colonial powers, with the particularly significant rise of anticolonialist nationalism. This was true within the fascist powers' sphere as well as beyond—and was a crucial factor in the grassroots developments that were to make the Third World such volatile terrain after 1945.

American war efforts proved decisive in ensuring allied victory—through both direct combat and an indirect role that stretched from Europe and Africa, to the Middle East and India, to East and Southeast Asia and the Pacific. The military and economic power demonstrated in wartime gave the United States a crucial role in the post-1945 decolonization process. This role had special characteristics. Americans saw themselves within a revolutionary tradition, and leaders like Franklin D. Roosevelt assumed that one of the world's first independent colonies would become a champion of further decolonization.[38]

The struggle against the Axis also helped to generate the Cold War—and this, in turn, had a considerable impact on the course of decolonization after 1945. On the one hand, for example, the whole question of colonialism came to be discussed in increasingly ideological terms—as one element in the global culture war between the "free world" and "totalitarian communism." On the other hand, the Cold War had a particularly important impact on the course of American policy. The anticolonial bias of the United States regularly became secondary to its anticommunism, with support mounting for the reinstallation of European colonial powers or even the direct American takeover of formerly European roles in areas like the Middle East and Southeast Asia.

# 3

# The Economic Impact of Decolonization in Southeast Asia

## Economic Nationalism and Foreign Direct Investment, 1945–1965

*J. Thomas Lindblad*

"The demands of nationalism appear to be irreconcilable with the obligations of a borrower." This was the dry remark offered by a contemporary Western observer when reviewing the prospects for American investment in Southeast Asia during the period of decolonization that followed World War II.[1] Simple as it is, this statement epitomizes a fundamental dilemma of the newly independent regimes in Southeast Asia at the time. There was an urgent need to restructure economies and to reduce the extreme dependence on world markets for primary products. This could be done precisely because national governments at home, and not colonial offices far away, were setting the priorities of economic policy. But structural transformations required massive injections of capital that was in short supply at home. Status as a colony was thus replaced by status as a debtor and recipient of foreign direct investment. Meanwhile, the assertion of national identity required that all traces of a colonial-like dependent relation be eradicated. This proved to be an insolvable problem facing several countries at the same time.

A survey of attempted solutions to this dilemma can focus on three major former colonies in Southeast Asia: Indonesia (independent in 1945), the Philippines (independent in 1946), and Malaysia (independent in 1957). They represent three different types of colonial heritage: the interventionist and ethically inspired Dutch one in Indonesia, the comparatively progressive American one in the Philippines, and the traditional liberal one in Malaysia. The economic impact of decolonization in these three countries is considered under four headings:

1. Challenges facing the national governments
2. Economic policies pursued by the national governments, especially with regard to foreign investment

3. Investment climate as it evolved over time
4. Actual development of foreign investment commitments

The discussion draws on contemporary observations made without the benefit of hindsight as well as later historical analysis. It should be mentioned that the statistical base for identifying magnitudes of foreign investment in this period is disturbingly weak. Much better estimates exist for either the preceding period (the late colonial situation prevailing up to 1942) or the subsequent period (the time of industrialization and economic growth running from the 1960s up to the Asian crisis in 1997).[2]

Several former colonies in the region are not considered here: Myanmar (Burma), Vietnam, Laos, and Cambodia. In these countries, conditions for foreign investment soon changed in such an extreme way that the whole question of trying to strike a balance between economic nationalism and the interests of foreign investors or creditors became senseless. In Myanmar, public resentment of foreign predominance in the economy did translate into a kind of partnership between government and foreign finance in the early 1950s, but this period proved to be only a first step toward expropriation and full state control of the economy. The division of Vietnam in 1954 into a communist North and an American-controlled South, on the other hand, created a situation in which warfare became the overriding concern behind economic policies.

## Indonesia: Achieving Full Independence

It was the well-known nationalist leader Hadji Agus Salim who shortly after the declaration of independence stated that the Indonesian revolution "has yet to enter its economic phase." This was no less true ten years after the declaration of independence, in 1955, when much of Indonesia's economic life was still controlled by foreign capital interests, Dutch corporations in particular. The story of what happened to foreign capital in Indonesia during the 1950s has been told several times.[3] It includes the *benteng* (fortress) policy to foster Indonesian entrepreneurship (launched in 1951), the subsequent deterioration of the economic climate for foreign firms, the escalating conflict with the Netherlands on the future of Irian Jaya (West New Guinea/Papua), the nationalization without compensation of remaining Dutch business interests in 1957–1958, Sukarno's shift to a "Guided Economy" in 1958, the "Confrontation" policy against Malaysia, and the expropriation of British and American firms from 1963 to 1965. The downward trend with regard to business prospects was only reversed with the downfall of Sukarno and the establishment of the New Order government in 1966.

Although it is tempting to take a global view of this episode in Indonesian economic history, regarding it as an interlude in which politics took precedence above economics, it is more instructive to consider the challenges, policies, investment climate, and investment flows separately in order to get a fuller understanding of the situation. Such an approach obviously also facilitates international comparison.

The economic challenges facing the Indonesian government in the 1950s were truly formidable. Per capita incomes were on the same level as in South Asia—lower than in 1939, possibly even lower than in 1929 or 1919. A structural retrogression had taken place in the economy with labor moving from more productive modern industries to low-productive pursuits in the traditional sector.[4] Poverty was widespread, with agricultural output only 19 percent higher than in the 1930s, a figure that should be compared to 37 percent in Malaysia or 45 percent in the Philippines.[5] Short-term problems were accompanied by the long-run need to reduce the high degree of dependence on exports of primary products, notably sugar, rubber, and tobacco. The extreme vulnerability of the Indonesian economy to price falls in world markets had been demonstrated very forcefully during the economic depression of the 1930s.

In short, Indonesia in the 1950s needed to grow fast, to industrialize, to invest heavily for the benefit of future economic growth, and, not the least important, to wrest control over the economy from the foreign, particularly Dutch, firms operating in the country. The conversion of a colonial economy to a national economy therefore carried two simultaneous connotations: industrialization and Indonesianization. The former aim had only seriously been contemplated by the colonial government toward the very end of colonial rule, in the late 1930s, whereas the latter aim did not necessarily imply a nationalization of means of production. Assertion of a national identity in economic life explicitly aimed at the reduction of Dutch control over much of the economy. The words of the brilliant Indonesian economist and later statesman Sumitro Djojohadikusumo, written during the War of the Revolution, were prophetic, "It was and it is unavoidable that under a nationalist government of a sovereign and independent Indonesia the factors working against Dutch predominance in the economy of Indonesia will gain tremendous momentum and become strong within a very short time."[6] This was clearly top priority in Indonesia under Sukarno.

As it turned out, the growth performance of the Sukarno period was better than the history sketched by New Order architects and memories of hyperinflation. The years of constitutional democracy (1950–1957), saw per capita incomes annually rising by 3.4 percent on average, which, accounting for an annual population growth of no less than 2.3 percent, implies an average increase of national income by 5.7 percent per year.[7] That is not bad by international comparison and it shows that contemporary designations of Indonesia as the "underachiever" or "chronic dropout" among developing countries do not do full justice to reality. The really poor growth performance, when per capita rates actually turned negative, only came after the shift to "Guided Democracy" and Guided Economy in the late 1950s—when, incidentally, Dutch business had already been squeezed out.

It was acknowledged from the start that overseas investment capital would be needed to finance the ambitious restructuring of the economy. Verbal tribute to this principle was paid by the Indonesian government in an official declaration in September 1950. By 1954, Minister of Finance Ong Eng Die (one of the very few Chinese Indonesians to ever occupy a cabinet post) announced that a plan would be made up for the role of private foreign capital in national economic development. But such a plan never saw the light.[8] In 1955, Indonesia's first five-year plan was formulated, with total investment targeted at 6 percent of the gross national product (GNP). Assuming a capital-output ratio of two to one, this would imply an increase in national income of 3 percent, or around 1 percent when accounting for population growth. The government contribution to the investment effort was set at 38 percent, to be financed at least in part by foreign aid or loans. Contemplating future five-year plans, Djuanda, the director of the Development Planning Board and later prime minister, assumed that the ratio of investment to national income could climb to 12 percent and eventually, by 1975, to 20 percent. To international observers, this appeared highly ambitious and scarcely realistic.[9]

In implementing the five-year plan, the Indonesian government often expressed ambivalence with regard to private enterprise. Sukarno's Guided Economy appeared to anticipate an essentially collectivist economic structure that, hardly surprisingly, aroused great concern among Western observers firmly convinced that foreign investment remained the major prerequisite for any kind of further economic development in Indonesia.[10] The eight-year plan, compiled by the newly installed Dewan Perancana Nasional (DEPERNAS; Council for National Planning), was presented in 1961 but did little to restore international confidence. The ratio of investment to the GNP was now set at 13 percent, but at the very high incremental capital-output ratio assumed to be 5.3, this only resulted in an income growth of 2.4 percent, barely sufficient to outpace the population growth. "Even a splendid performance is not likely to solve Indonesia's problems," one observer wrote.[11] Yet, even if DEPERNAS reverted to mass manipulation (including presenting an 8–part plan in 17 volumes, with 1,945 paragraphs symbolizing the day independence was proclaimed), it did not lose sight of Indonesia's pressing economic problems. The necessity of international cooperation was again reaffirmed even though circumstances had changed dramatically since the official declaration by the Indonesian government in September 1950.

Great changes had taken place in the climate for foreign investment apart from new policy initiatives and development planning. Grievances abounded in the early 1950s about heavy taxation, restrictions on capital movements (including repatriation of profits), demands for Indonesianization of staff, damages, thefts, squatter occupations, and, looming large in the background, the ill-defined threat of nationalization. By 1954, there was said to be "heavy disinvestment in foreign-owned estates" and one noted foreign observer bluntly stated that "Indonesia today offers meager prospects."[12]

Complaints continued throughout 1955, in particular with regard to banditry, illegal occupations, theft, and labor disputes. Giant American, British, and Dutch firms left or appeared to be preparing to do so, including General Motors, Proctor and Gamble, Imperial Chemical, Philips, and Billiton Tin.[13] The process of *Indonesianisasi* (Indonesianization, that is, Indonesians taking over senior management or supervisory positions in private companies) proceeded too fast for the taste of contemporary Western observers sharing the common expatriate conviction that access to foreign skills was indispensable to the functioning of the Indonesian economy.[14] Interestingly, former Vice President Mohammed Hatta publicly shared the concern about too rapid a transition to Indonesian leadership in private business.[15] In December 1957 and January 1958, matters went from bad to worse when most remaining Dutch firms were struck by a wave of nationalization. Historians have not yet reached agreement whether these actions were spontaneous, with tacit or subsequent support from Sukarno, or carefully planned by the Indonesian government.[16]

The fourth and final aspect to be considered here concerns the development of actual investment commitments. At the end of the colonial period, Indonesia was the foremost host country for foreign direct investment in Southeast Asia, accounting for more than one-half of the region's total. Estimated foreign capital stock approached $1.3 billion, of which two-thirds or more was held by Dutch firms.[17] British and American firms ranked second and third, respectively. A wartime estimate put commitments of the latter at $80 million, which was only marginally less than in the Philippines.[18]

The volume of foreign capital holdings at the end of the 1940s, when at long last the Netherlands acknowledged Indonesian independence, is not known with certainty. Although war damage had been substantial, leading Dutch firms were known to have invested heavily in reparations and restoration of production capacity—confident as they were that Indonesia would either remain a colony or provide safeguards for Dutch capital in case independence was achieved. An estimate of 3.1 to 3.5 billion guilders ($800 to 900 million) for Dutch investment alone as of 1950 suggests that nothing much had changed since the late 1930s, at any rate in dollar terms.[19]

The Korean War ushered in a boom for exports of primary products, such as oil and rubber. The Indonesian export industry benefited substantially as did foreign business firms. There is evidence that Dutch enterprises in particular switched to a short-run strategy geared toward pocketing as much profit as possible, while building up little for the future. Returns averaging $53 million were remitted from Indonesia to the Netherlands each year between 1954 and 1957.[20] Such remittances make clear that Dutch enterprises had lost their long-run confidence in the Indonesian investment climate. Many Dutch firms, in fact, kept hesitating between staying on in independent Indonesia and adjusting to the new conditions or exploring a reorientation toward other foreign destinations. They often ended up doing both.

Some divestment did take place in the course of the 1950s, but the decline was still rather gradual. In addition, the Indonesian oil industry continued to attract foreign capital, especially from Stanvac and Caltex, the two leading American producers and the main competitors of Royal Dutch/Shell. In 1959, accumulated American investment in Sumatra alone amounted to $400 million, an increase of 200 percent since 1949. However, almost 90 percent of these American-held assets were in the oil sector where Stanvac and Caltex increasingly enlarged their market shares at the expense of Royal Dutch/Shell.[21]

It is very difficult to adequately assess how much foreign investment actually remained intact in Indonesia as the investment climate under the Sukarno administration kept deteriorating. It appears probable that accumulated holdings were reduced significantly, perhaps to about one-half of their original magnitude, even before the Guided Economy was launched in 1958. A further steep reduction followed during the years 1956–1965. One of the small number of estimates puts accumulated holdings of Organization for Economic Cooperation and Development (OECD) investors in Indonesia at only $250 million in 1967—which is almost certainly too low, considering the American oil interests in Sumatra alone. By 1971, the accumulated value of OECD-held stock was cited at $900 million. This figure includes fresh investment initially entering the country after the Suharto government had taken over and following the passage of new liberal legislation for foreign investment in 1967.[22] The salient point, however, is that any total of foreign investment holdings between $250 and $900 million at the conclusion of the Sukarno period represented a very sharp decline since before the Pacific war or even 1950; this is true not only in nominal terms, but even more so in real terms in view of worldwide inflation rates during the 1950s and 1960s.

The final picture is a rather dismal one containing mutually exclusive challenges, economic policies that failed to convince, an investment climate that was deteriorating by any standard, and foreign investment that nearly collapsed. To contemporary observers, this appeared an unreasonably high price to pay for passing through the "economic phase of the Indonesian revolution." But is that really true? Full independence *was* achieved. Although this was only one of a series of identifiable goals, it was an especially important one. Independence did legitimize a national, unitary Indonesian government and it did provide a political basis for a national economic integration that had been a far cry from complete.[23] It is not unreasonable to argue that Indonesia had to take one step back in order to take one or even two steps forward at a later stage.

## The Philippines: Still under American Tutelage

Economic prospects looked bright for the Philippines when the country was granted independence in 1946. In terms of per capita income and a balanced economic structure, it was far ahead of its neighbors. Few could have predicted that Thailand would surpass it within a couple of decades.[24] The development economist Benjamin Higgins pointed out that net investment formed twice as high a share of national income in the Philippines compared to Indonesia (10 percent against 5 percent), whereas the government only had to contribute half as much to investment in the former country. Growth would almost surely be faster in the Philippines.[25] The heritage from American colonial rule added to the sense of promise. Because a class of Filipino entrepreneurs had been nurtured over the decades, the contrast with Indonesia's virtual lack of indigenous entrepreneurship or management skills could not have been starker. Last but not least, independence had been prepared well in advance: Manuel Quezon, the first Philippine president, took office *before* the Pacific war.

Still, challenges were not lacking. The economy suffered from the familiar dependence on exports of raw materials and industrialization deserved a high priority just as elsewhere in the region. The trade pattern was unbalanced, with an excessive orientation toward the United States, both for exports of primary products and for supplies of imported industrial goods. The process of Filipinization in economic life had really only started. Even if per capita incomes were twice as high as in Thailand or Indonesia, they remained a far cry from the level of developed countries or even British Malaya.[26]

The framework for economic policies in the Philippines was largely determined by safeguards of American interests laid down at the time of independence. The Bell Trade Act, or Philippines Trade Act, enacted in 1946, offered guaranteed reciprocal free trade between the Philippines and the United

States. Miguel Cuaderno, the governor of the Philippine Central Bank in the 1950s, was quick to observe that the unlimited duty-free access to American consumer goods removed any incentive to invest in import-substituting industrialization. According to him, investment amounts had been quite substantial in the late 1940s, but much of it was not directly related to increasing productive capacity.[27] The special trading relationship with the former colonial mother country presupposed that the peso was tied to the U.S. dollar, which in effect deprived the Philippine government of the possibility of pursuing an independent foreign exchange or trade policy.[28]

Conditions for a continued privileged presence of American business in the Philippines were created through the Laurel-Langley Agreement that remained in force until 1974. American firms were, to cite just one example, exempted from the requirement that mining activities had to be undertaken by firms with at least 60 percent Filipino ownership.[29] The great importance of this treaty, however, lay in the way business strategies of American firms changed as the protective umbrella of this treaty neared expiration. It was of greater significance than the various regulations specifically designed to attract new foreign investment that were brought together in the Investment Incentives Act of 1967. The Laurel-Langley Agreement allowed continuity while it encouraged short-run thinking on the part of American investors in particular.

An industrialization policy was formulated, along with efforts to increase Filipino participation in management and supervision. By the end of the decade, these efforts were judged to have been reasonably successful. There was also progress concerning the distribution of equity ownership by nationality. Of large firms, with a net capital in excess of 1 million pesos, only one-quarter was purely Filipino, but three-quarters had some Filipino equity participation.[30] This also applied to the financial sector. Of the twenty-seven new commercial banks set up between 1951 and 1966, all had Filipino owners.[31] Transfers of equity to Filipino owners at first usually took the form of joint ventures, in which the American partner supplied most of the capital— for example, the Goodrich tire plant was set up together with a Filipino business family in 1956. Later, in the 1960s, when the expiration of the Laurel-Langley Agreement neared, American firms began selling off equity in both mining and public utilities. Buyers were Filipino investors who, in turn, had often borrowed money from American banks in the first place.

The climate for foreign investment in the Philippines during the 1950s and 1960s was riddled with ambivalence. On the one hand, there was overt encouragement by the Philippine authorities and special protection for American firms. On the other hand, anticolonial or anticapitalist rhetoric gave rise to an atmosphere in which foreign investors felt less than welcome. This was usually linked to the demands for a more rapid Filipinization. One example was the slogan "Filipino First" chosen by President Carlos García in 1957, which did little to enhance his popularity with American business. Awareness that the special protection afforded under the Laurel-Langley Agreement was only temporary obviously added to the uneasiness. Foreign investment policies were allegedly designed to "accommodate basic nationalist aspirations of Philippine society and at the same time generate an inflow of foreign capital appropriate to Philippine goals of economic development and industrialization."[32]

Before the Pacific war, the Philippines had ranked third among countries receiving foreign direct investment in Southeast Asia, after Indonesia and Malaya. Estimates of American equity holdings varied from $164 million in 1935, to $135 million in 1943 (including portfolio investment), to $149 million in 1950.[33] Whatever the merits of these estimates may be, it is clear that the situation around 1950 was still very much the same as it had been in the mid-1930s. This underscores a fundamental continuity between the late colonial period and the years immediately after independence.

Investment by American firms gradually increased throughout the 1950s, reaching $230 million in 1955, $400 million in 1960, and $530 million in 1965.[34] This impressive expansion was in stark contrast with simultaneous developments in countries like Indonesia and must be attributed to the special protection offered under the Laurel-Langley Agreement. Despite all the rhetoric, actual inflows still took precedence above the assertion of economic nationalism.

American investment did change in character. The increase in total capital invested by American firms between 1950 and 1962 amounted to $266 million, from $150 million to $416 million. Increases in manufacturing and commerce alone, however, reached a combined total of $287 million. In other words, the rapid increase of American investment in these two sectors was accompanied by a withdrawal of American capital from other parts of the economy, notably mining, estate agriculture, and public utilities. The narrowing down of American investment commitments is even further accentuated when it is recognized that two-thirds of the increase, $185 million out of $287 million, were directed to oil refining (manufacturing) and the distribution of petroleum products (commerce).[35] This is a reminder of the one-sided focus on oil investment in Indonesia at the time.

The American-controlled segment of corporate business in the Philippines thus acquired a character of its own, distinctly different from both the more diversified Filipino and Chinese firms (of which the latter focused strongly on food processing manufacturing and trade).[36] The structural differentiation by ethnic origin arguably formed the most lasting outcome of the increase of investment, both foreign and domestic, in the Philippines in the decade and a half after independence. The narrow range of foreign capital investment is likely to have reduced the scope for spillover effects into other parts of the economy.

There was a slowdown of incoming American investment around 1970. This must be almost exclusively attributed to cautiousness in view of the nearing expiration of the Laurel-Langley Agreement in 1974, as very respectable profit rates of 16 to 18 percent per year were reported for American firms at the time. Despite the slowdown, however, foreign capital still occupied a prominent position in the Philippine business community by the mid-1970s, three full decades after independence. Foreign-affiliated firms then accounted for one-third of the top one thousand companies listed by the Philippine Securities and Exchange Commission. Half of them had a majority foreign equity share and one-third of them counted among the country's top two hundred companies in terms of performance.[37]

The picture at large for the Philippines after decolonization was a rather mixed one. Challenges were as acute as those elsewhere in the region, even if the starting position was relatively favorable. Economic policies were consistent, but obviously constrained by retained ties with the former colonial power. The climate for foreign investment was, apart from some rhetoric, reasonably good, especially for American firms temporarily enjoying special protection. It need not surprise us that actual investment rose but further expansion was stifled and contributions to economic development were restrained by the increasingly one-sided character of American investment. The Philippines remained under American tutelage for a considerable time also after independence. It did not attain full independence in economic policy making, but it also failed to reap the full benefits from access to foreign capital.

**Malaysia: Keeping in British Style**

When attaining independence after fierce internal strife during the Emergency period (1948–1957), Malaysia enjoyed the most promising economic conditions of all countries in the region. It was the world's single largest producer of tin, responsible for at least one-third of world output, and its share in world rubber production was still very impressive, about one-fifth, despite the rapid rise of the synthetic rubber industry in developed countries.[38] The peninsula was thinly populated, as were the two east Malaysian provinces joining the federation in 1963. Per capita incomes were the highest in Southeast Asia.[39] But behind the impressive façade, there were great challenges that promised to make the path of postcolonial nation-building a difficult one for decades to come.

One challenge was actually linked to Malaysia's main asset: its great capacity to generate foreign exchange earnings. These revenues were urgently needed to support the exchange rate of the pound sterling and the continuity of close links between British business and independent Malaysia became a top priority of Commonwealth economic policy. The very success in markets for primary products also turned into a liability in terms of militating against a rapid structural transformation of the economy. A transformation in favor of industry was necessary in the long run, but not in the short run. Economic policy makers in Malaysia, under the leadership of Tunku Abdul Rahman, had to simultaneously aim at several targets: benefiting from the old export industries while preparing for a new base of prosperity *and* cooperating with the British while making clear that Malaysia had indeed become fully independent.

Another challenge concerned the ethnic composition of Malaysian society. Indigenous Malays (*bumiputera*) formed a small majority of the population, which, incidentally became a large minority when North Borneo, Sarawak, and Singapore were added. But three-quarters were employed in the primary sector whereas 55 percent of the Chinese and 40 percent of the Indians were active outside agriculture. Chinese Malaysians accounted for two-thirds of all employment in the secondary sector, which was without doubt the most modern part of the economy.[40] To the Malay rulers, there was an urgent need for a massive redistribution of income away from the non-Malay modern sector to the rural Malay sector. To the Chinese and Indian minorities, this would constitute the cost of achieving an egalitarian society in which peoples of different ethnic backgrounds could live together. The positive discrimination inherent in the subsequent Malayanization of the economy was not always easy to reconcile with the needs of industrialization—as became evident in the 1970s and 1980s, when the New Economic Policy was being implemented.

The Malaysian government from the outset acknowledged the key importance of foreign direct investment in executing its ambitious plans for industrial development, starting with the promotion of import-substituting manufacturing.[41] Incentives were offered, especially in the vein of generous tax holidays accompanying so-called pioneer status for foreign firms. Legislation was laid down in the Pioneer Industries Ordinance and the Investment Incentives Act, coming into force in 1958 and 1968, respectively. But criticism abounded. One argument was that indiscriminate *ex ante* tax relief did not necessarily maximize inflows. Nor did it offer safeguards against unscrupulous firms out to make quick profits. Returns on British investment were known to be considerably higher in peninsular Malaysia than elsewhere in the Commonwealth. Total remittances of profits were disturbingly high, at an annual average of M$350 million ($115 million), but these officially recorded outflows obviously did not include transfers through overinvoicing or underpricing.[42]

Malayanization was pursued through various agencies, such as the Rural and Industrial Development Authority (RIDA), which offered credit and training facilities for potential bumiputera entrepreneurs. Yet, by 1965, when RIDA was converted into another type of agency, accomplishments outside the civil service, especially in commerce and industry, remained modest.[43] Part of the problem was in education, as in Indonesia, but much could also be ascribed to commonly held prejudices. In quite an extraordinary statement, one Malay ruler, the Yang di-Pertuan of Negri Sembilan, said to a British colonial officer that "to teach a Malay to keep a shop—you might just as well teach a chicken to swim."[44] The racial riots in 1969 made very clear that ethnic harmony and balance were still very far away.

The climate for foreign investment in Malaysia in the 1950s and 1960s was more influenced by banditry and terrorism during the Emergency than by any expression of economic nationalism in anticipation of or immediately following independence. Direct costs included physical damage to production facilities and outlays on protection, leaving aside casualties among personnel. The tin industry spent M$30 million ($10 million) on protection during the Emergency decade and rubber estates paid M$16 million ($5 million) for security in 1951 alone. In addition, indirect costs were incurred in the form of wage increases prompted by the duress and lack of safety.[45] Production was not seriously impaired, however. British business survived and Malaysia continued to generate export revenues. Still, if the Emergency did not result in a mass exodus of British capital from Malaysia, it may have discouraged new ventures.

Business was buoyant during the Emergency despite a far more systematic disruption of production than in Indonesia at the same time. This remarkable fact tells us that official nationalist rhetoric may have a greater impact on attitudes of foreign investors than daily disturbances that are condemned by the authorities as criminal acts. Some capital flight certainly took place during the Emergency, not only by British business firms, but also by Chinese and Indian (Chettiar) entrepreneurs who felt uneasy about the situation. Yet, this very period also saw a growth in consumerism, and even the leisure industry flourished.[46] The climate for foreign capital only improved in 1957 when peace was restored and direct incentives were offered. Conditions in immediate postcolonial Malaysia were clearly more comparable to those prevailing in the Philippines than to those in Indonesia.

On the eve of the Pacific war, Malaya ranked second among recipient countries of foreign capital, after Indonesia but before the Philippines. Its share in the region's total was about 14 percent. The composition by nationality of investor resembled that in Indonesia in the sense that the colonial mother country accounted for a very substantial proportion of the total, about two-thirds. The concentration on agriculture (rubber) and mining (tin) was extreme, with these two industries absorbing almost 90 percent of built-up foreign capital investment.[47] Thirty years later, by the late 1960s, the accumulated total stock of foreign capital in Malaysia (except Singapore) was reported at M$2.1 billion ($700 million) or twice as much, in nominal terms, as in the late 1930s.[48] This increase barely kept pace with the inflation during the postwar decades, however.[49] The important point, nevertheless, is that there was no steep reduction in accumulated stock of foreign investment as in Indonesia under Sukarno.

Gross domestic capital formation in Malaysia was only marginally retarded by the Emergency. The annual total from 1949 to 1953 amounted to M$486 million ($162 million), of which 65 percent was generated by the private sector. Above all, funds for private capital formation originated from domestic savings, though foreign inflows and transfers from the public sector played a supplementary role on occasion.[50] Yet, capital inflows into Malaya do not fully capture the contribution of foreign capital, since earnings reinvested by foreign-controlled enterprises count as domestic savings. Difficult to interpret as such data may be, they do convey an impression of the responsibility for fresh investment increasingly being taken over by the domestic capital market with foreign-held stock remaining largely intact. At the time of independence, British firms controlled three-quarters of the rubber estates, virtually the entire tin mining sector, and as much as one-third of the export and import trade.[51]

The continuity with the prewar period applied in particular to British business. This is borne out by the long-run trend in British capital investment over the 1950s and 1960s.[52] Nominal values of built-up investment stayed the same through the late 1950s and the gradual increase during the 1960s is likely to reflect an adjustment of book values to inflation. As well, the first decade of independent rule in Malaysia witnessed no exodus of British capital. This is easily understood when considering the benevolent climate for foreign investment and, as already mentioned, the exceptionally high profit rates. Returns on British capital, after taxes, in Malaysia approached 20 percent on average over the years 1955–1964 and amounted to 18 to 19 percent in both 1960 and 1970.[53]

The process of capital formation was accelerated during the first half of the 1960s, again in stark contrast with what was happening in Indonesia at the same time. The increase in capital stock between 1959 and 1966 amounted to 70 percent, with the fastest growth taking place in new machinery. There was a slight shift in favor of public as opposed to private investment, which in fact anticipated the state-financed Malayanization of means of production under the New Economic Policy. New foreign investment was slow in materializing, but strong foreign stakes in fixed assets were also retained in both primary export production and manufacturing.[54]

Foreign economic power coincided with ethnic imbalances to foster a great deal of concern about Malaysia's economic prospects by the late 1960s, notwithstanding the generous export revenues that were still forthcoming. In 1970, it was estimated that more than 83 percent of equity in limited companies in peninsular Malaysia was held by foreign firms (60 percent) and Malaysian Chinese (23 percent).[55] Even if such figures exaggerate the predominance of non-Malays (since all enterprises not organized along Western lines are left out), they underscore that the development strategy chosen by independent Malaysia to this point was untenable for the future. Malayanization in economic life therefore became tantamount to wresting economic power from both foreign and Chinese firms.[56]

The overall picture of the economic impact of decolonization in Malaysia looks rather different from elsewhere in the region. Challenges were arguably more complex and above all more contradictory than in other former colonies. Economic policies in the immediate postcolonial era met with little success, whether in terms of transforming the economic structure, redressing ethnic imbalances, or attracting new foreign investors interested in more than quick profit. The investment climate certainly deteriorated considerably during the Emergency, but improved as independence was attained and the Lee Kuan Yew government lent full support to the remaining foreign, especially British, firms. There was no steep reduction in foreign investment holdings, but neither was foreign dominance curtailed nor fundamental problems solved. Malaysia merely postponed more radical solutions.

## Conclusion

The conventional literature on decolonization tends to focus on political consequences, both for former colonies and former mother countries. Far less attention has been given to the urgency of a reorientation in economic terms in newly independent nations. The overview offered here shows how three major former colonies in Southeast Asia—Indonesia, the Philippines, and Malaysia—confronted the dilemma of economic reorientation and chose different options in their efforts to solve it. Four aspects of these postcolonial experiences were considered: the economic challenges, economic policies, investment climate, and actual development of foreign capital commitments.

All three former colonies felt the need to rid themselves of an excessive dependence on exports of primary products and to industrialize in order to secure economic growth in the future. In the short run, this was most pressing in the Philippines, but a bit less so in Indonesia and Malaysia. All three also felt compelled to assert their national identity in economic life as well as in other spheres. This was most urgent in Indonesia, where the very cohesion of the country as a unitary state was at stake.

Economic policies chosen varied quite markedly. The Indonesian option was the most assertive one, but also the one that proved least convincing. The special relationship with the United States was for the time being dictated by both the scope and substance of the Philippine policy, whereas the Malaysian one was riddled with compromise and eventually met with limited success. Indonesianization, Filipinization, and Malayanization formed different versions of the same conscious effort to foster indigenous entrepreneurship. The greatest success was experienced in the Philippines, drawing on a stronger colonial heritage in this regard.

The climate for foreign investment also varied considerably between the three countries and over time. The most dramatic deterioration was in Indonesia, whereas in Malaysia the climate actually improved as independence brought an end to the Emergency. In the Philippines, however, the trend was perceived to be the opposite one, with deterioration becoming evident as the special protection of American business drew to an end. In general, nationalist rhetoric appeared to cause greater alarm among foreign investors than lack of safety or the impact of volatility on daily operations.

In Indonesia, foreign investment outside the oil sector virtually collapsed, but in the Philippines and Malaysia the accumulated holdings of American and British firms, respectively, by and large remained intact. Special protection in the Philippines did result in some fresh American investment, but flows dried up as the end of protection came into sight. In Malaysia, new investment was conspicuously slow in materializing. Rates of return were impressive, especially in Malaysia, which suggests that foreign investment in the former colonies changed character, becoming more strongly oriented toward short-run gains than before.

Could things have turned out differently? Could a former colony in Southeast Asia have asserted its national identity in economic terms as strongly as Indonesia did while retaining the contribution of foreign capital to the economy as in the Philippines and Malaysia? This is a highly hypothetical question, but an intriguing one. When speculating about alternative options, it should be kept in mind that neither the Philippines nor Malaysia seem to have reaped the full benefits from their continued access to foreign capital. A significant portion of profits was repatriated, little new capital entered, and few opportunities emerged for an industrialization that could sustain future economic growth. The path of Indonesia was extreme and cataclysmic, of course, but perhaps the Philippine and Malaysian paths were not that much better if viewed from a longer historical perspective.

Figure 3.1    **Structure of Private Business in the Philippines by Ethnicity, 1961**

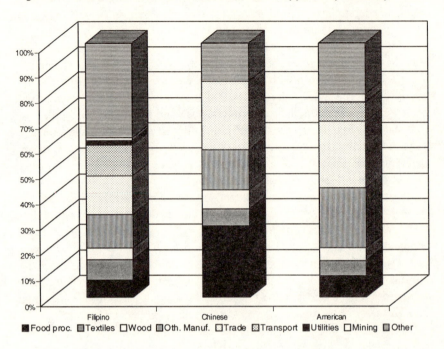

Filipino                  Chinese                  American
■Food proc.  ▨Textiles  □Wood  ▥Oth. Manuf.  □Trade  ▧Transport  ■Utilities  □Mining  ▤Other

Figure 3.2    **Private Capital Formation in Malaya by Origin of Funds, 1949–1953**

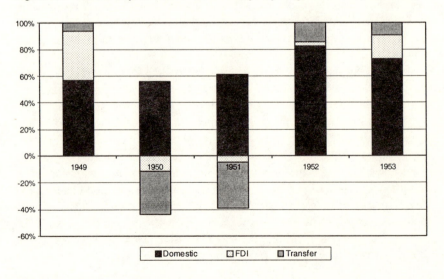

■Domestic    □FDI    ▨Transfer

Figure 3.3 **Stock of British Capital Investment in Malaysia, 1948–1968**

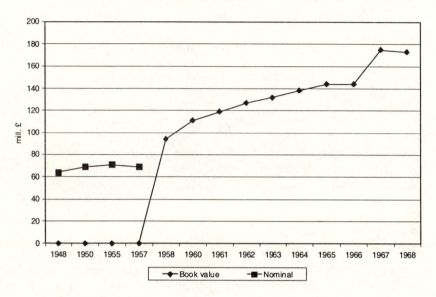

# 4

# Monarchy and Decolonization in Indochina

## Bruce M. Lockhart

One of the linchpins of French colonial policy in Indochina was the "protected monarchy," whereby Vietnamese, Cambodian, and Lao rulers reigned over all or part of their ancestors' kingdoms under French authority. In theory, of course, a protectorate implied indirect rather than direct rule, but given the tight degree of control that colonial officials exercised over the *souverains protégés*, the latter enjoyed little more real authority than the *indigène* civil servants of a directly ruled colony like Cochin China. The structure and functioning of the protected monarchies were largely regularized by the early twentieth century, though the French continued to make changes as they deemed necessary—inevitably with a view to consolidating their own power, rather than broadening that of the rulers.

The first dramatic changes came in March 1945, with the Japanese coup de force against the French colonial regime in Indochina, at that point still dominated by Vichy loyalists despite the fact that Charles de Gaulle was now in power in Paris and the Pétain government was no more. With Japanese encouragement, the three rulers—Bảo Đại (1925–1945), Norodom Sihanouk (1941–1955), and Sisavangvong (1905–1959)—declared independence from French rule.[1] Although the Japanese had done little more than replace the French in the role of all-powerful protector, the five months between the March 9 coup and Japan's surrender in August 1945 provided a "shot in the arm" for Vietnamese, Cambodian, and Lao nationalism and placed the French in the difficult position of having to reconquer their own colonies when the Japanese had already laid down their arms. (By Allied agreement, the northern half of Indochina was occupied by Nationalist Chinese forces and the southern half by British troops.) In Cambodia and Laos, the returning French were confronted with de facto independent governments under royal leadership. In Vietnam's case, the situation was complicated by the August Revolution that had brought the Indochinese Communist Party (ICP) to power and had obliged Bảo Đại to abdicate in favor of the newly established Democratic Republic of Vietnam.

The French spent the next nine years attempting to maintain some degree of authority over the colony that until 1940 had been under their complete control. They only definitively abandoned their efforts after the crushing defeat at Điện Biên Phủ in 1954; the Geneva Conference formalized a process for their departure from Indochina while leaving other key military and political issues unsettled. Prior to Geneva, the French toyed with various structures and solutions to forge a long-term relationship with the three Indochinese states. At the core of these various policies were the three rulers, who were meant to be the focal point of noncommunist nationalism and the recipients of a gradual independence to be crafted and bestowed by France. In the case of Cambodia and Laos, this approach was largely successful, and by 1953 both countries had received virtually complete independence, though their governments were still facing guerrilla movements within their borders. Bảo Đại was restored to power and remained there through the partition of Vietnam that followed the Geneva Accords; however, his political role was rapidly overshadowed by that of his last prime minister, Ngô Đình Diệm, who ultimately deposed him in a "popular referendum" in late 1955.

Against the backdrop of events between 1945 and 1954, what can be said of the success or failure of French decolonization policy in each of the three countries? Why, in particular, did the Cambodian and Lao royal families survive to dominate the political scene in their respective countries over the following decades while Bảo Đại (and his dynasty with him) vanished from the Vietnamese political stage?

**The Decline, Fall, and Resurrection of Bảo Đại**

On March 11, 1945, shortly after the Japanese coup de force, Bảo Đại issued a royal ordinance (*dụ*) proclaiming the independence of the "Empire of Vietnam." With Japanese approval, he chose the Confucian scholar Trần Trọng Kim as his prime minister and appointed a new cabinet intended to inject some "new blood" into the imperial government. The new regime faced serious obstacles, the most serious of which was the famine that had been rampant in much of Tonkin for several months and showed no signs of abating. Kim's government was only partially successful in its attempts to alleviate the widespread hunger among the population, since the Japanese continued to requisition large quantities of grain for military purposes. Moreover, the imperial government's authority was being directly challenged by the Việt Minh, the united front led by the ICP, which was aggressively expanding its influence through Tonkin and Annam during the final months of the war.

When the Japanese surrendered, the Việt Minh were sufficiently prepared to be able to seize power in the major cities and towns, and this August Revolution led to the proclamation of the Democratic Republic of Vietnam (DRV) on September 2, under the leadership of Hồ Chí Minh. The DRV cabinet lineup included Supreme Counselor Vĩnh Thụy— Bảo Đại's personal name. At the "invitation" of the Việt Minh leaders, the emperor had announced his abdication on August 25, following an earlier declaration that "[w]e would rather be [one of] the people in an independent country than the king of an enslaved country."[2]

Bảo Đại's role as supreme counselor remains poorly documented, perhaps because there is little to say about his activities over the next few months. He hovered at the edges of the political scene during the difficult first months of the DRV's existence, when the new government was having to cope with British and Chinese occupation forces as well as the returning French. His own account of these months suggests that he had only a minor role to play, and his contempt for the DRV government is quite clear. There is a story that at one of Hồ's most desperate moments in early 1946, he actually suggested to Bảo Đại that the two men exchange positions—perhaps to shift the blame for the impending agreement to be signed with France, which would allow its troops to reoccupy Vietnam in exchange for recognition of the DRV within the dual framework of an Indochinese Federation and a French Union, neither of which existed at that point. Within hours, Hồ changed his mind, however, and Bảo Đại remained supreme advisor.[3]

A few months later, Bảo Đại left for China as part of a DRV delegation whose objective was to pursue contacts with the Guomindang regime. The rest of the mission soon returned to Hànội, but Bảo Đại remained behind and then moved to Hong Kong, beginning a period of quasi exile that would last for nearly three years. By the end of 1946, open warfare had broken out between the French forces and the DRV, which withdrew from the capital and set up a resistance government in the rural areas that had been its original power base. The French occupied the cities but realized the need to create a regime that would ideally challenge the DRV while enabling the French to maintain a firm grip on the colony.[4]

In Cochin China, which had not been reintegrated into the DRV, the "infrastructure" was already in place: a separatist Republic of Cochin China that was the creation of Admiral Thierry d'Argenlieu, the French high commissioner whose determination to establish as many different Vietnamese political entities as possible had helped sabotage Franco-DRV negotiations throughout 1946. The French required something broader, however, and the former emperor (still cooling his heels in Hong Kong) seemed the most logical choice; thus, the "Bảo Đại solution" was born.

It should be pointed out that French policy makers were not unanimous in their enthusiasm for Bảo Đại. There was a certain sense that the events of 1945—his collaboration with the Japanese and his subsequent abdication— might have "discredited" him in the eyes of his people. (That French rule might have had a part in this does not seem to have occurred to anyone!) There was reportedly some talk of putting his son, Crown Prince Bảo Long, on the throne, while de Gaulle and a handful of other officials were in favor of bringing back the former emperor Duy Tân (1907–1916), who had been exiled for decades following his involvement in an anti-French plot. Bảo Long, however, was still an adolescent, while Duy Tân (usually referred to by his personal name, Vinh San) died in an airplane accident in the last days of 1945.[5]

Bảo Đại thus emerged as the most logical choice for a noncommunist alternative to Hồ and the DRV government. Almost immediately after the latter's establishment, d'Argenlieu was already talking about reestablishing the protectorate under a different name, and over the next year he became increasingly convinced that some form of monarchy under the former emperor was the only alternative to the communists. Léon Pignon, who became d'Argenlieu's political counselor and was one of the main architects of the Bảo Đại solution, came to a similar conclusion by late 1946.[6] Nor was the impetus exclusively from the French side: in 1947, anticommunist Vietnamese nationalists of various stripes were also making pilgrimages to Hong Kong to "consult" with Bảo Đại. Many of these nationalists were in exile in China, where they had formed a sort of united front in late 1946, but a number of political figures traveled from Vietnam to Hong Kong as well. By this time, Bảo Đại's links to the DRV government had been completely severed; he was subsequently tried and sentenced to death in absentia for treason.[7]

Over the next two years, the French and Bảo Đại (now in France) engaged in an awkward tango, without a clear sense of direction across the dance floor or even of just who was to lead; the result was a sort of diplomatic shuffle with a few instances of trampled toes. Bảo Đại, with varying degrees of coyness, indicated his readiness to resume some kind of leadership position, while the French dithered and quibbled over just how much authority he and his prospective government were to be given, as well as the important issue of whether Cochin China would be reintegrated with the rest of Vietnam. Finally, in March 1949 Bảo Đại and President Vincent Auriol signed the Élysée Agreements, whereby Vietnam (including Cochin China) became one of the three Associated States of Indochina, along with Cambodia and Laos.

The French National Assembly took nearly a year to ratify the Élysée Agreements—hardly an auspicious beginning for the new State of Vietnam. Britain and the United States hurried to recognize the new government—but most of its neighbors proved much more reluctant to do so, despite an urgent campaign by American diplomats on its behalf.[8] Over the next few years, Bảo Đại spent a good deal of his time in France, while the day-to-day affairs of state were handled by a series of prime ministers and the day-to-day war against the Việt Minh by French commanders. Bảo Đại initially inherited some of the elements of the Cochin Chinese regime, notably Nguyễn Văn Xuân, of whom Stanley Karnow provides the following pithy characterization, "Even in Vietnam, a nation known for its intrigue and political plots, he was famous for being almost totally untrustworthy. Superficially affable, smooth and cheerful, he devoted nearly all his time to conniving."[9]

Although Xuân's successors as prime minister—Nguyễn Phan Long, Trần Văn Hữu, Nguyễn Văn Tâm, and Bửu Lộc—were perhaps less venal, they generally had little more than strong anticommunism to recommend them. (A French observer gives a memorable description of the period, "Amidst blood, piastres [the currency of Indochina], luxury, tortures, heroism and dark plans, one found a fantastic gallery of characters, all driven by fate as in a Shakespearean drama. One saw the whole gamut of human types, from the cowardly to the fanatical, from the vile to the pure."[10]) The last prime minister of the State of Vietnam was Diệm, who was anticommunist, anti-French, and—once the circumstances were right—anti–Bảo Đại. Although Diệm's relations with Bảo Đại had long been complicated, in June 1954 the former emperor appointed him to succeed Bửu Lộc, telling him that "I am appealing to your sense of patriotism. You no longer have the right to avoid your duties. Vietnam's salvation requires it."[11]

French and U.S. policy makers alike, despite increasingly serious reservations about Bảo Đại's character and leadership (not to mention his personal finances), seem to have generally agreed on the need to keep him in place until roughly mid-1954. It is only after the Geneva Conference that French officials began to talk seriously to their American counterparts about "gradually eas[ing] Bảo Đại out of the picture," as one diplomat put it. The first step was to persuade him to remain in France, rather than returning to Vietnam, which was not a particularly difficult task. In the spring of 1955, the French seem to have reverted to the Bảo Đại solution as a way of stabilizing what was now South Vietnam during Diệm's violent confrontation with the sects, the idea being that the former emperor would act as arbiter between what was still legally "his" government and the forces opposed to his prime minister.[12]

By this time, however, the United States had the upper hand in influence over Vietnamese political affairs and was committed to supporting Diệm. Published American documents reveal a much greater ambivalence toward the prime minister, particularly among observers in Vietnam, than has generally been acknowledged. (Nor is there any indication that Diệm was either "chosen" by the Americans or "imposed" by them on the French and Bảo Đại.) Even so, as the political situation in South Vietnam worsened after the partition, the United States effectively threw in its lot with Diệm. The head of state, by contrast, was increasingly less appealing; his close ties to the Mafia-like Bình Xuyên were especially repugnant. Although General J. Lawton Collins, representing the United States in Sàigòn in early 1955, was ready to accept him as "the only person competent to provide [an] element [of] political continuity," this acceptance was conditional on his supporting Diệm in the latter's fight against the Bình Xuyên and other opponents.[13]

Once Diệm emerged the victor despite continued opposition from Bảo Đại and his supporters, the former emperor became irrelevant as far as the Americans were concerned. While the latter did not approve of Diệm's plan to depose his head of state and establish a constitution by referendum, it was the method rather than the purpose that they found objectionable. Acting on instructions from Secretary of State John Dulles, Ambassador G. Frederick Reinhardt (who replaced Collins) tried unsuccessfully to persuade Diệm that it would be more rational—and legitimate—to organize some kind of representative assembly to do the job instead. Once the referendum had taken place, however, they immediately accepted it as a fait accompli. Reinhardt concluded that "[i]t would seem to us that results referendum render unlikely Bảo Đại will be able to play significant role in future. That he so overwhelmingly repudiated in Free Vietnam means not only that he can expect little indigenous support but renders also improbable DRV regime or Communist bloc in general will consider Bảo Đại useful tool for their purposes."[14] With this epitaph, American interest in the Bảo Đại solution effectively ended.

The question, of course, is at just what point the French psychologically abandoned that solution once and for all. One suspects it was quite late in the game, given their general distaste for Diệm and their presumed realization that whatever the shortcomings of Bảo Đại and his political allies, these men represented their best chance of maintaining a counterweight to American influence in South Vietnam. They may well have held out the hope that he would somehow be transformed into a sort of Vietnamese Sihanouk who, despite his idiosyncrasies and personal caprices, would be capable of dominating the political scene, while functioning as an effective partner in the struggle against revolutionaries and, ultimately, in a postcolonial relationship with France.[15] Such a metamorphosis never took place, however, and Bảo Đại's rather abrupt exit from the political scene was effectively the final act of the French decolonization drama in Vietnam.

## Cambodia: Sihanouk on Center Stage

Although Norodom Sihanouk and Bảo Đại began in positions of relative parity in March 1945, their political careers evolved in somewhat different directions. Sihanouk declared Cambodian independence (under Japanese sponsorship) and assumed the title of prime minister along with that of king. In May 1945, he appointed as foreign minister Son Ngoc Thanh, a commoner who had been in exile in Japan after anti-French activities and who was to become his *bête noire* over the long term. Three months later, after a sequence of events that is still somewhat unclear, Sihanouk gave Thanh the premiership, which the latter held until the French arrested him in October. By this time, the French were returning to Cambodia, with the approval of some elements of the Cambodian elite.[16]

Sihanouk himself may have been unenthusiastic about the reversal of the independence he had proclaimed in March, but he bowed to the opinions of his conservative entourage rather than supporting Thanh against the French. While he expressed an initial determination to negotiate as the ruler of an independent country, the French were equally determined to return with full rights and, if necessary, to depose him if he stood in the way of this objective. Once Thanh was out of the picture, Sihanouk became more receptive to the advice of his Francophile courtiers, notably his uncle Prince Monireth, and he eventually offered the French a valuable Christmas present by annulling his earlier, Japanese-sponsored declaration of independence.[17]

In January 1946, the French and Cambodian governments signed a modus vivendi whose terms were roughly comparable to the agreement reached with the DRV two months later.[18] (Note that the March agreement with Hồ was not labeled a modus vivendi; this term was reserved for another document signed a few months later, after the final failure of negotiations in France.) Sihanouk had by now taken a back seat in the negotiations, which were handled by his conservative uncle Monireth. Cambodia began the process of drafting a constitution for a multiparty parliamentary system. The three political groupings that emerged were all led by princes of various ideological stripes; the most liberal among them was Youthevong, whose Democratic Party represented the most serious and articulate challenge to Sihanouk's domination of Cambodian politics. The Democrats had a strong showing in Cambodia's first elections later that year, but their strength was somewhat diminished with Youthevong's death (of natural causes) in 1947.

The next few years saw a series of changes in government that rather resembled those taking place in Paris, though the successive Cambodian leaders represented a much narrower political spectrum than their French counterparts. Sihanouk actually dissolved Parliament in September 1949, and two years passed before he allowed new elections to take place. Meanwhile, Cambodia was given incremental doses of independence at roughly the same pace as the State of Vietnam, with a preliminary proclamation of "independence within the French Union" in December 1948 and a formal Franco-Cambodian treaty in November 1949. On the political scene, the Democrats continued to frustrate Sihanouk's ambitions and strategies; as a result, in June 1952 he dismissed the Democratic prime minister and took full control of the government on the basis of a constitutional provision that all power emanated from the king.[19]

Sihanouk's problems were by no means confined to electoral politics; he also faced insurgencies in different parts of the country, some launched by loosely pro-Thai elements and others linked to the Việt Minh. Over the short run, these movements were targeting the French more than Sihanouk and his political system, but by attacking the slow evolution of Cambodian independence, they were of course questioning his policies and his vision for the country's future as well. One of the most vocal opponents in the anti-French resistance, moreover, was Son Ngoc Thanh, who had returned from exile in 1952 (thanks to Sihanouk's intervention on his behalf) and then joined the maquis, calling for a republican government. While no single one of these insurgency movements was strong or widespread enough to seriously threaten the government, they collectively represented a significant destabilizing force and a strong challenge to Sihanouk's authority.[20]

In 1953, as a result of these various political and military pressures, Sihanouk decided to launch his own personal "royal crusade" to persuade the French that the timetable for full independence should be accelerated. Through diplomatic contacts, a flurry of letters to French leaders, brief periods of self-imposed exile, and a call to arms to the Cambodian people, he pressured France to make the final concessions that would effectively bring colonial rule to a definitive end. His efforts bore fruit, not the least because Paris was by now too preoccupied with the deteriorating military situation in Vietnam to put up a fight in order to hold onto Cambodia, and in November 1953 the last steps were taken to grant the kingdom juridical independence. Sihanouk's victory was somewhat diluted by the continued presence of Việt Minh forces and their Khmer allies on Cambodian territory, but he had regained de jure sovereignty from the French. For the next few years, at least, his battles would be mainly against internal foes.[21]

### Laos: Royalty Divided

The situation in Laos under colonial rule was complicated by the fact that the royal family was not a unified institution: the ruling house in Luang Phabang was split between two rival branches, while a separate family line held sway in the southern region of Champassak. (This situation reflected the fragmentation of the former kingdom of Lane Xang during the early years of the eighteenth century; there had once been a royal family in Vientiane as well, but the Siamese had done away with their throne in the late 1820s.) Thus, on the one hand the Lao political stage was dominated by princes, but on the other hand they represented seriously differing political, regional, and family interests. At the time of the Japanese coup de force in 1945, all three of the royal lineages held positions of authority: King Sisavangvong was from the main branch of the family, while his viceroy was Prince Phetsarath, the fourth member of his lineage to hold that title. (The division between the two lineages, a result of Siamese manipulation of the order of succession, dated back to the mid-nineteenth century.)[22] Meanwhile, Prince Boun Oum of the Champassak line was de facto ruler of the southern provinces, which were administratively separate from Luang Phabang's authority.

These divisions were by no means healed by the Japanese assumption of power and the consequent declaration of Lao independence on April 8. Laos remained divided administratively and psychologically, with rivalry between Phetsarath (now prime minister) and Crown Prince Savang Vatthana and between the northern royal family and Boun Oum in the south. The situation was far from resolved at the time of the Japanese surrender, when the king declared that Laos would revert to being a French protectorate. In early October, after several weeks of maneuvering the king attempted to dismiss Phetsarath, who then proclaimed an independent Lao Issara (Free Lao) government (though not under his direct leadership) that deposed the king.

By now the French were returning, and the Lao Issara regime desperately worked to forge an alliance between various nationalist elements opposed to the restoration of colonial rule. Key players in these events were the sizable Vietnamese communities in Lao towns such as Vientiane, Savannakhet, and Pakse. These communities had already been infiltrated by the Việt Minh and had close ties to the revolutionary movement in Vietnam. The main bridge for the Vietnamese-Lao revolutionary connection was, ironically, another prince—Souphanouvong, a half-brother of Phetsarath who had studied in France and then worked in Vietnam, where he found both a wife and a political cause. Determined to help radicalize the Lao Issara movement, Souphanouvong returned to Laos with a group of Vietnamese soldiers and established a "Lao Army of Liberation and Defense" under his command. His position was acknowledged by the new government, but more moderate elements of the Lao Issara were far from satisfied with this new Việt Minh connection.[23]

Over the next few months, skirmishes occurred between returning French forces and various Lao and Vietnamese units, culminating in the bloody battle of Thakhek in March 1946, when French planes bombed and strafed hundreds of people who were fleeing across the Mekong. Souphanouvong was severely wounded but made it to safety in Thailand. Over the next few weeks, the French reoccupied Vientiane and then Luang Phabang. Just before the capture of Vientiane, the Lao Issara government invited Sisavangvong to retake the throne, but almost immediately they (including Phetsarath) had to flee the country when the French troops entered the city. Following the capture of Luang Phabang in May, the king once again proclaimed his acceptance of French rule, and Laos returned more or less to the status quo ante: a kingdom under France's sovereignty, though a modus vivendi similar to that which Sihanouk had signed now made Laos a constitutional monarchy within the French Union.[24]

The political evolution of the Kingdom of Laos over the next six years roughly paralleled that of Cambodia and, to a lesser extent, the State of Vietnam. Like Cambodia, Laos established a multiparty parliamentary system that saw a succession of governments headed by princes and elite commoners; one of the prime ministers was Boun Oum, who consented to participate in the national political process. A constitutional monarchy was formalized in 1947, when the first Lao constitution (promulgated in 1945 under the Lao Issara) was replaced by another charter. A Franco-Lao treaty was passed by the National Assembly in November 1949, and in October 1953 Laos was granted full independence within the French Union structure.[25]

Throughout the period 1946–1953, the royal government based in Luang Phabang and Vientiane faced challenges on one of two fronts. Across the Mekong in Thailand, a diverse grouping of Lao Issara elements remained in exile—and in opposition to the pro-French regime. Although they were involved in sporadic guerrilla activities on Lao territory, the strength of their movement was gradually diluted by deepening conflicts within the leadership, notably between Souphanouvong on the left and more conservative leaders on the right. Phetsarath was somewhere in the middle, unable to serve as a unifying force. Over the course of 1949, both men were expelled from the Lao Issara leadership; by the end of the year, the movement had been formally dissolved and most of the exiles returned to Laos and joined the royal government.[26]

Phetsarath remained in Thailand, a potential threat to the ruling family that never actually materialized. In the early months of the Issara government's exile in Thailand, he had still been considered a possible replacement for Sisavangvong, and he was sporadically wooed by both the French and the Vietnamese to join their respective Lao allies. As time went on, however, he became little more than a shadowy figure across the Mekong, although as late as 1954 American diplomats still viewed him with some suspicion. He finally returned home in 1956 and died three years later. The last years of his life were spent trying to restore unity to his divided country by restoring unity within his family.[27]

After the breakup of the Lao Issara government-in-exile, Souphanouvong and the rest of its more radical wing made their way to the Lao-Vietnamese border region and joined the revolutionary movement under Vietnamese sponsorship. Souphanouvong remained a key leader of the revolution until his death in the mid-1990s. During much of the twenty-year Lao civil war, he was in direct opposition to another half-brother, Souvanna Phouma, who emerged from the right wing of the Lao Issara to become a prominent "neutralist" and longtime prime minister. Crown Prince Savang Vatthana appears to have played a fairly important part in political affairs, at least through the time of the Geneva Conference. After succeeding his father in 1959, however, he assumed the largely ceremonial role of a constitutional monarch. The two half-siblings, along with Prince Boun Oum of Champassak, effectively dominated much of the political scene in Laos until the royal government was overthrown in December 1975.[28]

### Cambodia and Laos: Decolonization "Success Stories"

A study of French decolonization policy in Indochina during the period 1945–1954 must recognize at least two fundamental paradoxes. The first is that for much of this period, the French were not truly committed to "decolonization" per se, but rather to maintaining a firm grip over as much of their colony as possible and making the minimal concessions necessary to keep that part of their empire from falling down around their ears. At what point, then, can we speak of true "decolonization" in Indochina? Certainly not with the various agreements of 1946, which did little more than legitimize the reoccupation of the colony in conjunction with the withdrawal of British, Japanese, and Chinese forces. Perhaps in 1949–1950, when the Élysée Agreements and comparable agreements for Cambodia and Laos created the Associated States of Indochina, reflecting at best a grudging French recognition that more progress had to be made in making the three countries into viable noncommunist states.[29] Certainly by late 1953–1954, when Cambodia and Laos received full de jure independence within the framework of the short-lived French Union, followed by the final withdrawal of French troops following Geneva. By that point, Paris had had to acknowledge the reality that sooner or later Indochina would no longer be "French" and that true decolonization began. (It can be argued that this realization came earlier for Cambodia and Laos but, in the case of Vietnam, only with Điện Biên Phủ.)[30]

A second fundamental paradox is that the instruments of decolonization were essentially the same as those who had served the French so loyally—for the most part—under colonial rule: the *souverains protégés*. While in the State of Vietnam a group of nonroyal "politicians" like Nguyễn Văn Xuân had their part to play, their role was clearly subordinated to that of Bảo Đại as chief of state. In Laos, moderate political figures like Katay Don Sasorith and Oun Sananikone were to some extent overshadowed by Prince Phetsarath during the early months of the Lao Issara government and then by Souvanna Phouma and Crown Prince Savang Vatthana after 1949. The same was true in Cambodia, where Sihanouk and his relatives dominated the political process and were largely able to impose their will on those commoners who made it into high government offices. (The most viable "career path" for opposition figures, whether Son Ngoc Thanh or the future Khmer Rouge leaders, thus proved to be the maquis.) Rather than working to formulate a postcolonial political structure or cultivate a new generation of leaders, the French generally concentrated on maintaining continuity with previous policies.

Ultimately, Laos proved to be the best "case study" among the three for a comparatively smooth decolonization. Once Phetsarath was in exile and the main branch of the ruling house—the loyal Sisavangvong—was safely reestablished on the throne, it was relatively smooth sailing for the Franco-Lao relationship. Phetsarath's decision to remain in Thailand until the late 1950s virtually removed him as a significant obstacle to French plans for Laos's political evolution, even though his shadow hovered over the royal government as a potential challenge to its legitimacy. By the time the more moderate Lao Issara elements returned home in 1949, they had been effectively defanged by internal conflicts and by French willingness to grant Laos progressively greater autonomy, no matter how incremental.

Souphanouvong was a more complicated challenge, since from all accounts he combined considerable personal charisma with the authority attached to a member of the royal family. If he had remained an isolated rebel, he would perhaps not have gotten very far on his own, given that the rest of the royal family was committed to the French timetable for independence. However, his connections with the ICP (officially reborn in the early 1950s as separate Vietnamese, Cambodian, and Lao People's Parties) gave him wider revolutionary connections and stronger firepower than anything the Lao Issara could have achieved. Once he returned to Laos after the dissolution of the Lao Issara, he had to share the political stage with budding revolutionary leaders like Kaysone Phomvihane and Nouhak Phoumsavane, but his stature as the "Red Prince" gave him a kind of legitimacy and authority that none of the others could claim.

Even so, whether Souphanouvong and the Neo Lao Itsala[31] (the popular front established on the Việt Minh model in 1950, several years before the official birth of the Lao Party) were truly in a position to interfere with the kingdom's French-determined progress toward independence is another matter. The impact of the Vietnamese-created Lao revolutionary movement will be discussed later, but it should be pointed out here that for most of this period Souphanouvong was probably less well known in Laos than either

Phetsarath or the king and the crown prince. He had, after all, spent a good bit of his adult life outside the country and could not easily challenge their right to hold power.[32] A case can be made that it was only as Phetsarath's influence began to wane in the 1950s that Souphanouvong emerged as a more credible rival to the ruling family.

In general, French policy in Laos was to a large extent being borne along by the pace of developments in Cambodia and Vietnam. Plans for Cambodia got off to a relatively smooth start. For much of the 1945–1953 period, Sihanouk seems to have been a compliant partner in the decolonization process —as indeed he had been a compliant "protected ruler" since the French had put him on the throne in 1941. Until 1953, he seems to have been preoccupied mainly with domestic politics and his various rivals and opponents, in both Phnom Penh and the maquis. It was only in that year that he seriously challenged the French timetable with his "royal crusade" for Cambodian independence.

It is difficult to assess the influence of Sihanouk's "crusade" on the pace of decolonization in Cambodia. Secondary sources generally either maximize or minimize the impact of his actions depending on whether their authors are pro- or anti-Sihanouk.[33] It would be interesting to know whether (a) French plans for Cambodia and Laos were preceding at roughly the same pace and (b) Sihanouk's efforts significantly accelerated the granting of full independence to the two countries. However, the French could be fairly confident that the two royal governments, once independent, would not compromise with radical political elements and would be unlikely to renounce friendly ties with their former colonial rulers.[34] Thus, Paris would have little to lose by pushing ahead with de jure independence and did not have to fear that its long-term influence would be displaced by the Americans (a much greater concern for Vietnam).

Admittedly, the military situation in Cambodia and Laos in 1953, though not as perilous as in Vietnam, was far from encouraging. Chunks of Cambodia's territory were still under the control of various insurgents—notably the United Issarak Front, the Cambodian equivalent of the Việt Minh—while Laos in 1953 underwent a serious if relatively brief incursion by Vietnamese forces in support of their Lao comrades. Even so, by 1953 the French had little reason for fighting to hold onto Cambodia or Laos when they could "release" them into the arms of the French Union, at that time still assumed to be a long-term reality. It is likely that Paris would have preferred to wait until the revolutionary movements in the two kingdoms had been suppressed, presumably in conjunction with the defeat of the Việt Minh. The French government would have recognized, though, that completing Cambodian and Lao independence would also strengthen the legitimacy of those two governments, which would in turn hopefully weaken the insurgents' claims to be fighting for "true independence." Despite Sihanouk's eccentricities and mercurial temperament, he was recognized as a strong leader; the fact that he was not necessarily a democratic one was of much less importance.[35] Giving into his demands for full independence without a real "fight" thus strengthened his position domestically while maintaining Franco-Cambodian relations on a relatively even keel.

**Vietnam: A Case Study of Failure**

All things considered, then, Cambodia may be considered another successful example of decolonization from the French perspective, despite the "hiccups" of 1953. Vietnam, of course, is another matter, and the Bảo Đại solution was largely a failure. Not only were the French unable to create a viable long-term alternative to the revolutionary forces led by the Việt Minh and DRV, but also when Bảo Đại himself fell in 1955 he effectively dragged the French along with him, at least as far as their political influence in Vietnamese affairs was concerned.[36] There are several reasons why this was so.

The first and most fundamental issue relates to Bảo Đại's legitimacy as a former emperor. It is almost universally acknowledged that the Nguyễn as a dynasty and the Vietnamese monarchy as an institution had lost most of their prestige by the time of the August Revolution.[37] As mentioned earlier, the French had some sense of this in the early postwar years, but nevertheless Bảo Đại appeared as the most effective challenger to Hồ and the DRV. Although policy makers such as d'Argenlieu and Pignon initially spoke in terms of a full-fledged imperial restoration, ultimately this step was not taken, and Bảo Đại's tenure as head of state (Quốc trưởng) was characterized by a general ambiguity as to whether or not he was to be considered as a ruler. According to a June 1949 telegram from the U.S. ambassador in Paris, Bảo Đại was to be "chief of state, not emperor or monarch, pending popular consultation." Yet nearly two years later, the same ambassador reported that French Foreign Ministry officials had told him that the question of whether Vietnam would ultimately be a monarchy or a republic was still up in the air. Moreover, terms like "Cựu Hoàng" (former emperor), "Hoàng Thượng" (Your Majesty), and "tâu" (a particle used in addressing royalty) remained part of the official "discourse" of the State of Vietnam.[38]

This ambiguity appears in Bảo Đại's own memoirs as well. He says that in January 1948, shortly after a rather tenuous declaration that he had initialled together with French high commissioner Émile Bollaert, he demanded that "France give me back my title of emperor" and reunify the former Vietnamese kingdom. A few weeks later, one of the Cochin Chinese leaders now

"rallying" to Bảo Đại claimed that the latter's abdication in 1945 had occurred under duress and was therefore null and void, so that "legally [he] is
still the emperor." Commenting on this declaration, however, Bảo Đại claims
that he was not strongly in favor of a restoration since it would allow a return
to the status quo ante whereby the French controlled the monarchy.[39]

Whether or not he was to return to power as an actual sovereign, it seems
clear that the proponents of the Bảo Đại solution assumed that his imperial
stature was the most important component of his legitimacy as a leader (though
he criticized the French for "neglecting" precisely this "essential element").
In an October 1951 speech, French military commander General Jean de
Lattre de Tassigny affirmed that:

> His Majesty Bảo Đại [is] the symbol, the necessary support for Vietnam's
> unity. The Crown is the link which draws together this vast and richly var-
> ied country. . . . It is also the link which unites the Vietnamese State and the
> ethnic minorities. The emperor constitutes [a] unity [that is] stronger than
> differences, distinctives, and feudal loyalties. . . . [Y]oung and modern heir
> of an old dynasty, [he represents] Vietnam's historical unity, the hyphen
> between its past and its future, the guarantor of [its] unity since above
> social classes and political parties, His Majesty [represents] the whole na-
> tion, the people of Vietnam.[40]

Jean Letourneau made a similar observation to the U.S. ambassador in
Vietnam a year later, a comment that the latter repeated in a conversation
with Bảo Đại to assuage Bảo Đại's concerns that the French minister and
certain Vietnamese politicians "had republican preferences" and "believed
in the abolition of the monarchy and its replacement by a republic."[41]

No less ambivalent than Bảo Đại's personal position was the status of the
State of Vietnam that he led. He was intended, in effect, to be the "anti-Hồ,"
a rallying point for all patriotic Vietnamese who presumably saw through the
nationalist façade of the Việt Minh and DRV. (A French journalist at the time
expressed the conviction that "[a]s soon as H.M. Bảo Đại is back on the
throne of his forefathers, Hồ Chí Minh's armies will be nothing more than
gangs to be hunted down."[42]) Bảo Đại commented in his memoirs that by
1950, "I had appealed to all of the spiritual families [i.e., the Catholics and
the southern sects] and . . . I had a coherent group in hand. I could play the
entire keyboard of opinions." What this meant in reality, however, was a
congeries of individuals and movements of all political stripes—what the
French writer Lucien Bodard calls a "coalition de la piastre"—who had little
in common beyond a virulent hatred of the communists.[43]

Twentieth-century history shows that anticommunism alone rarely suf-
ficed as a cohesive national ideology, and the State of Vietnam was no excep-

tion. Bảo Đại's attempts to incorporate pro-French Cochin Chinese separatists, anti-French nationalists like Diệm, and religious sects like the Cao Đài and Hoà Hảo (which changed allegiances according to their strategic calculations at a given moment) seem to have been doomed to failure from the start.[44] The fact that his successive governments were not blessed with an abundance of men known for their talent and integrity only made things worse. In mid-1952, for example, when Nguyễn Văn Tâm was in the process of forming his first government, the U.S. consul in Hànội observed that "Tam's cabinet as composed so far bears [the] local reputation of being made up of persons qualifiable by one or more of [the] fol[lowing] epithets: pro-Fr[ench], opportunists, non-entities, extreme reactionaries, assassins, hirelings and, finally, men of faded mental powers."[45]

A third factor was geographical. Although a case can be made that most Vietnamese in Tonkin, Annam, and Cochin China shared a sense of national identity and a desire for reunification, decades of separation under colonial rule had left their mark. This was particularly true for Cochin China, whose political evolution as a colony had been significantly different from the two protectorates where the Nguyễn emperors' authority still theoretically held sway. While the administrative reunification of the southern provinces with the rest of Vietnam became a key issue, their psychological reintegration under the leadership of a former emperor was problematic, to say the least.[46] The south was the least royalist of the three regions, yet it became the main arena for the competing political forces that made up the State of Vietnam, and Sàigòn—not Hànội or Huế—was chosen as the de facto capital. There were logical reasons for this choice, as Sàigòn had acquired more political vitality and experience during the 1920s and 1930s, while Huế was viewed as a sort of sleepy royal backwater and Hànội bore the deep psychological imprint of the August Revolution and the DRV. Even so, to locate Bảo Đại's government in Sàigòn and pack it with Cochin Chinese politicians was not a strategy calculated to strengthen his hand. In this respect, his preference for Đàlạt and Ban Mê Thuột over his capital probably reflected his sense of alienation from Sàigòn as well as his preference for the various pleasures and diversions that the highland areas had traditionally offered him. A specific grievance was the long-standing French refusal to turn over the high commissioner's palace—the most potent symbol of French authority in Sàigòn—to the Vietnamese government.[47]

## Comparative Observations

During the colonial period, French sources tended to speak collectively of the *souverains protégés*, since most of Indochina was composed of royal protectorates and they tended to feel that issues affecting one ruler could have ramifications for the others as well. While it is not easy to determine the extent to which the French continued to think in these terms after 1945 (as opposed to viewing Vietnam, Cambodia, and Laos as separate entities), the monarchy remained the linchpin of an "Indochina-wide" approach to decolonization. As history has testified, however, French policy had varying levels of success in the three countries; in order to understand why, some comparative observations are in order.

The most obvious point, of course, is that power in Vietnam was being restored to a former emperor, whereas in Cambodia and Laos it had remained in royal hands with little or no disruption through the turbulent final months of the war. Despite the challenge from Son Ngoc Thanh, Sihanouk had remained on the throne, and even if he had caused enough trouble for the French to remove him, there was no question of abolishing the Cambodian monarchy. In Laos, while the ruling house in Luang Phabang was pushed off the scene for a few months following the king's refusal to cooperate with Phetsarath and the Lao Issara, it can be argued that the prominent role of Phetsarath signified that the royal family as a whole was by no means discredited. Indeed, until the final days of the Royal Lao government in 1975, princes such as Souvanna Phouma and Boun Oum, not to mention Souphanouvong, continued to dominate the political stage. Until the formal creation of Vietnamese-backed Lao and Cambodian resistance governments in 1950, even the ICP had to grudgingly consider the possibility of backing some form of monarchy in these two countries.[48]

Bảo Đại faced an entirely different situation. From the beginning, his Japanese-sponsored Empire of Annam had faced a direct challenge from the rapidly expanding Việt Minh guerrillas in the countryside. When Japan surrendered, the Việt Minh were able to take control of enough key locations to establish a provisional government and convince Bảo Đại to abdicate. His decision to do so and cooperate with the new regime appears to have enhanced his popular prestige and allowed him to maintain at least a façade of authority as supreme advisor to the DRV. (It may also have saved his life, since he could conceivably have met the same fate as his high-ranking minister and longtime apologist for the protectorate, Phạm Quỳnh, who was rounded up and shot.) A voluntary abdication to a revolutionary government is not easily reversed, however, and the physical transfer of his royal regalia to Việt Minh representatives brought an element of finality to the proceedings.[49] Many people would have felt at the time that the Mandate of Heaven (thiên mệnh) had indeed changed, and efforts by the French and Bảo Đại himself to persuade people otherwise—even if he returned to power as "head of state" instead of "emperor"—bore little fruit.

Bảo Đại's doubtful legitimacy at the individual level was hardly strengthened by French policy toward his State of Vietnam. Ellen Hammer, whose observations penned in 1950 were both incisive and prophetic, noted that "the impressive emphasis on legal formalities has obscured the facts that the new regime enjoys few of the usual attributes of sovereignty and that, indeed, Bảo Đại has yet to find a nation over which to rule."[50] It is widely recognized that one of the most crucial shortcomings of French policy was the unwillingness to endow Bảo Đại's government with precisely the "attributes of sovereignty" that could have made it a more credible alternative to the DRV. Hồ's government, after all, had functioned as a sovereign government in Hànội for sixteen months from 1945 to 1946 and continued to do so in the Resistance Zone, despite the obvious limitations that came with a rural-based guerrilla government. The DRV's declaration of independence over a—in theory, at least—reunified Vietnam was a hard act to follow, to put it mildly. As Paul Mus so trenchantly expressed it, "in 1945–46 we absolutely refused to give Vietnam the independence which we later granted it [through the Associated States structure], and so we found ourselves at war with a government which a physical majority of the nation followed or supported [the DRV] because it presented us with demands [independence, reunification] which we later credited the Bảo Đại government with forcing us to grant."[51]

The situation in Cambodia and Laos was radically different. Despite the growing strength of revolutionary movements during the decolonization period, they did not pose the same threat to the legitimacy of the monarchies. Not only had they never seized power as the Việt Minh did in Vietnam, they were much slower to expand beyond the ethnic Vietnamese minority and put down roots among the Cambodians and Lao. It was only during and after the wartime period that future Khmer and Lao communist leaders, such as Son Ngoc Minh (Achar Mean), Tou Samouth (Achar Sok), Kaysone, and Nouhak, appeared on the scene, and their real involvement with the ICP did not begin until after August 1945. While some official Lao histories have attempted to insert the party into a leadership role in the Lao Issara period of 1945–1946, their efforts are far from convincing, and there is no evidence that any ICP leader was on the scene in Vientiane or Luang Phabang. Souphanouvong was of course in the picture after his return in October, operating mainly in the south, but despite his ties to the Việt Minh, he was not an ICP member at the time.[52]

The authority of royal leaders in Cambodia and Laos was not seriously challenged by indigenous revolutionary forces until the establishment of alternative "resistance governments" in those countries in 1950.[53] Even then, it can be argued that the challenge remained more military than political. While the ICP-led resistance forces managed to gain control over sizable swathes of territory in both countries, their Vietnamese-style revolutionary programs had yet to resonate significantly among the Lao and Khmer, and the leaders who emerged out of the ICP were not yet in a position to compete with the Vientiane and Phnom Penh governments for political supremacy. The progress of Cambodia and Laos toward independence under French sponsorship, as discussed earlier, was steady enough to weaken the claims of the resistance to be fighting for "true independence."[54] It was only in the late 1950s, with the growing American involvement in Laos and the opportunity to partici- pate in coalition governments, that Souphanouvong and the Lao Party be- came a credible threat to the more conservative royalist elements. In Cambodia, this only really happened in the late 1960s, during Sihanouk's final years in power, and it should be noted that by that time the leadership of the Cambodian Communist Party was dominated by the Khmer Rouge group, most of whom did not owe their positions to earlier Vietnamese support.

A final problem for consideration is the historical and cultural framework within which the three monarchies were operating under French rule. I have argued elsewhere that the French fundamentally misunderstood Vietnamese kingship and its Confucian framework, and that they assumed that as long as they preserved the façade of imperial power and what they liked to call the "moral authority" and "spiritual powers" of the Nguyễn emperors, this would ensure the dynasty's continued legitimacy. In essence, French policy mak- ers—even those *annamitisants* who prided themselves on their understand- ing of Vietnamese history and society—overestimated the extent to which a ruling dynasty in Vietnam could remain viable through ceremonies and ritu- als when stripped of its actual power.[55]

If one compares the three "protected monarchies," there were no signifi- cant differences among them in terms of the political powers granted by the French either before or after 1945. Colonial officials in the 1880s came down particularly hard on the Vietnamese and Cambodian courts in order to im- pose their authority and quell potential opposition, but over the long run, the three protectorates were roughly equivalent as far as royal authority was con- cerned. Nor did the Cambodian and Lao ruling families produce more heroic *souverains protégés* than their Vietnamese counterparts. (On the contrary, two Nguyễn rulers—Hàm Nghi [1884–1885] and Duy Tân [1907–1916]— were deposed for rebellion, while a third—Thành Thái [1889–1907]—was also sent into exile, though apparently for perversion rather than subver- sion.[56]) How, then, does one account for the survival of two ruling houses and the fall of the third, in addition to the factors discussed earlier?

Part of the answer may lie within Theravada kingship, whereby the king's position as protector and patron of the religion was more important than any comparable role in a Confucian monarchy like Vietnam's. The French essentially supported Buddhism in Cambodia and Laos. Though they certainly sought to control the religion and ensure that it was not turned against them, they also recognized its value in promoting social stability and cultural identity; the latter function was particularly important since France was always wary of potentially threatening religious links between the Cambodians and Lao on the one hand and the Thai on the other hand. They may also have been aware of the long-term consequences for Burma of the British decision to remove the monarchy: the weakening of controls over the Buddhist Sangha and the destabilization of much of the traditional social order.

In Vietnam, by contrast, the French had sought to break the hold of Confucian culture over the elite through the abolition of the traditional examinations, the replacement of Chinese characters by romanized script, and the introduction of a bastardized Western-style educational system. (This was less an attack on Confucianism than an attempt to break cultural and psychological ties with China after the French had ended its traditional suzerainty.) These changes, combined with the intellectual ferment of a new generation of Southeast Asians exposed to Western ideas and values through various media, meant that Confucianism's grip over the Vietnamese was seriously weakened, and with it the authority of the monarchy. While Cambodia and Laos did experience cultural change and Buddhist institutions were not untouched by colonial rule (notably the declining role of the Sangha in education), neither development affected the prestige of their monarchies on a scale comparable to what the Nguyễn dynasty suffered. (In fact, by encouraging the two monarchies in their traditional patronage of Buddhism, the French were to some extent helping to buttress their authority.) Nor is there evidence of the same degree of ferment among Lao and Cambodian intellectuals, who were fewer in number and generally more Francophile than many of their Vietnamese counterparts.

The French consistently viewed the monarchy as the most viable—and most pliant—institution in all three countries. Consequently, from 1945 onward they anchored their policies of recolonization and then decolonization to that institution. In Cambodia and Laos, this proved a wise decision, all things considered, and France was able to make a relatively graceful exit that left power in the hands of a Francophile elite dominated by royals. In Vietnam, this was not to be the case: when colonialism fell—temporarily in 1945 and then for good in 1954—it dragged the monarchy with it.

# 5

# France and the Associated States of Indochina, 1945–1955

*Hugues Tertrais*

The dramatic Indochina conflict of the 1940s and early 1950s was a battle over decolonization: a long struggle between those who wanted it and those who resisted it. The French did not immediately appreciate the strength of Hồ Chí Minh's revolutionary movement when it was launched in the summer of 1945—and when they began to understand, they sought only to manage and channel the decolonization process in a way that would protect their own interests as far as possible. In this respect, the concept of the "Associated States" was a key component of French strategy. It deserves careful study, if only to show how France moved step by step toward failure in this period.

## The Associated States Project

The status of the Associated States was unique in the post–World War II French Union—and probably unique as a concept and as a mechanism in the process of decolonization overall. Indochina was the only territory in the entire French colonial empire that never supported Free France and Charles de Gaulle: it remained linked to Vichy even after the end of Vichy. In Asia, furthermore, it was the only European-controlled territory that collaborated with Japan—until Japan's March 9, 1945, coup, at all events. Ironically, however, Vietnam became one of the few territories where a new government seized power as a result of a nationalist uprising: the August Revolution and Hồ's September pronouncement in Hànội saw the magic word "independence" set fire to all parts of the country.[1]

The "Japanese coup" of March 9 quickly prompted French thoughts of reestablishing authority. A March 25, 1945, declaration unveiled a vision of postwar empire in which "freedom" would be obtained within a Federation of Indochina, a federation nested in a new French Union. To be sure, France's definition of "Indochina" was not immediately clear. The Indochinese Union of 1898, organized by Governor-General Paul Doumer, had consisted of five countries: Cochin China (directly administered by French officials) and protectorates over Annam, Tonkin, Laos, and Cambodia (with traditional rulers remaining partly in charge). But such an "Indochina-5" did not really exist after Japan tore up the protectorate treaties in March 1945. Was an "Indochina-4" envisioned instead? Were the French interested in reverting to the very earliest period of colonization, when a French Cochin China existed alongside Vietnam, Laos, and Cambodia?

Of course, grassroots nationalists had their own sense of identity. Those in Cochin China and those in the city of Sàigòn (where Trần Văn Giau headed the Việt Minh) both participated in the national uprising and considered themselves part of the national territory. The March 6, 1946, agreement between Hồ and France's envoy Jean Sainteny—which recognized a free Vietnam inside the French Union but left the status of Cochin China unsettled—failed, because the French were not ready to contemplate the kind of "Indochina-3" (i.e., one Vietnam, one Laos, and one Cambodia) that this development suggested.

Whatever the precise configuration of the new federation, France envisioned a series of reforms and initiatives for it. A plan to replace the Banque de l'Indochine that had issued currency since 1875 was prepared by the Banque de France in 1946, for example, prior to the break with Hồ. It was supervised by Jean Belin, the inspector-general of the Banque de France. Jean Monnet's ambitious modernization plan also included an Indochina section—the Bourgoin Plan—which set the industrialization of Vietnam as a goal. Such a concept had hardly been discussed in the 1930s. It grew out of calculations concerning the impact of Japan's collapse as the only industrialized country in Asia. Why not take advantage of this to develop new strengths and market opportunities?

The planning commission's report (published in 1948) identified six areas requiring attention: public infrastructure, agriculture, mining, energy, industrialization, and social infrastructure. In an environment "transformed by the Japanese defeat," it was argued, Vietnam had "plenty of manpower, skilled and industrious," as well as natural resources and raw materials. Indochina as a whole possessed "industrial potential" that would enable it "to establish large-scale industry."[2] The French plan put particular emphasis on irrigation and industry. With the aim of doubling paddy production, for example, agricultural hydraulics were to receive 25 percent of investments. Heavy industries like chemicals, iron, steel, and aluminum would also be developed, because they "constitute a great country's economic infrastructure" and "are yet lacking in Indochina." Two main industrial projects were planned: one in the north, near Haiphong, where coal mining would allow significant power supplies, and the other in the Cam Ranh area, near the sea and the Dalat-Da Nhim hydroelectric plant. It was expected that two five-year plans would see expenditures of 3 billion piastres (at 1939 value, the equivalent of $685 million), with 45 percent of the sum going into public infrastructure. In order to use economic development to strengthen linkages and associations with Indochina, the plans were designed to emphasize the federal character.[3]

## Building the Associated States

Because of the rupture with Hồ, France had to sacrifice some of its projects during the first three years of the conflict (1945–1948), but worked hard to save what it considered to be the most important: the federal structure of the Associated States. The federation was actually initiated during the second period (1949–1952). The third period (1952–1955) was characterized by increasing French difficulties to contain Indochinese nationalism and saw the final breakdown of the system.

During the first period, France tried to maintain an Indochina-4 policy in its negotiations with Hồ. On June 1, 1946, during the difficult discussions with the new Vietnamese president, Admiral Thierry d'Argenlieu, the French high commissioner, let Southern separatists proclaim an "autonomous Republic of Cochinchina" in the south chaired by Nguyễn Văn Trinh.[4] The reason for this move was to "Vietnamize" Cochin China. On October 1, 1947, ten months after the beginning of the war, General Nguyễn Văn Xuân became president of that republic. He changed the designation "Cochin China government" into that of "provisional Government of South Vietnam." However, secret talks with the former emperor Bảo Đại as an alternative to Hồ had been initiated. Like Hồ and virtually all Vietnamese, the former emperor demanded the territorial unity of the country, including Cochin China.

Why did the French choose Bảo Đại? Born in 1913 and educated in France, he had been on the imperial throne at Hue since 1926 when, pressured by the Japanese, he renounced the 1885 Protectorate Treaty with France on March 11, 1945. Under pressure from Hồ's representatives, he abdicated from the throne five months later (August 25, 1945). Thereafter, he served as "supreme adviser" to Hồ's government for a short time.[5] After Bảo Đại severed relations with Hồ and following the Hànội "clash" of December 19, 1946, between French and Việt Minh forces, d'Argenlieu's first thought was "to restore the institution of traditional monarchy."[6] The French military in Indochina expected that a new Bảo Đại nationalism would replace Hồ's influence. In the words of General Étienne Valluy, "A nationalist idea, but one which agreed with the principle of the French presence."[7]

The project of the Associated States was neither intended as a vehicle against Hồ's power, nor was it conceived as a supportive instrument for Bảo Đại. It had been inserted into the new French constitution of the Fourth Republic in November 1946 when the revolutionary Hồ was still the official leader of the Vietnamese government. But with the advent of the Cold War in 1947, France was only willing to negotiate with the traditional rulers of Indochina: Bảo Đại in Vietnam, Norodom Sihanouk in Cambodia, and Sisavangvong in Laos. France tried to salvage its concept of federalism together with its influence in Indochina by sidestepping Hồ.

The initial French project seemed doomed to fail. On December 7, 1947, on the cruiser *Duguay-Trouin* anchored in Ha Long Bay, the new French high commissioner Emile Bollaert and Bảo Đại concluded a provisional agreement on the independence and unity of Vietnam. Cochin China would be given to Bảo Đại instead of Hồ. Furthermore, the concept of independence, which had at first been anathema to France, was finally accepted, albeit in a circumscribed way. Ambivalences remained. Thus, High Commissioner Bollaert, who three months earlier had wanted to negotiate with Hồ, was forced not to use the term "independence" in his September 10, 1947, speech; Paris allowed it only in the Vietnamese translation (*Doc Lap*). Finally, the economic plan was never realized because of the war that had started in December 1946. All money that had been earmarked for development projects had already been spent on the military conflict. To cover the most urgent matters in spite of limited resources, a "special budget for Indochinese reconstruction and infrastructure" was created in April 1947. Since northern Vietnam (Tonkin) was firmly under the control of the Việt Minh, the French concentrated on the economic development of Cochin China, Cambodia, and Laos (the Indochina-3 formula).

In the period between 1949 and 1952, Bảo Đại was unable to achieve his goal of establishing himself as as an alternative to Hồ. He and his state apparatus became a war machine against the Việt Minh and a source of conflict between France and the United States. During these years, the Associated States of Indochina were established. On March 8, 1949, three years after the Hồ-Sainteny Agreement, and a few days before the foundation of the North Atlantic Treaty Organization, French president Vincent Auriol and Bảo Đại, henceforth chief of the State of Vietnam, exchanged official letters of recognition. Four months later, on July 19, France and Laos signed a general convention regulating bilateral relations. A similar treaty was concluded with Cambodia on November 8. As members of the French Union, they were able to build national armies and, with consent from Paris, to establish diplomatic relations with foreign countries. However, France remained very cautious: while the texts were made public, they were not published in the *Journal Officiel,* the proper organ for state treaties and laws.[8]

The military situation for France looked bleak. Returning from an inspection trip through Indochina three months after the Auriol–Bảo Đại Agreement, General Paul Revers, the chief of staff of the French armed forces, wrote, "On the eve of the inauguration of the Bảo Đại government, Vietnam is deeply divided. We control only part of the territory and less than half of the population. In the territories under control, terrorism is rampant. In the other areas, the Viet Minh have installed a government and an efficient administration; they have armed forces."[9] Therefore, Bảo Đại was supposed to consolidate his power in the territory under French control first, and then widen his control.

The status of the new Associated States was decided in 1950 at a conference in Pau, a small city in southwestern France.[10] Four delegations met: the French (headed by Albert Sarraut, president of the French Union Assembly), the Vietnamese (Nguyễn Trung Vinh), the Laotian (Phoui Sananikone), and the Cambodian (Sum Hieng). During the six months from June to December 1950, these four delegations had to overcome a multitude of problems, ranging from navigation on the Mekong River to currency issues. The goals of the conference were to transfer part of the French powers to the new states and to establish an economic, customs, and currency union, which would remain partly under French control. France maintained extensive advisory functions, especially in Cambodia and Laos. Moreover, the union consisted of not only the three Indochinese entities, but included France as well to ensure the lasting political and economic influence of French colonial power. The project centered on a common currency. A new bank of issue, the Institut d'Émission des États Associés, was to replace the old colonial Banque de l'Indochine. This institution, comanaged by the four parties concerned and chaired by the French Gaston Cusin, was supposed to work directly with the three national treasury departments of Vietnam, Cambodia, and Laos—all heirs to the Indochinese Treasury Department. Although it meant no genuine independence, the currency union was a move toward self-government and regional unity.[11]

However, one main problem remained: the war against the Việt Minh, an increasingly powerful enemy, especially since it was backed by Red China. In October 1950, during the Pau Conference, the Việt Minh people's army defeated the French expeditionary forces at Cao Bang, near the Chinese border, thus opening the way for Chinese advisors and matériel. In this deteriorating situation, with costs of the conflict rising yearly, the solution seemed to be twofold: first, to involve the new Associated States with their own "national armies," and second, to ask for substantial American support. Paris expected that in view of the Korean War, which had broken out in June 1950, Washington would be sympathetic to French demands for military aid. In exchange for greater autonomy, the Associated States mobilized their armies to fight the Việt Minh. In early 1949, when the French expeditionary forces numbered 130,000 men, the national armies were still very small: about 16,000 men in Vietnam, most of them former members of the old French Indochinese Guard, less than 5,000 men in Cambodia, and perhaps 1,000 men in Laos. The first plan to recruit Indochinese soldiers was devised in 1949, with the object of raising fifty thousand men in Vietnam alone.

In November 1950, just before the end of the Pau Conference, Jean Letourneau, the French minister for the relations with the Associated States, met Bảo Đại in Dalat and urged him to increase the number of troops to about 150,000. A few months later, on July 11, 1951, Bảo Đại, who had been convinced by General Jean de Lattre de Tassigny, the new French high commissioner and commander in chief, proclaimed a general mobilization in Vietnam. In 1952, the three national armies had grown to 176,000 men. In addition, there were 188,000 French soldiers (including tens of thousands of soldiers from the Maghreb and West Africa, as well as Foreign Legion troops). While the former were mainly used for "pacification," the latter fought the regular Việt Minh units.[12] Yet, the problem of financing the army remained. In early 1951, the French Foreign Office commented on the impact of the communist victory in China on the situation in Vietnam, "[With] the arrival of the Chinese communists to the Indochinese border in November 1949 and the recognition of Hồ Chí Minh by the Peking government . . . , military operations blew up to such a scale that their costs could no longer be supported solely by France."[13]

Following the diplomatic recognition of Hồ's Democratic Republic of Vietnam (DRV) by China and the Soviet Union, President Harry S. Truman extended official recognition to Bảo Đại's State of Vietnam (February 7, 1950). Meanwhile, the French government agreed to the conditions Washington attached to its military support for Indochina. In 1950, as part of the Mutual Defence Assistance Program, military equipment, such as weapons, munitions, warships, and fighter aircraft, was delivered to Indochina free of charge, partly for the French troops and partly for the national armies. The first delivery arrived on August 10, 1950, a month and a half after the beginning of the Korean War. In September, a Military Advisory Assistance Group was installed in Sàigòn to supervise the distribution of U.S. military aid. Finally, a Military Assistance Act was signed by France, the United States, and the three Associated States of Indochina in Sàigòn in December 1950. All equipment would go directly to the French military services and only a small group of French officers was authorized to communicate with their American counterparts. Military support was accompanied by an economic aid program for the Associated States. This program was highly contested, because the Truman administration insisted that economic support had to be distributed directly to the Associated States. This was unacceptable to the French, so they tried to delay the conclusion of the agreement as long as possible.[14] It was not until November 1951 that the treaty, which had been announced in May 1950, was finally signed.

American aid proved to be a double-edged sword for the French—and for the Americans as well. This can be inferred from a February 1950 U.S. State Department memorandum, "Most Indochinese, both the supporters of Bảo Đại and those of Hồ Chí Minh, regard independence from the French as their primary objective." At the same time, American observers feared a domino effect, "The choice confronting the United States is to support the French in Indochina or face the extension of Communism over the remainder of the continental area of Southeast Asia and, possibly, farther westward."[15] When the Griffin mission, President Truman's task force for an assessment of the economic needs of Southeast Asia, visited the Associated States in March 1950, Léon Pignon, the French high commissioner, suspected the Americans of launching "a comprehensive economic and cultural offensive" to eradicate French influence in Indochina.[16] Because "the failure of American policy in China is still recent," French officials did not accept any American interference in their own policy toward Indochina.[17] However, the contradiction between dependence on the United States on the one hand and interest in prohibiting American influence in Indochina on the other hand would grow in the years to come.

**The Failure of the Associated States**

On January 1, 1952, the joint Associated States Currency Institute began circulating the new currency, which retained its former name (piastre, in Vietnamese dông). But it seemed almost too late for a monetary and economic union of the Associated States. For one, the Pau system deteriorated rapidly. The first economic and customs meeting, held in Paris in April 1952, ended in a complete failure. The free movement of goods was a central principle of the Pau Agreement, but both the Cambodian and the Vietnamese governments quickly prohibited rice exports from their territories. Furthermore, at the end of the year the Vietnamese government declined to transfer its share of the monthly customs income to the Cambodian and Laotian governments. The 1952 and 1953 Intergovernmental Conferences, held in Sàigòn (July to September 1952) and Phnom Penh (January to March 1953), failed to formulate a common exports policy and ended with a fundamental Cambodian-Vietnamese disagreement over external trade and customs matters.[18] The awakening of Cambodian and Vietnamese nationalism contributed to the breakdown of the agreements. In particular, Cambodian elites objected to the cessation of Cochin China from France to Bảo Đại's State of Vietnam. In their view, the Mekong Delta belonged to the Khmer, who had settled there until the seventeenth and eighteenth centuries, when the Vietnamese took over and occupied that area.

Meanwhile, American assistance increased significantly. From 1950 to June 1953, three hundred American ships delivered a total of three hundred thousand tons of matériel, averaging two or three shipments of eight thousand tons per week. But military support brought its share of problems: slow delivery and varying quality of the equipment, which was sometimes old and never the best. However, despite these initial problems the French Union forces were modernized and homogenized. American military support increased threefold, from 40 billion francs in 1950 to 119 billion francs in 1953. In 1954, the United States covered fully 80 percent of France's war expenditures. In addition to military assistance, further financial aid to Indochina was agreed on at the February 1950 NATO conference in Lisbon: $330 million for the 1951–1952 fiscal year, and $410 million for the following fiscal year; combined, these two financial packages covered 25 percent of the cost of the war at that point.

France was facing too many problems in too many areas of the world and was finally forced to make some tough decisions. In Indochina, the military struggle against the Việt Minh no longer seemed to offer any chance of success, and the political dialogue with conservative nationalists grew increasingly difficult. The United States kept "pressure on the French to turn over more power to the native Indochina rulers in Laos, Cambodia and Vietnam."[19] Since both rearmament at home and the war in Indochina were more costly than envisaged, the French government was very worried about the budget.

In 1953, France appeared to show signs of disengagement. Therefore, another $400 million aid package to keep the French fighting against the Việt Minh was agreed on in April. The 1949 treaties between France and the Associated States were finally published in the *Journal Officiel*, and control over the Associated States relaxed. Moreover, on May 11, 1953, the piastre was devalued, a move that monetary experts had been demanding for quite some time. The devaluation in effect meant a significant liquidation of French economic interests in Indochina. Furthermore, on July 3, 1953, a solemn declaration by the French government promised "to perfect the independence of the States." Following the Cambodian "crusade for independence," launched by King Sihanouk, anti-French feelings greatly increased in Sàigòn, where a Vietnamese National Congress assembled in October 1953. Finally, in November 1953 the holding of a meeting of the High Council of the French Union, convened by President Auriol, took note of "the intention of Cambodia to break off the agreements establishing an economic, monetary and customs Union."[20]

France lost against the Việt Minh (the DRV), which won a decisive military victory against the French at Điện Biên Phủ in May 1954; a month later, it also lost politically vis-à-vis the Associated States, which now obtained full independence and new association treaties with Paris. Four years after the Pau Conference, a final meeting between France and the three Associated States took place in Paris from August to December 1954. Its agenda was to officially end the Customs and Currency Union and the quadripartite political system. On January 1, 1955, the three newly independent states issued their own currencies and replaced the piastre with the Cambodian riel, the Laotian kip, and the Vietnamese dông. Obviously, there were now two Vietnamese currency areas: the Republic of Vietnam in the south, the successor to the State of Vietnam, which was no longer headed by Bảo Đại but by Ngô Đình Diệm, and the Democratic Republic of Vietnam in the north, which had its own dông.

## Conclusion

There are differing interpretations as to when decolonization materialized. If we consider the departure of the French as the key event, 1954 would be the appropriate moment. The DRV people's army entered Hànội on October 10, and the quadripartite system linking France and the Associated States ended on December 29, 1954. But from both an international and Vietnamese perspective, the year 1945 seems more significant. First, the 1945 Potsdam Conference divided Indochina into two parts along the sixteenth parallel, but without France being represented at the conference. Second, after the Japanese coup and the 1945 August Revolution, French rule was already a thing of the past in Vietnamese public opinion. France underestimated the power of Vietnamese nationalism, and its recolonization appeared to be a military conquest, much like the initial effort to colonize Indochina in the nineteenth century. With the help of the British, initially it was not very difficult for General Philippe Leclerc's troops to gain a foothold in the south, where the British were in charge of disarming the Japanese. In the north, however, there was the dual threat of a Chinese occupation army and Hồ's government. Therefore, the French had to negotiate agreements authorizing the deployment of French troops both with the Chinese and with Hồ.

At the time, reconquest was the ultimate aim of the French.[21] But after the December 19, 1946, uprising, the Vietnamese people's army consolidated its control over the north. The French expeditionary forces were able to establish control over Hànội, but they never succeeded in reconquering the whole country. In January 1947, General Valluy compared the situation to the colonial conquest some sixty years earlier, "Our elders faced an anarchic society," he said, "where the strongest organized body was the province or some village community." Today, "we are facing a rule—even if irregular but efficient—centralized and organized into a hierarchy, with a pyramidal framework and backed by an ideology appealing to the masses."[22]

The question remains: What impact did the failed Associated States strategy have on the Indochinese countries? From a political viewpoint, one of its results was obviously the division of Vietnam. The "Bảo Đại solution" was an alternative to Hồ, but one that divided the Vietnamese people and pushed them into civil war. The risk was well known in France at the time. For example, during a parliamentary debate on the Cochin China issue, following the March 8, 1949 agreement with Bảo Đại, the socialist Gaston Deferre asked, "Does not the return of Bảo Đại to Vietnam involve the risk of unleashing civil war there?"[23]

Military mobilization did indeed fuel the civil war. The Vietnamese national army enlisted some 226,000 men in 1954, about as many as the French expeditionary forces (230,000 men). All in all, some 250,000 Vietnamese fought on the French side, including those integrated into French units. On the Việt Minh side, some 350,000 soldiers were involved. Moreover, military mobilization necessitated increasing taxes. Although both the State of Vietnam and the DRV obtained some international support, they had to collect taxes to finance their troops.

At the end of the war in 1954, two Vietnamese camps were facing each other, each with its own territory, police, economy, and currency. The Việt Minh dominated the north and the countryside, while the Bảo Đại camp was relatively strong in the south and in the cities, especially in Sàigòn. In 1950, 70 percent of the population was under Việt Minh control in the north, 75 percent in the central parts of the country, and only 15 percent in the south.[24] Bảo Đại versus Hồ meant south versus north, cities versus countryside, and trade versus agriculture. For these reasons, one can argue that the 1954 Geneva Agreement, concerning the partition of the country along the seventeenth parallel, only sanctioned a fact that the war had established.

How can we assess the failure of the Associated States from an economic viewpoint? Instead of the industrial projects envisaged in 1945, we can observe illicit piastre traffic during most of the war, especially in Sàigòn. With an exchange rate of 17 francs to the piastre and a true value of around ten to one from 1945 to 1953, the Indochinese currency was widely overvalued and illicit traffic with France was very easy. Instead of an Indochinese federation, there existed, at the end of 1954, four countries on bad terms with each other (North and South Vietnam, Cambodia, and Laos). Retarded development characterized the Indochinese countries during the whole period. The Associated States had been France's idea for transforming the old empire into a new entity of semi-independent countries. But the plan did not succeed because the French were neither able to win against the Việt Minh, nor to promote a noncommunist, French-friendly nationalism. In 1954, the only option was to leave a "Balkanized" Indochina, disrupted by revolutionary and conservative nationalism.

# 6

# The Indonesian Revolution and the Fall of the Dutch Empire

## Actors, Factors, and Strategies

*Marc Frey*

The Indonesian revolution and the fall of the Dutch empire rank among the most important developments in the history of contemporary Southeast Asia.[1] Following three years of Japanese occupation during World War II, the Indonesian nationalist movement swept away a colonial system whose foundations dated back to the end of the sixteenth century. The proclamation of independence on August 17, 1945, set in motion a struggle against colonial rule that involved both diplomacy and military conflict. The struggle for sovereignty, which ended only in late 1949 after two Dutch military offensives and a protracted Indonesian guerilla war, also caught the attention of the international community. For the newly founded United Nations, it was the first test of its conflict-resolution mechanisms. Following unsuccessful efforts at mediation by Great Britain during the first two years of the conflict, the United States assumed responsibility for the final resolution of the crisis by putting pressure on the Dutch to relinquish sovereignty over the island archipelago. Most importantly, the revolution of 1945 gathered sentiments of an Indonesian community and transformed them into a shared identity on which the Indonesian nation-state could be built. Decolonization was a multilayered process defined by actors, ideas, and institutions in Indonesia, in the Netherlands, and in the international arena. It is hardly surprising, then, that these complex developments have attracted a considerable degree of scholarly interest.

Historians of decolonization employ three categories to distinguish different levels of analysis: the "metropolitan," the "colonial," and the "global" dimension. These categories refer to historical developments taking place in the colonial powers, in the colonies, and in the world at large.[2] Approaching the topic from the "colonial" perspective, Audrey R. Kahin, George McTurnan Kahin, Jan Pluvier, and Anthony Reid, among others, argue that it was above all the unique blend of military activities (*perjuangan*) and diplomacy (*diplomasi*) of the Indonesian Republic that successfully secured indepen-dence.[3] Scholars who focus their research on the metropolitan perspective confirm this interpretation. For instance, H. W. van den Doel, C. Fasseur, Lodewijk de Jong, and Yong Mun Cheong find the strength of the republic gradually rising and that of the Netherlands slowly but surely diminishing. They also give credit to the republic's ability to employ military and diplo-matic pressure successfully. In contrast, they find Dutch policies to be in-flexible and uncompromising, and they argue that the Netherlands eventually lost the all-important sympathies of its closest allies, the British and Ameri-can governments. It was in particular the American shift in strategy from benevolent neutrality that favored the colonial power to one designed to bring Dutch colonialism to an end that was instrumental in forcing The Hague to acknowledge Indonesian independence.[4] In contrast to these findings, P. J. Drooglever and J. J. P. de Jong, also writing from a metropolitan perspective, argue that Dutch policies vis-à-vis the republic were much more flexible and open to compromise than previously thought. In their view, Great Britain strongly encouraged a weak Indonesian Republic to demand "100 percent *merdeka*" (independence). British occupation policies in late 1945, they claim, energized and unified a rather disparate group of nationalists and legitimized a poorly organized administration as the de facto government of Java, Sumatra, and Madura. Moreover, they blame the United States for thrusting premature independence down the Netherlands' throat.[5] This interpretation is challenged by those, who, writing from a global perspective, assess the influence of outside actors on decolonization in Indonesia. Frances Gouda, Gerlof Homan, and Robert J. McMahon, among others, find the United States consistently on the side of the Netherlands. Only when it became clear in 1949 that the Dutch military would not be able to pacify Java and Sumatra did Washington change sides and persuade decision makers in The Hague to consent to Indo-nesian independence.[6]

Any monocausal explanation for the success of the republic falls short of capturing the complexity of the specific historical setting in which the Indo-nesian revolution unfolded. But ultimately the colonial dimension determined the outcome of the conflict. It was indeed the republic's interplay between military action and diplomacy, as well as the pressure exerted by guerilla warfare, that was instrumental for securing success. It is improbable, how-ever, that without American intervention the transfer of power would have taken place in 1949. The global dimension of the conflict thus reinforced local developments on the colonial level.

Following some introductory remarks about Indonesia in 1945, this chap-ter seeks to define the major actors and to analyze their expectations, percep-tions, and interests. Particular emphasis will be put on the following problems:

What kind of designs and plans did the various actors have with regard to Indonesia? Which strategy did they employ to realize their aims and interests? How did the actors perceive one another, and what impact did this have on decision-making processes?

The proclamation of independence by Sukarno on August 17, 1945, and the establishment of a republic filled a power vacuum in Indonesia. This power vacuum had been caused by three factors: the sudden surrender of Japan, the lack of a sufficient number of Allied occupation forces, and the revolutionary changes in Indonesia. First, after three years of occupation during which the Japanese had established their version of a colonial regime, they found it politically expedient to encourage preparations for a transfer of power in Java. By August, deliberations for a republican constitution had progressed considerably. But the unexpected Japanese surrender on August 15, 1945, fundamentally changed the variables under which preparations for independence had taken place. Now, independence could be declared and secured on an Indonesian basis free of Japanese domination. Moreover, according to the terms of the surrender, Japanese troops were assigned with preserving order and security in Indonesia and preparing the ground for an Allied occupation of the islands. But in this the Japanese failed. At times, local commanders were unwilling to cooperate with the Allies. More often, members of Indonesian youth movements disarmed the Japanese and captured their weapons. Second, the Allies had not expected an occupation of Java and Sumatra in 1945, and they were completely taken by surprise by the sudden collapse of Japan. The British simply did not have a sufficient number of troops available for a speedy occupation of the islands. And third, the traditional ruling aristocracy that, to a large degree, had cooperated with the Dutch before the war, had either been supplanted by intellectual nationalist officeholders appointed by the Japanese or been forced out of office by youth movements formed during the war.[7]

It was thus a unique opportunity for both those Indonesian nationalists who had cooperated with the Japanese during the war as well as for those who had opposed the occupation regime. Many of the former had taken part in the constitution-making process initiated by the Japanese promise to grant independence to Indonesia. While there was sharp disagreement on the problem of collaboration with Japan, everyone agreed that the nationalists were now ready to assume administrative responsibilities. The moment was also seized by the revolutionary youth movements (*pemudas*). Formed as paramilitary groups during the occupation and thoroughly indoctrinated with anti-Dutch propaganda during the war, they represented the radical part of the nationalist movement. Many of them regarded a class struggle as a necessary corollary to the struggle for independence. In numerous places throughout

Java and Sumatra, the pemudas overthrew traditional hierarchies. Republican leadership was not uncontested either. In particular, Sukarno was challenged by Sutan Sjahrir, who criticized the president's wartime collaboration with the Japanese. In mid-November, Sukarno had to dismiss his cabinet, and Sjahrir, a widely respected intellectual who had the backing of the pemudas, became prime minister. This step initiated the transformation of the political order into a parliamentary system with a cabinet responsible to the legislature. However, Sukarno's charisma ensured that the president remained the most influential political leader. Nationalist leaders and youth movements shared a number of goals: both wanted an independent republic free from foreign domination, improved economic opportunities for Indonesians, and better living conditions (a point that was important in view of the wartime hardships).[8] But large segments of the youth movement envisaged a comprehensive social revolution involving a fundamental reevaluation of institutions, traditions, and values. Nationalist leaders, in contrast, were prepared to make compromises, with the traditional rulers as well as with the Allies. While scholars disagree on the level of cooperation between nationalist administrators and the pemudas, it is certain that tensions existed. In time, these tensions would increase as the republic struggled to find the balance between military action and diplomacy.[9] Sukarno's appeal to the masses and Vice President Mohammed Hatta's organizational skills ensured that the revolution did not turn into anarchy. By the end of September 1945, the republic's control extended over most of Java and Sumatra with a combined population of fifty-five million people, almost 80 percent of the Indonesian population. Towns and cities were no longer administered by the Japanese but by nationalists. But organization was still loose and uncoordinated, especially in Sumatra. In South Sulawesi and Bali, Republican governors worked hand in hand with the local aristocracy, but elsewhere in East Indonesia Republican influence was limited, especially in rural areas.[10]

For a variety of reasons, the Allies were completely unprepared for the situation they faced in Indonesia in the fall of 1945. The Southeast Asia Command under Admiral Lord Louis Mountbatten, assigned with the Allied occupation of Burma, Malaya, and Vietnam (up to the sixteenth parallel), had been assigned with the task to occupy Indonesia and disarm the Japanese only in mid-August. The decision to relieve General Douglas MacArthur and his Southwest Pacific Command of this responsibility had come as a great shock to the unprepared Dutch. Notwithstanding the fact that they had lobbied the British for a close cooperation of the colonial powers during the war, and despite the confident expectation that the British would facilitate a Dutch reconquest of Indonesia as best as they could, the Dutch would have preferred American assistance. MacArthur had more troops and better equipment, and could project much more power than Mountbatten.[11] Moreover, the Dutch had already concluded favorable agreements with MacArthur with regard to the administration of Indonesia during the occupation period.[12] All of a sudden, the Dutch had to deal with a British military that had fewer resources than the Americans and with a commander in chief whose favorable views of nationalist movements were well known.

But questions of command and troops were not the only problems the Allies faced. Another was information and analysis. Dutch advance guards who entered Batavia/Jakarta in early September believed that the assassination of Sukarno and Hatta would be sufficient to suppress all opposition to colonial rule. Others had a more realistic view and felt that most Indonesians were "strongly anti-Dutch."[13] Ch. O. van der Plas, a high-ranking official of the Netherlands East Indies Administration who arrived in early September, was deeply shaken by the widespread "hatred" toward the Dutch and concluded, "We have underestimated the extend of anti-Dutch policies as well as the result of years of anti-Dutch propaganda." Hubertus van Mook, the lieutenant governor-general, strongly urged Mountbatten not to recognize the republic "in any respect," because this "would create the greatest difficulties and bring confusion in the minds of all law-abiding Indonesians."[14] The British, however, refused this request. Mountbatten argued that British troops could only occupy key areas and would depend on the cooperation of Republican forces to disarm the Japanese. Moreover, in Burma the British had diffused a potentially explosive situation by working with Aung San and the nationalist leadership, and they saw no reason why the Dutch should not do the same. Finally, the British troops consisted mainly of Indian soldiers. With a view to repercussions on Indian politics and the morale of the soldiers, Mountbatten felt he could not force these troops into action against Indonesian nationalists. While British occupation forces landed in Batavia/Jakarta on September 29, the supreme commander urged the Dutch to negotiate with the Republican leadership. Mountbatten's request was powerfully reinforced on the same day by hundreds of thousands of Indonesians, who assembled in the capital to demonstrate against colonial rule and for independence.[15]

By mid-November, the patterns of the conflict were well developed. The republic demanded a recognition of sovereignty. Sukarno, Hatta, and Sjahrir, whom the Dutch regarded as an acceptable negotiation partner, realized that the Dutch would not voluntarily consent to independence. The Republican leadership was willing to compromise, play for time, and reach the desired aim in stages. Furthermore, leaders like Hatta and Sjahrir thought that Dutch advice, expertise, and capital would be needed for a couple of years to modernize the economy.[16] In contrast, young radicals and especially the communists envisaged a future completely free of Dutch (and Western) influence. In view of conflicting political visions and because of the multiethnic and multicultural character of Indonesian society, the republic promoted unity in diversity. Its ideological basis became Sukarno's Pancasila ("five principles"): nationalism, humanity, democracy, social equality, and belief in one god. Efforts were made to absorb the pemudas within the Army of the Republic of Indonesia (Tentara Republic Indonesia), and Parliament and newspapers provided platforms for a lively and controversial political discourse.[17]

The debate about Indonesia in the Netherlands and within the returning Dutch community in Batavia/Jakarta revealed a deep split with regard to the republic. Van Mook urged his government to introduce democratic reforms as soon as possible in order to present a progressive Dutch vision for Indonesia. Already in the prewar period, he had called for a "modern" colonial state, in which colonizers and the colonized would work together for the common good. Now, he felt circumstances dictated a devolution of power from The Hague to Jakarta, the indigenization of the administration, and gradual democratization. In contrast, most of the returning military, as well as many Dutch who had been interned during the war by the Japanese, felt that most of the Republican leaders were collaborators (Sukarno in particular), that the republic was illegal, and that they were entitled to revenge. Speaking for many, Admiral C. E. L. Helfrich, commander in chief of the Dutch forces in the Far East, declared, "This country has to be cleared of all the bad elements, even if they number 100.000."[18]

In The Hague, the strength of the republic and the degree of anti-Dutch sentiment was seriously underestimated. Decision making was complicated by factional stride and party arithmetic. An early armed intervention against the republic would have found the support of the cabinet, but resources were lacking. Experts asserted that Indonesia had contributed to the Dutch gross national product by some 14 percent in 1938, and the public believed that the country needed the Indonesian economy for reconstruction purposes. Equally important were considerations of prestige: Dutch politicians feared a loss of international influence and the relegation to a really small power. Therefore, negotiations with the republic were grudgingly accepted, but a military solution remained the favored option for the majority inside and outside of government.[19]

Utilities and public works were in Indonesian hands, and Republican forces guarded well over a hundred thousand Japanese soldiers in the rural areas of Java and Sumatra. Thus, the British quickly extended de facto recognition to the republic because cooperation was simply a necessity. A completely neutral position as desired by Mountbatten and Sir Philip Christison, the commanding general in Indonesia, proved impossible. In the urban bridgeheads the British had established, soldiers became targets of guerilla attacks as they were accused of facilitating the entry of the Dutch. In Surabaya, six thousand British-Indian troops fought a bloody battle with the urban population, the pemudas, and twenty thousand Republican soldiers before they could occupy the city, leaving thousands dead. After the battle, Indonesian leaders partly blamed the pemudas, but they also accused the British for fostering an aggressive climate. Increasingly, the British were perceived as surrogate conquerors and not as a disinterested occupying power concerned with winding down the Pacific war. Numerous instances where Dutch troops (about five thousand) had provoked clashes behind the British military shield confirmed this view.[20] Great Britain's prestige as an "enlightened" colonial power willing to grant independence to its dependencies was at stake. Neither the financial situation nor public opinion in Britain and elsewhere allowed for costly military adventures. Moreover, the situation in Indonesia seriously impeded the reconstruction of the whole region.[21] Surabaya therefore reinforced the British government's decision to bring the Indonesians and the Dutch together.

Similar concerns were voiced in Washington. Interested in an early resumption of raw materials exports from Indonesia, the administration urged the Netherlands to negotiate with the republic in a cooperative and friendly spirit. Officials in the State Department argued that it was imperative to involve Sukarno and Hatta, because otherwise radical elements could trigger a civil war. Washington's attitude reflected its long-term strategy toward colonialism. It envisaged cooperation between the nationalists and the colonial power in the interest of economic and political modernization, the gradual emancipation from colonial rule, and continued close relations between sovereign states in the future. In short, the United States called for an adoption of the "Philippine model."[22]

What caused the Netherlands government to finally enter negotiations with the Republican leadership was the realization that the Dutch position in Indonesia was simply too weak to resist British pressure to negotiate. Because Sukarno was regarded as a collaborator of the Japanese and a henchman of the Indonesian communists, van Mook was instructed not to talk to the Republican president but to seek "moderate" leaders.[23] Negotiations, though, were only one part of the Dutch strategy. Comparable to the Indonesian approach—military pressure and diplomacy—the Netherlands prepared themselves for war in Indonesia. If negotiations with the republic were to fail, a military solution would be imposed. Since it was estimated that a sufficient number of Dutch troops (seventy-five thousand) would not be ready to fight before January 1947, the search for a peaceful resolution of the conflict was the only choice in the meantime.[24] Negotiation positions and aims were far from clear, though.

To placate American anticolonial sentiment, the Dutch queen Wilhelmina in December 1942 had promised autonomy and "complete partnership" for the colonies after the war.[25] But this lofty announcement had not been followed up with more concrete plans. It was not until the fall of 1945 that the first Dutch outlines for future relations between the Netherlands and Indonesia were worked out.[26] Acknowledging that Indonesian nationalism constituted a "problem," and following a reform-oriented speech by van Mook in November, J. H. A. Logemann, the Social Democratic minister for overseas territories, presented a constitutional outline on December 24. The document envisaged a "Commonwealth of Indonesia composed of territories possessing different degrees of autonomy." A Parliament (people's council or Volksraad after the prewar institution, which had had only advisory powers) made up of representatives of the territories and elected by a franchise "progressively extended as circumstances permit" would have legislative powers in conjunction with a governor-general appointed by the queen. The Parliament could not, however, force the resignation of the executive. There were to be imperial institutions—in which Indonesian representatives would be in a minority—for foreign policy and matters of common interest. Finally, the document stated that "after a certain lapse of years the relationship . . . will be reconsidered on the basis of a complete and voluntary partnership."[27] In every respect, the document fell short of the conceptions of the republic. In fact, the Dutch effectively ignored its existence altogether. It offered neither democratic structures nor franchise for all Indonesians. By simply reiterating the queen's wartime promise to form a "complete partnership," it projected the onset of decolonization well into the future. In fact, it foreshadowed the highly controversial federalist policies that van Mook relied on from mid-1946 in an effort to divide and rule. The constitutional outline reflected the paternalistic attitudes of Logemann, van Mook, and many other Dutchmen concerned with Indonesia. With regard to timing, van Mook thought that "autonomy" could be granted after a period of twenty-five years and independence "within the working life of the rising generation." Logemann envisaged a "long process" preceding eventual Indonesian independence. Sukarno was right when he complained that most of the Dutch had not changed their "mental outlook" as against 1942.[28]

It was this mental outlook that eventually thwarted British efforts to mediate a settlement. In March 1946, a compromise came into reach. Sjahrir gave up his demand for Dutch recognition of the republic's sovereignty over Indonesia as a whole and was prepared to accept the de facto sovereignty over Java, Sumatra, and Madura only. He also agreed to cooperate with van Mook in the formation of a federally constituted Indonesia in which the Dutch would play an important role. But there were strong oppositional forces to Sjahrir's accommodating policy. Pemudas continued to harass Dutch civilians and soldiers and bedeviled the republic's effort to project an image of stability and "good governance." Moreover, Sjahrir was criticized for neglecting Indonesian interests. But it was the Dutch government that effectively torpedoed the compromise. Contrary to van Mook's expectation that The Hague would accept Sjahrir's position, the government was adamantly opposed to recognizing the republic's de facto sovereignty over Sumatra. It refused to acknowledge the all-important role of the republic in Indonesia, and its chief aim remained a commonwealth of Indonesia as part of the Kingdom of the Netherlands.[29] The subsequent breakdown of negotiations in late April weakened the position of those Indonesians who had been willing to cooperate with the Dutch and destroyed what faith had remained in the Dutch resolve to effect a "complete partnership."

Because of military weakness and British pressure to resume negotiations, The Hague sent a high-level commission to Indonesia to seek a peaceful settlement with the republic in August. At the same time, the military buildup continued. In July 1946, Australian and British forces left all areas outside of Java and Sumatra to the Dutch army. This provided van Mook with the opportunity to accelerate a program of federalism. Since prewar times, he had been convinced that a federal state would be the best solution for the multiethnic and multicultural Indonesian society. In 1946, however, federalism was first and foremost a strategy to encircle the republic and erode its influence outside Java and Sumatra.[30] In the Dutch conception, federalism was identical with fragmentation. It was designed as an instrument to retain Dutch sovereignty over the islands while devolving authority to autonomous entities. At a conference in Malino (South Sulawesi), hand-picked delegates from Borneo, Sulawesi, the Moluccas, and the Lesser Sundas duly consented to van Mook's plan to organize the previously existing small administrative units into two large states, Borneo and East Indonesia. But even among this pro-Dutch group, anticolonial sentiments were widespread. While acknowledging the need for continued cooperation with the Netherlands in the future, the delegates, most of them members of the aristocracy or of the prewar administrative elite, insisted that independence should come after a transitory period of ten years. Moreover, analyses by the Dutch intelligence service showed that it would be difficult to transform these infant states into functioning administrative units able to provide a counterbalance to the republic. The basic reason for the weakness of the newly created states, the report went on, was the widespread longing for unity in Indonesia and the awareness of a common identity symbolized by the republic.[31]

The impending withdrawal of the remaining British troops at the end of 1946 prompted London to urge the two sides to negotiate again. Alarmed by reports from Southeast Asia, the Foreign Office feared that once British troops had withdrawn, the Dutch would seek a military solution. Whitehall was convinced that the Netherlands could not win this struggle in the long run; meanwhile, a colonial war would also destabilize Britain's position in the region.[32] There were thus important reasons for the British to see the conflict ended. British-mediated negotiations led to a cease fire in mid-October and to a draft agreement initialed on November 15. In the so-called Linggadjati Agreement (named after the hill station where the negotiations had taken place), the Dutch for the first time recognized the de facto sovereignty of the republic over Sumatra, Java, and Madura. This important concession on the part of the Dutch was reciprocated by the Republican assent to became part of a federally constituted United States of Indonesia, in which Borneo and East Indonesia would have the same legal status as the republic. A joint interim government headed by the Crown was to be formed no later than January 1, 1949.[33] Eventually, the two sides signed the agreement in March 1947; by then, however, "interpretive material" (Sjahrir) and supplementary declarations from both sides had led to fundamentally conflicting opinions on the letter and spirit of the agreement.[34] In fact, as van den Doel concludes, "two different accords" were signed: The Republican leadership consented to the formation of a sovereign federal state in which the Republic of Indonesia would play the dominant role, and it envisaged a loose cooperation with the Netherlands in a more or less symbolic union. The Netherlands, on the other hand, wanted a strong union with a range of political responsibilities in which the republic would have a subordinate position.[35]

By the time the Linggadjati Agreement was signed, British troops had left and conditions for peaceful cooperation had deteriorated. To the chagrin of the Dutch, the American and British governments extended de facto recognition to the republic. The Indian government and a number of Arab countries did the same.[36] The republic was now an internationally recognized autonomous state held responsible for the administration of Sumatra, Java, and Madura. Since the end of January 1947, Dutch trade regulations amounted to a blockade of the Republican territory. This economic squeeze aggravated an already tense food situation. Deteriorating living conditions fueled anti-Dutch resentment, especially in urban areas, and increased the resolve of the pemudas to wage guerilla attacks. Moreover, following the British withdrawal (Batavia/Jakarta was finally cleared in December 1946), Dutch military had moved into the major cities. After the signing of the Linggadjati Agreement, Republican leaders argued that since the Dutch had recognized de facto sovereignty, they should remove their troops from areas under Republican control. Still more matters were in dispute. Sjahrir's government strongly objected to the creation of the states of Borneo and East Indonesia and complained of numerous truce violations. Sukarno summed up the essence of the conflict by arguing that "the Dutch say that independence follows the establishment of order and peace. We say that order and peace follows independence."[37]

The Dutch position with regard to Indonesia was motivated by a number of considerations and convictions. For one, the vast majority of the Dutch categorically rejected any notion of ultimate independence. This reflected the fear of losing a very valuable source of national income. It was, moreover, an outgrowth of the belief of most of the leading politicians, regardless of party affiliation, that a Netherlands stripped of its colonial empire would lose what influence it had in the international system. These "rational" arguments were reinforced by a deep-seated and widespread paternalism that in some instances turned into outright racism. Van Mook, for example, found the republic's organization "childish." P. J. A. Idenburg, a high official in the colonial administration, regarded the republic as fundamentally "irrational" and opined that "the typical Javanese-Hinduistic syncretism" was responsible for the creation of an "imagined reality" that colored the perception of the Republican officials. General S. H. Spoor, supreme commander of the army, felt humiliated by the fact that he had to converse with his Indonesian counterparts on equal footing. Admiral Helfrich found order turned upside down and concluded that a degrading situation had arisen in which "the roles of whites and colored on Java had been turned around." Leading military and most civilian officials were convinced that Indonesians were inherently incapable of governing the country, so much so that van Mook frequently complained about the colonial mentality and behavior of his subordinates.[38] Perceived qualities like childishness, irrationality, and superstition were stereotypes that effectively "orientalized" Indonesians.[39] At the same time, these notions legitimized a Dutch self-perception colored by feelings of ethnic and cultural superiority. The belief in the ethnic and cultural superiority of Europeans and the constant recreation of enemy images informed the "mental maps" even of reform-minded Dutch officials like van Mook.[40] In the Netherlands, Willem Schermerhorn, a former prime minister and chief negotiator of the Linggadjati Agreement on the Dutch side, noted in his diary, "The Dutch people [are] torn by a difference in their perception of the situation, as well as by all kinds of emotions ranging from jealous possessiveness to a kind of national pathos."[41] Informed by these sentiments and convictions, discontent with the situation in Indonesia produced an overriding desire to impose order—not a negotiated order built on compromise, but a Dutch-defined order.

The corollary to divide and rule in the periphery was war in the center. The generals had advocated military action right from the beginning of the difficulties with the republic. A war plan had been drawn up by March 1946 and preparations had progressed throughout the year.[42] The acquisition of weapons and munitions posed no insurmountable problem. In the spring of 1946, the U.S. government prohibited the use of former lend-lease material in Indonesia. But just a few weeks prior to the decision, Washington had transferred large amounts of weapons, among them over sixty planes, armored trucks, and tanks to the Dutch. In addition, throughout the year the Netherlands were able to procure weapons and munitions in Great Britain.[43] At the end of 1946, war was a constant theme in the political debates in The Hague and within the Dutch community in Indonesia. By May 1947, moreover, the financial situation of the kingdom had become so desperate that a raid to secure plantation products (rubber, palm oil, and quinine) in Republican territory seemed an economic necessity.[44] In other words, the Dutch military lived off the land that it claimed to protect.

Following a fact-finding mission by L. J. M. Beel, the prime minister, and J. A. Jonkman, the minister for overseas territories, war became a certainty.[45] Consultations with the Americans and the British revealed their aversion to a military solution of the conflict.[46] But convinced that the international repercussions of a war could be ignored and that London and Washington would tacitly understand The Hague's rationale, the Dutch offensive (disingenuously called "police action") against the republic started on July 20, 1947. The supreme commander, General Spoor, was confident that his spearhead strategy would achieve the military aims in a short period of time.

Indeed, Dutch troops encountered almost no resistance to the occupation of West Java, East Java, Madura, Semarang, Medan, Palembang, and Padang.[47] But within a week, van Mook pressed The Hague to also occupy Jogjakarta and to erase the republic from the political map. Meanwhile, Spoor reported increasing difficulties, ambushes, and sabotage.[48] It did not take long to recognize that the aim of the offensive, namely to bring the republic to its knees and to force "moderate" Indonesians to cooperate, had failed.

Save for the economic aspect, the offensive did not improve the Dutch position vis-à-vis the republic. Republican administrators refused to receive orders from the Dutch and launched what amounted to a massive campaign of civil disobedience. Moreover, reports indicated that the offensive had cost the Dutch sympathies in East Indonesia. In terms of military capabilities, the republic was only lightly affected because its troops had simply melted away and regrouped in inaccessible territory. Comparable to the French experience in Indochina, the Dutch controlled the cities, and convoys could move along the roads. But the countryside remained in the hands of the Republican army and the pemudas.[49]

In the international arena, the Dutch had miscalculated as well. With the support of the United States and Great Britain, the UN Security Council passed a resolution on August 1 calling "upon the parties to cease hostilities and to settle their dispute by arbitration or by other peaceful means."[50] Moreover, the Australian-sponsored document asked the two parties to keep the council informed.[51] The resolution amounted to a major diplomatic defeat for the Netherlands. First, the wording clearly suggested an equivalence of the two sides, thus adding to the international standing of the republic. Second, the Security Council's demanding further information made the Netherlands accountable for actions it considered to be an internal affair. Third, international pressure forced The Hague to abandon any thought of occupying Jogjakarta. But despite the international outcry, the Dutch felt strong enough to virtually ignore the Security Council's resolution.

Within the newly occupied areas, the pacification campaign continued. Prime Minister Beel and van Mook pressed for a continuation of the offensive. A petition signed by leading officials of the colonial administration even called for an outright liquidation of the republic (though it did not say how).[52] Meanwhile, the United States ensured that the Security Council did not set up an arbitration commission, as envisaged by Australia and the Indonesian Republic, but a Good Offices Commission (GOC), whose suggestions would not be binding. Moreover, Washington ensured that the Security Council did not call on the Netherlands to remove its troops from territory previously under the de facto control of the republic. This move in effect sanctioned the use of force and tacitly legitimized the Dutch argument that the dispute was an internal affair. At the same time, however, Washington made clear its interest for a peaceful resolution of the conflict and its aversion to military action.[53]

The GOC, which consisted of a Belgian and an Australian representative (nominated by the Netherlands and the republic, respectively) and was headed by the American history professor Frank Graham, arrived in Indonesia in late October 1947. The commission sensed that prospects for a compromise were slim. The Dutch complained about the refusal of Republican administrators to cooperate and accused Jogjakarta for making large parts of Java and Sumatra ungovernable. They also blamed the Republican army for countless acts of sabotage and terror, and they insisted that the campaign to assassinate collaborating administrators had to end. For its part, the republic suffered from a severe economic crisis caused by the Dutch blockade and aggravated by food shortages and tens of thousands of refugees. Moreover, the Republican prime minister Amir Sjarifuddin, who had succeeded Sjahrir just prior to the Dutch offensive, condemned van Mook's policy of creating a new state in East Sumatra. Until May 1948—and in blatant violation to existing agreements with the republic—van Mook founded a total of thirteen states governed by minority leaders or the aristocracy and sustained by the

Dutch military. In most of these governments, Dutch advisers were the real rulers. Under these circumstances, both sides entertained completely divergent visions for the future of Indonesia. The republic continued to demand recognition by the Dutch and independence as soon as possible. The Netherlands, on the other hand, pressed for a tight union of the Indonesian states with the Crown, in which foreign policy, defense, finances, economic policy, and cultural affairs were to be jointly administered.[54]

By the end of December 1947, Graham felt that in order to avoid another Dutch offensive, he had to force the two sides into an agreement. Given the military superiority of the Dutch, he suggested a compromise that temporarily sanctioned the conquests of July and August. However, Graham envisaged an eventual return to the status quo ante (Republican control over Sumatra, Java, and Madura), an end to the creation of Dutch-sponsored states, and free elections in which the Indonesians were to choose their own destiny. The prospect of an exchange of the bullet by the ballot and the conviction that the republic would win in free elections eventually made the Indonesians accept his proposals. It was even more difficult to persuade van Mook and The Hague. The Dutch consented only after Washington had threatened to withhold Marshall Plan aid. The Renville Agreement, named after the negotiation location, the USS *Renville* and signed on January 17, 1948, under UN auspices, favored the Dutch in the short term, while it held out the promise of independence in the future. The compromise reflected Washington's attitude toward the conflict. Because the Netherlands was such a "strong proponent" of U.S. policies in Europe, the State Department felt it could not press for an "immediate and complete withdrawal" of the Dutch. A "limited period" of Dutch sovereignty could stabilize Indonesia and stimulate much-needed trade. Washington hoped that this interval could be used to provide Indonesians with expertise in governing. The notion of a period of "tutelage," during which the Indonesians would be prepared for independence, reflected a vision representative of U.S. policy toward the colonial world.[55] The agreement, though, rested on the assumption that the Netherlands would have "opportunity during interim period to convince Indo[nesian]s of their mutual dependence on each other."[56] Given the past record of the Dutch, it was doubtful whether they would seize the opportunity.

The republic had signed the agreement for the simple reason that the Americans had so dearly wanted it. The points that favored the republic all depended on the questionable willingness of the Dutch to abide by the terms of the agreement. But its leadership was also well aware of the favorable aspects of the agreement. The republic had demonstrated its sense of responsibility vis-à-vis the United Nations and American public opinion. Moreover, the Renville Agreement signaled the continued interest of the United

States in Indonesian affairs. American involvement, they hoped, would slowly but steadily work in the republic's favor. For the moment, however, Jogjakarta's acceptance of the agreement caused a major political crisis in the republic. On January 23, 1948, Sjarifuddin's government resigned because of strong opposition to the agreement from both the left and right wings. By March, Sjarifuddin himself had become highly critical of it. Under his leadership, the Front Demokrasi Rakyat (FDR; People's Democratic Front) united the Sayap Kiri (left wing) of the republic's political spectrum. It advocated a nationalization of the economy and called for a close cooperation with the communist camp. Sukarno, however, strongly objected to an alignment with the Soviet Union. He realized that the republic depended on the support of the United States, and he felt that this policy would ultimately be successful. He therefore appointed Vice President Hatta to head an emergency cabinet answerable only to the president, not to Parliament. Hatta, an economist with a rather conservative outlook, had already gained the trust of the international community by advocating what Western commentators called "moderate" policies.[57] For the international standing of the republic, the internal political polarization proved to be a blessing in disguise.

By mid-1948, it was obvious that the Dutch did not honor the Renville Agreement any more than they had the Linggadjati Agreement.[58] This behavior increased opposition to the Dutch within the areas under their control, and it spurred unrest and discontent within Republican territory. Even the ruling elites of the federal states became more and more critical of the Dutch. Dissatisfaction with the continuing instability and the political uncertainties was voiced at a conference in July, where representatives from the Dutch-sponsored states debated the future of federalism in Indonesia. The delegates agreed that the position of the republic should be a subordinate one (thus favoring the Dutch viewpoint). But at the same time, the conference called for an interim federal government existing only of Indonesians and for a Dutch high commissioner with very limited powers. That was certainly not what van Mook wanted. In The Hague, a newly elected government felt that the lieutenant governor-general's strategy had ended in political bankruptcy, and in mid-August the government decided to replace him as soon as possible.[59] His successor, however, soon realized that van Mook had not pursued policies detrimental to the Dutch position but had simply been driven by events.

The republic also encountered increasing political difficulties. In August, Musso, the veteran leader of the Indonesian communists, arrived in Jogjakarta from years of exile in the Soviet Union. Musso had been one of the leaders of an abortive communist uprising in 1926. Since then, he had spent most of his time in Moscow as a revolutionary in exile. Within weeks, Musso united the left-wing opposition, including the FDR, under the banner of the Partai Komunis Indonesia (Indonesian Communist Party) and positioned himself as the most outspoken and powerful critic of the Republican leadership's strategy of diplomasi and armed struggle.[60] He called for "A New Road for the Indonesian Republic" (thus the title of his party program) and for an alliance with the Soviet bloc.

The confrontation between the Republican leadership and Musso's communist opposition came to a head in mid-September, when troops stationed in Surakarta declined to follow orders and refused to demobilize. Loyal troops were rushed to the city and were able to put down the mutiny within two days. But local communist cadres in Madiun played on the discontent of these troops and declared a people's front government. Musso and the communist leadership were completely taken by surprise; it is therefore unlikely that the rebellion, as has occasionally been suggested, was instigated by Moscow. A radio broadcast by Sukarno in which he called on the people to choose between the legal government and Musso left the communist leadership with little room to maneuver and forced it to join the rebellion. Ultimately, the people's front government was unable to attract a sufficient number of followers in Central and East Java. On September 30, Musso, Sjarifuddin, and others left Surakarta because of an advancing Republican army. Musso was killed four weeks later, and near the end of the year Sjarifuddin and others were arrested and killed as well.[61] The suppression of the rebellion demonstrated the loyalty of the major part of the armed forces to the political leadership. It showed that Sukarno and Hatta were able to act decisively and that they were regarded as leaders by the vast majority of the Javanese population. Moreover, as Reid writes, the suppression reflected "a conceptional break between national and social revolution." At the time of the declaration of independence, both had been seen as mutually reinforcing. Hô Chí Minh followed this model with success (and at great costs) in Vietnam. Sukarno and Hatta chose differently. They postponed social revolution for an indefinite period of time and positioned the republic squarely in the noncommunist camp.[62]

The Madiun uprising was observed with great interest by the Dutch and the international community. Former prime minister Beel, in Batavia/Jakarta since mid-September to succeed van Mook, could not conceive of anything better for the Dutch position in Indonesia, "It is now or never. As soon as it appears that the Republic is unable to undo Madiun and takes sides with these Communists, we have to act. There is no doubt about that. It would be disastrous if we would not seize this god-sent and unique opportunity."[63] Beel deliberately aggravated the crisis by expelling Republican officials and administrators and their families from Batavia/Jakarta. But if he had hoped for increased discontent and Republican disorder, he was mistaken. His move only stiffened American resolve to end the crisis in Indonesia.[64]

American diplomats in Batavia/Jakarta had been critical of Dutch actions in Indonesia for quite some time. Their efforts to renew negotiations and to develop a partnership had been torpedoed more than once by an uncompromising Dutch colonial administration. But State Department policies still clearly favored the Dutch. U.S. actions at the United Nations and policy guidance for the in-country diplomats revealed that American policy toward Indonesia was still determined by the following factors: Washington felt that it needed a strong Netherlands, both for economic and strategic reasons (recovery of Europe and the formation of an anticommunist bloc). Therefore, all criticism had to be weighted against the possible repercussions of Dutch noncooperativeness. Moreover, paternalistic notions were not confined to the Dutch. Many policy makers in Washington believed that nationalists in the emerging Third World needed a period of benevolent tutelage before they could govern their countries without the advice of colonial powers or Western countries in general. But with regard to Indonesia and its leadership, a remarkable change in perception had taken place. Uncertainties about the ability of the Indonesian leadership to govern and the republic's position toward communism had given way to great disappointment about the Dutch. For months, the conviction had gained ground that Sukarno and Hatta were respectable and respected leaders and that they were politically "moderate" (meaning noncommunist and pro-Western).[65] The Madiun uprising confirmed these notions and helped bring about a significant change of policy.

By the end of September, the contours of a new American policy toward the Dutch-Indonesian dispute became apparent. Negotiations with the Netherlands for a loan of $100 million were suspended, because Washington, for fear of being accused of an unneutral act, did not want to destabilize Hatta's position in any way. Moreover, the State Department urged the Dutch to lift the blockade of the Republican territory and to allow for American imports of textiles in order to enhance Hatta's credibility vis-à-vis an impoverished population. And it hinted at the possibility that with American support the UN Security Council might "impose a solution" should the Netherlands continue to present "dishonest" accusations and "inflammatory" demands.[66] By mid-December, when numerous indications pointed to another Dutch offensive against the republic, George Kennan, the State Department's director of the policy planning staff and chief architect of containment policy, called for a de jure recognition of the republic should the Dutch "persist in sabotaging negotiations." His analysis reflected Washington's shift toward a global Cold War policy:

The Dutch cannot successfully re-assert their authority over and stabilize Sumatra, Java and Madura. The choice therefore lies not between Republican and Dutch sovereignty but between Republican sovereignty and chaos. We know that chaos is an open door to communism. Hatta, Sukarno and the present moderate leaders of the Republic are the only ones who can supply it [a friendly Indonesia]. But if they are to do so they must be able to stand and deliver what they have promised the Indonesian people—independence, whether immediately or by stages.[67]

Why were the Dutch unwilling to seriously negotiate with the republic, and why did they launch a second offensive? In discussions with Hatta and other Republican leaders in October and November 1948, Dutch politicians held out the prospect of an "independent," federally constituted and democratic Indonesia. But this vision was still a prospect for a distant future. For the time being, The Hague insisted on a high commissioner with extensive veto powers and a union in which the Netherlands would be the supreme arbiter of the Dutch-sponsored artificial territorial entities. The legalistic language of the Dutch discourse on the future of empire could not conceal the paternalism, the occasional racism, and the simplifying comparison between the good-intentioned Dutch and the devious Republicans. Dutch sentiment was well expressed by E. M. J. A. Sassen, the new minister of overseas territories. He felt it was his obligation to "support and help those seventy million to enter a new phase of their history." Dutch assistance and guidance would be necessary for years to come, because the Republican alternative would be chaos and communism. Therefore, action was necessary. "Lethargy," argued General Spoor, would impair Dutch credibility in the eyes of "the Asian."[68] The aim of the Dutch offensive was not to force the republic to accept the Dutch demands, instead, Beel wanted to erase the republic from the political and mental map of Indonesia. Correspondingly, he gave orders not to use the term "Republic" any more.[69]

The offensive of December 18, 1948 (euphemistically termed "second police action"), went straight to the heart of the republic. Its capital Jogjakarta was occupied without much resistance, and the Republican leadership was taken into custody and exiled to other islands. Within days, the major cities in Java were occupied as well. While the Dutch military considered the offensive a success, international reactions were highly negative. To preempt an Indian or Soviet initiative, Washington promptly demanded an emergency session of the UN Security Council. On December 24, a resolution called for an immediate cease-fire, the withdrawal of the Dutch troops, and the release of the Republican leaders. Simultaneously, the Truman administration cancelled Marshall Plan aid for the Dutch colony.[70] The worldwide reaction as well as the all-important American response was one of unanimous condemnation. In Washington, the Central Intelligence Agency concluded that now was the time to act, "The rich resources of Indonesia and the goodwill of its more than seventy million peoples are at stake. The development of conditions favorable to the USSR in Indonesia appears now to require, as a countermeasure, a consistent application of positive and sympathetic US influence."[71]

In view of strong U.S. pressure, the Dutch cabinet had no choice but to signal its willingness to comply to the terms of the UN resolution. It declared to halt the offensive within days and offered to cooperate with the Security Council. At the same time, however, it decided to drag out further negotiations with the international community as long as possible. And in contravention of the resolution, it regarded the republic as nonexistent.[72] This stance, however, proved impossible to uphold.

The Security Council renewed its call for a return of the interned Republican leaders to Jogjakarta. On January 28, it went even further and suggested that an interim government be established by March 15, that elections should be held no later than October 1, and that a transfer of sovereignty to the United States of Indonesia should be effected no later than July 1, 1950.[73]

Developments in Indonesia also worked to the detriment of the Dutch. Throughout January, it became clear that the federal model that the Dutch had created would not function the way it had been conceived. The states remained weak, presided over by an elite that had mainly cooperated with the Dutch before the war. The majority of the Indonesian population sided with the republic and the leading politicians of the federal states began to shift their allegiance. Moreover, the zigzagging of the Dutch—the launching of the offensive and the sudden willingness to cooperate with the Security Council—led many to lose trust in Dutch credibility and seek cooperation with the Republican leadership.[74]

Thus, Beel complained bitterly about the numerous fence-sitters and the general noncooperativeness of the people. Contrary to the positive evaluations of General Spoor, the military situation deteriorated as well. Ambushes, sabotage, and terror increased, and by mid-February the Dutch faced widespread guerilla activity in Java.

All in all, Dutch casualties during and after the second offensive were higher than the total for the preceding period (1,275 as opposed to 1,251 between 1945 and December 1948). In comparison, however, Indonesian losses were dramatically higher; some estimates run as high as 120,000, among them many civilians who died in air attacks.[75]

Apart from international pressure, the popularity of the republic, and the military situation, there was a fourth aspect that influenced Dutch decision making: finances. Military expenditures had reached 20 percent of the total budget. Without additional American assistance, the Netherlands simply could not sustain the costs of war anymore. But foreign assistance was not in sight. In view of the widespread opposition to the Dutch offensive in the United States, there was not the slightest chance of an American loan. To the contrary, in March 1949 the Truman administration warned the Dutch that it would also have to cancel all Marshall Plan aid earmarked for the Netherlands in case of a further noncompliance with the Security Council resolution. The threat of a financial embargo proved decisive.[76]

With the assistance of the GOC, now headed by the American diplomat H. Merle Cochran, the Dutch and the republic commenced negotiations in April 1949. Two months later, Sukarno and Hatta could return to Jogjakarta. In mid-August, a cease-fire came into effect, and the two sides decided to convene a roundtable conference. Even earlier, conferences between the Republican leadership and federalists had demonstrated the high degree of identity and unity among the Indonesians. Both parties agreed that the republic should exercise authority over the whole of Java, Sumatra, and Madura. Furthermore, the states would not create independent armies but would accept the Republican army. In turn, the republic acquiesced in a federal order for Indonesia. Technically, there were thus two Indonesian delegations present at the roundtable conference that began on August 23 in The Hague. In practice, however, there was not much disagreement between the Republican and federal delegates.[77] The policy of divide and rule had ended in a complete failure.

At the roundtable conference, the Indonesian delegates succeeded with their vision of a loose, largely symbolic union between two sovereign states. This conception had already been discussed in the negotiations leading up the Linggadjati Agreement. Back then, though, the Dutch government had felt strong enough to ignore an arrangement in which the Crown would only be a symbolic head of the union. With respect to the other two major stumbling blocks of the conference, however, the Dutch were more successful in implementing their viewpoint.

The second issue concerned the debts incurred by the Netherlands East Indies. The Dutch argued that Indonesia should assume the total debt, which amounted to over 6 billion guilders (approximately $1.7 billion). The Indonesians were willing to shoulder all debts incurred before 1942 as well as those funds that had been made available to the Indonesian people since then. But they declined to take over the costs of the Netherlands Indies Civil Administration as well as those of the two military offensives and the occupation forces. The compromise Cochran presented pleased neither side, but the sum of 4.3 billion guilders ($1.3 billion) was grudgingly accepted.

The third issue was the question of West Irian (West New Guinea). This large but sparsely populated territory had been an integral part of the Netherlands East Indies before the war. After 1946, however, the Dutch came to regard the island as a refuge of Dutch colonialism, notwithstanding the fact that it was neither of value economically nor suited as a resettlement area for Dutch planters and the Dutch Indonesians. It did not even possess intrinsic military value for the Netherlands. But the Dutch Catholic Party, which formed the coalition government at The Hague together with the Social Democrats, claimed that the territory could become a fertile field for missionary activities.[78] The reason why the Dutch insisted on retaining the island was political as well as emotional: retaining a semblance of empire served to underwrite the Dutch claim to be a middle power in the international system. Moreover, West Irian was important simply because the Indonesians wanted it so much. Since the issue threatened to bring about the collapse of the conference, Cochran suggested to postpone a solution and renegotiate the issue after one year.

The three contested issues would seriously affect Dutch-Indonesian relations during the 1950s. But when the conference ended on November 2, it had achieved its principal aim: the transfer of power on December 29, 1949.

Within months, the federal states dissolved themselves and consented to the formation of a unitary republic, which was proclaimed by Sukarno on August 17, 1950, five years after the declaration of independence. Regarded by many Indonesians as a legacy of colonialism, the union was defunct from the start and was unilaterally abrogated by Indonesia in 1956. West Irian troubled the relations even more, and the stubborn retention of the territory negatively influenced Indonesia's relations with other Western powers as well. It was not until 1962–1963 that the transfer of power took place, following American pressure on The Hague and a subsequent mediation by the United Nations.[79]

The success of the Republic of Indonesia to achieve independence and sovereignty was the result of many factors. The international context was important for two reasons. First, the republic profited from Cold War tensions. Already before the second military offensive in December 1948, the United States regarded the Republican government as more capable of guaranteeing order and security in Indonesia than the Dutch military. The Madiun rebellion, moreover, had demonstrated to Washington that Sukarno and Hatta were able to suppress communism and were willing to secure order and stability. Security interests and positive attitudes toward the republic translated into pressure on the Dutch to retreat from Indonesia. Second, Indonesia was the first important colonial issue to be debated by the UN Security Council. It provided a forum of expression for the republic that was recognized throughout the world. The invocation of the principle of national self-determination as laid down by the Atlantic Charter in 1940 proved to be a powerful weapon that could not be ignored by the members of the Security Council. (This is why France refused to discuss Indochina in the United Nations). Moreover, global public opinion favored the republic and forced the Netherlands to account for its actions. American pressure was instrumental in forcing The Hague to enter into negotiations for a complete transfer of power in 1949.

The metropolitan dimension needs to be taken into account as well. While there were conflicting Dutch views on Indonesia and its future, there was a broad consensus that the Netherlands should play an important role in the country's stakes for a long time to come. The only exception was the small Communist Party, which demanded Indonesian independence throughout. But discrepancies between the Social Democrats and the Catholic Party were never a dividing issue in the debate about colonialism. In contrast, the financial situation of the country had a significant impact on decision making. By 1949, the costs of war surpassed the actual and potential economic value of Indonesia for the Netherlands. This realization strengthened the resolve to negotiate, and it led to an emphasis on safeguards that would protect the Dutch economic position in an independent Indonesia.

In the final analysis, however, developments in Indonesia (the colonial dimension) itself were decisive for the outcome of the struggle. Granted, the sudden collapse of the Japanese occupation and the slowness of the Allied occupation were factors that clearly favored the republic. More importantly, though, the Republican leadership successfully applied a mixture of diplomasi and perjuangan to the conflict with the Netherlands. The guerilla activities following the two offensives created conditions under which a Dutch military victory proved impossible—otherwise a second offensive would not have been necessary. Its diplomacy, on the other hand, was successful in the projection of credibility, both on the local and the global level. Finally, the republic's strength derived from the fact that it was the sole political agent that was able to represent a common Indonesian identity, an identity that had evolved prior to World War II and that captured the imagination of the vast majority of the Indonesian population during and after the Japanese occupation.

# 7

# Theories and Approaches to British Decolonization in Southeast Asia

*Karl Hack*

This chapter surveys approaches to British decolonization, in the context of Southeast Asia, in order to see how far new paradigms and ways of linking old models might be profitably explored. This is no easy task, as even the terminology reveals. "The End of Empire," withdrawal, decolonization, disimperialism, the rise of nationalism, imperial decline, the transfer of power—there are almost as many names for the end of British imperium, as there are for the region itself: the Nanyang or Nanyo, the Malay Maritime World, or East Indies, or, somewhat late in the day, Southeast Asia.

The surfeit of descriptions at first suggests a historiography in its prime, requiring only the filling in of detail. Yet, a surplus of terms can also suggest a lack of conceptual clarity and a host of unintegrated perspectives. If "imperialism" is no word for scholars, "decolonization" is a harlot of a word. It pleases so many needs that readers can never be sure of its real meaning. What is decolonization? A limited postwar transfer of sovereignty and the immediate struggles over this? The removal of colonists and eradication of their alien cultural forms? The dismantling of a British system of world power? The eradication of levers of "informal" imperial influence? Or a long-term process of Asians reasserting autonomy by mastering Western discourses and the global market?

This chapter reexamines the nature of decolonization through three main questions. First, what was the nature of Southeast Asia as a region and its relationship to other structures and areas? Second, can we identify an emerging pattern to the historiography on British-influenced territories, and how might we adjust this? Third, how useful is the idea of "withdrawal" in 1968. Did decolonization really come to a rude full stop, dividing time neatly into a European- and American-dominated imperial period, and the postcolonial Asian-dominated world of Association of Southeast Asian Nations?

## Southeast Asia: Geographical and Temporal Contexts

It is well established that the concept of Southeast Asia as an interrelated region came to the fore during World War II.[1] There is also a tendency to think of decolonization as belonging mainly to the postwar period, with the years 1914–1941 being a time of "nationalism," and 1870–1914 an era of "new" or "high imperialism." But should the British adoption of Southeast Asia, and the story of the region's decolonization, be located in wider contexts and longer time frames? After all, the Philippines became a Commonwealth with a good measure of internal self-government in 1935, and Burma achieved a similar level of self-government effective from 1937. Both developments suggest that a "post-1945" focus might miss the boat by a good few years.

One wider and longer process might be called, if only for heuristic purposes, the "long Asian conflict" of the 1920s or 1930s to 1949. The concepts of a "Pacific war" (1941–1945) or a "World War II" (1939–1945) arguably do not suffice here. From an Asian perspective, this period of intense conflict stretched back at least as far as Japan's unofficial invasion of China in July 1937, if not its seizure of Manchuria, or the communist-nationalist split in China in the 1920s. If this was a conflict over the identity of East Asia, with nationalist, communist, and imperialist forces all in the arena, it ended, at the earliest, with Mao Tse-tung's declaration of the People's Republic of China on October 1, 1949.

It was Japan's "forward movement," as part of this wider conflict, that forced Britain to consider Singapore's defense as linked to Malaya's, Malaya's to Thailand's, and Thailand as pressurized by the Japanese basing of forces in French Indochina in 1940–1941. Britain abandoned earlier models of defending Singapore as an isolated entrepôt and naval garrison, and developed instead a prototype domino theory that saw the region as one strategic theater, with each country's defense interlinked with the next, if only by aircraft ranges. This notion of regional interrelatedness, belatedly taken up by the United States in 1949–1950, was signaled by the formation of the Anglo-American Southeast Asia Command (SEAC) in 1943.[2] It was worked out through the appointment of Lord Killearn (Miles W. Lampson) as the Foreign Office's special commissioner for Southeast Asia (1945–1948). He was charged with helping to coordinate postwar rehabilitation, as well as encouraging gradual Western decolonization and Asian-Western partnership. In 1948, his post was abolished, but the regional tradition continued with the appointment of a British commissioner-general for Southeast Asia, responsible alike for coordinating the defense and closer association of British territories and for regional diplomatic policy. In turn, he chaired meetings of the British Defense Coordinating Committee (Far East), which surveyed policy almost from China to Sri Lanka.[3]

From the British perspective, the notion of "Southeast Asia" coalesced as a by-product of the forward movement of Japanese imperialism, which in its full schizophrenic glory had a second identity, as an anti-Western, anti-imperialist crusader reclaiming the south for Asians and building a "Greater East Asia Co-prosperity Sphere."[4] In addition, it also threw up Asian, as well as specifically communist, notions of an area between India and China, such as Tan Malaka's 1946 term "Aslia" for the area within a fifteen-hundred-mile radius from Singapore.[5]

The same Japanese forward movement that reshaped British diplomatic policy, also impacted on colonial planning. It was crucial in crystallizing British intentions to decolonize in entirely new ways. It was the capture of Singapore on February 15, 1942, that kick started British planning to restructure the politics of its territories.[6] But even before defeat, the Japanese movement had affected British territories by inspiring the Nanyang Chinese there to boycott Japanese goods and to form salvation associations in the 1930s. These events further reminded Malays, "Indonesians," and Burmese of the need to organize and alerted them to the possibility of outside pressure in their favor.

The Burmese youth who styled themselves *thakins* (a term meaning "master" and usually reserved for Europeans) are an excellent example of Southeast Asia's intimate integration with both the long Asian conflict and Indian developments; that is, with overlapping East Asian and South Asian circles of decolonization. The thakins formed a Freedom Block with mainstream politicians after the 1939 outbreak of war. With the thakins of the Dobama Asiayone already following the Indian National Congress in demanding full independence rather than self-government, the Freedom Block made cooperation with Britain conditional on promises of independence. Some thakins fled repression for Japan in 1940–1941, coming back with the Japanese invasion of 1941, only to turn their army from supporting to fighting Japan in 1945. Finally, their Anti-Fascist Peoples Freedom League (AFPFL) garnered enough popular support along the way to pressure Britain into granting independence by January 1948.[7]

The same long Asian conflict patterned British policy and demanded regional approaches, after as well as before the Pacific war. Even the conflict's last throes had dramatic effects. The communist surge through south China in 1948 turbocharged British attempts to start what became the Colombo Plan of 1950. This was a cooperative framework to encourage development in South and Southeast Asia and through that, eventual politico-military cooperation with the West and against communism. Starting with Commonwealth countries, Britain hoped this would ultimately harness American resources. As Nicholas Tarling notes, then, the Cold War in the form of Asian, communist "liberation" movements, itself a symptom of the wider Asian struggle, complicated rather than changed Britain's basic regional approach.[8]

In this way, the 1930s to 1949 conflict, over the nature of East Asia, framed "decolonization" in British-dominated areas of Southeast Asia. Before the conflict, each territory was dealt with in isolation, but as it intensified in the mid–1940s Britain appointed a governor-general for British territories in Southeast Asia in 1946 to promote the formation, however distant, of a Dominion of Southeast Asia. This was because plural societies and fractured microstates had proved indefensible in 1941, with Britain's failure to recruit more Chinese and Malays to its own defense a startling omission. Britain returned in 1945 determined to foster new "nations" for bigger states: to "unite and quit" where before it had ruled the divided.[9] The conflict thus saw Britain to come down on the side of rigorous state-building, in an ongoing debate about the competing claims of state-building versus obligations to protect traditional rulers and peoples—such as the Malay sultans and people—and to honor agreements based on informal rule.[10]

Britain's imperialism in the Malay Peninsula always had of course an emphasis on state-building and infrastructure, on "development." The appointment of British advisers to the Malay states from 1874 was specifically intended to foster "good government," with British residents' advice to be binding—to be "acted on"—on administration and revenue. Despite the imposition of British as well as Malays as district officers, the system theoretically remained one of advice, conceptually not totally different to Thailand's use of foreign advisers. The formation of the Federated Malay States (FMS) from four territories in 1896 was in a similar vein of state-building, as was forcing Johore to take a British general adviser in 1914, despite its self-modernization, but in the light of increasing development and internal financial strains.[11] This process was coming to maturity by the 1920s, when indirect rule was yielding to direct, and opium taxes to other revenues. The 1920s and 1930s saw the British try a variety of tactics, centralization and decentralization included, to persuade sultans of the five unfederated Malay states to join the FMS, all to no avail. There was also discussion of how to acknowledge the increasingly settled nature of much of the Chinese population.

So, the Japanese forward movement, by its thrust and by its failure, accelerated these tentative moves toward rationalization, bureaucratization, and building more inclusive state structures. Britain's Malayan Union scheme of 1946—for a unitary, centralized colony with Chinese offered citizenship on generous terms—was an extrapolation of existing trends. At the same time, Japanese imperialism, by its brutality—its *kempeitai, romusha,* and *sook ching*—by its economic collapse—tearing countries from their export markets and plunging them into hunger—and by its propaganda and mobilizing, made peasants and kampong dwellers into potential revolutionary material, while forging new links between elites and masses.[12] Hence, all colonial powers, when they returned, were met with more assertive forms of nationalism.[13]

Britain's response to the Asian branch of the Cold War should be seen against this background. The years 1948–1950 were to see communist victory in China, the outbreak of the Korean War, and revolts in Burma, Malaya, the Philippines, and Indonesia.[14] Hence, some scholars have seen Britain as gradually accepting, in the late 1940s, that Southeast Asia had to be defended against the rising tide of communism. On a wider plain, Ronald Hyam argues that "[t]he whole process of decolonization is best interpreted within the geopolitical context of the Cold War. The long-term aim with respect to future relations with Afro-Asian countries was to ensure their alignment with the West, thus containing communism."[15] Tarling, by contrast, notices how Britain's regional approach predated the Cold War and continued in old grooves, even if with new complexities.

Yet, as John Gallagher and John Darwin remind us, twentieth-century British imperialism, far from declining uniformly, sometimes intensified. So it was after 1945 in Southeast Asia.[16] This is not altogether surprising. With retreat from South and East Asia (excepting Hong Kong), Singapore was now more than ever at the center of Britain's focus. At the same time, Britain emerged from World War II a great power relative to all but the superpowers, producing nearly a third of the industrial output of noncommunist Europe in 1950.[17] Hence, Britain also saw decolonization in terms of ensuring that the quarter of the world it was to withdraw from should remain locked into capitalist global systems and Western friendship.[18]

The period 1945–1948, however, differed from the decline of 1921–1941, in that Britain rediscovered the confidence to see itself as a regional trendsetter or coordinator. With Japan out of the way, China locked in civil war, and British decolonization in India giving Britain the moral high ground, Britain might act as pivot between East and West. The revival in confidence was soon dented. Indian independence made use of Indian troops difficult even before August 1947, and the failure of France and the Netherlands to find middle ground with nationalists undermined hopes for Western cooperation. In the face of increasing instability and growing communism, Britain reverted to its prewar type. After SEAC's rundown, Britain chose to commit words, not soldiers and resources, to the cause of wider regional stability, preferring concession (as on extraterritoriality in interwar China and Thailand or recognizing communist China in January 1950) rather than confrontation. Its own resources were shepherded for imperial territories, where the Cold War had its greatest impact on British actions by an indirect route, tying down forty thousand troops fighting Chinese-led communists in the Malayan Emergency (1948–1960).[19]

The confirmation of continuity in Britain's stance, of the same underlying processes bridging the Pacific war and the Cold War, can also be seen in the adoption of similar defense plans in 1941 and 1951. In response to Japanese and communist forward movements, respectively, Britain adopted plans based on invading southern Thailand the instant Thailand looked like it was falling, in order to secure a sort of Asian Thermopylae across the narrow Isthmus of Kra. In both cases, diplomatic interest in the region nevertheless saw resources corraled in and for British territories only.[20]

We might also note that the years 1931–1949 or even 1927–1949 remain a relatively short period. It would hardly register a blip on an *Annaliste,* or Braudellien, radar tuned to the long duration. It is worth asking how far we should see this period, in its turn, as encircled by a wider process, one of general Asian interaction with, and assertion against, the industrializing and increasingly aggressive West of the nineteenth century. A period that stretches back at least to the 1850s and had three main gravitational fields: India, China, and Japan.[21] This linking of decolonization to imperial advances is not as far-fetched as it might at first seem. Marc Ferro, for one, notes how colonization and decolonization are not necessarily sequential events, but are often synchronic. Here, this means the opening of Japan, China, and Thailand to larger-scale European trade from the 1850s that also involved Japan's and China's attempts to adapt the best in Western discourses, discourses that need to be interpreted as everything from accounting through "Orientalism" to political ideas.[22] However we label this wider process, it is clear that globalization, imperialism, and latent "decolonization" jostled together from an early stage. In a sense, the "new nationalism" of cultural revival, and later of secular parties, was to be the child of the "new imperialism" of the free or at least expanded world market and of the enforced export of Western norms of bureaucratic standardization, government, and justice.[23]

Another way of linking imperial expansion to contraction is to take the argument over whether there was a new imperialism in the nineteenth century, and join this to debate on decolonization. John Gallagher and Ronald Robinson's classic 1953 article "The Imperialism of Free Trade" argue that British imperial motives remained unchanged in the mid-nineteenth century. Noting the period of the 1860s when Britain was reluctant to take on new colonies, even suspicious of the costs of existing ones in West Africa, they argue there was no period of British "anti-imperialism." Instead, to paraphrase and develop their argument, Britain always preferred free trade where possible, informal imperialism when necessary, and formal empire if unavoidable. For them, the level of imperialism needed would be sufficient enough to ensure the smooth integration of areas into the world economy. If this is the case, the new imperialism of the nineteenth century might be considered to be a function of the cumulative expansion of world trade and Western industrialization and bureaucratization that underpinned and increased with it. The "new" in new imperialism would reflect the transition to a more demanding Western attitude and more intrusive flows of trade, rules, and people called forth: whether Chinese workers from the 1860s or missionaries and explorers in midcentury Africa and Auguste Pavie in Indochina.[24] In reverse, Peter J. Cain and Anthony G. Hopkins and Tarling all seem to hint that decolonization was made possible if not probable for Britain when these countries, or the Third World in general, had become more securely anchored into the capitalist global system and capable of managing credit.[25]

There is a further link between the interpretation of Gallagher and Robinson and later analyses of British decolonization. Both argue the timing of expansions was due to peripheral crises. They express this in terms of collaborative relationships. Western countries and traders formed relationships with key elite groups in areas such as Malaya or Egypt. These relationships disturbed the local balance of power, undermined the financial solidity of the state, or simply called forth resistance against the collaborating elite. The result was that a crisis on the so-called periphery developed, which forced the hand of metropolitan imperialists anxious to defend accumulated interests. That the "official mind" of London officials and politicians often reacted because they perceived the crisis as threatening "strategic" interests (the Suez Canal, the Cape route, British paramountcy in the Malay Peninsula, or the principle that internationally contracted debt must be honored) did not change the initial locus and nature of the crises.[26]

Another way of looking at this is to ask how far and in what ways crises at the periphery were in turn caused by globalization and by local states' attempts to modernize, resist, or otherwise deal with this phenomenon. Key British imperial interventions, those that according to Gallagher and Robinson triggered a chain of strategically linked gains, happened when these attempts broke down. So, intervention in Egypt in 1882 followed Egypt's cumulative failure to deal with debt accrued in the pursuit of development; British intervention in the Malay states in the 1870s followed the intensification of disputes there following massive Chinese immigration to the likes of Larut, Lukut, and the Klang valley. Then, in the Gallagher and Robinson chain effect, the defense of Egypt started a stream of acquisitions down the length of the Nile, and the Pangkor Engagement with Perak replicated throughout the Malay Peninsula. Though the official mind often reassured itself that it was acting to prevent other countries from being drawn in—preempting other imperial powers—it is notable that for the Malay states in 1874 the very specter of a strategic threat seems to have been engineered by Straits Settlements (Singapore, Melaka, Penang, and Province Wellesley [modern Perai]) businessmen. Likewise, there would have been no Egyptian or Malayan crisis for an official mind to mull over but for the perils of modernization and globalization, refracted through the Suez Canal and Egyptian society in one case, and the tin-bearing soil of western Malaya in the other.[27]

On this theme, Vladimir I. Lenin and John Hobson, not to mention Cain and Hopkins, may confuse matters by suggesting that the official mind was moved by the need to export capital or by the existence of gentlemanly capitalists in Whitehall, willing to intervene abroad in support of finance if not finance capital.[28] The banal reality was that London might respond to overall financial interests (the needs of sterling, the inviolability of debt repayments, and so forth), while freely ignoring individual companies in both imperial advances and retreats.[29] Hence, British companies had little effect in modifying decolonization in Malaya or Ghana, but in the 1960s Brunei's oil was sufficient reason not to bully its sultan too much over accelerating democracy and not to threaten the termination of the Anglo-Brunei defense agreement.

More to the point, so-called peripheral crises happened precisely because these areas were peripheral to, and had problems coping with, a much larger global economy that threatened to swamp them. Again, decolonization has occasionally followed a not dissimilar logic: cumulative problems with globalization or interactions with the global system cause a crisis, which when refracted through metropolitan politics triggers decolonization.

Arguably, Indonesia, knowing this might be a price for international help, decolonized East Timor in 1999 partly as a by-product of its mismanagement of globalization and Suharto's resultant fall in 1998. Again, Indonesia was relatively insignificant to the world economy, and East Timor was economically trivial to Indonesia. There was a parallel here to the final Dutch decolonization of Indonesia, where the waning of American support and possible threat to American aid helped push the Dutch to face the obvious and accept Indonesian independence in 1949. As with the Cold War and Britain, the impact of globalization on actual imperial policy was, and is, often indirect. For Britain itself, cumulative relative economic decline contributed to successive and worsening sterling crises, until those of 1966 and 1967 persuaded a reluctant Labour government to announce it would end its fixed military presence at Singapore.[30]

Meanwhile, in the Malaya of the 1870s again, Chinese labor flows, in response to conditions at home and the demand for tin abroad, were to prove crucial. We could argue this immigration—one might almost say colonization—of frontier space was threatening to burst the vessels of the Malay states by injecting new, virtually self-governing Chinese communities such as that at Kuala Lumpur.[31] Following this logic further, decolonization, or even avoidance of colonization, happened as unsubjugated states struggled to modernize while retaining independence, as with Thailand after its 1850s trade agreements, and Japan if not China, or as already imperialized populations, casting aside early, futile attempts at traditional resistance, adapted and used Western discourses. Hence, the later arrival of classes of the *ilustrado-new prijaji* type for each colony, the lawyers—the Gandhis, Lee Kuan Yews, Tunku Abdul Rahmans—writers, and teachers—the Rizals and U Nus—fits into a longer play, and an ironic one. The better a Western country accomplished the "white man's burden," the quicker it called forth its own undertakers. Or, in a less deterministic vein, the more rapidly it increased the costs of resisting nationalist demands, costs it could nevertheless take on, as France and the United States did in Vietnam, and the Dutch in Indonesia.

This broader conception, in which imperialism and globalization are themselves the taproots of decolonization, allows Britain's relations with Thailand and the latter's attempt to bureaucratize while balancing foreign advisers to take their proper place. Thailand's self-modernization resulted in its modern and export economy being dominated by Britain, with rice exported to British territories in Indian-supplied jute sacks, and rubber processed or exported by British-owned facilities in southern Thailand and Penang. Its drive to rid itself of extraterritorial rights for foreigners saw a culmination of bureaucratization, began by King Chulalongkorn (1868–1910), and Thailand only really emerged from the shadow of "informal British dominance," presumably something a shade less intimidating than "informal imperialism," in the 1920s to 1930s.[32] Again, decolonization of "informal" imperialism or dominance relates closely to issues of globalization and state-building. Imperial expansion and deimperialization were coterminous.[33]

Historians' choice of terminology sometimes obscures the synchronous nature of these developments. It is important to note that the words "nation" (people and community) and "state" (institutions supporting infrastructure and procedures) are different, though overlapping. While both Cold War America and colonial powers were deeply committed to state-building, nation-building was relatively neglected in the former period and a matter more for rhetoric than practical action in the latter. Indeed, we could speculate that this is one root of the American tragedy in Vietnam. Britain was told in 1954–1955 that Ngô Đình Diệm had to be recognized, regardless of doubts, as the South Vietnamese premier. Far too much direct interference in nation-building would destroy the credibility of the process and the West's favored contacts. The United States could tip the political balance for or against individuals, sometimes, but it could not fundamentally restructure "nations" or control the relationships between elites and their "nations," except by the application of extreme force. Force that in its turn might damage the fabric it was designed to weave.[34]

The British attempt to build a postwar "Malayan nation," with all its vicis-situdes, was arguably both unusual and outrageous in having the clarity and foresight to attempt "nation-building" as well as "state-building." Finally, the idea that the West, or at least the United Nations, came to support the "nation-state" after 1919 is also fraught with ambiguity. Witness British at-tempts to create new multinational nations from distant territories, rather than keep the shape of preexisting imperial components such as North Borneo or Sarawak, and the UN complicity in handing over West New Guinea to Indonesia in 1962–1963. Nation-building and nation-delineating was often ridden roughshod for state-building purposes, and so postcolonial elites could "inherit the Raj" intact. Postwar, postcolonial entities emerged more often than not as "nations-states," not "nation-states." All of which begs the ques-tion of further decolonization in the future.[35]

Finally, it is worth noting that themes of colonial-era state-building, and the concomitant creation of the roots for modern-style nationalism, in no way assume a "Whig" idea that empire was but a manifestation of progress and development, a sort of International Monetary Fund before its time. The "dual mandate" notion so rooted by the 1920s and 1930s—that Britain should both develop and yet protect "native" peoples and forms—infamously con-tributed to the economic marginalization of some groups, such as rural Malays, "protected" by gazetting land as for agricultural purposes only, and keeping rural education practical, vernacular, and limited.[36] Sir Frank Swettenham's passion for immigration, in his long service in the Malay states and Straits Settlements, totally ignored the dangers of creating John Furnivall's "plural society." A laissez-faire attitude to provision of services meant health was often worst at the forefront of capitalist development, and state-formation throughout colonial Southeast Asia relied heavily on opium taxes right up to the 1920s. Again, though, events look different in the longer perspective. The very reliance of colonial states on revenue farming and opium speaks of the fragility of state-building enterprises in this period of the first truly glo-bal economy, whether attempted by colonial or Asian states.[37]

In addition, we might ask if many of the same tensions were not revealed again in the post–1970s' wave of globalization and the new international divi-sion of labor. Malaysia and Singapore increasingly took in large quantities of foreign labor in the latter period. For countries such as Thailand and the Philip-pines, one might ask if there are parallels between their domestic and export exploitation of female workers, earning crucial foreign exchange as prostitutes or maids, and taking the pressure off poorer regions, and that of Japan from the 1870s to 1920s.[38] Should Indian restriction of labor export, and Japanese re-striction on overseas prostitution by the 1920s, be seen as early decolonization or early attempts to veneer globalization with moral imperatives?

Either way, these links between globalization, bureaucratization, and state-building, and between these and nation-building and decolonization, have been noticed before. Elsbeth Locher-Scholten makes the argument that Dutch new imperialism flowed from the increasing demands of a more industrialized, bureaucratized Europe, and Jan Aart Scholte tries to link the same theme to decolonization by tracing how international changes helped mold the idea of Indonesia. What is missing in all of these ingredients is an attempt to synthesize them into a more digestible form, to systematize their application, and to work out how long time frames need to be.[39]

Nevertheless, it could still be argued that much of the previous discussion is packaging, a conceptualization of well-known details and trends. To reiterate this chapter's opening point, the plethora of names for decolonization and Southeast Asia might suggest little need for radical deconstruction of models. It might be argued the historiography is characterized by increasing sophistication and consensus, well leavened by concepts such as the nation as imagined community, the second colonial occupation, nation-building, the "Grand Design," regionalism, counterinsurgency, and withdrawal.

## The Emerging Pattern of Historiography on British Decolonization in Southeast Asia

The emerging pattern of the historiography on British decolonization in Southeast Asia can be summarized briefly. It acknowledges the new nationalism of the early twentieth century but, noting its weakness, traces substantive decolonization from the fall of Singapore and the impact of the Japanese occupation, through a British second colonial reoccupation of 1945–1946, nationalist reassertion by the United Malays National Organization (UMNO) in Malaya and the AFPFL in Burma, to independence for Burma (January 1948), Malaya (August 1957), Malaysia (September 1963), and on to a final full stop with the 1968 British decision in favor of "withdrawal" by 1971. This picture identifies cultural revival and ethnic and linguistic identities stirring between 1900 and the 1930s as early solvents of empire. It sees them as egged on by modern education and by the expansion of communications and penetration of the state under new imperialism. Buddhism and the Young Mens Buddhist Association of Burma were to Burma what Islam, the Kuam Muda, and early journalism were to the Malay states. Such identity politics, partly defensive against Indian (in Burma) and Chinese (in Malaya) immigrants, gathered pace and cemented into secular politics in the immediate prewar period.[40] The new *prijaji* of Malaya—journalists, teachers, and the occasional aristocratic lawyer or administrator—were matched by equivalents in Burma.

But such nationalism supposedly lacked a convincing bite. Burma progressed to internal self-government effective from 1937 largely as a by-product of Indian nationalism, falling in a "South Asian" sphere. If Indian provinces were to have responsible government under local ministers, Burma as an Indian province would anyway have merited the same.[41] Hence, its advance, accompanied by separation from India, happened despite fissuring nationalism, not because of the young students calling themselves "thakins" and demanding complete independence. In Malaya, pan-Malayan meetings of the many Malayan associations had only just begun by the late 1930s. In both countries, problems of ethnicity, whether of Shan and Karen hill-tribe areas in Burma or the Chinese and Indians in Malaya, complicated matters. The Straits Settlements colony, however riven by Kuomintang and communist cells, also remained a vessel filled by different visions, rather than a location for any distinct regional and Southeast Asian–inspired national identity. Brunei, Sarawak, and North Borneo scarcely registered on the Richter scale of decolonization. Indeed, both looked like museum pieces, with company rule in North Borneo and the personal Brooke dynasty in Sarawak.[42]

On this schema, it was World War II, and the British response to that conflict, that changed things. Britain's answer to humiliation—130,000 personnel lost in the Malayan campaign and Burma overrun in 1942—was pure hubris. The small, fractured, weak, ethnically riven, plural societies Britain had controlled and protected in the prewar period were to be reengineered in a "second colonial occupation." This term encompassed not just a return, but an increase in the scope of intervention and number of officials. Burma, twice incinerated by war, was to undergo three years of direct rule after reconquest, before resuming progress to full independence. Though AFPFL power over workers and veterans soon turned that into a scuttle, such was the plan.[43] Meanwhile, the Malay states, never before British colonies, but sovereign states whose sultans promised to ask and act on the advice of British residents and advisers, would lose their sovereignty in a new Malayan Union colony on April 1, 1946, absorbing also the Straits Settlements of Penang and Malacca. Singapore, it is true, would remain outside the union, but only while a new governor-general for Southeast Asia prepared the ground for what later on would be called the "Grand Design." That is, Malaya would be joined with Singapore, now a separate colony, with the protectorate of Brunei, the old Brooke kingdom of Sarawak turned Crown colony in 1946, and the old company territory of North Borneo, now also made a Crown colony. Britain, in a delightful paradox, started its program of building a Malayan nation and measured decolonization by creating, in 1946, no less than four new colonies.[44]

This apparent paradox is explained by Britain's desire to spawn not tottering microstates, but politically, financially, and militarily strong successor states. If decolonization was to strengthen Britain and perpetuate its world role, power had to be passed to such strong states, possessing populations united by a shared, imagined sense of nationality that overarched ethnicity, sufficient people, and resources to support armies and universities alike, and led by elites well disposed toward Britain. Ultimately, ideally, these could be pulled together into one dominion. Creating such a "Dominion of South East Asia" required, ironically, intensified imperial involvement within the territories, and regionally the creation of a propitious environment for new states to be born into.

Yet, while requiring more British intervention than ever before, the vision of extending dominion-type relations to future postimperial states and of looking for new "collaborative" elites for a postcolonial era also required flexibility and appeasement even on the lines extended to China, Japan, and Thailand between the wars. Once Britain had decided to let India, Ceylon, and Pakistan go quickly and reap the benefits, it was difficult, both psychologically and in terms of overall conception of decolonizing areas into a new Commonwealth, to change track. Once the elephant had crashed through, the tail was likely to follow.[45]

This is not to say that British plans went off smoothly. Met with Malay anger and with the fear of amok in mind, the Malayan Union of 1946 was soon replaced with a federation in February 1948, the Malay states regained their sovereignty and Malay sultans their veto power, and Chinese citizenship was curtailed. But Britain retained a strong, federal center and its aims— of state-building, of nation-building, and of trying to encourage a united "Malayan nation"—edged the Malays' sultans and newly formed UMNO toward it rather than browbeating them.[46] Never losing sight of these aims, Britain formed a Joint Consultative Committee between Malaya and Singapore in the 1950s and tried to keep financial and citizenship legislation in line and to coordinate administrative matters between the three Borneo states.[47]

That the wider federation took a backseat in the late 1950s was not, for the most part, due to British disinterest, but to its attitude toward so-called collaborative politics and its resulting tendency to put the micromanagement of local politics to the fore. Tarling notes Britain's desire, from the war, to construct a new "partnership" between Western countries and their Asian colonies, one that might persist into a postcolonial period. This foreign policy view was reflected in a colonial desire to change old trusteeship relations, with Britain providing an iron frame of top European administrators to keep plural societies in balance, into partnerships with potential postcolonial elites. Put bluntly, Britain did view imperialism, as well as decolonization, along the lines Robinson suggests, at least in part. It viewed decolonization not as a set of formal or constitutional arrangements, nor as loyalty to one or more traditional elites, but as a constant search for local elites who could deliver stability if not development alongside "collaborative" or at least genial relationships.[48] Hence, Britain usually responded quickly as new elites demonstrated power, whether Aung San and the AFPFL in Burma, or the Alliance of the UMNO and the Malayan Chinese Association (MCA) in Malaya.

As the Alliance of the UMNO and the MCA, and later the Malayan Indian Association, emerged triumphant from the 1951–1955 Malayan elections, Britain accepted the acceleration of independence they demanded. A 1956 constitutional conference paved the way for Malayan independence in August 1957, with continued British aid, investment, and defense bases and rights. Britain also accepted the alliance position, as it was not ready to consider any wider federation. This despite Britain having hoped for a more genuinely cross-communal party, rather than an alliance of communal organizations, but partly because the alliance proved staunch anticommunist partners against the mainly Chinese-led insurgency of 1948. The stalling of the Malaysia project from 1955 to 1961 thus reflected this British notion of decolonization as managing collaborative relationships, just as the idea's resurrection in 1961 was made possible by Malaysia's fear that Singapore, if left alone, might turn communist.[49]

The following construction of Malaysia, inaugurated in September 1963, then delayed a further rundown of British military power in the region, which Malaysia had been supposed to facilitate. This was because the Indonesian "confrontation" of Malaysia (1963–1966) tied down larger than ever forces. Once that was aside, however, a British Labour government decided on withdrawal under pressure of recurrent financial crises.

Here, then, is a historiography rich in detail, with documentary collections for both Burma and Malaya, detailed studies for territories as underpopulated as Sarawak[50] and Brunei,[51] and even papers on issues such as Penang secessionist desires.[52] Here is a historiography that presents common themes across territories, employs a rich range of concepts, and seems equally strong on nationalist detail. It is true that works focused on British policy have, however fairly, attracted the accusation that they might be writing "colonial records" history.[53] But for every work from an imperial perspective, there is another that traces a nationalist story, or one focused on one subnational community or class, such as Chinese tin miners or Malay peasants.[54] The likes of W. R. Roff, Anthony C. Milner, and Ariffin Omar trace the emergence of a new Malay political identity, notions of loyalty to a new *bangsa Melayu* displacing loyalty to *kerajaan,* to sultan and individual Malay states.[55] The interaction of fears of Chinese dominance, inspiration by Islamic reformism, new elites, and a rising vernacular press, all mixed up by the war and supercharged by British attempts to abolish Malay sovereignty, has been more than adequately traced.[56]

Tim Harper's unveiling of the social and cultural underpinnings to political Malaya in the 1940s and 1950s alone is kaleidoscopic. He produces a vast tapestry of Chinese tapping rubber on the forest frontier, and of an explosion of publications: from the *Sejerah Melayu* in comic strip form to the provocative Malay-language daily *Utusan Melayu* (circulation thirty-five thousand by 1958), and from big publishers to tiny outfits in improbable places like the Trengganu fishing village of Marang.[57] All this to show that the Malayan Emergency "emerged from elemental forces from below," with these same forces dictating communal political formations despite British plans to create a united Malayan nation. Here, in Harper, is a vision that incorporates colonization of space (the forest frontier), and a complex interplay between imperialist plans and the reality on the ground. Harper argues the forms and structures that Britain hoped to use to forge a cross-communal "Malayan" identity were hijacked. Entrenched identities and wartime disruption meant "papers attacked Britain, unions became politicised, politics communalised, and a colonial Emergency emerged from 'elemental forces from below: a spiral of violence.'"[58] In short, "both sides were reacting to events."[59]

Here is a historiography that emphasizes the social, the national, and especially the communal, so that imperial policy comes to be seen as reacting to events on the ground. This helps to explain some of the puzzles of decolonization, such as the gap between postwar plans to minimize British forces East of Suez, the reality of forty thousand troops tied down in the Malayan Emergency (more in the confrontation), Britain's plans for three years of direct rule in Burma collapsing into rapid independence, the Malayan Union dying ignominiously, and Britain accepting the communally based alliance when it had hoped to build politics out of a new sense of a "Malayan nation." By itself, however, the picture is still incomplete. Each strand—nationalist, colonial, counterinsurgency, communist, radical, and so on—still tends to emphasize one approach, with few works attempting to synthesize the divergent strands.[60]

For instance, while it is true Britain often retreated from detailed policies, even principles perhaps, it could be argued that this was the better to preserve core strategic interests. While Britain could bend gracefully before the winds of change, it could also fight and even defeat opposition movements, ignoring Azahari and his Partai Rakyat Brunei in Brunei until the December 1962 revolt allowed them to be extinguished, and deporting and even executing communist insurgents and some of their supporters in Malaya. It was capable of adroit management of "hearts and minds" measures, down to

General Sir Gerald Templer, the high commissioner, inviting villagers to Kuala Lumpur, and psychological warfare, but it was also capable of parading dead communists around kampongs in the Malayan Emergency. It was also willing to stall nationalist advances on occasion, as when it allowed a 1956 Singapore constitutional conference to fail rather than give up control of internal security. The traditional contrast between British policy and other European powers, emphasizing British pragmatism and flexibility,[61] and the need to nurture the elites most capable of delivering stability locally, in the hope of winning their postcolonial cooperation, is thus acknowledged. However, other aspects have to be taken into account.[62]

Indeed, more radical historians argue British interventions were not primarily to counter communism and disorder, but to prevent radical Asian nationalists disrupting British interests. They see Britain as using force to "manage" nationalism, remove "radical" nationalists, and so court more pliant elites. Michael R. Stenson, for instance, maintains that labor regulations, deportations, and the closing down of political space virtually forced Malayan communists to revolt in 1948.[63] These radical narratives imply Britain sought out moderates, whether democratic or feudal, provided such groups would "leave British businessmen on Malaya's rubber plantations, Malayan dollars in the sterling pool, and Royal Navy ships berthed in Singapore." This was true elsewhere in the empire: Britain accepting Malay domination rather than racial equality in Malaya, supporting "feudal" rulers in the Persian Gulf states, balking at forcing Brunei's sultan to democratize his country in the 1950s and 1960s, toppling a democratically elected government in British Guiana, and secretly colluding with Israel and France in order to try and topple Gamal Abdel Nasser in the humiliating Suez debacle of 1956.[64]

What dictated the thin line between pragmatism and obstinacy? No one factor was present in all cases. Oil-rich Brunei was strategically unimportant after the Malaysian federation. Britain clearly stalled constitutional advance in Singapore, in 1956, because of internal security and geopolitical reasons, yet in January to February 1956 agreed that Malaya might advance to independence, despite the continuing Emergency and subversion. Burma was scuttled in the face of AFPFL power to disrupt by means of violence or union action, despite good political and military reasons for thinking it was neither stable nor ready for independence. Britain did, it is true, continue the long imperial tradition of forming federations as a prelude to greater local autonomy and strength, but it also let the Malaysia project stall from 1955 to 1961, and was ultimately excluded from the final negotiations for Singapore's departure from Malaysia.[65] Whether or not Britain stayed or went, and whether its state- and nation-building policies progressed or mired seems almost random. What is needed is clearly a composite but flexible model, one that at least gives some notion of how the different elements fit together. To focus on genial complicity in Malayan decolonization, for instance, without juxtaposing Brunei and Singapore, can only be one-handed clapping.

As we have already seen, the "strategic" or geopolitical paradigm is helpful in explaining purely British reactions, but it is still limited, especially in the way it can reduce Asian developments to so many additional inputs into the strategic calculations of the official mind. Critically, Singapore's strategic value did not change much between its 1956 and 1957 constitutional conferences, yet in 1956 Britain wanted to retain ultimate control of internal security, and in 1957 it agreed to submit this to an Internal Security Council where a Malayan member would hold the balance between Britain and Singapore. Indeed, by 1957 Britain had decided it should consider simply giving Singaporean politicians control of internal security if necessary to have a successful conference, while retaining the power to suspend the constitution. It explicitly recognized that ultimately "strategic" success might mean putting the needs of local politics first.[66]

What is needed is a model that can hyperlink the various imperial, globalization, colonial records, radical, counterinsurgency, diplomatic, and nationalist strands into a coherent account. One possibility is a modified version of John Darwin's argument. This holds that Britain saw "decolonization" not as withdrawal or termination of empire, but as shifting from one means of maintaining a system of world power to another. The project was not a resounding success, simply because it proved even more difficult for a declining power to maintain informal imperialism, which required the distribution of benefits or threat of force, than formal empire. According to this model, the precise shape of decolonization is dictated by interactions between three levels affecting this system of world power: metropolitan politics, international power and ideas, and locality and nation.[67]

Such a model of Britain seeking to guard its international power, or indeed Hyam's doctrine of geopolitical primacy, makes sense, but only if two modifiers are added. First, the official mind's notions of power or geopower must be widened. Second, the debate on whether officials were gentlemanly capitalists first, or strategic and political planners by nature, sets up an unreal dichotomy. At least three components were identified in London, and from time to time, as making up *power:* first, military hardware, bombs and bases (or base rights), or tanks and strategically located territories such as Singapore; second, economic strength; and third, collaborative or positive relationships. Contrary to Hyam's notion of two levels of decisions, with planning in London the highest level, and conceived of almost solely in terms of geopolitics, all these factors could operate either in Asia, or London, or both. It is utterly clear that Malaya's economic value—its dollar-earning rubber and tin was the life-support drip for the sterling area—was to the fore of planners' minds in the mid–1950s. It is equally clear economics was prominent in considering Brunei in 1966–1967. Yet, economics, in the form of domestic crises, also operated in the metropolis, especially from 1965 to 1968.

The notion of Britain managing what it saw as a system of world military–economic–collaborative power cannot be reduced to a calculus or a neat tabulation. For instance, favored local elites became more and more powerful as independence accelerated. As their ability to impose costs on Britain rose, the claims of strong, noncommunist elites became almost irresistible, given Britain's ultimate goal of friendly postcolonial elites. Thus, strongly placed local elites had a great deal of scope to dictate the emerging shape of postcolonial politics and to force accelerated decolonization. Yet, if strategy, or sometimes economics, became on occasion a prominent enough concern, Britain could and did slow or hasten the process accordingly. Had the alliance determined to recognize the Malayan Communist Party in December 1955, when the Tunku met Chin Peng face to face, Britain would almost certainly have tried to apply the brakes, with what results we can only guess.[68]

**The End?**

We know, of course, that the Tunku did meet Chin Peng, that he presented the latter with little choice short of surrender on British terms, and that the British retreat continued to Malayan independence in 1957. But the story is not usually seen as ending there. It seemed as if Britain had achieved Darwinesque decolonization, changing its world system of power from the basis of formal to informal imperialism.[69] Defense agreements continued with Malaya (1957), Brunei (1959), and then Malaysia (1963). These certainly contained some derogation of Asian sovereignty, as in the Anglo-Malayan Defense Agreement of 1957, which in theory gave Britain the right to use Malayan bases to defend British territories in the East, and the impact of tens of thousands of British and British-employed military personnel on Singapore. As late as June 1965, Labour prime minister Harold Wilson declared Britain's frontiers lay in the Himalayas. In October 1967, the sheikhdoms of the Persian Gulf were assured Britain would honor its commitments to them. Yet, between 1965 and January 1968 the Wilson government gradually cut away its East of Suez capability. In April 1967, it decided to close the Singapore bases by the mid-1970s. Finally, in January 1968 Wilson announced that Britain's East of Suez role, excepting Hong Kong and Brunei, would end earlier still in 1971.

We are not interested here in why Britain took these decisions. What we are interested in is what sort of an end this was, and what this says about "decolonization."[70] Technically speaking, it was not the end of formal empire or imperialism, since by September 1963, at the latest, Britain had relinquished all formal control over Singapore, as it passed into Malaysia. All that remained was a defense agreement with Malaysia, which allowed Britain to continue using Singapore for defense purposes. The case for this being the end of informal imperialism is stronger, but still slight. The defense agreement did give Britain some scope to claim it could use Singapore without consent, though it called for consultation. Britain also continued to operate bases, employing thousands of people and underpinning a great deal of the economy. Above all, however, this was "decolonization" in the sense employed by Darwin, defined as "a partial redeployment and redistribution of British and European influences in the regions of the extra-European world whose economic, political and cultural life had previously seemed destined to flow into Western moulds."[71] That is, as changes in European systems of world power, in this case the change being a "termination."

But was it a termination? Historians as perceptive as Anthony Reid endorse this clear demarcating of European imperialism and Asian postimperialism, saying, "the 1960s and 70s brought to completion the decolonization of the region."[72] Yet, Britain's presence died a much longer, lingering death. Even in 1968 Wilson did not admit that withdrawal meant the end of a world role. In a draft personal message for President Lyndon B. Johnson, he said Britain had to make the cuts if it was to secure a new, long-term role "on the world stage" and "when I say quote the world stage unquote I mean just that."[73] On January 16, 1968, Wilson told Parliament there would be total withdrawal from East of Suez in 1971, but even then he confirmed there would be a European-based capability to intervene in the Far East and troops in select dependencies after 1971.[74] Wilson's caveats aside, his Labour government fell in 1970, and the 1970–1974 Conservative government entered new "Five Power Defense Agreements" with Australia, New Zealand, Malaysia, and Singapore in 1971 that allowed loose cooperation. True, the returning Labour government of 1974–1979 did finalize withdrawal from Singapore's bases by 1976, even though the Five Power arrangements persisted, and Britain helped set up an International Air Defense System effective by 1971, with British army Gurkhas remaining in Hong Kong until their 1997 transfer to China and Brunei.[75] The dispatch of British Gurkhas— those improbable remnants of the Raj—from their base in independent Brunei to help police East Timor's emergence from Indonesian control in late 1999 provides a symmetry even Hollywood might find implausible.

If the British "system" of bases and power terminated in 1976, only to be replaced by the defense of individual territories and defense politics, winning and helping friends by small-scale assistance, this is a relatively trivial point. More importantly, this brings us back to our starting point, that the terminology and concepts chosen may have an insinuating effect on analysis. For whatever the British withdrawal of 1965–1976 was, it was not decolonization in the most pedantically narrow of definitions: the undoing of "colonization," understood as the peopling of territory by aliens or at least by their cultural and other forms. It is true that "colony" has come to mean virtually any formal, overseas European imperial state, but in the process it has obscured a vital distinction.

Ferro's *Colonization* makes this distinction clear. He self-consciously separates "colonization" and "imperialism," noting that "[c]olonization is associated with the occupation of a foreign land, with its being brought under cultivation, with the settlement of colonists."[76] As such, colonization would be both more than imperialism, which need not involve actual settlement, and less, in that settlers can arrive before or in the absence of an imperial state, or indeed any state.

If this were the case, there would be a good case for distinguishing three levels of change. First, decolonization, the reshaping of *space* "colonized" by different groups, languages, and forms, both in the sense of the hardware of domination (people and land) and the more intractable software (ideas, curricula, and languages). Decolonization of such "space" could vary from a change of official language, through the absorption of culturally distinct communities by devices such as common national curricula and school systems, to, at worst, the brutal ethnic cleansing of communities. In contrast to this decolonization, there is deimperialization. Deimperialization can be further separated into the second category of change, the ending of formal empire, and the third, the ending of informal imperium.

Each type may demand a slightly different approach. Take "decolonization" in the narrowest sense. It is notable for being the most difficult form of deimperialization, the one that has had least success and the one most often evoked to justify the politically motivated persecution of minority groups in possession of coveted resources, however politically powerless they might be. Decolonization in this sense might mean affirmative action in favor of Native Americans or Maoris, a process of reconciliation with Australian aborigines, European colons fleeing Algeria in 1962, or the Zimbabwean government driving out white farmers in 2002. The fact that many of the latter may have bought their farms on the open market place can be conveniently brushed aside by the rhetoric of decolonization.

In Southeast Asia, where there has been relatively little colonization in the original sense of large-scale settlement by Europeans, such spatial colonization might refer to the Chinese in Malaya and Singapore or the Javanese and Sumatrans spilling out to other islands in Indonesia during the "New Order" period. Wherever such settlement raises issues of cultural, political, or economic dominance, the control of space, defined to include concepts such as "economic" space as well as merely land itself, may become an issue. A history of decolonization in this sense might feature Burmese, Malay, and non-Javanese responses to subcolonization of economic space by Indians, Chinese, and Javanese, or the struggle, by first Britain and then the People's Action Party, to ensure that Singapore defined its own multiracial and new national identity, rather than succumbing to internationalist communist or narrowly Chinese images of what Singapore should look like. Clearly, some aspects of the Chinese presence in Southeast Asia could be seen as an example of such colonizing of space, of overseas communities replicating alien social and cultural structures in new areas. Harper's book on Malaya, for one, could be reinterpreted in this way. In effect, it presents the Malayan Emergency as fought by the last wave of such Chinese "colonizers," who, left stranded by the tides of history on the Malayan forest frontier, and with no "colonial" or pro-Chinese state to protect them, turned to the Malayan Communist Party to protect them against dispossession and to integrate them into global events on terms they found comprehensible and advantageous.[77]

The point about some movement constituting a colonization of space might stand despite many, if not most, Chinese becoming sojourners, Straits Chinese, *peranakan* (merely transiting), or mestizos (blending into rather than marking out local space). It also stands despite the label "Chinese" being a convenient term for people speaking different dialects such as Hakka, Hokkien, or Teochiu, and notwithstanding the early twentieth-century attempts to promote Mandarin. The Thai Chakri dynasty, with its part-Chinese lineage, and José Rizal, with his ilustrado family's mestizo origins, show just how far Chinese could and did become part of a joint Asian project of modernization and decolonization, rather than minority and alien workers, entrepreneurs, and "essential outsiders."

This reinforces the point that a partial writing of "decolonization" might not, or at least should not, simply be a tale of Malay versus Chinese, with the *bumiputera* being reinforced by embracing Sumatrans and others of first- or second-generation immigrant status, but also of a battle in Singapore to decide whether a "Chinese" identity would prevail, one communism tapped into in the 1950s, or a new, more multicultural "imagined nation."[78] This story might also concentrate on postcolonial societies' engagement with something more tenacious than mere settlers or imperialists, the software of colonialism: books, languages, customs, judicial systems, social structures, attitudes, and more. Arguably, the most successful decolonizing states have not been those that decolonized most, but those that recognized which aspects of this software *not* to decolonize. This blending of new definitions and perspectives on colonization and decolonization, as not just West versus East, but as an aspect of Asian and Western flows, of a globalizing economy, and as involving Asian–Asian issues, too, means "decolonization" is now, as well as then.[79]

While it might be sensitive to see such parallels between contemporary Southeast Asia and issues of European decolonization, is it without value? The crucial point here is that such comparisons need not imply value judgment. To see issues such as West Papua or, far more problematically, Acheh in the historical context of decolonization is not to predict outcomes, any more than seeing Basque, Breton, or Northern Irish problems in this context would predicate the breakup of European states as inevitable or right. Nor does acknowledging that Burmese or Malays may have seen decolonization in terms of opposition to colonization of space by Indian or Chinese forms and businesses involve any judgment on whether that was, or is, right. It would be difficult, however, to assert that such issues of decolonization, or regional issues that carry the latent threat of decolonization, have been confined to history quite yet.

# 8

## British Attitudes and Policies on Nationalism and Regionalism

### Nicholas Tarling

Colonial Southeast Asia had been created under the aegis of the British, the primate power of the nineteenth century. It was in substantial part the result of their attitudes and policies that, despite their primacy, the region, always divided, was divided anew. The territories they secured, or over which they acquired protectorates, were limited to Burma, the Straits Settlements, the peninsular Malay states, and the three states of northern Borneo. They favored the continuance of the Dutch empire in the archipelago, and they accepted the establishment of the French in Vietnam, Cambodia, and the eastern parts of Laos. They supported the continuance of an independent Thai kingdom. They also supported the continuance of the Spanish regime in the Philippines. When it was overthrown in the 1890s, they did not intervene, but accepted the intervention of the United States, as opposed to a German alternative. The United States indeed became one of the colonial powers, though, envisaging self-rule and independence for its acquisition, it was a colonial power with a difference. The involvement of the potential superpower was in fact a guarantee of colonial Southeast Asia. It stood in the way of the Japanese, who were established in Taiwan beginning 1895.

Though often originating in rivalry, the colonial regimes in Southeast Asia had much in common. Among them, however, there was little coordination, though there was some local cooperation against communism in the interwar period. They treated nationalism among those they ruled in different ways. If the nationalists in the Philippines benefited from distinctive American policies, those in Burma sought to take advantage of the achievements of their neighbors in India, and a substantial measure of self-government was secured in the 1935 constitution. Always cautious, the Dutch, on the other hand, had become more cautious after the 1926–1927 uprisings, and the French failure to make any gestures to the moderates conduced to communist leadership of the nationalist movement. Nor, of course, were the nationalist movements marked by regional collaboration. Colonial frontiers stood in the way—the Dutch thought Manuel Quezon's visit quite dangerous—and the movements were shaped by influences from the metropolis or from nonregional sources.[1]

It was only in the face of the intensification of the Japanese threat after the outbreak of World War II in 1939 that the British began to consider the region as a whole. They recognized that what happened in one part of the area affected what happened in others. That was particularly obvious when, after its "strange defeat" in Europe, France came to terms with the Japanese in 1940–1941. The affairs of the British Empire in the Far East, Duff Cooper reported, were being conducted "by machinery that has undergone no important change since the days of Queen Victoria."[2] He advocated the appointment of a commissioner-general, and was himself made resident minister when the Pacific war broke out. It was in the course of that struggle that the term "Southeast Asia" came into common use, applied as it was to the Allied command set up in 1943 under Admiral Lord Louis Mountbatten and based in Sri Lanka.

The experience was still in mind when the conflict ended. The British appointed a special commissioner in Southeast Asia, responsible to the foreign secretary, as well as a governor-general for their own territories, though they later amalgamated the two offices. That was one illustration of their belief that a regional approach should succeed the imperial approach. It was sustained not only by the experience of invasion and war, but also by the prospect of famine and disorder in the immediate postsurrender period. It persisted as an element in British policy into the succeeding phases, marked by the onset of the Cold War, the triumph of the communists in China, and the outbreak of the Korean War.

There is another continuity. The centerpiece of the British Empire in Asia had been India. Southeast Asia—particularly, but not solely, Burma—had been seen from an Indian perspective. Soldiers from India dominated the Allied forces in Southeast Asia, as the Kranji War Memorial in Singapore vividly demonstrates, and India was an essential source of matériel as well as manpower in the liberation of Southeast Asia. The role of Indian soldiers in the reoccupation was crucial, both making it possible and limiting what the British could do in Burma, in Indonesia, and in Vietnam. Initially, even so, the British looked for the continuance of this role in the subsequent phase. Partition ruled it out. Satisfactory defense agreements could be made with neither successor-state. Pakistan was too weak, and any deal with it would alienate India. "India showed little interest in military discussions" anyway.[3]

That did not, however, mean that India lost its importance in British policy. The British still hoped that India would play a positive role in promoting the stability of South and Southeast Asia. What was now needed was to win its support by Commonwealth-style diplomacy. The British recognized that, as an independent state, India would have policies of its own. After all, the empire had itself been a kind of dual monarchy, in which the policies dictated by a concern for India's security had not necessarily coincided with the policies of the world's first industrial power. What had to be emphasized was what the British and the Indians had in common, rather than what divided them. India, of long-standing influence in Southeast Asia, would offer an example of a stable noncommunist government. Its influence would counter that of China.

This concept seemed the more valid inasmuch as the British had also recognized that their position in postwar Southeast Asia could no longer rest on an imperial framework: even if feasible, mere restoration was insufficient. "A crushing defeat . . . was inflicted on British arms" in Malaya and Singapore, as H. F. C. Walsh, the British consul-general in Batavia, put it in 1942, and the fall of the Netherlands East Indies was "no less spectacular. . . . The Europeanised 'Far East' has gone, and the organisation of European activities there in the future will have to be rebuilt on entirely different foundations from those prevailing before 1939."[4] Wartime planning hardly even recognized the extent on the changes required. At the end of the war, however, it was clear to the British that their future in Southeast Asia must depend on coming to terms with the nationalism that either the interregnum had promoted or to which it had offered an unprecedented opportunity. That, of course, had precedents in British policy in the attempts, for example, to come to terms with the Chinese in the 1920s, and was being replicated in India itself. Britain's interests, it was believed, could be put on a new footing if leadership was offered to moderate nationalists in territories that might sustain viable states. At the same time, Britain could help provide the resources, expertise, and security such states would need in a dangerous world.

If such a policy were to succeed—and to win the backing of India—it had to be followed by the other colonial powers, France and the Netherlands, whose return the British had facilitated. If they did, moreover, it would enhance the prospects that Southeast Asia would become, in the phrase Lord Killearn (Miles W. Lampson), the special commissioner, used in 1946, "a region of peace and orderly progress."[5] At the same time, it would make it possible to reconcile Britain's policies in Europe with its policies in Asia. In the imperial period, they had been marked by tension, though in general European policy took priority. In postwar Europe, France and the Netherlands were allies of Britain. It was desirable that their policies in Asia coincided rather than clashed. Britain supported the return of the other colonial powers to Southeast Asia, but their attitudes and policies, like Britain's, had to change.

Late in 1945, Britain's Civil Planning Unit suggested "that it is in our over-riding interest to see the establishment of just and stable systems of Government wherever possible in the Far East, and that in South-East Asia especially it is unlikely that this objective can be attained without our continuing to play a leading part in the settlement of difficulties between the native peoples and our Allies."[6] In Netherlands India, the British endeavored to make their support conditional on Indonesian-Dutch negotiations. In the case of French Indochina, they were able or willing to exert less pressure. Negotiations over the Anglo-French treaty of Dunkirk took place almost simultaneously with the Franco-Vietnamese clashes of late 1946.

There were indeed a number of obstacles. Dutch leaders and their electorate tended to identify the future of their state with the retention of Netherlands India. "We know," as the clandestine Anti-Revolutionary Party publication *Trouw* put it in 1944, "that our country, if deprived of the Indies, would be a small and insignificant state which would be pushed about within the great turmoil of international relations."[7] Netherlands India was also seen as essential to economic postwar recovery: it had added 8 percent to the Dutch gross domestic product in the interwar period.[8] In the case of Indochina, the economic arguments were less compelling, though, as Thomas A. August points out, its colonies had become more important to France in the depression.[9] Returning to Indochina, however, was connected not only to Charles de Gaulle, but also to the restoration of French grandeur after the humiliations of the war.

There were structural factors, too. The British had a two-party system, and the first postwar Labour government had a substantial majority that could take bold initiatives. No such position was obtained in the Netherlands: postwar governments were based on Catholic-Labour Party coalitions, and that tended to limit a concessionary policy. Politics in Paris were, of course, even more fractious than in The Hague. At some critical points in the Indochinese imbroglio, there was no government in Paris at all. That left the making of policy to men on the spot, influenced by the colons, men who thought *deux coups de fusil* would suffice. Sometimes, governments were so weak that they did not want to risk trying to get backing for their policies from the elected Assembly.

The constitutional obstacles are, moreover, sometimes given too little emphasis. J. H. A. Logemann, the Dutch minister for overseas territories, observed that the British task was easier than that of the Dutch: Britain had no written constitution, while to amend the Dutch constitution required a two-thirds majority.[10] Nor could the French readily follow the British Commonwealth pattern. "[I]t is not part of the pattern to try to incorporate the local population by cultural change into a large super-national empire," as Thomas Henry Silcock later put it, "but rather to introduce piecemeal a num-

ber of British institutions, modified to local circumstances as they seem necessary, with the ultimate object of building up a separate state which will
have permanently absorbed along with its own local characteristics certain
British institutions."[11] "Lacking any sort of powerful dynastic bond such as
England and the dominions possess in the king, France and her possessions,
in order that their association or their union be durable, needed to develop
between them a bond as strong, if not stronger, but a republican bond," as
Michel Devize put it.[12] At the very same time as they were attempting to
negotiate with the Việt Minh leaders, the French were indeed engaged in
drawing up the constitution for the French Union. That made for rigidity in
both spheres.

"Britain now finds herself confronted in an acute form with the problem
of maintaining friendly co-operation with the Dutch without putting herself
into antagonism with the general cause of nationalism in Asia," ran the Civil
Planning Unit's paper. It presciently added, "This problem may continue to
be a serious one after the British forces have been withdrawn." Indeed, after
the conclusion of the Linggadjati Agreement, the British had to press for its
signature. Michael Wright of the commissioner-general's office in Singapore
preached to L. J. M. Beel and J. A. Jonkman, the Dutch ministers, when they
called early in May 1947. "We looked forward to the close co-operation of
the Dutch as well as others, but always on the basis of a European/Asiatic
partnership." At this point, the Soviet Union was not active in Southeast Asia
on a major scale. There was a short-term opportunity to make "a reality of a
partnership between Asiatic people concerned and Western countries."[13] Esler
Dening of the Foreign Office offered similar advice in The Hague. The British in India and Burma and the Dutch in Netherlands India were "fundamentally faced with the same problem and had the same opportunities. The days
were past when we could hope to rule in Asia by force even if our peoples
wanted to do so which they did not." But the peoples of those areas had "a
background of British and Dutch traditions . . . we had . . . an opportunity of
getting in on the ground floor of the new Asia if we played our hand prop-
erly."[14] The first police action nevertheless followed. Ernest Bevin, the British foreign secretary, thought the Dutch might break the Indonesian Republic,
but that would only mean unrest and guerrilla fighting as in China. "He wanted
to bring this great area of South East Asia, impinging upon India and Ceylon,
out of turmoil."[15]

Enjoying limited success with the Dutch, the British hesitated over pressing the French. They were "notoriously sensitive" to influences from the
outside, which were "liable to produce prejudicial and unsatisfactory results."
The outbreak of fighting at the end of 1946 did not shift the British view. "I
do not think it wise to intervene at present," Bevin wrote.[16] Eventually, the

position would deteriorate. In Netherlands India, it was possible to point to a moderate noncommunist leader with whom the Dutch might reach a deal and so avoid the rise of a less moderate leadership. That was less easy in the case of Vietnam, since the ruthless French prewar approach had undermined the moderates and in fact given the communists an opportunity. Had Mohandas Gandhi tried civil disobedience in French Indochina, he "would long since have ascended into heaven," as Hồ Chí Minh put it.[17] In the early postwar phase, negotiation might still have been possible. Its failure was coupled by the increasing tendency to present the developing struggle in Cold War terms. Though without much conviction, the French turned to the "Bảo Đại solution." The British thought that Bảo Đại had little chance of winning over noncommunist nationalist support, especially as the French remained reluctant to concede the Associated States of the French Union any real power to determine their destiny. Indeed, it was hard to press them to do so, since French forces were still necessary to fight the Việt Minh, which the British, too, increasingly said was an arm of international communism.

The French had undermined the protection of the colonial Southeast Asia in 1940–1941. Now, they stood in the way of a regional approach. "From the point of view of the Far East we should like to see closer collaboration with the French. But adjacent territories have tended in the past to look somewhat askance at French colonial activities in Indo-China, and in face of present nationalistic tendencies in Burma and Malaya . . . it is advisable not to press too strongly for the time being."[18] "We must not appear to be ganging up with Western powers against Eastern peoples striving for independence," Dening wrote early in 1947. "Rather our aim should be to contrive a general partnership between independent or about-to-be independent peoples and the Western Powers who by their past experience are best able to give them help and, in our case, to some extent, protection. Owing to political conditions in the N.E.I. and Indo-China, this process of consultation and cooperation with these areas must be a gradual one."[19]

The advance of the Cold War made the process more necessary but also more difficult. In face of the Soviet threat in Europe, Bevin took the initiative in creating the Western European Union. "We have consistently pursued a more liberal Colonial policy in South-East Asia than either of the other Metropolitan powers concerned," wrote Kenneth Christofas. "There is a great danger that, if our alliance with the other Western powers in Europe were to be correspondingly reflected in our behaviour in the East, we should lose the sympathy of the Asiatic peoples by whom 'Colonialism' and 'Imperialism' are considered a far greater menace than Communism." The emergence of the Western European Union, as Wright put it, "makes it still more difficult to get away from the pattern of purely European collaboration, which it is desirable to avoid."[20] It was in this context that Bevin began to look to the Commonwealth countries, particularly India, in respect of the Southeast Asian region. At the Commonwealth prime ministers' conference in October 1948, he pointed to the unsettled conditions there. Could Commonwealth countries help its pacification? "[T]here should be some regular means of consultation between Commonwealth countries interested in that area with the object of helping to put the political and economic life of the countries of South-East Asia on a firm footing, based upon internal stability and freedom from the menace of Communist attack." The recent attainment of independence by India, Pakistan, and Ceylon "meant that their collaboration in such an approach would be of special value and influence." The remarks secured positive comments from Herbert Evatt and Jawaharlal Nehru, who said that Indonesia and Burma had sought India's counsel.[21] This was the germ of the Colombo Plan. But it finally emerged in a context that had been further modified and assumed a yet wider purpose.

The deterioration of the situation in Southeast Asia—marked by the challenges to the newly independent government in Burma and the declaration of the Malayan Emergency—seemed all the more serious as the Chinese communists approached victory. Bevin asked his officials what the implications would be. There was nothing Britain could do to combat the advance of communism in China itself, they concluded. The main task was to build up resistance in neighboring countries by resolving political disputes, such as that between India and Pakistan over Kashmir and those in Indochina and Indonesia, and by improving the economic position of Southeast Asia as a whole.[22] Communist success in China, they thought, would be "a grave danger to Malaya," increase the difficulties in Indochina, and possibly worsen the disorder in Burma. Cooperation among the governments of the area would be difficult to achieve, though desirable. Australia, New Zealand, India, and Pakistan, all with "a vital interest in the peace and prosperity of South-East Asia," would, for example, be "unwilling to join in any activities involving support of the French and Dutch Governments in this area." Britain would be "in the best position to act as the co-ordinating factor."[23]

Early in 1949, however, India seized the initiative by calling a conference on Indonesia following the second Dutch police action. It expressed "the opinion that participating Governments should consult among themselves in order to explore ways and means of establishing suitable machinery . . . for promoting consultation and cooperation within the framework of the United Nations."[24] For the British, Sir A. Nye, the high commissioner, suggested the conference was a challenge, but also a opportunity.[25] Like his colleagues at the Foreign Office, Malcolm MacDonald, the commissioner-general, favored "an understanding and reasonably sympathetic attitude." The "movement towards Asian cooperation" had probably come to stay. "If we try to put too much of a break on it, we shall not stop it, but merely turn it into a critical and even hostile mood toward us. By giving it such sympathetic support as we wisely can we shall help to lead it along paths of moderation and co-operation with the Western democratic peoples."[26]

Britain alone had "the experience and the ability to knit the South East Asia region together," Dening argued. An India-led movement would either become anti-Western or it would fail.[27] "If we wait too long, we may find ourselves no longer able to influence the situation," Bevin told the prime minister. "There are so many difficulties in South East Asia that a purely political approach may meet with no success. It seems desirable therefore to approach the problem more from the economic angle, since in the economic field there is a good deal which the West has to offer the East, thus providing a solid basis for co-operation." A regional conference, not necessarily confined to Commonwealth states, but with Britain as a participant, might "pave the way to regional co-operation, in the first place in the economic field. Later possibly this might lead to some kind of regional security arrangement."[28]

MacDonald came to London late in May 1949. Defense, he argued, was the prime objective, for triumphing in China the communists "would probably try immediately to crumble the anti-communist front in South East Asia while the going was good." There was no question that something like the recently concluded North Atlantic Treaty Organization (NATO) pact would appeal to Nehru. Nor, MacDonald thought, could he be expected to take part in a conference together with the French and the Dutch. "Why . . . should we not hold a Conference limited to Commonwealth Powers, amongst whom India would play a leading part? . . . While we were developing co-operation within the Commonwealth in South East Asia the French and the Dutch might disappear from the scene as Colonial Powers and so facilitate a wider Conference."[29] A conference of foreign ministers at Colombo in January 1950 became the venue.

There, Bevin did not advocate a pact, "[T]he right policy was for the like-minded countries with interests in the East to keep in close contact and be ready to help each other in resisting any attempts to hinder peaceful development on democratic liners. He recognised the close-interdependence of East and West and stressed the great need for the expansion of capital development and food production in the less developed countries." Nehru preferred "mutual consultation and co-operation" to a pact.[30] In the event the conference—with the aid of Spender and Jayawardene—came down somewhere between the two, envisaging what came to be called the Colombo Plan.

"[N]ot much could be accomplished," Spender argued, "without considerable assistance from the United States. This was not likely to be forthcoming unless South-East Asia showed itself willing and able to help itself."[31] The British had indeed seen the venture as a step toward involving the United States in the defense of Southeast Asia. There, where it had divested itself of the Philippines, its role had so far been a limited one, largely centered on the attempts to bring about a settlement between the Dutch and the Indonesians following the first police action. The Americans, Bevin had suggested late in 1948, would not accept any responsibility for Southeast Asia. "Nevertheless I feel that it would be a good idea if they can be brought to associate with us as far as possible in stemming Communism in South East Asia."[32] The initial soundings were not encouraging. "They have burnt their fingers so badly in China," wrote Hubert Graves at the Washington embassy, "that they are at present in a very cautious mood."[33] Nevertheless, when the cabinet reviewed its policy for the Colombo conference, "it was suggested that it should not be impracticable to maintain the political influence of the United Kingdom in South East Asia, while arranging for the United States to provide much of the capital investment that was required." The experience of the Americans in China might make them receptive to suggestions for collaboration on the basis of British experience and U.S. capital.[34]

The attitudes and policies the British were developing to counter the communists in Southeast Asia were not seen as inconsistent with the recognition of the communist regime when it assumed power in China late in 1949, and the British proffered it in January 1950, just before the Colombo Conference was held. They wanted to retain Hong Kong and to trade with China. They also conceived that treating the Central People's government like a normal government might encourage it to behave like one, rather than like an outlaw or a subordinate of the Soviet Union. At a deeper level, Britain's recognition of the communist regime was consistent with the pragmatism of its diplomatic tradition, which could only be emphasized by the loss of its primacy. It was much less easy to reconcile the relationship it had been developing with the United States (since its primacy was challenged at the end of the nineteenth century) and which had become closer during World War II. Generally, it sought to associate its policies with those of the United States, while avoiding complete dependence. But the United States, frustrated by the failure of its policy in China, did not recognize the new regime, and British and American polices were thus at odds in the Far East.

In this context, Britain's policies in South and Southeast Asia took on another dimension. There, it aimed to respect, though also to shape, the attitudes adopted by the independent or soon-to-be independent nations. In particular, it recognized the importance in itself and, in respect of its influence over others, of India. India, too, recognized the Central People's government. India and Britain, it was clear, had something in common. Less obviously, the attitudes and policies of India and of other nations in South and Southeast Asia became a means through which Britain might influence the policies of the United States. The notion that it must do so became all the more important when it ceased to be merely a matter of funding development.

With the opening of the Korean War, still greater issues were at stake. Britain endorsed the U.S. position on Korea in the summer of 1950, though, heavily burdened by its NATO commitment, it was at first reluctant to send ground troops.[35] The action of interposing the Seventh Fleet between the mainland and Taiwan, which Britain found much less acceptable, put off the chances of accepting the Central People's government into the comity of nations. The United States was now once again stirred into action in the Far East, but that made it more necessary, not less, for Britain to try to influence its policies. A provocative policy toward China might prompt it to take Hong Kong and to intervene in Korea or elsewhere. An extended conflict in the Far East—whether or not they had given the signal for it—might give the Russians an opportunity in Europe and even lead to general war, with the possible use of atomic weapons.

Before World War II, British policy in East Asia had been constrained by its need for security in Europe and by its relationship with the United States, which had ruled out a compromise with the Japanese, then the chief threat to the status quo. For such a compromise could only be reached at the expense of the Chinese, and in defiance both of the long-standing sympathy the United States expressed for their cause and of the principles for which the United States stood, as set out, for example, in Henry Stimson's nonrecognition doctrine in respect of Manchuria of February 1932 and Cordell Hull's statement at the opening of the undeclared war in July 1937. If Britain had defied the United States, it might have secured a Far Eastern Munich. It would, however, have damaged Anglo-American relations. Though there was no guarantee of support from the Americans in a European crisis, the chances of securing it could not be risked by making a deal in a region of lesser priority that would alienate the Americans.

The current position, though very different, was not without its similarities. Britain had to go along with the United States in the Far East, lest it risk alienating its guarantee of ultimate support in Europe. Yet, while renewed American interest in Asia might be welcome, the form it took expanded the difference between American and British policies on China. Britain's line had been to combine recognition of the new government with opposition to its expansion elsewhere through a closer association among the new nation-states of South and Southeast Asia and through a closer relationship with them, initially built on acceptance of their nationalism and contribution toward their development. That line remained. But it also became a means by which Britain might shape American policy. In that sense, it emphasized what Britain and India had in common.

The approach was set out in a paper Bevin presented to the cabinet at the end of August 1950. Since the end of the war, it began, Britain's policy in South and Southeast Asia had been to "encourage the legitimate aspirations of the peoples of that area for independence." Supporting nationalism was indeed "the best possible counter to communist subversion and penetration." The United States had seen South and Southeast Asia as "primarily a British interest." Only during 1949 did it become disposed to give Southeast Asia more attention, "largely owing to the Communist threat," and Britain hoped that it would be prepared to contribute to economic development. In the Far East, by contrast, the Americans had "tended to be a law unto themselves": they had not consulted others, yet their policies were without clear direction. The initial reaction in Asia to the U.S.-led and UN-sponsored intervention in Korea had been positive, but second thoughts had followed, and India was specially worried "lest American action should jeopardise the friendly relations which India herself is bent on establishing with China. But the feeling is probably more widespread that the United States is intervening in Asia and seeking to determine its future in a way unpleasing to the peoples of Asia and likely to be to their detriment. Though countries like Siam and the Philippines pay lip service to the United States they are not themselves held in high repute. India, on the other hand, has an undoubted influence on Asian opinion." There was a "distinct possibility" that, unless U.S. policy took more account of Asian opinion and susceptibilities, "we shall find that Asia is gradually alienated from the West, which could only be to the benefit of the Soviet Union."[36]

China, Bevin went on, was the subject of bitter controversy in the United States, and the prospect of elections in November made the situation more acute. The American public was likely to be "irrational" and unreasonable toward Britain where its policy diverged. The problem was to persuade the United States "not to adopt policies in relation to the Far East which will fail to command general support amongst friendly nations and which will antagonise Asia." Britain's methods must not be "obtrusive," nor should the onus fall on Britain alone. Bevin's plan was to try to get the State Department to agree to consult with other powers, especially the Commonwealth and France and possible some other European countries. The next step would be to get the support of other friendly members of the United Nations, and so build up a common front against any attempts of the Soviet Union to create a split. "The task will obviously be a difficult one, but it offers the best hope of reconciling United States and Asian opinion and of enabling the Commonwealth to keep in line with the United States. Only by pursuing this course can we hope to avoid open divergence with the United States on China and the related question of Formosa, and the unfortunate consequences which might ensure in the present highly-charged atmosphere in the United States."[37]

The Korean War did in fact expand, thanks in part to General Douglas MacArthur, the "mad satrap," as Gladwyn Jebb called him, and the Chinese introduced "volunteer" troops.[38] The anxiety of the British government increased, particularly when it seemed that President Harry S. Truman contemplated the use of atomic weapons. In the event, however, the conflict was contained, the satrap was dismissed, and truce talks began. In the meantime, British attitudes and policies remained within the framework that Bevin had set out, even when the Labour government was displaced by Conservatives in the election of October 1951.

The same was true in Southeast Asia itself. In Malaya, effective measures against the communists were adopted even before the Conservatives combined both political and military power in a "strong man," Sir Gerald Templer, and they were the more effective because they were placed in a political context. Malaya was in fact set on a faster track toward self-government and independence.[39] In the chaos that beset Burma after independence, the British stood by the Rangoon government, despite the distrust that the Karen insurgency provoked, and by the poor relations between Ne Win and the British Services Mission provided under the defense agreement of 1947. The British also pressed for the withdrawal of the Kuomintang troops that penetrated Burma from 1950. Covert American support did not cease with the dismissal of MacArthur. But the British insisted that their presence, an invitation to intervention by the Central People's government, also promoted instability and prevented the Burmese government from focusing on it.[40]

Coming to terms with Indonesian nationalism was made more difficult by the West New Guinea dispute, inasmuch as Australia, an essential Commonwealth partner, opposed its transfer to the republic on security grounds. But, if the Dutch had otherwise "disappeared from the scene" as a colonial power in Southeast Asia, to borrow the phrase MacDonald had used in advocating the Colombo Conference, the French had not. Indochina still stood in the way of the kind of regional approach the British had long contemplated. Indeed, the Korean War made it seem essential that the French should continue their struggle. Even if the Central People's government confined itself to aiding and training the Việt Minh and did not overtly cross this border, the communists might come to power. And the British—with World War II again in mind—believed that it would be difficult to "hold" the rest of Southeast Asia in that event. Neither the United Kingdom nor indeed the United States was, however, prepared to send in its own forces. That might indeed provoke Chinese intervention. There could be no more Koreas.

The continued role of the French made it difficult to pursue the regional diplomacy that the British had been following. That was evident, for example, in the debate within the Foreign Office on the prospects of a regional defense pact. It had been dismissed on the ground that no new commitments could be made and that, given the "determined neutralism" of India, and also Burma and Indonesia, it would be seen as a white man's pact, underwriting French colonialism. The conclusion of the Australia, New Zealand, and United States Treaty revived the debate, and Dalton Murray was inclined to discount the effect of a treaty on India.[41] The matter was reconsidered when the Conservatives' election pamphlet "Britain Strong and Free" called for a "NATO for the Far East." A minute by J. C. Petrie rather sought to square the circle.

> What would appear to be required . . . is a purely South-East Asian treaty of friendship, not openly anti-communist or even purely "defensive," and in which the stress would be laid on promoting closer economic, political and social collaboration between the parties. Within this alliance there might be provision for mutual defence planning in case of attack in which the United States, France and the U.K. would participate, with Australia and New Zealand.[42]

India, Petrie thought, "might take the lead in the regional alliance, and possibly take part in the defence planning."[43] "This kind of thing we are always working towards," Murray commented in the margin, "but even the Colombo Plan has had only limited success and there is really not much to make these countries cohere—except the immediate external threat which some of them refuse to recognise." Lord Ismay, the new secretary of state for Commonwealth relations, thought, however, that the idea needed more political preparation. "India would probably react violently to the proposed Defence Pact, and might take the lead amongst the Asian states in denouncing it."[44]

The consistency of British policies and attitudes was again illustrated—alongside their problematic nature—when the Foreign Office studied the implications of the U.S. presidential elections late in 1952. "British policy," as R. H. Scott put it, "is to maintain a firm and united front against communist aggression and at the same time to search for a modus vivendi." He looked, as in Europe, for "normal contacts with the communists, though of a distant and formal kind, and a collective Pact for the defence of the free world against them."[45] Recognition was not, however, on the agenda of the new U.S. administration, nor any deal that implied further "losses" to the communists. The talk was of "massive retaliation" and of "unleashing" the Chinese nationalists, which alarmed the United States' allies as much as its opponents.

The divergence between U.S. and UK policies became still more apparent in 1954 when it became evident that the French could or would not continue the struggle in Vietnam and the move toward a settlement in Korea became the occasion for a similar move in Indochina. John Foster Dulles called for "united action." The ambiguity of the phrase aroused apprehension. There was a dispute with Sir Anthony Eden that might be compared to that between Stimson and Sir John Simon, the British foreign secretary in 1932. At a meeting in London in April, Eden apparently agreed to an immediate examination of the possibilities of a collective defense, and then insisted that it could not proceed before the convening of the conference in Geneva. His argument related first to the attitude of India, and then about Pakistan, Burma, and Ceylon at the Colombo Conference. The minutes rather supported Dulles. "Quite apart from any question of texts," Eden told his ambassador in Washington, "I should have thought any one could have foreseen the reactions . . . on the Colombo Conference, . . . to say nothing of Geneva." Increasingly, the Americans neglected "the feelings and difficulties of their allies," creating "mounting difficulties for anyone in this country who wants to maintain close Anglo-American relations. We at least have constantly to bear in mind all our Commonwealth partners, even if the United States does not like some of them."[46] Moving ahead without those powers would only alienate them. It was recommended that the discussion about collective defense should be deferred.

It was indeed taken up after the conclusion of the Geneva agreements. It is striking, but quite understandable, that the British made efforts to square the circle, trying to win the assent, even the participation of the Colombo powers. Except in the case of Pakistan, participation did not eventuate. Eden nevertheless approved the Manila Treaty. "From the wider standpoint of meeting Americans without giving Colombo Powers reasonable grounds for grievance the Treaty is a diplomatic triumph."[47] The hope that other Southeast Asian countries would join persisted. The main obstacle, James Cable argued, was that they saw it as "entirely an instrument of American foreign policy." It was an argument, he thought, against making Bangkok the seat of the treaty, since Thailand was seen as an American puppet.[48]

British foreign policy has been criticized for its emphasis on a world role and, in keeping with more recent fashions, for its lack of "strategic thinking." Neither accusation seems quite just. So far as Asia was concerned, Britain's attitudes and policies were quite thoroughly developed and articulated, and both were consistent and adaptable. They also took account of Britain's weakness. The illusion lay in the belief that they could influence U.S. policy. However, this influence was held in check by strict limits. Perhaps, too, they overestimated India's strength. The differences between Eden and Dulles, though they became personalized, were not merely personal. Nor was it even, perhaps, a matter of the disparity of power. The differences should be seen in the context of differences of approach, to which the disparity of power contributed. As before the war, so now, the United States could take its stand on principle, and it put no priority on coming to terms that sacrificed this principle. Britain, by contrast, inherited a more pragmatic tradition, and its weakness disposed it all the more to seek compromises by diplomacy and to look for the modus vivendi.

# 9

# The "Grand Design"

## British Policy, Local Politics, and the Making of Malaysia, 1955–1961

*Tan Tai Yong*

In September 1963, Britain ended colonial rule in Singapore, Sarawak, and Sabah (North Borneo), by amalgamating these ethnically distinct states with the newly independent Malaya to form an expanded federation known as Malaysia. The making of Malaysia was an important landmark in the postwar history of Southeast Asia. It marked, in a single stroke, the end of the formal British Empire in Southeast Asia (excepting Brunei); yet, at the same time, the very formation of a "Greater Malaysia" provided for the establishment of a sizeable Commonwealth bastion centrally positioned in Southeast Asia, which provided that crucial link in an extensive British strategic and military presence stretching from Aden to New Zealand.

In itself, the making of Malaysia, although a relatively small state compared to Indonesia to its south and Thailand to its north, represented state-formation on quite an ambitious scale. It essentially entailed the integration of four distinct entities—in terms of historical development, ethnic makeup, and varying stages of political and economic development—into a single unified nation-state. There was little historical basis for Malaysia, and the new state came into being following a seemingly short period of deliberations and negotiations. Official talks on the formation of Malaysia began in earnest in 1961, and two years later, the Federation of Malaysia was established. The problems of such a contrived yet complex exercise in state-building, within a relatively compressed preparatory phase, was evident no more than two years after its formation, when Singapore, which was merged with the federation in September 1963, separated from Malaysia in August 1965 and became an independent state in its own right. Indeed, the breakup of Singapore from Malaysia has continued to plague relations between the two countries, and the historical interpretations of the reasons and circumstances leading to separation have been grist to the mill of the on-and-off strained relations between Singapore and Malaysia for the past thirty years. The making of the Federation of Malaysia, therefore, forms an epochal episode not only in the history of the region, but also in features very strongly in the national consciousness of present-day Malaysia and Singapore. In view of this, the reasons for the formation of Malaysia and the circumstances leading to it need deeper excavation. Why and how did Greater Malaysia come about in 1963?

By most accounts, the formation of Malaysia has often been attributed to a bold initiative taken by Tunku Abdul Rahman, the Malayan prime minister, in 1961. On May 27, 1961, at a Foreign Correspondent's Association luncheon meeting at the Adelphi Hotel in Singapore, the Tunku sounded the possibility of bringing the territories of Singapore, Borneo, Brunei, Sarawak, and the Federation of Malaya "closer together in political and economic cooperation." Although the idea of a union between Malaya and the Borneo states had been floating around United Malays National Organization circles from about 1956, and was already well established by 1960, this public announcement by the Malayan prime minister has often been taken as the genesis of the Malaysia idea as a "practical and realistic proposal," one that saw fruition two years later, in September 1963.[1] The main reason for the Tunku's initiative was essentially political: he had to overcome his earlier reluctance for a merger with Singapore in an attempt to avoid the risk of having a "Cuba in his Malayan backyard."[2] He had come to accept that an independent, Chinese-dominated Singapore, which might become increasingly oriented toward Peking, would be a greater danger to Malaya than a Singapore, which, if brought into the federation, he could exercise political control over. Years after the event, the Tunku admitted that he had also harbored the romantic notion of his newly independent Malayan federation offering a natural beacon of freedom, attracting the other still colonized states in the region to come into association with it as the way toward freedom. As he recalled in 1975, "Merdeka brought such happy years to Malaya, such peace, progress and prosperity, that it was only natural that other States in the region, which were still 'British' should look towards Kuala Lumpur, the glint of freedom in their eyes, thinking of ways to come into closer association."[3]

Such a view may have been indicative of an elder statesman reminiscing personal glories in the twilight of his political career, but it does generate the impression that Greater Malaysia was borne out of the initiative and will of the Tunku.

While the Malayan premier may have triggered the processes that led to the formation of Malaysia, political impulses for a return of Singapore to the Malayan fold had already been evident in Singapore long before 1961. David Marshall, Singapore's first chief minister, and Lim Yew Hock, his successor, had both pursued the merger objective during their respective tenures in office in the 1950s. Although taken out of the Malayan Union, and later the federation, after World War II, politicians in the little island colony knew instinctively, and perhaps pragmatically, that the political future of Singapore lay in a remerger with the federation up north. While the timing was not quite right and the circumstances far from propitious in the 1950s, with Malaya under Emergency rule and inching gradually toward independence on its own, political leaders in Singapore from Marshall to Lee Kuan Yew knew that they had to somehow keep alive the hopes of a merger. Chief Minister Marshall had in December 1955 made an official request to the British government to use "its good offices with the governments of the Federation of Malaya and the States of Sarawak, Brunei and North Borneo to urge the consideration of a federation of all these territories and Singapore," while Lim Yew Hock had repeatedly spoken of how union with the federation would solve Singapore's economic problems, but was aware, at the same time, that the Tunku would not countenance union because of the Chinese factor.[4] Although in opposition from 1955 to 1959, the People's Action Party (PAP) had shared the conviction that merger was a political objective, which a responsible government in Singapore had to pursue. When it was elected to office in 1959, the PAP and Prime Minister Lee became the chief advocates of the merger with the federation, and it was a policy they pursued to a successful conclusion in 1963.

An alternative view has it that it was not so much the Tunku or the advocates of the merger in Singapore, but the British that were the driving force behind the formation of Greater Malaysia. This interpretation argued that Malaysia was indeed made in London, and its outcome was an expression of a successful attempt at imposing a form of British neocolonialism in Southeast Asia.[5] This view argued that the transformation of the erstwhile British colonies in Southeast Asia into a new Commonwealth state was indeed a remarkable feat of British decolonization in the 1960s. In Malaya, the British were able to conspire with a local elite that they had created to establish a postcolonial entity in Southeast Asia that would continue to maintain British commercial and strategic interests in the region. Following this, the British attached the strategic colony of Singapore, thereby assisting the noncommunist PAP government in defeating its communist foes, and in the process preserving the important military bases in Singapore well into the late 1960s. In a single stroke, the British, too, managed to solve the problems of the "politically undeveloped" states of North Borneo and Sarawak, by allowing them independence as part of the greater Malaysian state. Indeed, Malaysia worked so well that it came to be argued that the new state represented a very successful attempt by the British to impose a form of neocolonialism in Southeast Asia.

Anthony J. Stockwell challenges the neocolonialism theory by pointing out that while the idea of Malaysia did not clash with British objectives of regional consolidation, in reality, "Britain lacked the power locally to secure control over its continuing interests in the post-colonial period."[6] He further points out that British interests in the region had changed from economics to security, and that policy makers in Britain were precisely keen on Greater Malaysia because it offered a solution to the problem of maintaining regional security at minimum cost to British taxpayers. Finally, Stockwell maintains that the inspiration and initiative for Malaysia came from the federation and Singapore, and that Britain merely "followed their lead, but never commanded the heights from which it might assert mastery over the planning and execution of the "Grand Design."[7] Stockwell's conclusions are supported by some recent research: Karl Hack, for instance, asserts pithily that " the reason for federation . . . had much to do with local developments, little to do with British plotting."[8]

This chapter suggests that while the idea of Greater Malaysia did not necessarily constitute an attempt at imposing British neocolonialism in Southeast Asia, the formation of a "Dominion of Southeast Asia" had long been a British desire as it seemed to offer an attractive political solution for Southeast Asia in view of Britain's "reluctance to hold its defense umbrella over the area for a moment longer than was necessary."[9] But far from being a carefully laid out plan for decolonizing in Southeast Asia, the Grand Design remained very much an idea that lurked in secret files until events on the ground, namely political developments in Singapore, intervened. Although the plan was first conceived in the immediate aftermath of the war, it only sprang to life in the late 1950s, and thereafter, drawing on local initiatives and interests, the British were able to dovetail their objectives with developments in Malaya and Singapore, thus bringing about a mutually beneficial arrangement in the form of the Federation of Malaysia. Reflecting on events when he was the UK commissioner of Singapore and British commissioner in Southeast Asia, Lord Selkirk recounted that "Whitehall in fact took no initiative until the Federation had been proposed, first in private and then in public, by the Prime Minister of Malaya and immediately supported by the Prime Minister of Singapore. . . . It was only after the proposals had been endorsed by all the territories concerned that Whitehall gave its full cooperation to the establishment of the Federation and sought to make it a success."[10]

In suggesting that Whitehall merely followed the lead provided by the leaders in Malaya and Singapore, Selkirk was perhaps understating the role played by the Commonwealth and colonial offices in effecting Malaysia. Although the Tunku's May 1961 announcement had made Malaysia a practical proposition, the deal was, at that point in time, far from done. What

followed from the announcement was a complex exercise involving complicated negotiations of the terms by which Singapore would merge with the
Malayan federation as well as the intricate maneuverings by which the Borneo
Territories were cajoled into joining Malaysia. In all of this, without the role
of an "honest broker," played admirably by British officials in the region, the
Malaysian enterprise, riven as it were by doubts, disagreements, and distrusts, would have been aborted at an early stage. In the upshot, the idea of a
greater federation of Malaysia, shelved for the greater part of the 1940s and
1950s, surfaced with a full vengeance in the late 1950s when the full impact
of the Suez crisis and political instability in Singapore came to be appreciated by London. Thereafter, riding on political developments in Singapore
and Malaya, the British were able to broker a deal, which eventually saw the
integration of Singapore and the Borneo Territories (excluding Brunei) into
the Malayan federation to form Malaysia.

## British Postwar Policy in Southeast Asia

The idea of a federation of proximate, if disparate, territories, as an objective
of British policy in postwar Southeast Asia had been discussed in British
official circles from as early 1945. When the British returned to their empire
in Southeast Asia in 1945, their primary aim was to reestablish security and
stability, thereby creating the necessary conditions for rehabilitation and economic revival. In pursuing these objectives, the British sought to base their
policies on a regional approach.[11] The consolidation of regionalism—based
on security pacts, policy coordination, and economic cooperation—was regarded as essential to the stability of the region, and its natural corollary was
the coming together, eventually, of the states of Southeast Asia into a regional bloc. Indeed, the appointment of Malcolm MacDonald as secretary-
general in Southeast Asia in 1946, with certain authority over the four
governors, was essentially aimed at preventing the British dependencies in
the region from drifting in different directions.

An ultimate union of the British territories in Southeast Asia—Malaya,
Singapore, and the Borneo Territories—was, therefore, regarded from very
early on as a long-term British objective there. In a 1952 minute on "Malaya," J. J. Paskin, the assistant undersecretary of state responsible for the
Hong Kong and Pacific and Southeast Asia Departments of the Colonial Office, commented that "from 1945 onwards it has been Colonial Office policy
that there should be closer association between (a) the Federation and
Singapore, and (b) the Borneo territories; and there was also hope that there
would ultimately be a union of the Malayan and the Borneo territories."[12]

Indeed, in the 1940s and early 1950s it had seemed that it was part of

Britain's grand plan for the region that there would be "no apportioning of self-government to the territories individually, but in blocs."[13]

The idea of a single dominion made up of British dependencies in Southeast Asia was articulated as the Grand Design, and because it was likely to be anchored on the Federation of Malaya, it was alternatively known as "Greater Malaysia." Regionalism seemed to offer the best solution to British policy makers who had to contend with the pressures of having to plan for decolonization in Southeast Asia on the one hand, and having to ensure stability in the region, particularly in the context of defense and security considerations in Asia generated by the Cold War, on the other. With the emergence of communist China as the major power in Asia, as well as problems in the fringe of Southeast Asia, in Burma, Vietnam, and Indonesia, it was crucial to British interests in the region that the process of decolonization should ensure that its colonies be turned eventually into faithful Commonwealth members. A federation of Britain's erstwhile colonies in Southeast Asia into a single dominion, or the Grand Design, was seen as the best guarantee of that.[14]

The concept of the Grand Design, referring to the desired end of British policy in Southeast Asia, through the amalgamation of Malaya, Singapore, Sarawak, Brunei, and North Borneo into a single political entity, was taken to denote an overall game plan (but not a time table) for decolonization in Southeast Asia. It envisaged as a first phase the merger of Singapore with the federation, to be followed by the association of the colonies of Sarawak, North Borneo, and the protected state of Brunei. Finally, in the third and ultimate phase the desired British objective was for an amalgamation of these two regional blocs into one single political unit.

Throughout the late 1940s and early 1950s, however, the Grand Design remained a vague concept, and it never really generated much active interest, nor gathered its own momentum.[15] British governors and high commissioners spoke about the possibility of integration or amalgamation in conferences on the political future of British colonies in Southeast Asia, but the idea never obtained serious official consideration, nor were there any concrete plans, detailing the timing or manner of the withdrawal of the British from the region, ever laid out or submitted as a firm policy proposal to Whitehall.

That the Grand Design did not elicit excited response from policy makers and the men on the spot did not necessarily reflect a lack of belief in the feasibility of the concept. Indeed, there was almost unanimous agreement that as an "ultimate objective" there was little that was disputable. Right across the region, unification, rather than dispersion, seemed to be the shared desire of the colonial officials.

Although Singapore and the federation were separated in 1946, the British had stated that it had been no part of their policy "to preclude or prejudice in any way the fusion of Singapore and the Malayan Union in a wider union at a later date."[16] The colonial office had always had in mind that Singapore and Malaya would one day merge and "had on many occasions blessed the idea in public," for without merger, it failed to see any hope for Singapore's economy.[17] More fundamentally, there were concerns that an independent Singapore, on its own, would quickly fall prey to the communists.[18]

Likewise, the possibilities of closer association of the colonies of Sarawak, North Borneo, and the protected state of Brunei had been canvassed for a number of years, both in the Borneo Territories as well as the United Kingdom. British policy makers felt that the three territories were individually very vulnerable "both because of their geographical position and the racial make-up."[19] It was also felt that their powerful neighbors, China, Indonesia, and the Philippines, "all have, or could easily work up, interests of one kind or another."[20] Individual independence for these territories would have rendered each too vulnerable, and was considered, therefore, unworkable.

In 1957, local opinion in Brunei, Sarawak, and Sabah came out openly, if mildly, in favor of some form of closer association and of there being some public discussion to explore the idea. Sir Robert Scott, the commissioner-general in Southeast Asia, and Sir Anthony Abell and Sir Roland Turnbull, the governors of Sarawak and North Borneo, respectively, at that time strongly urged that the initiative should then be taken and that local discussion should be encouraged, although London had not given "firm direction" on the policy to be pursued there.[21]

In December 1957, the secretary of state for the colonies authorized the governors of Sarawak and North Borneo to initiate public discussion on closer association in their territories. Indeed, William Goode recalled that his brief in going to North Borneo in the 1950s as governor was to work for a closer association between the Borneo Territories as a preliminary to the ultimate aim of a greater federation with Malaya and Singapore.[22] But, a caveat was quickly added: an association of North Borneo and Sarawak would be regarded as unfeasible unless Brunei, with its oil money, would be part of the federation. The sultan of Brunei, at that time, showed no enthusiasm for participation in talks for closer association with North Borneo and Sarawak alone.[23] It was, therefore, envisaged that, in the long run, if these territories were to achieve independence on a viable and effective basis, they should be included in some wider association that would involve Singapore and Malaya.[24]

The belief in the Grand Design notwithstanding, developments on the ground seemed to suggest a reverse trend. Instead of the territories being drawn closer together, they seemed to be pulling apart. The first objective of merger between Singapore and the federation receded into the background by the mid-1950s, owing to quite distinct but not unconnected political events in Singapore and Malaya. In Singapore, it was the growing influence of the communists and procommunist movement in the political arena and the radicalization of Chinese politics that raised much concern in the federation, itself embroiled in a desperate struggle against a determined and well-organized communist insurgency. Under the circumstances, merger between the two territories could not be contemplated, and the whole idea was eventually put on the back burner when independence had to be conceded to the federation in 1957. Even after independence, the Federation of Malaya was not prepared to contemplate absorbing Singapore for fear of the destructive effect that such a merger would have on its Malay and Chinese population. There were also deep, inherent distrusts between the tiny Brunei sultanate and its neighbors in North Borneo. Religious, territorial, ethnic, and historical animosities, compounded by the reluctance to share oil wealth, all contributed to limiting any real progress toward closer association.[25] Senior colonial officials in the Borneo Territories admitted that while the Grand Design had laudable objectives, it was "too neat and pat a scheme that seemed to gloss over many obvious pitfalls," and there were differences in political systems and patterns of trade that had to be overcome if any association were to be made workable.[26]

Notwithstanding these developments, it should be noted that the British never abandoned their idea of a Grand Design for Southeast Asia. The idea was revived at the end of the 1950s and gained an added degree of currency and urgency in British circles, fueled essentially by their concerns about the impending independence for Singapore, especially in the wake of Malaya's independence. With the imminent constitutional development in Singapore leading inexorably to a diminution of British rule and eventual independence for the island colony, the Colonial Office became increasingly concerned that the British military bases located there should not be jeopardized, especially by the communists who seemed to be gaining political ground over the moderates. The only way to secure the bases was to ensure that Singapore would not turn "Red," and the best way to ensure this was to make certain that it became part of the staunchly anticommunist Malaya.[27] A merger between Singapore and the federation and subsequently the incorporation of the Borneo Territories would do much, so the British reasoned, to secure a key area in Southeast Asia. A stable federation would reduce the dangers that the smaller units might be affected piecemeal by subversive elements either from within or outside the borders. Most importantly, from the British point of view, the formation of an anticommunist federation would provide some degree of stability in Southeast Asia, thus enabling the British to reduce internal security responsibilities in the region.[28]

Consequently, after a series of visits to Singapore and Malaya by Duncan Sandys, secretary for commonwealth relations, John Profumo, secretary for defense, and Admiral Lord Louis Mountbatten, chief of the British Defense Staff and admiral of the fleet, the British were sufficiently encouraged that the gestures and responses from the local politicians indicated that the Grand Design was now very much on the cards. Indeed, in July 1960 the secretary of state for the colonies submitted a memorandum to the Colonial Policy Committee calling for the British government to accept as the "ultimate aim of her policy the development of a political association between Malaya, Singapore and the Borneo territories." On October 20, 1960, a meeting was held at Kuching, Sarawak, and arising from the conclusions of that meeting and further discussions at the Eden Hall Conference in January 1961, in which the views of the governors of Sarawak and North Borneo, as well as the high commissioner of Brunei, Kuala Lumpur, and Canberra, and the British ambassador to Indonesia were represented, Lord Selkirk presented a number of recommendations.[29]

The British government would work toward bringing about a closer political association between Malaya, Singapore, and the three Borneo Territories, but the progress toward this goal "would be gradual and adjusted to the rate of political evolution in the Borneo Territories." As a first step, ties between North Borneo and Sarawak should be strengthened with the intention of the two territories eventually forming a single unit, and if Brunei chose to join in, it would be encouraged. Concurrently, the British would encourage "any development leading to co-operation between Malaya, Singapore and the Borneo territories," and "should avoid political or economic developments . . . which would cut across the idea of an ultimate association of the five territories." Whenever opportunities arose, the British should discuss the matter in confidence with interested parties such as the Tunku, Lee, and the sultan of Brunei, and after with the support of these protagonists, the British should issue in public statements to the effect that "a broad association between the Federation and Singapore and the Borneo territories [had] great possibilities for the future of the area."[30]

On April 18, 1961, the question of the Grand Design was considered at a meeting of the Colonial Policy Committee, during which it was decided that subject to the views of the governments of Australia and New Zealand, the British government would accept the development of a political association between Malaya, Singapore, and the three Borneo Territories as "an ultimate aim of policy." As they saw it, the Grand Design was "the most likely policy to satisfy long-term United Kingdom interests in the region."[31] This was confirmed by a comprehensive defense report submitted by the Joint Planning Staff, after taking into consideration the views of the Foreign, Commonwealth Relations, and Colonial Offices.[32]

Having enunciated their policy, the British decided to take a cautious approach to the whole scheme, realizing that the plan would only succeed if it had the full support of the Malayan and Singapore political leaders. Lord Selkirk, the commissioner-general of Southeast Asia, was, therefore, advised to push along the matter of a merger between Singapore and Malaya with their respective leaders. This was the critical part of the puzzle: if the British could succeed in sealing an agreement here, the rest would be easy—the Borneo Territories would have to fit somehow. As the chiefs of staff were later to admit, from the British viewpoint, the "principal objective of Malaysia" was the merger of Malaya and Singapore.[33] In any case, to planners in Whitehall, a greater Malaysian federation incorporating North Borneo, Sarawak, and Brunei would also produce a satisfactory solution to the problem of the future constitutional status of the three Borneo Territories, while at the same time reduce claims on the territories by Indonesia or the Philippines. Federating with Malaya and Singapore would provide the most sensible path toward self-government status within the Commonwealth.

## The PAP in Power: Independence through Merger, 1959–1961

In Singapore, the British found in Lee Kuan Yew an ardent advocate of merger. Lee had been deeply convinced on the need for a merger from the very outset of his political career, believing it to be absolutely vital to the survival of a noncommunist and prosperous Singapore. Indeed, he had argued that the frontier between Singapore and the federation was a "freak man-made [one created] by the fancy of planners and map-makers in London," and that "the relentless logic of geography and the force of historical, ethnic and economic forces all point to the inevitability of merger."[34]

History and geography aside, Lee was convinced that separate independence for Singapore would be a "dangerous illusion." Lee's belief in the necessity of a merger was borne out of a hard-nosed assessment of the economic realities facing Singapore. The rapid growth of the island's population, coupled with a declining entrepôt trade, had posed a serious economic problem, especially as opportunities for employment failed to increase at a corresponding pace.

Entrepôt trade, the mainstay of Singapore's economy, was threatened by several countries choosing to engage in direct trading themselves and, in some cases, by taking measures to protect their own industries. Industrialization seemed to be the most viable option for Singapore, if it were to create enough jobs for its young and fast growing population as well as cut its dependence on the entrepôt trade.

But in this, Singapore faced three principal difficulties: first, there was the competition that it had to face from the federation in attracting investors; second, there were the tariffs set by the federation that acted as a barrier to the entry of Singapore-manufactured goods into the federation markets; and third, investors were invariably drawn to areas of low labor costs outside Singapore. Several of Singapore's fledging rubber footwear manufacturers, for instance, facing fierce competition from Japan and Hong Kong, had to move from Singapore into the federation to secure tariff protection.

There seemed to be no simple solution: If Singapore were to be forced by circumstances to restrict imports of goods that competed with the island's industries, it would have to compromise the island's free port status. For political reasons, Singapore would have wished to exclude Malayan products from its protective duties, but it could not do so under the General Agreement on Tariffs and Trade rules unless it formed either a customs union, which would involve Singapore adopting a tariff similar to the Malayan tariff, though the level would have to be lower, or a free trade area between Singapore and the Malayan federation.[35]

There were other problems. For industrialization to be viable, a large market was needed. The internal market in Singapore was simply too small to sustain a highly capitalized process. While the Federation of Malaya would have been Singapore's natural market, its tariff barriers made Singapore's goods uncompetitive as they crossed the causeway. In view of this, the Singapore government viewed with urgency the advantages of integrated industrial development in the context of a common market with the federation. However, suggestions for a common market failed to impress the federation government, which saw little to gain from it. Kuala Lumpur had pointed out, quite rightly, that a common market would involve observing similar customs duties and that as long as Singapore completely retained its free port status, a common market would give a preponderant advantage to it. The Malayan federation would have nothing to gain from a common market that would open its own markets to goods manufactured in Singapore but that in turn gave it no advantages in the Singapore market, which it did not already possess. The logic was certainly incontrovertible. The Federation of Malaya had a normal range of tariffs on imported goods, including those bought from Singapore, while the latter, as a free port could only collect duties on alcohol, tobacco, and petroleum intended for domestic consumption. Goods manufactured in the federation thus enjoyed free entry into Singapore, while goods made in Singapore had to pass through a tariff barrier before they could be marketed in the federation. If a common market was not going to work, Singapore's hopes for economic survival, it seemed, would have to rest with a merger with Malaya.

In addition to economic pressures, there were powerful political reasons, from the PAP's perspective, for early independence through a merger. Chinese chauvinism, fed by economic frustrations and the popular appeal of anti-imperialism (especially with the British enjoying full rights of occupation, control, and use of the bases on the island), had created a conducive environment for the political left, particularly the procommunist radicals. Indeed, by 1960 there were growing signs that the influence of the communists was growing stronger and more pervasive. For the embattled prime minister of Singapore, a merger with Malaya was critical to strengthen his defenses against the communist influence.

From its inauguration in 1954, therefore, the PAP had adopted, as its main policy, independence for Singapore through merger with the Federation of Malaya. From the outset, however, it had realized that the possibility of achieving this aim in the context of the times seemed remote. The PAP knew that the present alliance government in Malaya was antimerger because it was afraid that the inclusion of one million Chinese from Singapore would upset the racial balance of power in the federation and was inherently distrustful of the Chinese-supported "leftists" in Singapore. Based on that assessment, the PAP realized that it had to first allay these fears in the federation before it could create the necessary conditions for a merger.

While in the opposition benches between 1955 and 1959, the PAP demonstrated its readiness to cooperate with the federation government when Lee took the politically difficult position of supporting the institution of the Internal Security Council to control security in Singapore. He knew that this would please Kuala Lumpur, and had rationalized that as the PAP's ultimate aim was to effect a merger between Singapore and Malaya, "it was only logical that the Federation be given a decisive voice in the affairs of Singapore, including its security."[36] Lee pursued this line persistently. At the PAP's annual general meeting held in Singapore on August 4, 1957, he defined the party's long-term policy as the establishment of "an independent democratic, non-Communist, socialist Malaya";[37] later that year, following the constitutional talks in London, Lee maintained that independence for Singapore was not possible until a merger with the federation was achieved; and just before the 1959 election, he had obtained an undertaking from key PAP players— Lim Chin Siong, Fong Swee Suan, James Puthucheary, and Devan Nair (all four who had been detained by the Lim Yew Hock government in 1956)— that they would support the making of a noncommunist Malaya and that merger was the way to independence.[38]

In 1959, the Lee-led PAP scored a decisive victory in the general election that brought internal self-government for Singapore. As independence through merger had been a major part of the PAP electoral platform in the 1959 election, Lee saw the resounding electoral victory of the PAP in that election as a public and popular endorsement of the merger objective. It was regarded as a national endorsement for government, which he now headed, to go on a re-lentless pursuit for a merger. Convincing the Singapore electorate and his political opponents of the need for a merger was one aspect of Lee's political battle; it was another trying to convince the federation government to want to merger with Singapore.

Therefore, it is hardly surprising that Lee, from 1955, had been persuad-ing the Tunku on the need for a merger between the two territories. Lee had argued that the Singapore problem was an integral part of the wider Malayan problem, and that "it was easier if [the Tunku] were to include [Singapore] in his overall calculations . . . than if he were to try to pass the problem child to the British."[39] Gradually, as Lee explained, "the unpleasant facts were placed before the Federation Government. . . . What had been publicly known was that Malaya was vital to Singapore. But what we did not emphasize . . . was that Singapore was vital to their survival."[40] However, each time Lee men-tioned merger as a possibility, or as a desirable objective, the Tunku would be quick to deny any possibility of a merger in the foreseeable future and to point out that Malaya had to first settle its own racial policies. For a long time, therefore, the Tunku decided to shut his ears to all suggestions of a merger.[41] The Tunku was deeply distrustful of the political policies of the Singapore government, believing the latter to be too lax in its attitude toward communism, and was, therefore, suspicious of any proposals for any action that might be interpreted as the first steps toward a political merger of the two territories.

Because the PAP's declared aim of independence through merger with the federation was vulnerable to destructive criticism from Lee's political oppo-nents, owing to the federation's lack of interest in any union with Singapore, Lee was keen to explore the idea of a route to independence through a wider political association that would include the Borneo Territories. Indeed, both the federation and Singapore government had independently been taking an active interest in the Borneo Territories, and following a meeting with the governors of these territories, the commissioner-general recommended in October 1959 that discreet encouragement should be given to the interests that the prime ministers of both the federation and Singapore had been tak-ing in the wider association with these territories.[42]

There was little doubt that Lee was attracted by the idea of a larger group-ing both as a solution to his own dilemma and as a desirable development in its own right. Through the Grand Design, he was having more success in talks with the federation ministers on the basis of a Malaya-Singapore merger with the three Borneo Territories coming in as a counterweight. It seemed that the Grand Design was the only method by which the Tunku could be persuaded to accept Singapore. However, Lee was advised that it would be politically inexpedient to switch his line too rapidly from merger to Grand Design; any change on his part had to be gradual and must be presented as an expansion rather than an abandonment of previous ideas, or else he might be regarded as a political opportunist.[43] Nonetheless, after a seven-day unofficial visit to Sarawak and North Borneo, he hinted at his new approach when he announced that "it would be worthwhile for the Borneo Territories and Singapore to stick together."[44]

In early May 1961, Lee, on the encouragement of British officials, produced a paper on the Grand Design, which he sent to the British and federation ministers for consideration. In his paper, Lee listed two alternatives for the constitutional future of the British territories in Southeast Asia. The first was for the territories to each achieve individual independence and to function as separate, independent political units. He then pointed out that if this alternative developed, merger between Singapore and the Federation of Malaya would be abandoned as a political objective, and "power in Singapore would pass to a China-minded group with strong cultural and economic links with Communist China."[45] A procommunist government would emerge that would eventually achieve independence for Singapore with the help of communist China. With such a development, he warned that British interests and security in Southeast Asia would come under considerable threat.

The other alternative was for the establishment of a larger federation comprising the territories of Malaya, Singapore, and the Borneo Territories. This, Lee argued, was the most satisfactory solution for the peoples of the territories concerned, and also one that the British could accede to. In broad outline, the scheme was to use the stable Malay-based federation government as the sheet anchor of the whole of this region. Each of these states could then be left to elect its own government based on its existing state arrangements, with the government of the Federation of Malaya, by virtue of its larger population, controlling the government of the larger federation. The powers of the larger federation government would include defense, foreign affairs, police, security, and such matters like currency and common economic development. To protect the susceptibilities of the Borneo peoples and the present balance of power between Singapore and the Federation of Malaya, provisions would have to be built into the constitution to ensure that voting by citizens of the respective three states could only be done in their own states. This safeguard would prevent upsets in the balance of power.[46]

To the government of Singapore, therefore, merger with the federation promised not only economic viability for the small island state, but more fundamentally its survival from the communist threat. There was no doubt in the mind of Prime Minister Lee that "the Communists could only be beaten if it was clear that Singapore could not have independence except through merger."[47] In fact, Lee considered that the weakness of his government, which was highlighted by the defeat of the PAP candidate at the hands of maverick assemblyman Ong Eng Guan at the Hong Lim by-elections, was essentially the result of uncertainty in Singapore about the road to independence. Lee was convinced that the only way for him to restore his fortunes was to obtain a decision in favor of the Grand Design. In this situation, Lee regarded it as essential that he make some progress with the federation, and in informal talks with Tun Abdul Razak, he tried persuading him that the federation should make some rather more forthcoming statement on the Common Market in order to generate some feeling of euphoria in regard to relations between Singapore and Malaya.[48] Lee was realistic enough to realize that Singapore could not expect any positive gestures from the federation at this stage; the Tunku's position on a Singapore-Malaya merger had been made clear to him several times before. But he argued that the federation must not destroy the hope of eventual merger, nor encourage any idea that Singapore could be independent on its own.[49] Lee's remarks on the merger drew a response from ministers in the federation, who suggested that it would be helpful if Britain made clear its long-term policies for its territories in Southeast Asia.[50]

By 1961, it seemed that the Tunku had changed his mind, as he spoke for the first time of the need for a political and economic association with Singapore. Lee reacted at once, not wanting to let the opportunity pass. He warmly welcomed the proposal for a Greater Malaysia in his National Day Rally speech on June 3, 1961, though not fully aware of the real difficulties that he would have to confront in securing the merger with the Malaya:

> By the ties of sentiment as well as business, we in Singapore have always been closest to the Federation of Malaya. If merger and independence can come sooner and easier through the Borneo sister territories coming in together with us into political integration with the Federation, then we support it for it would also mean that we would have a larger and more powerful economic base for our new nation. . . . We welcome and support the declaration of the Prime Minister of the Federation of Malaya that it is inevitable that we should look ahead to this objective of closer political and economic association between the Federation, Singapore, Brunei, Sarawak and North Borneo.[51]

But why had the Tunku changed his mind?

### The Tunku's Stand on the Grand Design

Prior to 1961, the Grand Design made little leeway because of the reluctance of the Malayan leadership to contemplate any sort of union with Singapore. As mentioned earlier, the Tunku had all along opposed the idea of a straightforward merger with Singapore alone because he had regarded Singapore as a "communist power-house"[52] and was fearful that the infusion of the island's Chinese population into the federation would upset Malaya's delicate racial balance. And it was not just the one million Chinese that the Tunku was unwilling to incorporate into the federation; rather, it was a radicalized Chinese population of which he was most afraid. Indeed, the Malay majority in the federation had long been concerned that there was an inordinate proportion of Chinese sympathizers in the Malayan communist movement. As it was the Malays on whom the Tunku must ultimately depended for political support, he was not about to undermine his own position by allowing the merger with Singapore.[53]

While rejecting the idea of a simple merger between Singapore and the federation, the Tunku was very much more receptive to the idea of a Grand Design.[54] Hitherto, the Tunku had argued that the interests of the federation would best be served by keeping Singapore separate, and should the situation in the island colony should get out of hand, the federation[55] could easily insulate itself from the effects by physical means, such as the closure of the causeway, and by relying on friendly Western powers. Alternatively, if the British wanted the Malayans to take on board the problematic Singapore, they would have to concede the Tunku's Greater Malaysia plan first.

The Tunku's interests in forming a grand federation of Malaya and the British colonies in North Borneo preceded the federation's independence, and on many occasions he had raised the possibility with British representatives. Immediately after independence, the Malayan prime minister pursued the idea further when it was announced in a BBC broadcast that he was favorable to the idea of extending the Malayan federation to the Borneo Territories, if these territories wanted this. In January 1959, he broached the idea of some sort of political union between the Borneo Territories, the Federation of Malaya, and Singapore to MacDonald, and later that year, while in Sarawak and North Borneo en route to the Philippines, he had openly suggested that the long-term future of the Borneo Territories should lay with Malaysia.[56] He mentioned his government's fear of the Singapore Chinese reinforcing the Chinese in Malaya with the effect of establishing in due course a Chinese political predominance, and hence his reason for not willing to contemplate a merger of Singapore and Malaya. But he was open to the idea of a "Five Power Federation," whereby the non-Chinese populations of the three Borneo Territories would serve as a counterweight to the Singapore Chinese.[57] It was obvious that the Tunku "looked upon the indigenous races of the Borneo Territories as almost Malays," and his appeal for the territories there to enter into some form of federation with Malaya was made on the grounds that "all Malays should stand together."[58]

In June 1960, at the Commonwealth prime minister's meeting in London, the Tunku suggested to Lord Perth (John David Drummond) of the Colonial Office that "although merger was unacceptable to the Federation government, a package deal, including Singapore and the Borneo Territories was another matter." In his overall plan, the Tunku indicated a particular keenness on Brunei, attracted as he was to the valuable addition of oil-rich Brunei to the federation treasury, and had attempted to forge links with the Brunei administration by seconding Malayan officers to fill key posts in Brunei.[59] He was further lured by the prospects of a doubling of the federation's territories if Brunei with Sarawak could be reunited and then brought together into the Federation of Malaya. And while he was interested in the integration with Brunei and Sarawak, also partly because he believed the two territories had racial affinity with Malaya, he was clearly less enthusiastic about North Borneo and Singapore, where the Malays formed a minority within a non-Malay major-ity.[60] He was thus quite happy to let the British retain North Borneo for de-fense purposes, as a "British fortress" colony outside this association. However, this was rejected on the grounds that retaining North Borneo as a Crown colony was an impractical proposition in the event that Sarawak assumed self-government status as part of the Malaysian federation. It was thus de-cided that the Tunku would not be given encouragement on this score. As far as Singapore was concerned, the Tunku would prefer the British to remain in control, as at present, for as long as possible.[61] By 1960, the Tunku's strategy was becoming increasingly clear: sooner or later the Federation of Malaya would be faced with the decision of a merger with Singapore and when that should happen, the Tunku and his Malayan ministers would demand the Borneo Territories as "the necessary sugar to sweeten the pill of Singapore."[62]

With Singapore as the main stumbling block, Malayan ministers began canvassing British officials of the need to dangle the Borneo Territories as an incentive if they were to have any chance of persuading the Tunku to accept a merger with Singapore. The Malayan minister for the interior had, on the sidelines of the Internal Security Council meeting at the Cameron Highlands on June 25, 1960, held a private conversation with H. T. Bourdillon, deputy commissioner in Singapore, in which he reiterated the possibility of a merger with the federation embracing Singapore and the Borneo Territories.[63] Razak, the federation deputy prime minister and minister for defense as well as rural development, had a more sophisticated plan. He proposed a three-stage plan in which Sarawak and Brunei, united under the sultan of Brunei, would be brought into Malaya in the first stage. Following this, North Borneo would be brought into the federation in an association similar to Penang or Mal-acca. Finally, Singapore would be brought in, but under special status and on different terms from the other states in the federation.[64]

It was only toward the end of April 1961 that the Tunku, possibly sensing that the British would be forthcoming to a wider federation involving the Borneo Territories as well, seemed ready to discuss questions of a merger with Lee.[65] Lee, advised perhaps by British officials that the Tunku was beginning to listen, took the opportunity to visit Kuala Lumpur several times to press his Grand Design on the Tunku. The situation was indeed becoming critical, both for Lee and the British government. The former needed to offer some evidence of constitutional advance before 1963, when the Singapore constitution was due for a review, while the latter did not want to be faced with the prospects of having to transfer power to a procommunist government in Singapore. But there was optimism in the air, as Lee believed that Razak was already converted to the idea of a merger with Singapore, albeit under a broader federation with the Borneo Territories, and he could in turn be expected to break down the Tunku's prejudices on Singapore.

There was little doubt that the British "in their own pragmatic ways, helped" to bring the Tunku to this point of view. He was constantly reminded by British officials, not the least by Harold Macmillan himself during the Commonwealth prime ministers' conference in early 1961, of the very real danger of a "batik curtain" in Singapore if steps were not taken to deal with the communist threat in Singapore.[66] The timing was critical, too, the Tunku was reminded. In 1963, when the constitutional review was due, Singapore would demand independence, which the British would be hard put not to grant. And once Singapore was given its constitution, the British would have to adhere to it themselves, which would preclude them from taking an active part in using undemocratic measures for the purpose of frustrating communism.

But the Tunku was probably weighing the options himself. It was apparent to him that the situation in Singapore was changing and that a constitutional review was due in 1963. The increasingly slender hold on government by the PAP highlighted the ever-ominous threat that Singapore would soon have a communist-led government. This, and the realization that the British would not be able to look after Singapore indefinitely for him, led him to give serious consideration to a possible merger.[67] That the Tunku was already preparing for a major decision was reflected in remarks that he was reported to have made to *Reuters:*

> On the question of merger between Malaya and Singapore, the Tunku said, there would be no problem if the politicians in Singapore had not been given too much rope. The British in Singapore have not been firm enough— they have wanted to please everyone and politicians and trade union leaders have been allowed to do what they want. Because of this and because

the government in Singapore is now powerless to do anything in this matter, the people are looking to the Federation. I do not know what we can do but the time has come to do something.[68]

To the Tunku, the risk that support for Lee in Singapore was rapidly dwindling was palpable, and if a general election should be called, there were fears that it would easily be won by the Barisan Socialis, which was, in the Tunku's judgment and that of all his advisers, a classical communist front manipulated by Lim Chin Siong, who was regarded by the Malayan leadership as a hardcore communist. Once Singapore was freed from British rule, the Tunku foresaw "that Peking and Moscow would establish Missions in Singapore, and that as soon as the Communist powers had provided Singapore with the necessary guarantees, economic and military, British rights and interests in Singapore would be liquidated. . . . He therefore fears for Malaya's own security and integrity. . . . [I]n short, if Singapore is to be saved from communism, the Tunku himself must do it."[69] This reasoning led to the Tunku's historic announcement in May 1961. It should be emphasized that his announcement, at that stage, did not amount to a formal proposal for a "Greater Malaysia." It nonetheless served to momentarily prop up the PAP's position in Singapore and set the stage for the British government to realize their Grand Design.[70]

All that remained to be done was to ensure that agreements be reached between Singapore and Malaya on the terms of the merger, and for the Borneo Territories to be convinced that joining the proposed federation of Greater Malaysia was their best bet for political and economic advancement. All this had to be settled by 1963, when Singapore's constitutional future had to be settled. As it turned out, despite often acrimonious negotiations between the Malayan and Singapore leaders, an inconclusive commission of enquiry in the Borneo Territories, a political revolt in Brunei, whose leaders eventually decided later on to sit out of the federation, and threats of military reaction from Indonesia, Malaysia came into being in September 1963. And what emerged out of the entire exercise?

Singapore, which was the object of the entire initiative, left Malaysia in unhappy circumstances in 1965, although the communist threat that drove the British into action in the first place did not materialize. The Tunku was left with the Borneo Territories, while Brunei, which was the real prize that the Tunku was eyeing, remained outside Malaysia. Britain had hoped that a federation of its dependencies in the form of a Greater Malaysia would lessen its defense commitment in the region, but instead, it ended up having to deal with confrontation from the Indonesians. And finally, despite doing all that had to be done to safeguard the Singapore bases, the British decided to pull out of their bases less than eight years later.

# 10

# Making Malaya Safe for Decolonization

## The Rural Chinese Factor in the Counterinsurgency Campaign

*Kumar Ramakrishna*

### The Malayan Emergency: Prevailing Orthodoxies and Persisting Questions

It has long been a canon of Malayan historiography that the Emergency, the euphemism for the twelve-year-long insurgency of the Malayan Communist Party (MCP), was effectively neutralized by countermeasures in the socio-economic, military, and political spheres. The conventional wisdom holds that the hearts and minds (HAM) of the public were won largely through resettlement away from exposed, vulnerable, and ramshackle squatter areas on the fringes of Malaya's ubiquitous jungle, into economically viable, well-equipped, and secure "New Villages."[1] A second perspective suggests that the imperial British habit of applying "minimum force" in counterinsurgency operations, by reducing the risk of collateral damage to life and property, also contributed to weaning the people away from the MCP.[2] Complementing the dominant HAM narrative have been additional explanations: the increasing sophistication of the Police Special Branch in penetrating communist cells and gathering intelligence;[3] effective civil-military cooperation in war executive committees at federal, state, and district levels;[4] a shift from early large-scale operations to small-scale patrolling on the jungle fringe reliant on good intelligence, in tandem with increasingly well-mounted food denial operations;[5] and, as recent historiography avers, effective population control of the Malayan public that severed vital Malayan Races Liberation Army (MRLA) logistics lines.[6]

The aforementioned factors, however, occupy subsidiary positions within the dominant paradigm; ultimately, it is suggested that the Emergency was won because of political factors: first, the Conservative government in London agreed to confer on Malaya its constitutional independence, while after Merdeka (independence) the dominant Malay elites voluntarily shared power with, and thereby guaranteed the basic political rights of, the non-Malay immigrant constituencies. In particular, citizenship and the right to vote secured the allegiance of the hitherto disaffected Malayan Chinese community on whom the mainly Chinese communists relied for moral and material sustenance.[7] Complementing this overarching political explanation is the tendency in the historiography to suggest that the Emergency was all but over by the end of May 1954, when General Sir Gerald Templer, the high commissioner, left Malaya. Indeed, the remaining six years up to the formal end of the Emergency in July 1960 are regarded as representing nothing more than a "large-scale mopping-up operation."[8]

There are three major problems with the prevailing orthodoxy, the most fundamental being the common assumption that in the ultimate analysis political advance provided the vital impetus to the successful defeat of the communist insurgency. Given that the community most affected by the excesses of the MRLA, the rural Chinese, was, as shall be seen, relatively apolitical, it is unclear exactly how the promise of self-government and citizenship compelled it to support government.[9] Second, while the HAM of the public certainly needed securing in order for government to win the counterinsurgency contest, surely the HAM of the terrorists themselves had to be secured in order to end the war through mass surrenders and the collapse of the terrorist organization. However, the prevailing orthodoxy virtually ignores the campaign to win terrorist HAM.[10] Third, in relation to the last point, in downplaying the period after Templer's departure as a relatively unimportant if long mopping up process, the dominant paradigm, while certainly illuminating how the Emergency was eventually won by government, does not at all explain how the conflict was terminated. In particular, the literature is unable to satisfactorily explain the climactic mass surrenders of 1958 that in the words of Anthony Short, a historian of the Emergency, virtually ended the war.[11]

**The Two Malayan Emergencies**

The argument that the resolution of the Emergency essentially required the British and the Malay elites to guarantee Chinese political and constitutional rights in an independent federation is incomplete. While this paradigm may capture how the educated urban Chinese were won over to the British-Malay plan for an independent Federation of Malaya, it does not explain how the allegiance of the much more numerous and hence strategic rural Chinese was secured. To fully understand how the Emergency ended, we must first recognize that there were in fact two separate if parallel Emergencies: the political and the operational, and while the two were conflated in real life, they need to be teased apart for the sake of analysis in order to better appreciate their particularistic dynamics. The political Emergency represented the campaign by the British to build a multiracial, stable, and anticommunist Malayan government as the necessary prelude to decolonization. Much has been written to elucidate how an independent Federation of Malaya was born out of the occasionally tumultuous interactions between the Colonial Office, successive high commissioners, the United Malays National Organization (UMNO), and the Malayan Chinese Association (MCA). The political Emergency was successfully concluded on August 31, 1957, with the declaration of Merdeka.[12]

However, the official end of the Emergency only arrived on July 31, 1960. That there was a delay between the attainment of independence and the formal end of the Emergency offers prima facie evidence that at least to the men on the spot, rather than the nebulous and inconsequential mopping up process frequently portrayed in the literature, something more tangible had to be obtained before a concrete sense of closure could be achieved. Hence, for scholars to make sense of how the Emergency truly ended requires the recognition that the political dimension of the campaign was not the only dimension of consequence. There was another—the operational Emergency, the counterinsurgency campaign against the MRLA in the rural areas, that until Merdeka ran parallel but quite separate from the political Emergency. The operational affected the political in that progress in the counterinsurgency campaign expedited Malayan constitutional advance. This is why High Commissioner Donald MacGillivray made the crucial announcement to the Federal Executive Council at the end of November 1955 that the continuation of the counterinsurgency campaign at the low level of intensity by then prevailing would pose no obstacle to Malaya's progress toward Merdeka.[13]

However, while an increasingly effective counterinsurgency campaign reinforced constitutional progress, the converse was not a cut and dried affair: the political did not necessarily affect the operational. In other words, political reform and constitutional advance toward Merdeka did not ipso facto confer the initiative on government in the shooting war. This is because the community most affected by the revolt, the rural Chinese, was not at all impressed by political rights, but—as argued later on—by physical and socioeconomic security. Hence, the operational Emergency to a very large extent possessed its own internal dynamic, turning on the rural Chinese factor. Rather than being analytically and haphazardly spliced together with the political Emergency, as in the current historiography, the operational campaign therefore deserves individualized and deeper analysis. It can be divided into three phases: the first, from June 1948 to December 1951, represented the strategic stalemate era as both government and the MCP matched each other in alienating the rural Chinese; the second phase, from January 1952 to June

1955—the rural Chinese HAM phase—was dominated by government's attempts to win and hold the confidence of the strategic rural Chinese community; and the third period, from June 1955 to December 1958—the terrorist HAM phase—was defined by the contest between government and the MCP for the HAM of the remaining hard-core terrorists.

## The Rural Chinese Factor

The contention that the rural Chinese community represented the center of gravity of the operational Emergency is amply supported by available evidence. A 1949 communist document entitled "The Present Day Situation and Duties of the Malayan Communist Party" noted that because the MCP had failed to make headway with the "city population," it had to rely for its supplies on the "Chinese rural population."[14] The latter consisted of the tin miners, rubber workers on plantations and in factories, unskilled and semi-skilled workers in various crafts, and, in particular, the "genuine squatters": those Chinese who engaged in full-time farming. Government officials recognized that these rural folk were the "most important group of all" in the insurgency, because they resided on the jungle fringes and were consequently in contact with communist cadres lurking nearby.[15] For instance, a June 1954 study found that 61 percent of a sample of surrendered terrorists (surrendered enemy personnel [SEP]) had been rubber tappers "readily accessible to MCP influence." Similarly, a 1953 study of another SEP sample found that most of the latter had been farmers, laborers, carpenters, and, in particular, rubber tappers, all of whose "geographical location" had increased their exposure to the communists. Yet another 1956 study of a further SEP sample also concluded that most of these had been unskilled tappers.[16]

These rural Chinese, whose forebears had hailed from southern China, possessed as W. L. Blythe noted, a "cosmogony" that was essentially "material." They were a simple, uncomplicated people, who generally wished "to be left alone to earn their living" and did "not want their lives complicated by politics either Chinese or Malayan."[17] Consequently, what they sought was not so much political rights but rather physical and socioeconomic security. While this assertion may appear controversial, it would not have been to contemporary observers, to whom the relatively apolitical nature of the average Chinese peasant was readily apparent.

On the one hand, even somewhat removed high officials like Chief and later Prime Minister Tunku Abdul Rahman noticed that in contrast to the "Chinese business man" and the "Chinese top people in the town," Chinese New Villagers "didn't care very much" about the "political consequences of independence."[18] For his part, Attorney General Michael Hogan felt that the

Chinese peasant "was just worried about his bowl of rice," and he did not think that many were "particularly conscious or anxious" about "constitutional change at that time."[19] More reliable than these offhand reminisces were the observations of the small coterie of European Chinese-speaking officers who mingled closely with the ordinary Chinese. For instance, the Secretary for Chinese Affairs (SCA) for the Pahang region, scoffing at the "ludicrous" suggestion that the rural Chinese were disloyal to Malaya, asserted instead that "they scarcely can realise the place exists." He argued that their "world" was "their village, their rubber estate, a village in China perhaps, the struggle to make a living—and fear."[20] In addition, W. J. Watts pointed out that what the rural Chinese wanted was not "political rights" but rather that government should be "intelligent, scrupulously just and efficient." He emphasized that the former squatter, "fully wrapped up in his struggle for existence," tended to ask: "What value is it to me if I became a Federal citizen?"[21]

Because the rural Chinese were generally apolitical, they had little in common with the wealthier, English-educated, and politically active Chinese businessmen like Tan Cheng Lock, Khoo Teik Ee, Tan Siew Sin, and Ong Yoke Lin, who formed the core of the MCA. In fact, one Chinese affairs officer lamented that "many of the top leaders in the M.C.A. have very little knowledge of what is happening among the rural Chinese or the Chinese in the small towns and villages."[22] Even before the inauguration of the MCA in February 1949, Blythe, the SCA for the Malayan Union, observed in September 1948 that it was "quite absurd" to expect the Chinese members of the legislative and executive councils to act as the conduit between government and the mass of the rural Chinese.[23] Certainly, despite its physical presence in and material contributions to the New Villages, the MCA never struck deep roots therein. In this context, Heng Pek Koon's contention that the MCA was an "ideal 'power broker'" between government and the Chinese squatters is somewhat debatable.[24] It is thus hard to escape the conclusion that ultimately, given the centrality of the rural Chinese to the counterinsurgency campaign, the MCA, a largely urban phenomenon, was in fact less crucial to the operational Emergency than the MCP and government, both of which respectively possessed, and would come to possess, relatively deeper and more durable penetration into the rural areas.

The generally socioeconomic motivations of the rural Chinese community as a whole shed useful light on the factors determining the entry and exit behavior of that segment of the community actively engaging the Security Forces: the terrorist rank and file themselves. It was estimated that about 10 percent of the MCP/MRLA rank and file were "hard-core" "fanatics" who were utterly dedicated to the party and its quest for power.[25] These disaffected individuals, perceiving that they had been "bullied" by "government," "police," and "robbers," duly seized the MCP's offer of a "short cut to power." In fact C. C. Too, a key Malayan government Psychological Warfare Section expert, pungently observed that any notion that these Chinese had signed up with the communists to advance Malayan "equality" or "democracy" was quite simply "bullshit."[26] The hard core aside, 20 percent of the rank and file were composed of former Malayan People's Anti-Japanese Army (MPAJA) guerrillas who had been recalled to service and given less important tasks than the hard core, while there was also a "good proportion" of "congenital thugs" out for "plunder and rapine for its own sake." Nevertheless, by far the largest group of terrorists—one estimate by a communist masses executive put it as high as 70 percent—had decamped in the jungle not out of a desire to free Malaya from the grip of British imperialism, but rather to flee police repression following the outbreak of the Emergency.[27]

This needs amplification. A June 1954 government study found that for most SEPs, fear of the police or even the terrorists themselves had merely been the "last straw," or the "proximate reason" for jumping into communist waters. For some time prior to entry into the jungle, like a "swimmer" drawn to the very "edge of the pool," the mainly rural Chinese SEPs had already gravitated toward the MCP due to disenchantment with the socioeconomic dislocation of postwar Malaya. The country had been characterized by poverty, the breakdown of family relationships due to the Japanese occupation, and, more importantly, the acute lack of opportunities to improve one's lot in life. In view of these circumstances, the MCP, which dominated Malayan politics in the postwar years, appeared to offer a potential avenue to a better quality of life.[28] Hence, twenty-five SEPs who had entered the jungle in 1948–1949 conceded that they were not particularly interested in the political future of Malaya and did not believe in the ideals of communism either. They had nailed their colors to the MCP mast for "personal reasons": the belief in the communist promise that life in the jungle would be attractive and that they would enjoy social security, self-advancement, and a sense of belonging to a seemingly progressive organization. In fact, a "common refrain" among the SEPs was that they had been "too busy trying to earn a living" to worry about politics; the main topic of conversations at coffee shops, labor lines, and unions had been work and how to make ends meet. Another sample of SEPs confirmed the predominance of "felt economic needs," noting that they had been attracted by the "material aims and promises" of the communists that in the jungle they would enjoy everything from better food and clothing to women, cinema, sports, and games. The communists had also promised that after the revolution the rank and file would enjoy a better standard of living and educational and work opportunities. It cannot be overemphasized: What the mass of MCP recruits had sought from communism was not the classless society but rather the accoutrements of a better life.[29]

Little wonder then that once the MCP proved that it was in the habit of not keeping its promises, defections resulted. Of a sample of 343 Chinese SEPs who surrendered between January 1949 and June 1953, the highest percentage —almost a third—admitted that they had left because of "dislike of [MCP] leaders." In fact, from 1954 it was recognized in government circles that the terrorist body remaining in the jungle comprised the hard core and the more committed terrorists; those individuals who had felt badly let down by the MCP had all but surrendered. A 1953 study of fifty-eight SEPs amplified how the gaping chasm between communist words and deeds alienated many recruits. The selfishness of the leaders, their failure to keep promises, their complete callousness and indifference to the lower ranks, and their "bluffing lectures and propaganda" were all mentioned as causes of discontent or disgust, together with the inequality and irksome restrictions imposed on the rank and file.[30] In other words, the terrorists defected when they lost confidence in the MCP leadership. Losing confidence in the party, however, did not ipso facto mean transferring allegiance to government. As far as the terrorists and the larger rural Chinese public were concerned, by the end of 1951 government was little better than the communists.

## Phase 1: Strategic Stalemate (June 1948 to December 1951)

By the end of 1949, one and a half years after the declaration of the Emergency, MRLA terrorists had killed 655, abducted 250, and wounded 360 civilians; in 1950 and 1951, they perpetrated 10,400 terrorist-inspired incidents.[31] Moreover, in an effort to deter the public from cooperating with government, terrorist tactics were calculatedly brutal: in Plentong in Johore, terrorists shot dead a Chinese squatter, hacked his wife to death, set alight their hut, and threw the slain couple's eight-year-old daughter into the flames. In Kampar, Perak, a Chinese girl was butchered by having a nail hammered through her head. A 1952 police report pointed out that this "senseless cruelty" was not at all "isolated" but typical of "hundreds of similar incidents" throughout the country.[32] Of especial importance, the rural Chinese bore the brunt of communist terror, "presumably because they presented both the greatest hope and the greatest danger." Subsequently, in issuing its confessional October 1, 1951, directives, the MCP itself conceded that its campaign of "economic sabotage and terrorism" since 1948 had damaged its image with the rural Chinese community.[33]

But that did not mean that the latter seesawed toward government by default. As Too observed, the ordinary Chinese villager had never had a positive concept of authority, given centuries of gross abuse and neglect by government officials, soldiers, and "persons dressed in uniform." In fact, in China the soldier and the bandit had been perceived as equally representative of "oppressive authority."[34] Compounding matters in the first years of the Emergency was the absence of formal government contact with the squatters. The old Chinese Protectorate, set up in 1877, had up until World War II kept government in close touch with the ordinary Chinese, and Protectorate Taijins (elders) acted as the official "finger on the pulse" of the Chinese community. But after the war, the Protectorate had been abolished and its place taken by a solitary SCA for the Malayan Union with no "field officers" and who consequently "sat on a cloud with no terrestrial contacts" with the Chinese.[35] Much closer contact had been utterly necessary to rebuild British prestige following the ignominious capitulation to the Japanese in 1942.

Moreover, rural Chinese-government relations, having become dangerously distant during the difficult postwar years, worsened even further following the outbreak of the Emergency, thanks to the behavior of the police and army.[36] A severe shortage of Chinese-speaking personnel in a mainly European-officered Malay force created a communications vacuum in which crass stereotyping flourished: because most terrorists were Chinese, ordinary Chinese villagers tended to be regarded as "hostile" and were often treated roughly. Thus, SCA for the state of Kedah felt that new police officers especially ought to be educated "to correct false impressions and prevent many serious mistakes in the future through ignorance."[37]

The prevailing assumption in government circles up to 1952 was that because of a supposed "streak of hysteria" in the Chinese makeup and the so-called secret society complex, the Chinese were deemed to be afraid of intimidation organizations like the MCP. Hence, it was argued that the only way to extract compliance was to make them "fear Government more than they fear the Communists."[38] This "bashing the Chinese" mentality ultimately precipitated not merely Security Force excesses as at Batang Kali in December 1948, but also harsh Emergency measures that fell largely on the rural Chinese: in particular, individual detention and deportation (Emergency Regulations [ER] 17[1] and 17C), mass detention and deportation (ER 17D), and by the end of 1950 collective punishment (ER 17DA) that involved communal fines and curfews. By February 1951, 2,800 Chinese had been deported to China, and by the end of that year, of 25,641 Malayans detained more than 28 days under the Emergency Regulations, 22,667 were Chinese.[39] The resulting Chinese backlash against government compelled MCA president Tan Cheng Lock to implore the visiting secretary of state for the colonies to advise Kuala Lumpur not only to reduce "the number of offences committed by the Security Forces against the general public especially in the rural areas," but also to do more to "build up an attitude of love, confidence and trust of the people as a whole toward itself and avoid doing anything to antagonize them or alienate their sympathies in any way."[40]

## Phase 2: Winning Rural Chinese HAM (January 1952 to June 1955)

Given the utterly lamentable state of relations with the rural Chinese up to the end of 1951, it was painfully obvious that government had to work hard to win over the community. In this respect, it was fortunate that the new high commissioner and concurrently director of operations was General Sir Gerald Templer, who arrived on February 7, 1952, and who was to have an enormous impact on the country.[41]

Templer grasped the complex situation in Malaya with "incredible speed" and as early as April declared in a speech to the Chinese Chambers of Commerce that government could only win "by enlisting the support of the Chinese villagers."[42] In October, he declared that government "cannot win this battle" without "information," and the "ordinary simple people" had to have "confidence" in government before they would give information.[43] Two months later, the most important measure to build such confidence was inaugurated: Operation Service, a massive public relations campaign aimed at transforming police attitudes toward the Malayan public in general and the rural Chinese in particular.

The brainchild of Police Commissioner A. E. Young of the London Police —who had come in as part of Templer's "new broom" in February—Operation Service called on policemen—who were the agents of government in most frequent and direct contact with the rural Chinese—to seek every opportunity, big or small, to demonstrate that they were friends of the people. To create a sense of urgency among the police, Young decreed that promotion would henceforth depend not merely on good performance of routine tasks, but also the cultivation of a good "relationship with and attitude to the public."[44]

The police responded by engaging in a plethora of good "deeds of service"—the rate from 1953 onward was twenty thousand a month—such as summoning a doctor for a member of the public, giving information on the functions of government, visiting schools, and even in some cases delivering a baby when no midwife was available. Almost inevitably, some observers considered Operation Service a "gimmick," while a government study as late as June 1954 noted that it was still too early to expect the Chinese to forget the years 1948–1949, when Security Force misdemeanors were at their height.[45] Nevertheless, other Malayans considered the campaign the "best and most important thing" government had attempted, while the Secretary of State for the Colonies Oliver Lyttelton, though initially dismissive, ultimately acknowledged its charged symbolic significance, especially in the context of relations between a largely Malay police and the Chinese public.[46]

In fact, even before Police Commissioner Young attempted to reorient police attitudes toward the Chinese, another observer had noted in July 1952 that not merely the police but all government representatives needed to engage in the "personal approach" toward "the people in the New Villages and the kampongs," so as to win their "confidence."[47] Moreover, Templer's incoming director-general of information services, the former grammar school headmaster A. D. C. Peterson, commented in August that all government departments had to become "propaganda-minded" in order to "win the confidence" of the public. Peterson added that what was needed was "an extremely vigorous propaganda effort, carried out in accordance with a coherent plan, by all Departments and levels of Government."[48]

In January 1953, Templer subsequently extended Operation Service to other branches of government. Hence, the Post Office Department launched Operation Courtesy and the Medical Department followed suit.[49] Over time, Operation Service became ingrained as the modus operandi of all government departments, and "throughout the Templer and MacGillivray period the government was fully aware that its policies and practices had to match its pronouncements."[50]

In the final analysis, the real value of Operation Service was not that it enabled government to secure rural Chinese confidence overnight, but rather that it represented a very specific, concrete attempt to recondition official attitudes toward the Chinese—something that was critically necessary in the wake of the gross errors committed between 1948 and the end of 1951.

Concerted attempts to transform official attitudes and behavior toward the Chinese public were matched by propaganda-minded policy adjustments as well. One policy that badly needed closer scrutiny was detention. Soon after his arrival, Templer voiced concern that many detained Chinese were in effect innocent. Fortunately, given the winding down of resettlement, the progress of the New Villages, and the steadily expanding administrative coverage of the rural areas, it became possible to rely less on the detention instrument.[51] Hence, under Templer detention figures began a steep decline: while in February 1952—the month he arrived—there had been 6,483 Chinese detained under ER 17 (1), this figure was slashed to 1,614 by December 1953. Furthermore, the number of all persons detained under ER 17D (mass detention and deportation) fell from 2,037 in January 1952 to nil by December 1953.[52]

In 1953, moreover, Templer made three further decisions that were intended to project the idea that government was the provider of rural Chinese needs and wants: first, on March 17 he abolished the dreaded ER 17D; second, on September 3 the first White Area—in which all Emergency restrictions were removed and the public could live normally once more—was inaugurated in Malacca, to great public acclaim;[53] third, Templer did away with the unpopular measure ER 17DA (collective punishment). He had used the regulation when he first arrived in Malaya, notoriously at Tanjong Malim in March, in dealing with villages that had been implicated in terrorist incidents but failed to cooperate with the Security Forces subsequently.[54] However, he had done so in that and a few other instances in order to establish his credentials as a no-nonsense leader who was determined to set things right in Malaya. Thus, to a large extent Templer's tough, even brutal stance at Tanjong Malim, Permatang Tinggi, and Pekan Jabi represented a "publicity stunt" and his ruthlessness "was intentionally exaggerated in reporting to achieve the maximum deterrence with the minimum force."[55] Significantly, Templer abolished ER 17DA on November 25, 1953, and in May 1954 he admitted publicly that he had never been very comfortable with the measure and found it "very difficult to estimate" its effectiveness.[56]

Importantly, Templer also consolidated Lieutenant-General Harold Briggs' resettlement policy.[57] He was fully aware that some New Villages were inadequately protected and served by insufficient amenities. For instance, he ensured that by March 1953, 218 of the New Villages that had active Min Yuen (the clandestine terrorist logistics network) were given perimeter lighting.[58] He also formulated a checklist to measure the quality of life in the New Villages, which included criteria such as some agricultural land for full-time farmers, land titles for house plots and agricultural holdings, an adequate water supply, a school and teachers' quarters, a village community center, places of worship, good roads with side drains, and reasonable standards of sanitation and public health. Village security was also enhanced through intensified training of special constables and the Home Guard. Inevitably, not all New Villages met these standards and flourished.[59]

Nevertheless, the true contribution of the New Villages toward securing rural Chinese confidence was that they created a relatively secure environment in which the Chinese could come into intimate contact with government Taijins. Hence, as John Davis noted, while the New Villages were clearly imperfect and the Chinese consequently had complaints, all administration was built on complaints.[60] Hence, the germane point was to whom the Chinese were complaining. Increasingly, from 1952 onward, the Chinese could bring their problems to European Chinese-speaking district and resettlement officers, Chinese assistant resettlement officers (AROs), state SCAs, ethnic Chinese affairs officers, and assistant Chinese affairs officers at the district level.[61] These government staff were greatly assisted by the Red Cross, St. John's Ambulance, and Christian missionaries, who provided clinics, vocational training, and adult literacy classes.[62]

The tremendous appeal of these Taijins cannot be overstated. They made government real and tangible to the New Villagers, and the AROs in particular, who lived in the New Villages, were readily available to help with their everyday problems. Moreover, some of the European Chinese-speaking state SCAs like Adrian Alabaster and Gerald Jolleye were very well liked by the New Villagers, while N. L. Alexander frequently reduced the Chinese to "fits of laughter." So popular were these Taijins that when the MCP accidentally killed Jolleye, the New Villagers were "horrified." The Red Cross "misses" were similarly "appreciated" and "popular" with the New Villagers and the communists took care not to attack their vehicles.[63] From the middle of 1956, moreover, the staff of the Emergency Food Denial Organization, who oversaw central cooking, were given a wide berth by the communists because of their popularity with the Chinese in the New Villages and estates.[64]

While Karl Hack is therefore correct in suggesting that resettlement meant enhanced government control of the rural Chinese community, resulting in a better flow of intelligence, he misses a crucial variable interposed between population control and increased intelligence: Chinese confidence.[65] By the beginning of 1953, against the background of a steadily improving security situation and reduced overall terrorist activity, population control, the weeding out of communist cells in most New Villages and estates allowed government Taijins and welfare organizations to dominate them, thereby enhancing Chinese confidence in government.

Templer left Malaya at the end of May 1954, but the official attitude he encouraged—the general concern to be propaganda-minded and to project through words and deeds that government was the provider—was continued first by High Commissioner MacGillivray and later the Tunku. Thus, figures for detentions and deportations continued to drop drastically and White Areas continued to spread throughout the country, positively enhancing government's image with the public, including especially the rural Chinese. For instance, by the end of 1956, there were only 337 people in detention, while a meager 76 persons were deported in the first 6 months of 1957. Moreover, by the end of 1957, 3.5 million people were living in White Areas.[66]

In addition, in mid-1956 the stringent food control policy that had been introduced by Briggs in June 1951 in order to cut off the flow of supplies to the terrorists was modified and its effects on the public were ameliorated by the introduction of central cooking of rice. Because cooked rice—in contrast to uncooked rice—was bulky, spoiled quickly, and consequently could not be readily smuggled out to the starving terrorists by communist supporters, the mass of the New Villagers, estate workers, and miners could eat as much rice as they wished instead of making do with the austere Operational Rice Ration they had so disliked.[67]

Furthermore, the Police Special Branch by mid-1955, thanks to a better information flow from an increasingly appreciative public, was able to perfect the technique of the surgical swoop on New Villages and estates so as to detain Min Yuen and communist supporters without inconveniencing the mass of innocent villagers among whom they harbored. The latter, mindful of the not too recent past when they could have expected collective punishment in the form of communal fines and curfews that impacted on both the guilty and the innocent, were naturally only too thankful. The new, discriminating approach was perfected by November 1956 during Operation Tartan Rock in Johore, which eliminated the Min Yuen network in Kulai, Senai, and Scudai New Villages through a precisely calibrated cordon-and-search operation, leaving unmolested the mass of the villagers.[68]

By the end of 1954, Lieutenant-General Geoffrey Bourne, the new director of operations, observed that although there was a discernible improvement in the level of public cooperation with the Security Forces, the problem was that there was still a general air of what Peterson called "a reasonably friendly apathy." Bourne felt that government's problem was only marginally military in nature. He observed that "the political or psychological side of the struggle is three-quarters of the problem" and that this essentially involved "persuading the people to help the government."[69] The biggest task facing government was therefore to get the rural Chinese to be more proactive in its support for the counterinsurgency effort. In this respect, the cumulative impact of government efforts to project the image of the provider began to bear fruit. At the end of 1954, even while some officials were complaining about public apathy, a government study nevertheless detected "evidence that Operation Service may be producing a change in the attitude of the people toward the Government and notably toward the Police."[70]

Within months, this burgeoning rural Chinese confidence found tangible expression in the form of the good citizen's committees (GCCs). Following a Police Special Branch swoop that eliminated the Min Yuen in the town of Banting in Selangor in March 1955, the grateful Banting Chinese formed a GCC with the help of State Information Officer Jack Hackett. The basic task of the GCC was to rally public support behind government, and to this end in April two hundred Banting residents gathered at nearby Sungei Manggis New Village to watch nine Banting GCC members take turns firing a twenty-five-pounder of the Ninety-third Field Battery at MCP positions eight miles away. By June, the first large-scale public processions were appearing on Banting's streets, and the Banting "bug" had begun to bite, with Triang and

Kerayong New Villages in Pahang firing twenty-five-pounders as well—and keeping expended shell casings as souvenirs. So successful were the GCCs that by the end of 1955 the movement was extended throughout Malaya.[71]

The growth of the GCC movement—hitherto neglected in the extant literature—was to have a decisive impact on the communists. Already on the strategic defensive since the end of 1951, the MCP had hoped to preserve sufficient organizational cohesion to continue prosecuting the armed struggle at a lower intensity while gradually devoting more resources to subversion of schools, unions, and left-wing political parties.[72] As noted earlier, by 1954 the terrorist ranks were filled largely by harder-core terrorists who were committed to the cause. This hard core was recognized by government's Psychological Warfare Section as a militarily weaker but "psychologically tougher" target.[73] However, by late 1954 and certainly by 1955, even these hard-core terrorists, including ranking cadres like state committee members, were defecting, citing loss of hope in a final victory as the key reason.[74]

There were good reasons for this loss of terrorist confidence. The Indochina cease-fire of July 1954 suggested that the seemingly inexorable southern advance of international communism had been checked, enabling the "imperialists" to devote their full resources to Malaya.[75] Second, successful Security Force operations involving the food denial strategy, evolved by Briggs and improved by Templer and Bourne, obliterated the Communist Terrorist Organization (CTO) in the key state of Pahang by early 1955.[76] The third reason, which became increasingly significant by the end of the year, was the GCC movement, which strongly suggested that the public was moving from a position of "reasonably friendly apathy" to overt identification with government. To the hard-core terrorists, it was extremely vital that in their adverse strategic circumstances some degree of public support remained intact. When these extremely pragmatic men and women recognized that this was not forthcoming, they refused to carry on. Hence, by the end of 1956 it was noted that in districts where the people publicly denounced the MCP, terrorist gangs rapidly collapsed.[77]

Furthermore, by 1957 GCCs were penetrating even into extremely "bad" areas: Broga, Semenyih, Tanjong Malim, Ulu Langat, and Pusing.[78] For instance, in August 1957 the Tanjong Malim GCC organized a mass plunge by two thousand people, flanked by the Security Forces, into the jungle in order to get district committee member Chi Lui to surrender. Significantly, Tan Boon Jin, the GCC chairman, declared that it was "stupid" of the terrorists not to give up and that the people had "enjoyed" themselves.[79] Tan's remarks are pregnant with significance, for they illustrate that by the mid-1950s government was clearly enjoying the confidence of the public, especially the rural Chinese, and was even winning over former hard-core communist supporters. Certainly, the late Richard Clutterbuck, who was in Malaya during the crucial period 1956–1958, recalled that by that time the ordinary Chinese "desperately wanted the violence to end, and were generally very co-operative."[80] The GCC movement thus gave the public "a feeling of strength in number and unity," and both promoted rural Chinese confidence as well as gave tangible expression of it.[81]

## Phase 3: Winning Terrorist HAM (June 1955 to December 1958)

If it took years for government to build sufficient credibility with the mass of the rural Chinese, it was no easier with the terrorists. Many squatters and tappers had after all decamped in the jungle to escape police repression, and a 1954 study found that fear of the police had been an even greater motivator of entry behavior than fear of terrorist threats in almost every state.[82] While those who entered the jungle may not necessarily have believed communist blandishments that life would be better inside, once they were deterred from emerging because the Emergency Regulations stipulated that bearing arms was a capital offence punishable by death—and there was precious little faith in the ability of the police to be sympathetic. Indeed, stories of "gross ill treatment" of captured terrorists by the police filtered into the jungle, which only enhanced the feeling that "death was everywhere," and the only prudent option was to remain in the jungle.[83]

In these circumstances, High Commissioner Sir Henry Gurney's September 1949 amnesty, which promised nonprosecution only to those not guilty of involvement in capital crimes, proved particularly vague and hence impotent in attracting surrenders. However, once Hugh Carleton Greene became head of the Emergency Information Services in September 1950, the situation changed. The month before, Gurney, desiring to encourage more wavering terrorists to defect, had decided to indefinitely postpone the prosecution of SEPs who did not qualify for clemency under the 1949 amnesty terms. Greene immediately seized on this by promulgating a policy of "fair treatment" of all SEPs. Accordingly, beginning in December Greene sent out SEPs on lecture tours to the rural areas in order that they were seen to be well treated, thereby suggesting that government was genuine in its assertions of fair treatment. Greene, however, made no promises that SEPs would never be prosecuted at a later date; the emphasis was on how they were being treated in government custody.[84]

Templer carried on the fair treatment policy, and while he continued to resist calls for a formal declaration of nonprosecution for all SEPs, he did seek to publicize to wavering terrorists that if they came out they could ultimately take up civil employment, learn a trade at Taiping Rehabilitation Center, join the Information Services, enlist in the Special Operations Volunteer Force (SOVF) made up of former terrorists operating in the jungle against their former comrades, or engage in agricultural work at the Kemendore Agricultural Settlement.[85] Following Templer's departure, High Commissioner MacGillivray persisted with the fair treatment policy, and in March 1955— in order to forestall UMNO-MCA pressure for a new amnesty as it was felt that the timing was not appropriate—government formally and publicly clarified that all SEPs were detained for three months after surrender, following which they were either rehabilitated or joined the Security Forces voluntarily.[86]

By this time, the MCP was very anxious: as noted earlier, the unfavorable external environment, the strategic retreat within Malaya itself, and the emergence of the GCC movement in April 1955 clearly suggested to the remaining terrorists that they were no longer backing the winning horse. Furthermore, government's unequivocal public declaration in March that it in effect never prosecuted SEPs, in conjunction with its established practice of routinely parading clearly well-treated SEPs in New Villages and estates, sharply augmented its by-now significant fund of credibility with the terrorists. In other words, the latter were slowly accepting that government kept its promises.[87] In these circumstances, the central committee realized that the idea of defection must never have been more seductive to its rump rank and file. To Secretary-General Chin Peng's credit, he did not panic: if the armed struggle was no longer tenable, he decided that the communists would then emerge from the jungle, but on their terms, rather than government's. Hence, the MCP launched the so-called political offensive in June 1955, offering to lay down arms in return for legal recognition of the party. Chin Peng sought to snatch a political-psychological victory from the jaws of military catastrophe.[88] It was at this point that the operational Emergency transited from the public HAM to the terrorist HAM phase: the government-MCP endgame in which the prize was the allegiance of the remaining hard-core terrorists.

Government's response to the June MCP offer was therefore to present alternative exit terms: the September 1955 amnesty guaranteed nonprosecution for all SEPs, regardless of crimes committed under communist direction. Government reserved the right, however, to investigate all SEPs; those who genuinely gave up communism would ultimately be reunited with their families. Meanwhile, SEPs who wished to be repatriated to China would also have their requests considered. However, those who wanted to remain in Malaya but refused to recant communism would have "restrictions" imposed "on their liberty."[89] However, when the Tunku agreed to meet Chin Peng at Baling in Kedah at the end of 1955 to clarify these terms, the latter cunningly exploited this, advising the rank and file to ignore the amnesty because at

Baling the party would be able to secure better exit terms. This had the effect of nullifying the amnesty and it was withdrawn on February 8, 1956.[90] At Baling, moreover, Chin Peng rejected the amnesty outright and demanded that in return for a cease-fire there should be legal "recognition of the M.C.P., no detention, no investigation and no restriction of movement" of SEPs. The Tunku disagreed, insisting on the MCP's dissolution, and the talks broke down.[91]

Subsequently, throughout 1956 and 1957 the tussle for the HAM of the hard-core terrorists intensified. The MCP insisted that as time passed and Merdeka drew nearer, the will of the government and people of Malaya to continue the struggle would flag, and they would pay the MCP's price for ending its revolt: legal recognition.[92] The Tunku's riposte was that even as Merdeka approached, the resolve of the government and people to stamp out communism would be undiminished, and he urged the terrorists not to be duped by the MCP's hollow promises. Finally, following the independence of Malaya on August 31, the Merdeka Amnesty was inaugurated on September 3 and was intended to last till the end of the year. It promised nonprosecution for all SEPs regardless of what they had done under communist direction and every opportunity for regaining their place in society if they were sincere in professing loyalty to Malaya. In particular, with Chin Peng's insistence at Baling on no investigations and restrictions in mind, the text of the amnesty pointedly declared that those who did not wish to forswear communism would not be interrogated but simply repatriated to China. They would also be fairly treated while awaiting repatriation. That government was bending over backward to win over the terrorists was evident even in the terminology used. Instead of "communist terrorists" and "surrender," the more dignified phrases "MCP personnel" and "wishes to leave the jungle" were inserted.[93]

The Merdeka Amnesty produced immediate results: by December, the Tunku was able to announce that the surrender rate since October had been forty a month; prior to that it had been eight a month. Meanwhile, Chin Peng had written to the Tunku on October 12 suggesting a second round of peace talks to obtain "a just and fair agreement to end the war." The Tunku had replied on November 8, agreeing to a preparatory meeting and asked Chin Peng to provide more details.[94] It was obvious by early December, however, that Chin Peng, as he had done so two years earlier, had thrown up the hope of fresh peace talks in order to ensure his weary rank and file that he would be able to get better exit terms than the Merdeka Amnesty at the new peace discussions.[95] The Tunku thus announced on December 6 that if he did not hear from Chin Peng by the end of the month he would call off the proposed talks. Chin Peng finally replied on December 9 and proposed to send two representatives for preliminary talks, but added that the question of surrender did not arise. The Tunku's immediate response the same day was that there was therefore no purpose in meeting at all. He also dismissed any possibility of peace talks and extended the Merdeka Amnesty by another four months.[96]

By early 1958, the terrorist rank and file were fully aware of the Tunku's decision and realized that there was not going to be better exit terms because the Tunku was not going to give Chin Peng a forum to secure such terms—hence, the liberal Merdeka terms were the best being offered. Little wonder that in the new year the remaining CTO members in the last "black" states of Johore and Perak crumbled completely in Police Special Branch operations. Over a hundred terrorists, including a state committee member, four district committee secretaries, seven district committee members, and ten branch committee members, gave up in south Perak between October 15, 1957, and July 10, 1958, bringing the total number of surrenders to 304 in that area alone since the inauguration of the Merdeka Amnesty.[97] In Johore, Hor Lung, a central committee member, surrendered, prompting the collapse of the MCP Southern Bureau and generating 160 SEPs.[98] By the end of the year, in Chin Peng's own words, the MRLA was "hard up" and "finished." It was thus in December 1958 that the MCP introduced the demobilization policy, enabling MRLA men to give up party membership and leave the jungle with severance pay.[99]

Victory in the operational dimension of the Emergency—the rural insurgency—was contingent on whether government could win over the extremely important rural Chinese public and terrorists—and this depended not on abstract political reform but on the provision of the tangible, material benefits of physical and socioeconomic security. Furthermore, the military campaign was certainly not "all over bar the shouting" when Templer left in 1954. The true end of the operational Emergency arrived only in December 1958, when Chin Peng decided to demobilize the MRLA.

Three factors explain why government won the operational campaign: first, the MCP alienated the strategic rural Chinese community through its ill-conceived terror campaign and forfeited the capacity to win the shooting war by the end of 1951; second, through deliberate attitudinal and policy changes government was able to transform its lamentable image of the first four years and wean the rural Chinese away from a posture of "reasonably friendly apathy" by mid-1955; and third, against a background of external and domestic communist reverses, the Tunku's refusal to give Chin Peng the opportunity to better the Merdeka Amnesty terms proved to be the trump card in government's post-June 1955 contest with the MCP for terrorist allegiance. Hence, a deeper understanding of the individualized dynamics of the operational campaign, when added to our extant knowledge of the British–UMNO–MCA bargaining that led to Merdeka, provides a fuller picture of how the Emergency was not merely won, but also terminated. In particular, a detailed understanding of the operational dimension helps us flesh out that much neglected mopping up period following Templer's departure. Thus, Malaya was made safe for decolonization in two stages: while the political Emergency ended on August 31, 1957, the operational campaign ceased with the MCP demobilization policy of December 1958. Government, however, became aware of the latter only in mid-1960, prompting the Tunku to formally end the Emergency on July 31.[100]

# 11

# "Nationalism" in the Decolonization of Singapore

*Albert Lau*

Of the "multitude of explanations" on the subject of decolonization, the role of indigenous nationalism is perhaps one that has often been advanced. The emergence of an "irresistible mass nationalism," as John Darwin puts it, "is commonly seen as the decisive moment in the defeat of colonial rule. Once nationalist leaders had begun to rally mass support for independence, the days of colonialism were numbered." He adds, "Nothing seemed more natural in retrospect than that the new educated elites in the colonies should have come to resent alien rule; that their resentment should have come to be shared by the mass of the population; and that with mass support behind them the nationalist leadership should have been able to dictate the timing of colonial withdrawal."[1] Yet, in the decolonization of Singapore, the role of indigenous nationalism would seem to be ambiguous. Until the outbreak of the Pacific war, a mass-based indigenous nationalist movement had not emerged on the Singapore political landscape. When semblance of such a movement emerged after 1945, commentators still do not agree about its role in ending British rule in Singapore. More intriguing are questions about its nature and character, whether the "nationalism" that arose after the war could be seriously considered as indigenous or "Singaporean."

The development of an indigenous nationalist movement against British rule in Singapore was long in simmering. Singapore began as a collection of immigrant communities, differentiated not only by race, but also by culture, and without a common sense of identity or belonging, or strong roots to the island—all of which made a common "nationalist" tie-up against British colonial rule before 1945 very unlikely to succeed, if not highly improbable altogether. The stability and security that British rule wrought to Singapore, on the other hand, provided a favorable climate for the commercial and economic pursuits of the plural communities of Singapore and discouraged anticolonial agitation.

The threat to British power, nevertheless, existed and its main source lay potentially in the China-born Chinese community. With their growing numbers and economic prowess, the Chinese soon became a rising political force in nineteenth-century Singapore. By 1836, as a consequence of the influx of immigrants from China, the Chinese had become the largest community in Singapore, overtaking the Malays. Invariably, the main challenge to British rule in nineteenth-century Singapore, as Governor Harry Ord reported to the colonial secretary in October 1868, arose mainly from the "turbulent nature of its larger Chinese population and their proneness to break out into disorder."[2] While the riots were not directed against British rule per se, but rather against bloodletting by rival Chinese gangs, they damaged British prestige by revealing their inability to cope. As Edwin Lee points out, "Chinese riots were trials of strength conducted with impunity as if the government did not exist, as well as contests of will with the government, underlined by attacks on government targets."[3] More significantly, "The riots caused men to raise their eyebrows, and ask the terrible question which officials in the nineteenth century had to live with, as to who the real rulers of Singapore were: the Chinese or the British?"[4] By the end of the nineteenth century, the question was settled in favor of the latter, with the passing of the Societies Ordinance of 1890 and the consequent deregistration of the secret societies. Although the secret societies were never totally eradicated and continued to operate underground, they never became the serious political challenge that they had once posed.

From the late nineteenth century, however, Singapore's plural communities experienced a new cultural awakening wrought largely by external stimuli arising from the lands from which they hailed. Until then, the vast majority of overseas Chinese, for instance, paid only scant attention to developments in the motherland. It was, after all, the very political turmoil and economic hardship that had driven them in the first place to seek refuge and opportunities in Singapore. But China's humiliating defeat by Japan in 1895, the Reform Movement it subsequently inspired in 1898, and the events leading up to the Chinese Revolution in 1911, stunned and revived interest among the overseas Chinese in their motherland and gave Chinese politics a national significance it never had before in Singapore.

In a reversal of its previous policy of branding emigrants as criminals, the Ching government, followed by the reformists and Sun Yet Sen's revolutionaries, increasingly courted the overseas Chinese for their financial and political support and to bind them to China's causes. The setting up of the Chinese consulate in Singapore in 1872 and the arrival of Chinese national leaders and political activists to Singapore, including Sun and the reformist leader Kang Yu-wei in 1900, helped to bring China's pressing problems closer to their countrymen. Direct appeals for financial and moral support on patriotic grounds offered the overseas Chinese a channel for heightened, if indirect, political participation in the affairs of the homeland.[5] Sun's revolutionaries founded numerous organizations like the branches of the Tung Meng Hui in Malaya in 1906 to propagate his ideology. China's failure to consolidate after the 1911 revolution kept interest in the motherland alive and awakened a new sense of affinity with China. Branches of the Tung Meng Hui were transformed into those of the Kuomintang (KMT), the first legal political party in Malaya, in 1912 after the setting up of the mother party in China in the same year.

Such concern toward China reached new heights after the Versailles Peace Conference in June and July 1919 granted Japan the former rights of the Germans in Shantung province, and was aroused again after Japan's invasion of Manchuria in 1931 and China from 1937. Numerous anti-Japanese boycotts were staged to protest Japan's aggression against China. Relief aid donations were collected by organizations specially set up for this purpose, such as the China Relief Fund under Tan Kah Kee, a well-known businessman and philanthropist.[6] Brought together by a common concern for China, Chinese from all walks of life were sensitized politically as never before to developments in the land from which they had hailed.

From the turn of the century, there was also a "growing realization, though slowly, of a racial identity" among Singapore's Malay community inspired in part by Islamic reformist ideas from the Middle East, but also arising from changes from within the community itself.[7] Freed from the influence of a traditional aristocratic social structure, and living within an open, commercially vibrant, urban metropolis—"an important breeding ground for new ideas and new ways"—the Singapore Malayo-Muslim community, although the only minority Malay community in the Malay world, enjoyed a liberality that was not as easily available to their kith and kin on the Malay Peninsula.[8] As social mobility within the community was no longer tied to aristocratic privilege but dependent on religious piety and wealth, a small proportion of Arab Muslims, who were highly respected for their religious learning and commercial acumen, and Jawi Peranakan, who were prominent in Malay journalism, were able to rise to positions of community leadership and to exercise an influence that far outweighed their demographic status.[9]

By the early decades of the twentieth century, however, this soon changed, fueled in part by frustration among the majority Malays within the Malayo-Muslim community over these non-Malay Muslim "foreigners" assuming leadership positions within their community and also dominating them economically. Concern for the strength and status of the Malay community in the face of growing Chinese economic and social power provided another source of anxiety. The Singapore Malay Union was founded in 1926 partly out of such frustrations, and its constitution kept non-Malay Muslims out of the organization.

This process of awakening took a further turn with the advent of Islamic reformist ideas from the Middle East and the controversy these sparked within the Malayo-Muslim community between advocates of the reformist Kuam Muda and those of the conservative Kuam Tua. Accusing the traditional religious elite of not adhering to true Islamic teachings and keeping the people in ignorance, the Kuam Muda reformers, through their *Al-Imam* periodical, exhorted Malays to cast off the shackles of *taqlid buta* (the blind acceptance of customary authority) and to practice instead *ijtihad* (the use of reasoning and one's intelligence to ascertain truth). Although much of the bickering occurred in the peninsula, Singapore, as the only sizeable urban concentration of Muslims in the Malay world, and one where the hold of the traditional *ulama* was less strong, afforded not only a ready audience for these new reformist doctrines, but also offered "sanctuaries or sniping posts for those who were in conflict with the religious authorities in the states."[10] Like the Chinese, the Malays had become a more politicized community by the early decades of the twentieth century.

The Indian community remained "politically quiescent" throughout most of the interwar years.[11] There were few issues that actually roused the Indians from their "traditional docility."[12] Indeed, visiting legislators from India had observed that conditions in Singapore were not so bad and that the Indian laborer was far better off than elsewhere.[13] Although a Singapore Indian Association had been established in 1923 to "promote the welfare of the Indians in Singapore," it suffered from fluctuating membership and did not seem to have caught the imagination of the Indian public.[14] The few occasions that the Indian community was prompted to act politically were, as in the other two communities, usually in response to external stimuli. Heeding the call by E. V. Ramasamy Naicker, a visiting southern Indian dravidian reformist in 1929, to organize "self-respect" associations to overthrow the existing caste-dominated social structure and spread the message of social reform, a Tamil Reform Movement, for instance, was started in Singapore by several non-Brahman caste Hindus in 1932.[15] But, as Visandakumari Nair observes, "The Tamil community in Singapore generally tended to exhibit much reluctance—a reluctance borne of conservatism—in responding to the association's appeals for radical social and religious reforms."[16]

By the mid-1930s, influenced by the resurgent nationalism in India and the visits to Malaya by prominent Indian nationalists like Jawaharlal Nehru (1937) of the Indian National Congress, Indian political consciousness in Singapore had also been awakened, but the realm of political awareness appeared to have been situated more in the peninsula where the bulk of the Tamil laborers worked on plantation estates rather than in Singapore. The Singapore Indian Association soon became involved in the formation in 1936 of the mainland Central Indian Association of Malaya (CIAM)—which had close links to the Indian Congress Party in India—with the object of safeguarding the political interests of Indians in Malaya.

The political awakening that was becoming evident among the dominant Chinese and minority Malay and, to a lesser extent, Indian communities by the first two decades of the twentieth century, however, did not constitute a serious political challenge to British power. In the final analysis, an externally oriented nationalism was also not entirely unfavorable to the British. So long as Chinese, Indian, or Malay political activities were directed outward and away from British colonialism, there was no danger to British primacy. Much of the political awakening was also still confined largely to the small minority of the politically active in the various communities and was concerned more with chauvinistic appeals—the strengthening of their own ethnic identity and societal interests—than with nationalistic ideals. To use A. D. Smith's conceptual categorization, it was, in short, really more "ethnic" than "territorial" nationalism.[17]

Attempts to rock the British boat would also have to overcome the inherent conservatism of immigrant communities still motivated largely by economic pragmatism and, therefore, sensitive to "limits" beyond which their political participation could not transgress. Chinese and Indian merchants were not about to destabilize the political milieu and sacrifice their commercial enterprises for the chaos of revolution. In their reckoning, British rule had afforded the much appreciated political stability for their businesses.[18] The Singapore Indian Association, for example, carefully avoided challenging British rule since "most [of its] middle class members were civil servants or merchants who depended on the good will of the government." Its leaders were "paragons of loyalty" to the Crown. Indeed, on its first anniversary in 1924, the association's premises were decorated with five hundred Union Jacks. It also went out of its way to welcome the duke of Gloucester on his visit to Singapore in 1927, "which greatly pleased the British authorities," passed a resolution in 1929 pledging loyalty to the king, celebrated King George VI's coronation in 1936 with a dinner, and raised funds from within the community to contribute toward the Malayan Patriotic Fund and the Colonial War Fund to support Britain's war efforts in 1940.[19] While Indians in Singapore were also involved in CIAM, they were mainly demonstrating solidarity with their kith and kin in Malaya rather than campaigning for their own political agenda.[20]

Mainstream Malay activists, too, were conscious of such "limits" to their political agitation. Singapore was very much a Chinese city and Malay nationalism realized it still needed British power to mediate its interests. British rule in Singapore was thus to be supported, not undermined. The Singapore

Malay Union (SMU), for instance, never made any mention in its political agenda of restoring the sultanate in Singapore, even though its inaugural meeting was held symbolically at the Istana, Kampung Glam, which once housed Sultan Hussein of Johore, "to remind those invited of the Malay raja who had once ruled Singapore." Instead, throughout its history, the SMU was "markedly cooperative and loyalist in its demeanor toward the government, giving tea parties to greet and farewell arriving and departing governors, presenting loyal addresses, and organizing appropriate functions to mark such British royal occasions as the Silver Jubilee of King George V."[21] As one Malay wrote in 1928, "Regardless of what others may think of their position, the Malays are quite satisfied with present arrangements, as they know full well that if they get rid of the British, they will be worse off under some other power who would be sure to overrun the country and trample down the Malays the moment they are by themselves."[22]

Without strong community support for anticolonial activism, the danger to British power from the radical fringe was also largely containable. While the outbreak during World War I of the Singapore, or Sepoy, mutiny of February 15, 1915, by disgruntled Indian soldiers of the Fifth Light Infantry had been represented as marking the beginning of political extremism in Malaya, it left no strong legacy of radical anti-British or anticolonial agitation in the Indian community.[23] The Punjabi Muslim soldiers had mutinied on the eve of their departure to Hong Kong, after they heard rumors that they were really being sent to fight fellow Muslims in Turkey. They attacked their British officers and went on a rampage against the European community at large. The mutiny stunned and jolted British pride but, with no community sympathy and mass support in Singapore, it was suppressed within ten days. Radical Indian political activism resurfaced again only in 1941, not in Singapore but in Malaya, where a series of strikes erupted in Klang rubber estates in March and May. The strikers demanded not only higher wages, but also better treatment and living conditions. They also demonstrated anti-European and anti-British sentiments. The influence of Indian nationalism was evident. Laborers on estates, observed the inspector-general of police, "began to wear Gandhi caps. Congress flags were being flown, and even demands sent to the management of estates to fly Congress flags at the entrance to Estates."[24] Vigorous police action, however, quickly crushed the uprising.

The issue of rights, however, found little resonance in Singapore where Straits-born Indians, like all British subjects, enjoyed the same opportunities as other Straits-born Asians to compete for posts in the Straits civil service. Local-born Indians in the Malay states, however, were discriminated against in competition for official posts that favored a pro-Malay policy. Sectarian divisions within the Indian community along class, caste, and ethnic lines was a further check to a cohesive Indian nationalist force emerging to threaten British rule the way the KMT and Malayan Communist Party (MCP) did.

Political extremism within the Chinese community was dealt with just as decisively. Preemptive strikes by the colonial power against revolutionary left-wing groups from the KMT to more extreme anarchists and communists crippled them before they could pose a major threat to British rule in Singapore. After the first alliance between the KMT and the Chinese Communist Party in 1924, the British started to look on the increasingly communist-infiltrated local KMT as a subversive movement that was harmful to their interests in Singapore and Malaya. Distrustful of the "Bolshevik leanings" of the KMT in Malaya, and fearing the latter's potential for becoming a "tolerated *Imperium in Imperio*" in the wake of massive anti-British demonstrations in China and Hong Kong resulting from the May 30 incident in Shanghai in 1925, the British took the decision to ban the KMT from operating in Malaya and Singapore in the same year.[25]

Of greater concern to the British authorities, however, were the communists. In 1928, following the establishment of the Nanyang Communist Party, the forerunner of the MCP established in mid-April 1930, the communists were already calling for a "Singapore under the Red regime."[26] As the only major local organization with a distinctly "Malayan" emphasis, and without any aversion to the use of revolutionary violence, the MCP afforded the most serious challenge to British rule in Malaya and Singapore in the interwar period. However, close monitoring by the Police Special Branch kept the MCP at bay in its early years.[27] Arrests in 1930 and 1931 deprived the party of almost its entire central committee and in 1934 the Special Branch succeeded in planting one of its agents, Lai Teck, into the leadership of the communist camp, a coup that would eventually have disastrous consequences for the party.[28]

From 1936, however, the MCP was able to regroup and launch a major comeback. Capitalizing on labor issues and resurgent Chinese nationalism, the party was able to deepen its industrial base and broaden its mass support. By fomenting a climate of unrest and disorder, primarily through organizing massive strikes between September 1936 and March 1937, and again between October 1939 and September 1940, the MCP threatened the British authorities with, in the words of the deputy governor, "upheaval and even revolution."[29] Taking advantage of the burgeoning National Salvation Movement of the Chinese community that emanated from the Sino-Japanese conflict of 1931 and that culminated in the outbreak of the Sino-Japanese War in July 1937, the MCP further expanded its anti-British activities "cloaked in the disguise of patriotism."[30] With the outbreak of World War II in Europe, the MCP called for a general "Malayan national emancipation."[31]

But despite MCP efforts, a general "Malayan" response against British rule did not materialize. Preemptive police action and deportation of MCP leaders consistently undermined the effectiveness of the movement.[32] Furthermore, the MCP's latching onto Chinese nationalism, while tactically expedient, was strategically disastrous as it alienated members of the other communities from supporting the movement. Though the party had made inroads in winning some of the radicals in the English-speaking Indian community in Singapore—the Special Branch noted, for instance, that an Indian branch of the MCP existed in Singapore in 1937—it was unable to recruit Malays into its rank and file.[33] The MCP soon became a Chinese-dominated movement, which further circumscribed its attraction to the other races. Even its support among the Chinese population was affected when the KMT, in a circular published in the *Sin Chew Jit Poh* on March 18, 1940, urged all Malayan Chinese to support Britain and not to participate in any MCP-sponsored anti-British activities.[34] The KMT move, noted the Special Branch, "[tore] from the Communist Party the cloak of patriotism" and had "possibly the most far reaching effect" in curbing MCP influence.[35] But the MCP still remained a long-term threat to the colonial authorities. As Governor Shenton Thomas warned in 1940, "Communism exists in Malaya and it is too much hope that it will ever be completely eradicated."[36]

The relative absence of strong indigenous challenges to British rule was also a reflection of the measure of the colonial power's success in finding local collaborators within the various communities to help underpin its governance of Singapore. No empire could do without its indigenous collaborators and the British found theirs in the local-born, English-educated, and domiciled, particularly the Straits Chinese, community. Unlike the China-born and the Chinese in the Malay states, the Straits Chinese enjoyed British subject status in an imperial colony, which they deemed as superior to those of their brethren in the peninsula, and therefore had a greater stake in wanting to preserve their special constitutional position in Singapore. Proud of their "British" heritage and brought up to identify with British culture, the Straits Chinese were generally pro-British and willing supporters of British rule, even though, like all Chinese in Malaya and Singapore, they were not unaffected by the politics of China or the ethnic revival this had stirred among the Chinese during the early decades of the twentieth century. If they were drawn to associate culturally with China, politically, however, they remained loyal to the British Crown and grounded to Singapore.

They were rewarded with appointments to the various public bodies like the legislative and executive councils, where their voice could be heard. Though the slow pace of political progressivism in Singapore (while understandable from Britain's perspective because of the volatility and imprint of

Chinese national politics on local affairs) often piqued them—the Straits Settlements ranked quite near the bottom in the scale of political advancement among British colonies—the Straits Chinese sought change from within, and not without, the system and based their claim for political rights on the strength of their loyalty to the British Crown.[37] Their willingness to pursue their demands within the limited and ineffectual channels provided by the British, and not to challenge them with a less pleasant alternative, meant that there was little hope of their demands being met except at the pace dictated by their colonial masters. The Japanese invasion of Malaya in 1941, however, was to radically alter this relationship.

In a campaign lasting a mere seventy days, invading Japanese forces had inflicted what Winston Churchill called "the greatest disaster to British arms which our history records": the capture of Malaya, including Britain's "impregnable fortress" in Singapore on February 15, 1942. The Japanese conquest of Southeast Asia has often been portrayed by scholars as an important watershed in the region's history, particularly in its impact on the development of anticolonial agitation.[38] By destroying the psychological equilibrium that upheld colonial rule, it is argued, the Japanese occupation sparked off a mental revolution that led to the emergence of anticolonial nationalism and the dismantling of the colonial edifice that had sustained Western rule for over a hundred years. It also contributed to the removal of the procolonial collaborators from the political scene and the raising of a new class of anticolonial elite who spearheaded the struggle for independence after the war. More significantly, it is argued, Japanese policies resulted in politicizing the masses and transformed the elite nature of nationalism before the war to one that was mass-based in its aftermath.[39]

That the speed of Britain's humiliating defeat at the hands of a numerically inferior invading army was shattering to locals is not in doubt. Many of Singapore's postwar political leaders, for instance, attributed their political awakening to the Japanese conquest and the occupation years. As Lee Kuan Yew observed, "The British built up the myth of their inherent superiority so convincingly that most Asiatics thought it hopeless to challenge them. But now one Asiatic race had dared to defy them and smashed that myth."[40] Lee called the war the "single most traumatic experience" in his life and attributed that experience to his subsequent political awakening. Lee's assessment was shared by S. Rajaratnam, "The Japanese in three short years destroyed beyond repair the seemingly indestructible administrative and psychological machinery of imperial control which otherwise would have taken us many decades to tear apart."[41] For Said Zahari, the war had brought a "new awareness . . . in my mind that my country should not be left forever in the clutches of imperialist power."[42] Fong Sip Chee expressed it this way:

The defeat of the British colonial power at the hands of the Japanese . . . left us in no doubt that the British were not invincible. Their interests in Singapore were pegged to serve the wider interests of the British Empire. It was a lesson to Singaporeans that Singapore could be abandoned by her colonial masters if they thought it expedient to do so. Nationalism was rife. Singaporeans began to realize that it was our duty and in our interests that we looked after our own affairs and charted our own destiny. Indeed, it was a national awakening and emergence from a political twilight zone.[43]

As Fong had already alluded to, the war had not just sparked off a mental revolution, but it had also convinced a new group of politically conscious Singaporeans and Malayans that a new political order would have to be established in the country. It was from this group of new elite that the future leadership of the nationalist movement was to emerge.

The war years did not just inspire and produce a new class of radical leaders; they also created a new radical left-wing environment that made the growth of anticolonial nationalism possible. Proestablishment, right-wing groups gradually lost the prominence they enjoyed before the war. Most of the traditional Chinese leaders in Singapore, for instance, lost their positions within the Chinese community.[44] Those who were not purged in revenge killings by the Japanese sought safer havens outside the country and were cut off from their countrymen.[45] Those who had collaborated with the Japanese were tainted by the stigma of collaboration and were discredited after the war. As Cheah Boon Kheng sums up, "Traditional Chinese leaders either had fled the country or were forced to cooperate with the Japanese if they remained. Consequently, the prewar elites were discredited and frequently despised."[46] Into the vacuum created by their demise came the left-wing social revolutionaries who had assumed the leadership of the anti-Japanese resistance struggle during the war. The postwar political environment consequently saw a pervasive shift to the left as a result of their rise. This had one important implication: only political groups that were left wing and anticolonial could continue to survive in this new environment.

But while the war had radicalized segments of both the Indian and Malay communities, its aftermath also saw varying degrees of success in subsuming these new elements under a wider anticolonial movement. During the war, radical Indian political opinion on the island had coalesced momentarily behind the charismatic Subhas Chandra Bose, who led the Japanese-sponsored Indian Independence League (IIL), based in Singapore, and its military wing, the Indian National Army (INA), with the objective of liberating India.[47] But it was unable to ride on its anticolonial momentum in the war's aftermath. With the surrender of the Japanese in August 1945, many of the IIL and INA leaders were charged by the British for collaborating with the enemy, which left a serious leadership vacuum among those in the Indian community.[48] Bose himself was killed in a plane accident on his way to Tokyo in August 1945.

Within the Malay community, a new radicalism had also emerged and found political expression in the establishment of a Malay Nationalist Party (MNP) branch in Singapore in February 1946.[49] Drawing inspiration from the Indonesian anticolonial revolution, the MNP, which had been inaugurated earlier in Perak in November 1945, sought to mobilize the Malay community for a possibly similar and violent anticolonial struggle to achieve full independence for Malaya and the subsequent union between Malaya and Indonesia to form a larger Malay political unit—an *Indonesia Raya* (Greater Indonesia) or *Melayu Raya* (Greater Malaya).[50]

But the MNP's radical agenda and those of its associate organizations found little resonance among the Malay masses or moderate Malay opinion in Singapore, who sought to revive the prewar loyalist Singapore Malay Union instead. Conscious of the community's minority status and political vulnerability in a Chinese-dominated Singapore, moderate Malay opinion was concerned that the MNP's program would "spell disaster for the Malays in Singapore."[51] As the Malayan Security Service reported, the Singapore MNP had found difficulties "in getting the local Malay community enthusiastic."[52] In February 1947, the MNP had opened the way for forging a broad-based anticolonial nationalist movement through its sponsorship of the Pusat Tenaga Rakyat (PUTERA, Center of People's Power), a coalition of mainly left-wing Malay associations. These in turn cooperated with conservative elements like the Associated Chinese Chambers of Commerce and were allied in a united front with its non-Malay partner, the Pan-Malayan—later All-Malaya—Council of Joint Action, whose members included the Malayan Democratic Union (MDU), formed in December 1945 by English-educated intellectuals in Singapore. However, the movement's prospect dimmed after the British met their challenge head-on and brushed aside the coalition's proposal for a "People's Constitution" that was unveiled at a mass meeting in Singapore in September 1947. Despite its initial tactical success in organizing a nationwide *hartal* in October 1947, which brought "commercial life . . . to a standstill" in Singapore, the coalition's campaign could not be sustained without strong ground support and eventually fizzled out.[53]

Not all within the group, particularly the more conservative elements like the Associated Chinese Chambers of Commerce, whose involvement had made the use of the *hartal* weapon possible, were comfortable with what they saw as the increasing radicalism of the movement or the dire consequences of eventually challenging British rule. With the unveiling of the colonial fist and the outlawing, before the end of the year, of the Singapore branch of the Angkatan Pemuda Insaf (API; Generation of Aware Youth), the MNP's radical youth wing—whose slogan "*Merdeka Dengan Darah!*" ("Independence Through Blood!") deeply worried the British—Malay radicalism in Singapore was kept on the defensive.[54] With the declaration in Singapore in July 1948 of a state of Emergency, following the outbreak of the communist insurrection in Malaya the month before, the political space for anticolonial agitation was reduced even further and the Singapore MNP was eventually forced to dissolve the party in May 1950.[55]

Of the anticolonial forces to emerge after the war, the strongest, however, was the Chinese-dominated MCP, which exerted a commanding presence over the political landscape between 1945 and 1948. During the last days of the Malayan campaign, the MCP had formed an alliance with the British for the purpose of mobilizing the local Chinese population for civil defense and to help in the military defense of Singapore Island. Armed by the British after the fall of Singapore to play a fifth column role behind Japanese lines, the MCP emerged in the war's aftermath strengthened, both militarily and politically. "As the only political organization prepared for an active anti-Japanese insurgency," observes Cheah, "it attracted wide-spread support among the Chinese who suffered greatly from the brutality of the Japanese."[56] For its role in the anti-Japanese resistance movement, the MCP was publicly rewarded and recognized by Admiral Lord Louis Mountbatten, the supreme Allied commander, after the liberation of Singapore. Given that the political aim of the MCP—the swift ending of British rule—had not changed, it was perhaps inevitable that the anticipated clash between them was only a matter of time. Its prewar ban lifted, the MCP took advantage of the liberal environment to continue its anticolonial campaign through its mass organizations. It won many to its cause, not only the Chinese educated, but also from among the English-educated social revolutionaries who saw the communist revolution as representing the only path at that time through which they could attain their objective of an independent Malayan nation.[57] After the British responded with tough countermeasures to its subversive campaign, the MCP in June 1948 took up an armed struggle against them, a fateful decision, as it turned out, because the MCP courted British repression and was never permitted to operate openly again.[58]

From 1948 to 1954, the stage was passed to right-wing groups as the British, conscious of how the outbreak of the communist insurrection or Emergency had further radicalized the political environment through the near state of war it engendered, started to clamp down on left-wing groups and activities. The hardening colonial response deradicalized public debate and thrust into the forefront of the political stage a right-wing elite. When elections were held in 1948 and 1951, it was the pro-British, right-wing, gradualist Progressive Party, led by English-educated lawyers like C. C. Tan and John Laycock, that emerged as the key player.[59] The Progressive Party had no mass base and succeeded only because the size of the electorate was limited to British subjects. Its political demise was inevitable, for it was a rightwing party operating within a left-wing environment. It was to meet its Waterloo in the 1955 elections.

From 1955, with the MCP almost beaten in the jungle war, the British decided to encourage more democratic participation in order to counter the attractions of communism. On the basis of the new Rendel constitution that they introduced in 1954, which increased the number of elected seats from nine to twenty-four, and with the lifting of the restrictive political environment, left-wing parties made a significant comeback. In both the 1955 and 1959 elections, left-wing parties came out the winners—the Labour Front (LF), led by David Marshall, in 1955 and the People's Action Party, led by Lee, in 1959.

In the final analysis, what the three and a half years of Japanese conquest and occupation had done was something that would have possibly taken many decades on its own to accomplish. Indeed, as Rajaratnam opined, it was the Japanese occupation that had "contributed unwittingly to the emergence and triumph of nationalism in a Singapore and Malaya which for 155 years had remained politically passive and would have so remained for another 155 years."[60] The war had facilitated—as no other event before had been able to do—the rise of an indigenous nationalist movement in Singapore and Malaya.

If the Japanese occupation had contributed significantly to the emergence of indigenous nationalism, it is not all that clear, however, that it was Singaporean nationalism that was awakened. If implicit in the word "nationalism" is the concern with the "nation," then the conception of the Singapore "nation" has to be clarified. Was an independent Singapore "nation-state" an option? Since 1946, Singapore had been severed completely from the Malay Peninsula to become a separate colony under the revolutionary Malayan Union scheme devised by the British during World War II.[61] While the colony's separation paved the way for the development of a separate Singaporean "territorial" nationalism, the nationalist forces that had emerged from 1945 were fighting more for Malaya's, and not Singapore's, independence and were apparently harnessing Malayan nationalism to achieve that end. Ever since Singapore's separation from the Malayan Union in 1946, all the major political forces in Singapore had, as one of their political objectives, a merger between the island and the mainland. As W.E. Willmott notes, "Viewed in the light of the collective sentiments involved, it is possible to recognize that the struggle against British colonial rule did not produce Singaporean nationalism because all those who participated in it felt that the colony was an integral part of the British possessions on the peninsula."[62]

The MCP, for instance, as its name suggested, was "Malayan" in its orientation, as was the MDU, which had established branches in the mainland. Since its inception, the People's Action Party (PAP) had always stood for a united Malaya inclusive of Singapore. To Lee, Singapore's exclusion from Malaya was the result of a "freak man-made frontier. . . . Had the British heeded the history of the peoples of Malaya and geography and economic realities," he said, "they would have put Singapore into the Malayan Union, just like Penang and Malacca."[63]

For Singapore, a merger was urgent as the alternative prospect of the island surviving either economically or politically as an independent state was bleak. Devoid of natural resources and confronted by a growing population requiring jobs, Singapore needed the federation "hinterland" to provide a bigger common market for its goods. Its leaders were also not confident that Britain would grant independence to a Singapore state that was neither economically nor politically viable. As Malaya moved toward independence beginning in 1955, Kuala Lumpur had even less interest in a merger with Singapore. Only then was a Singaporean nationalism deliberately forged. Marshall, in his constitutional talks in London in 1956, had on his agenda an independent Singapore. And in 1959, after Singapore achieved self-government, there was a deliberate effort to develop national symbols like the national flag and anthem.[64]

Was decolonization "inevitable" after the war? It is far from clear that the British saw a reduction of their roles in Southeast Asia after 1945. They had recognized that the world had changed, but few realized that they had to adjust to the changed circumstances, until quite late in the day. Though the British had justified the Malayan Union scheme under liberal guises—to make Malaya safe for decolonization—it was, in actual fact, an exercise in late colonial annexation, with British strategic interests very much in the colonial mind.[65] Nor did the British, like the Dutch in Indonesia, believe that a "colonial" war was unwinnable—if the Emergency could be considered as an indigenous nationalist uprising.

By the time World War II ended in August 1945, the British were clear that they wanted to remain as a key player in the global game, but they also knew that their resources would not be able to match their imperial commitments. Retaining the empire was integral to the British desire to play a global role, since without it, Britain would be reduced to the level of a second-class power. The hard truth was that Britain indeed no longer had that capacity to act globally. The Pacific war had already demonstrated beyond doubt that Britain could not ensure the security of its overstretched empire, and it appeared even more unlikely that it would be able to fulfil that role in the new postwar world at a time when major fault lines, unleashed by the war, were appearing in the imperial structure. The challenge before the British, therefore, was to manage Britain's imperial interests in a way that would maximize the economic and political returns and minimize the drain on British resources. British pragmatism dictated that they cut their losses where Britain's position had become untenable.

As for Malaya and Singapore, it was clear that the British initially had every intention of returning as rulers and to remain so into the foreseeable future. True, the empire in Malaya this time around had not remained untouched by a major world war, and Britain had been inflicted with its most humiliating defeat at the hands of the Japanese forces. It was unlikely that the British could simply pick themselves up from where they left off in February 1942 as though nothing had happened in between. War had unleashed new forces that the British recognized, but that they were not yet prepared to accept. The British were returning to stay, as the introduction of the Malayan Union scheme and the detachment of Singapore as a separate British colony demonstrated. Whatever new forces that had been unleashed, Britain apparently believed that, as before, collaborators could be found and their position in Malaya and Singapore would remain relatively uncontested.

On the Malayan front, Britain, after some initial hiccups, had found its collaborators in the right-wing Malay mass base, led by United Malays National Organization (UMNO),[66] while, in Singapore, the pro-British and right-wing Progressive Party, which advocated a gradualist approach to independence in collaboration with the colonial power, was in the forefront of the political stage in the early years. Conscious of the need to manage political change and expectations and to counter the attractions of communism in the battle for hearts and minds during the Emergency, the British had encouraged greater political participation. Beginning in 1948 in Singapore and 1951 in the federation, elections were progressively introduced. In 1955, elections were held both in Singapore and the federation. While the first federal elections in July convincingly ushered the UMNO-led Alliance Party into power, the Singapore elections a few months before, in April, saw the defeat of the pro-British Progressive Party. Overnight, the British lost their preferred indigenous collaborators in Singapore, their hopes for managing a leisurely pace of political development dashed, for the two parties that made significant gains in the election came from the Left—the LF and the PAP, both fervently anticolonial and socialist in orientation. They demanded a swift, not gradual, end to British rule in Singapore.

But both parties had inherent dilemmas that made them vulnerable to British exploitation. The LF government that came into power in 1955 did not have sufficient seats to form the government. It had fought the election with the expectation of being only an opposition in the legislative assembly, but was inopportunely thrust into power in a constitutional mold meant for the gradualist Progressive Party. Weak and trapped in a government that required it to work closely with the colonial power, the LF soon found itself being divested of much of its left-wing and anticolonial credentials. The PAP was also caught in a dilemma, for right from the beginning the party was divided between two ideologically diverse factions with incompatible ends and means. While the moderates under Lee wanted to reach their objective of an independent, democratic, and socialist Malaya through the constitutional process, the more radical elements led by Lim Chin Siong were not averse to the use of violence to achieve their vision of a communist Malaya. For the moment, both needed each other. Lee needed the mass-based anticolonial front that was under the communists, while the latter needed the cover provided by the PAP for its subversive activities. Collaboration was fraught with danger for it cast the PAP as a stooge of the MCP and provided the British and the LF government with good reasons to close down the party. The vulnerabilities and weaknesses of the two parties, in the meantime, afforded the colonial power tremendous political leverage in its dealings with them. British support made the difference between whether a particular political party remained in or out of power. Until 1956, in the absence of palatable alternatives—the PAP was still not ready—the British worked behind the scenes to "to keep Mr. Marshall in position."[67]

How successful indigenous nationalism could prevail against entrenched colonial powers would depend very much on the kind of pressure it could exert and the colonial powers' capability and willingness to meet indigenous demands or to suppress nationalist uprisings. Indeed, mounting a political campaign for independence was most likely to be successful where the colonial rulers, for their own reasons, had already decided not to stonewall the demand for self-government or independence. Marshall failed in his attempt to gain independence for Singapore at the London constitutional talks in 1956 precisely because he did not understand the limits beyond which the Colonial Office would not go. While he was insistent that Singapore be granted independence, he was unable to assure the British that their strategic interests on the island would be safeguarded.[68] On Marshall's demands, Thomas Lloyd, the Colonial Office's permanent undersecretary, had this to say, "The strategic importance of Singapore combined with the serious security threat and the unstable political situation seem to me to make it impossible for HMG to concede complete independence in the normal Commonwealth pattern."[69]

By refusing his demands, the British thereby ensured his resignation and his replacement by his deputy, Lim Yew Hock, as chief minister—an appointment, Marshall alleged, that was "planned by [the Colonial Secretary] Lennox-Boyd whilst we were still in London."[70] Unlike Marshall, Lim was prepared to work with the British to achieve his constitutional goals, even if that involved the launch of a series of anticommunist purges from September to October 1956, prior to the opening of new constitutional talks in London. Lim's collaboration, however, came with a high price. While the timely anticommunist purges against its extreme Left helped the moderate PAP faction under Lee to consolidate, it ironically undermined the credibility of the Lim government that, to all intents, had been perceived increasingly by the Chinese mass base as the "running dogs" of the British.[71]

By 1959, the PAP had also showed the British that it was able to win the mass ground after it trounced its opponents in a landslide victory in the Singapore elections that saw the island achieving self-government. The British had also decided that the moderate wing of the PAP under Lee's leadership was the local group that was best equipped to safeguard British interests. According to Lee, Sir William Goode, the last British governor of Singapore, "watched every move, every speech, every statement. He was in the Assembly with us, watching me, the difference between me and Lim Chin Siong. . . . He was calculating in terms of twenty, thirty, forty years and trying to get a group of people to emerge who can hold the situation."[72] It is likely that in Singapore's path to independence, the British remained very much the de facto power brokers.

# 12

# Franklin D. Roosevelt, Trusteeship, and U.S. Exceptionalism

## Reconsidering the American Vision of Postcolonial Vietnam

*Mark Philip Bradley*

Just a few months after the Japanese attack on Pearl Harbor, President Franklin D. Roosevelt expressed doubts about French colonial rule in Indochina and initiated plans to place Vietnam under some form of international trusteeship. By mid-1942, discussions were underway within the State Department on possible forms of international supervision for the development of indigenous political and civil society in postwar Vietnam. From 1942 onward, Roosevelt vigorously pressed members of the wartime alliance to support trusteeship, winning the support of Chiang Kai-shek and Joseph Stalin. At the same time, American officials in southern China were increasingly drawn into discussions about trusteeship for Vietnam. By the spring of 1945, however, the United States had retreated from these efforts, abandoning plans for the international supervision of Vietnam's transition to independence and acquiescing to the return of the French to Indochina.

Roosevelt's dogged pursuit of trusteeship for Indochina during World War II has often been viewed as a peculiarly quixotic personal crusade.[1] While scholars debate Roosevelt's culpability for the quiet death of trusteeship in the spring of 1945, most wistfully agree that postwar American diplomacy toward Vietnam marked a sharp break with Roosevelt's wartime plans for Indochina. But if Roosevelt's advocacy of trusteeship ended in failure, its significance lies not in a story of what might have been. Rather than a didactic parable of a pacific alternative to the increasingly bellicose character of the subsequent Cold War in Vietnam, trusteeship marked the full articulation of a persisting American vision that transcended Roosevelt's personal crusade.

Not all American policy makers shared Roosevelt's certainty that trusteeship was the best tool to realize America's imagined postcolonial Vietnam. But they did embrace the assumptions that underlay his larger vision. Roosevelt and the wartime American policy makers in Washington and southern China who framed the American vision of postwar Vietnam believed that the Vietnamese were innately incapable of self-government, that French rule had done almost nothing to correct these deficiencies, and that the dislocations of the Pacific war offered the opportunity to arrest the stagnation of Vietnamese civil society by providing the Vietnamese with tutelage in American political, economic, and social models.

Embedded in the harsh judgments of World War II–era American policy makers was a broader discourse on the proper relationship between what was seen as the backward character of nonwhite peoples and the more progressive West. American images of Vietnamese society reflected a fundamental belief in racialized cultural hierarchies that had underlain the American encounter with nonwhite peoples at home and abroad since the mid-nineteenth century.[2] Much of the vociferous critique of French colonialism rested on the widespread notion of the unique success of the American colonial project in the Philippines and the superior claims of American models to reshape the lives of backward peoples.

But if their assumptions were in part rooted in a domestic context, Roosevelt and wartime American policy makers also displayed strong commonalties with the patterns of perception and behavior of European colonialists. Notwithstanding the anti-French rhetoric of wartime policy makers, their deprecating assessment of Vietnamese society was grounded in a wider Orientalist discourse on the non-Western "other" through which, as Edward Said and others argue,[3] Western imperial powers used a culturally constructed conception of the negative essence of colonized peoples to denote Western superiority and reinforce imperial military and economic dominance. Although wartime Americans often celebrated what they saw as their own exceptionalism as a colonial power, their apprehensions of Vietnam and visions for its future pointed toward the shared rather than the antithetical nature of colonial discourse and practice in Europe and the United States. If the transformation of the incipient American vision for Vietnam eventually encountered serious and ultimately insurmountable obstacles, these efforts and the assumptions that guided them reveal the centrality of a shared Euro-American colonial discourse in the American construction of a postcolonial Vietnamese state during World War II and in its aftermath.

## "Benefiting the Owner": Roosevelt and Trusteeship

At a July 21, 1943, meeting of the Pacific War Council, the interallied working group that oversaw military operations in the Pacific theater, President Roosevelt addressed the members of the council assembled in the Cabinet Room of the White House:

Indo-China should not be given back to the French Empire after the war. The French had been there for nearly one hundred years and had done absolutely nothing with the place to improve the lot of its people. . . . Probably for every pound they got out of the place they put in only one shilling. . . . [W]e ought be help these 35,000,000 people in Indo-China. Naturally they could not be given independence immediately but should be taken care of until they are able to govern themselves. . . . [I]n 1900 the Filipinos were not ready for independence nor could a date be fixed when they would be. Many public works had to be taken care of first. The people had to be educated in local, and finally, national governmental affairs. By 1933, however, we were able to get together with the Filipinos and all agree on a date, namely 1945, when they would be ready for independence. Since this development worked in that case, there is no reason why it should not work in the case of Indo-China. In the meantime, we would hold Indo-China as a trustee. This word cannot even be translated into some languages. It means to hold for the benefit of the owner.[4]

Roosevelt's remarks before the Pacific War Council were not his first mention of plans for international trusteeship in Indochina. But the sentiments they convey aptly characterize his approach to the creation of a postcolonial Vietnamese state. Roosevelt saw French rule in Vietnam as a particularly egregious example of colonial failure. Traveling with his son Elliott to Casablanca, a journey that brought him intimate views of the poverty and disease in French Morocco, Roosevelt reflected on French colonial rule in Vietnam, "Why was it a cinch for the Japanese troops to conquer that land? The native Indo-Chinese have been so flagrantly downtrodden that they thought to themselves: Anything must be better than to live under French colonial rule!" In his remarks before the Pacific War Council, Roosevelt argued that the French acted solely in their own economic self-interest in Vietnam and had done nothing to "improve the lot of the people." It was a refrain that he would repeat many times in wartime discussions of trusteeship for Indochina with the Chinese, the British, and the Soviets. In a meeting with Stalin at the Tehran Conference in November 1943 where he won the support of the Soviet leader for trusteeship, for instance, Roosevelt told Stalin, "that after 100 years of French rule in Indochina, the inhabitants were worse off than they had been before."[5]

Underlying Roosevelt's hostility toward French policy in Indochina was not so much opposition to colonial rule itself as a sense that the French had not upheld the obligations of a colonizing power. In one of his earliest statements on French colonialism in Vietnam, Roosevelt observed that "the French did not seem to be very good colonizers." French conduct in Indochina, he suggested, "was at considerable variance with general practice of Great Britain and the United States to encourage natives to participate in self-government to the limit of their abilities."[6] Roosevelt made explicit some ten months later the critical role French failure to reform Vietnamese society played in his assessment of Indochina's future, arguing "that we must judge countries by their actions and that in that connection we should all avoid any hasty promise to return French Indo-China to the French."[7]

Roosevelt was also certain that the Vietnamese were unable to govern themselves, an assumption that rested in part on his belief that the failed policies of the French had left the Vietnamese unprepared for independence. But his use of the word "naturally" to introduce his assertions before the Pacific War Council that the Vietnamese were not yet ready for self-government and required external improvement suggests his perception of Vietnam's political immaturity was also refracted through a prism of racialized cultural hierarchies. Roosevelt's direct knowledge of indigenous Vietnamese society was extremely limited. In one of the few instances in which he described the Vietnamese, Roosevelt called them "people of small stature, like the Javanese and Burmese" who were "not warlike," a comment that recalled contemporary American perceptions on non-Western societies as feminized, weak, and permeable to outside influence.[8] In presenting Vietnamese society as analogous to the Philippines before American colonial rule, Roosevelt linked his vision of Vietnam to the broader and familiar American beliefs that posed a natural division between the stasis of non-Western societies and the dynamism of the West. The reductionist analogy Roosevelt used to join Vietnamese and Filipino societies may have seemed particularly compelling because he viewed Vietnam as another backward Asian society in need of development on more progressive Western lines.

The interconnections Roosevelt drew between Vietnam and the Philippines were central to his conception of Vietnamese development under trusteeship. Roosevelt's brief before the Pacific War Council that the success of American policy in the Philippines demonstrated there was "no reason why it should not work in the case of Indo-China" illustrates his often-expressed faith in the universality of American models and the ease of their cross-cultural transfer. But his emphasis on gradual evolution toward full independence in the Philippines suggests he saw the process of political and social development in Asia as very slow. In Roosevelt's view, some forty-five years would elapse between the coming of American rule to the Philippines and independence. Roosevelt argued that in 1900, not only were the Filipinos unprepared for independence, but a date could not "be fixed when they would be." Even after thirty-three years of efforts to build public works and provide education in "local, and finally, national governmental affairs," Roosevelt continued, both American and Philippine elites agreed that the Philippines would not be "ready for independence" until 1945.

Roosevelt's description of American efforts to guide the Philippines toward independence at the Pacific War Council indicates that he envisioned the transformation of Vietnamese society under international trusteeship would be guided by the same gradualism and moderation that had characterized U.S. colonial policy in the Philippines. These lessons from the American experience in the Philippines certainly informed Roosevelt's presentation of a timetable for trusteeship in Vietnam. In conversations with Chiang Kai-shek and Stalin later in 1943, for instance, Roosevelt raised the Philippine analogy to suggest that trusteeship "would have the task of preparing the people for independence within a defined period of time, perhaps 30 years."[9]

Roosevelt's emerging vision of postcolonial Vietnam was not, however, as sharp a departure from prevailing colonial norms as his rhetoric sometimes suggested and he himself appeared to believe. The easy links Roosevelt drew between his plans for Vietnam and American policy in the Philippines should not obscure the failure of the American colonial project in its own terms. As one leading scholar of American colonialism in the Philippines argues, the three central policies undertaken to transform Philippine society in the American image—preparing the Filipinos to exercise governmental responsibilities, providing primary education for the masses, and developing the economy—"failed . . . to bring about fundamental change," challenging "the widely held myth . . . of the United States as an essentially successful colonial power."[10] Nor did Roosevelt's views, shared by many who would make wartime American policy on Vietnam, acknowledge the inherent similarities in American and European colonial aims and practices. What Americans celebrated as "benevolent assimilation" in the Philippines both sanitized the violence of colonial conquest and presumed the backwardness and inferiority of their Filipino beneficiaries. If American colonial tutelage in the Philippines was a transitional stage to independence, as another scholar recently argues, "self-rule was not the product of a social compact among equals but the result of sustained disciplinary measures requiring the colonized to submit unstintingly to a pedagogy of repression and mastery."[11] Despite Roosevelt's belief that trusteeship in Vietnam marked a revolutionary break from the colonial past, the shared Euro-American beliefs that underlay the American approach to the Philippines and Vietnam belied his exceptionalist claims.

## Debating the Instruments of Change: Postwar Planning and Vietnam

As President Roosevelt worked in 1943 to advance his plans for international trusteeship in Indochina, members of the State Department's postwar planning staff began to craft their own proposals to prepare Vietnam for independence and self-government. The final recommendations of State Department planners favored a more limited role for the United States in Vietnam's future development than the one envisioned by Roosevelt, but their deliberations on the necessity for political, economic, and social change in Vietnam were infused by the same broader assumptions that guided Roosevelt's plans for trusteeship as well as his insistence that American models could best direct Vietnam's future development.

The most sustained wartime discussion in Washington of Indochina policy took place in the Subcommittee on Territorial Problems, one of the many committees in the State Department's labyrinth postwar planning apparatus. In meetings held in November 1943, the subcommittee took up the question: "Should Indo-China be restored to French sovereignty, with or without conditions?" For these discussions, its regular membership was supplemented with representatives from the Division of Far Eastern Affairs and several members of the policy planning research staff who were to serve as area specialists. None of these specialists had particular training on Vietnam, but three of them—Kenneth P. Landon, Amry Vandenbosch, and Melvin K. Knight—did bring some knowledge of Southeast Asia and French colonialism. Landon, a former missionary in Thailand for ten years, had recently joined the State Department's Division of Southwest Pacific Affairs. Vandenbosch, a University of Kentucky political scientist who was the leading American scholar on the Dutch East Indies, and Knight, an economic historian who had published works on French colonial rule in North Africa, were members of the research staff. Isaiah Bowman, a noted Johns Hopkins geographer and an important advisor to President Roosevelt on colonial issues, chaired the subcommittee.[12]

The subcommittee initially took up a review and discussion of working papers prepared by Vandenbosch and Knight on French colonial practices in Indochina and the capabilities of indigenous peoples to govern themselves. In their critical assessments of French colonialism and Vietnamese society, which met with general agreement among the members of the subcommittee, Vandenbosch and Knight echoed the views of President Roosevelt. Subcommittee members believed that French practices in Vietnam "fell short of the standards set by most of the other Western European powers." The committee also shared Roosevelt's views that the Vietnamese were not yet ready for independence. Their impressions of Vietnamese political immaturity, like those of Roosevelt, were partially grounded in perceptions of the failures of French colonial rule. French unwillingness to prepare the Vietnamese for eventual self-government, subcommittee members argued, represented a sharp departure from what they believed to be prevailing colonial norms. Vandenbosch told the subcommittee that the "Dutch had done much better by their colonies than had the French" as "the Indonesians had made more rapid progress in the direction of self-government under the Dutch than had the populations of Indo-China under the French." A sense of the superiority of American policies in the Philippines also shaped the subcommittee perception that French failure to guide Vietnamese political development had violated a fundamental obligation of colonizing powers. Assistant Secretary of State Adolph A. Berle, another subcommittee member, observed that "self-government, as was indicated by our experience in the Philippines, depended . . . on the policy which the government pursued."[13]

The subcommittee's perceptions of Vietnamese political immaturity also rested on assumptions of Vietnam as an inferior society, although it emerged more elliptically in their deliberations. In a discussion of Vietnam's "backward political development," Knight told subcommittee members "it was doubtful whether the Annamites . . . would have been any better off had the French not taken them in hand." Vandenbosch called French rule the "glue" that held Vietnam together, adding "it would not be possible to conduct any government in this area" without it. The subcommittee's contemptuous perceptions of Vietnamese nationalism did not reassure them that Vietnam was capable of self-government. Members of the subcommittee expressed sympathy with the frustrations that had produced nationalist sentiment in Vietnam, as they believed French colonial policy had done little to advance Vietnamese political or socioeconomic welfare. But their unfavorable impressions of nationalist politics reinforced their sense that the Vietnamese lacked the abilities necessary to immediately govern themselves. As Vandenbosch told the subcommittee, the nationalist movement was "limited" to a small number of educated elites who were unable to win the support of the peasant masses.[14]

The idea that indigenous political traditions or abilities might permit the Vietnamese to govern themselves in the postwar period was almost inconceivable to the members of the subcommittee as a revealing exchange between Knight and Bowman illustrates. Despite his derisive portrait of Vietnamese political culture, Knight somewhat timorously suggested that the Vietnamese might be capable of self-government without external direction. Bowman, with the apparent assent of the committee, immediately pressed Knight to elaborate. Did Knight really believe the chances of self-government in Vietnam were good? When Knight replied "it would be a good bet," Bowman questioned him further. Under Bowman's continuing pressure, Knight began to back away from his initial assertion, suggesting "it was probably difficult for an old culture to be reformed along modern lines." But he added the "case was still open as to whether it was governable." Not satisfied, Bowman pressed him again. Finally, Knight conceded "while at some future time Indo-China might be made self-governing" that time had not yet arrived.[15]

There was considerable debate and disagreement, however, over the appropriate policy to promote Vietnam's eventual movement toward independence, with advocates of international trusteeship pitted against supporters of a vaguer international accountability for the restoration of some from of French colonial rule. A minority of the subcommittee embraced President Roosevelt's proposal for international trusteeship in "recognition of the failure of France to provide adequately for the welfare of the native population." A majority of the subcommittee members raised a number of objections to international trusteeship for Indochina. Several members questioned the efficacy of employing an international administrative agency to effect reform in indigenous society. Trusteeship, one member argued, would be "experimental in character and of doubtful effectiveness." Although French administration "was maintained at a low level of competence," he continued, "the long experience of the French in the colony could be utilized to good advantage during the period of postwar development." Several members also asked how France could be required to relinquish its sovereignty over Indochina when the British and the Dutch were likely to maintain their colonies in Southeast Asia. Advocates of trusteeship argued that France was a special case as it had not been able to protect itself and its colonies at the outset of the war. Moreover, they suggested, "the difference of physical strength was so great between France on the one hand and Great Britain on the other" that France could only retake Indochina with the assistance of Allied military forces and would thus be bound by the wishes of the other powers.[16]

While the uncertainties of the wartime situation prompted it to reject the form of international trusteeship, the subcommittee remained committed to the goals of reforming French colonial practices and preparing the Vietnamese for eventual self-government. In place of trusteeship, the majority of the subcommittee supported a combination of incentives and constraints aimed at placing postwar French colonial rule under "international accountability." Confident in the powers of international suasion, they believed the establishment of a regional commission in Southeast Asia, a colonial charter for Vietnam, and the preparation of annual reports by the French would reform French colonial practices in Indochina and hasten the emergence of a self-governing Vietnamese state in a more realistic manner than the "idealism" of international trusteeship.[17]

More important than the debates over the mechanisms by which to guide Indochina toward postwar independence, however, were the common assumptions that informed proposals for trusteeship and commissions, charters, and reports. Both proposals shared Roosevelt's unwavering belief in the applicability of American political values and institutions for organizing the postwar Vietnamese state and tutoring the Vietnamese in principles of self-government, as well as the moderation Roosevelt believed had marked America's successful policy in the Philippines. Advocates within the State Department for international trusteeship wholly reflected this Rooseveltian vision. The fullest extant outline of American plans for trusteeship in Indochina, contained in a March 1944 working paper drafted mainly by the Division of Southwest Pacific Affairs, went far beyond Roosevelt's somewhat cryptic vision of how trusteeship would actually work. It called for the establishment of an executive, a legislative, and a judicial branch under joint control of the Vietnamese and international trustees; for the creation of a civil service board to oversee training in local and national governmental affairs; for immediate voting rights for indigenous peoples; and for a constitutional convention that demonstrated the depth of American faith in the cross-cultural transfer of its political institutions. The twenty-year period of trusteeship before granting Vietnam full independence recommended in the working paper also suggests the persistence of the gradualist Philippine model in shaping State Department policy toward Indochina.[18]

But the combination of a regional commission, a colonial charter, and annual reports that increasingly dominated State Department planning for postwar Indochina also firmly rested on the use of American models to slowly correct the perceived weaknesses in French colonialism and Vietnamese society. Discussion of the ways in which the colonial charter and annual reports would serve as conditions for a return of French colonial rule most fully reflected the American vision of political and economic liberalization in Vietnam. State Department planners suggested that the French be asked to promise to establish local and national representative institutions, provide for indigenous suffrage, expand educational and occupational opportunities, and develop local industries. The shared assumptions joining Roosevelt's advocacy of trusteeship and the deliberations of State Department planners were also fully reflected in American reporting on Vietnam from southern China and the recommendations of field officers concerning Vietnam's future development.[19]

## "Subservient Annamites": Wartime American Reporting on Vietnam from Southern China

In a December 1942 cable to Washington, Clarence E. Gauss, the U.S. ambassador to China, reported that he had seen a letter protesting the arrest by Chinese authorities of a Vietnamese nationalist leader. A year would pass before Gauss and his embassy staff realized whom the Chinese had arrested.

Gauss relayed a letter in a December 1943 dispatch to the State Department from the Central Committee of the Indochina Section of the International Anti-Aggression Association. The letter asked Gauss for assistance in the "immediate and unconditional" release of "Hu Chih-minh . . . in order that he may lead the members of the Association in activities against the Japanese." The "Annamite" in question, Gauss told the department, "was apparently" the same person whose arrest he had reported the previous December.[20]

Gauss's December 1943 dispatch, the first mention by any U.S. policy maker of Hồ Chí Minh, reveals the limitations on American wartime reporting on Vietnam and its dismissive perceptions of the Vietnamese. The embassy staff did make inquiries into the reasons for Hồ's continued detention, apparently unaware he had been released by the Chinese some four months earlier. But the name Hồ Chí Minh meant nothing to Gauss and the embassy's political officers. Nor did Gauss see the need to reply to the "Annamite organization" or further investigate its activities. The French delegation at Chungking, which was a primary source of information about the Vietnamese for American officials in southern China, had assured him it "was of little importance," probably one of the "Annamite organizations under the auspices of the Kuomintang" representing nothing "more than an attempt by the Chinese to make a show of their friendly feelings for subject peoples in Asia."[21]

Gauss and the U.S. embassy in Chungking were one of several critical sources of American political reporting on Vietnam from wartime China. While Indochina remained occupied by the Japanese, American diplomatic, military, and intelligence personnel responsible for following developments in Vietnam did so largely from Chungking or Kunming in southern China. Planning documents from the Office of Strategic Services' Morale Operations (MO), designed to discredit the Japanese and disseminate pro-American propaganda to the Vietnamese, offer one important and typical example of appraisals from the field of Vietnamese society and its perceived receptivity to American models. Because MO planners saw their task as an extension of psychological warfare, they sought to identify what they termed "Annamite mentality." The starting point for these analyses was the assumption that "Annamite reasoning" was fundamentally different than "our own," reflecting the division between Western and Asian thought processes inherent in the prevailing beliefs in racialized cultural hierarchies. As one member of the MO planning team for Indochina remarked, "The stimuli from . . . reality can and do produce stereotypes in the minds of the natives quite different from those produced in our own minds."[22]

In the discussions of the Vietnamese role in American psychological warfare strategies by MO planners, the characteristics most commonly ascribed to the "Annamite mind" were almost always negative and condescending.

One MO report noted it was "futile" to attempt to win over the Vietnamese to the Allied cause by "propagandizing" them that a Japanese defeat would ultimately benefit Vietnam as it was "part of the fundamental psychology of Annamites to be interested only in ventures which promise a quick turnover." Reports that presented the "individual Annamite" as "a rather vain person" and urged MO campaigns to "[f]latter the pride of the Annamites by telling them that without their co-operation the Japs would not be able to do a thing" were lauded by MO senior planners as raising "an excellent, and well-taken, point."[23]

Another MO planning document suggested that the "subservience" and "mercenary proclivities" inherent in Vietnamese society were barriers to the successful establishment of an indigenous underground organization:

> The Annamites have been a subject race for so many years, by the French, and the Chinese before them, that they have no organizing ability or initiative. . . . They are quite incapable of developing an organization of any kind, certainly not an underground. Being suspicious of each other and practicing trickery among themselves, any organization they have ever attempted to create has always broken down from the incapacity of its members to pull together. An underground organization would fall apart before it ever got going. . . . The mercenary proclivities of the Annamites is another hindrance to the development of a successful underground. The Annamites will do anything for money but they cannot be expected to take risks from ideological motives.[24]

Propaganda leaflets were potentially more effective strategies, MO planners argued, because "Annamites love to talk," "enjoy lengthy discourses or lectures," and responded best to "emphatic" or "exaggerated words which qualify force."[25]

These deprecatory images of Vietnamese society also shaped the assertions of MO planners that Vietnam would be highly receptive to American direction. "The Annamites are used to obeying," one report argued. "Instructions, advice, pleas or recommendations coming from Americans would be effective because they are authoritative. The Annamites recognize authority." Another report suggested that because the "Annamites are very much impressed by physical strength, courage and skill," they particularly enjoyed American films about "cowboys" and "test pilots." The report also stressed "they are *very much impressed by mechanical perfection*, such as frigidaires, reconditioning units, guns, plants, etc., and for them the word 'American' is synonymous with perfection in all that is modern industry."[26]

In late summer of 1944, as Americans in southern China began to encounter for the first time representatives of the Việt Minh, the organizational vehicle through which Hồ and the Vietnamese communists would seize power in Vietnam in August 1945, their perceptions remained very unfavorable. A Việt Minh delegation in Kunming met with American officials in August and September 1944 and provided the basis for the first American reports on the existence of the Việt Minh, its organizational structure, and its program for national independence. Their American audience was unimpressed with what it learned. William Powell, the representative for the Office of War Information in Kunming, reported on several meetings with the Việt Minh and called them "rather naïve politically" and "not too well organized." Commenting on the history of Vietnamese anticolonialism that representatives of the Việt Minh had given him along with appeals for American assistance, Powell patronizingly remarked:

> The whole document . . . certainly is a touching appeal. Any coherent appeal from an oppressed people who wish to rule themselves is touching. However, from conversations with these leaders themselves, and with well-informed foreigners here, I think there is little doubt but what they are not ready for complete independence. They've had little experience in modern government . . . and probably will require quite a bit of tutelage before they can completely run their country themselves in as responsible a manner as a modern post-war government must be run.[27]

William Langdon, the U.S. consul at Kunming, was even more critical of the Vietnamese, dismissing the Việt Minh as a group of "no real importance in the Indochina questions" after his own meeting with their representatives in September 1944. Langdon reported to Washington that they "lacked the spirit and aggressiveness one would expect of revolutionaries" and "did not impress [him] as having proper knowledge of the world or a sufficient grasp of the international situation." They were not, he argued, "far enough advanced politically to maintain a stable society or familiar enough with administration, jurisprudence, science, industry, finance, communications operation, and commerce to run a state on modern lines."[28] The tenor of Langdon's recommendations, which closely followed diplomats in Washington who argued for a conditional restoration of French rule in Vietnam, fully reflected the prevailing American assumptions of French colonial failure, Vietnamese inadequacies, and the promise of American models. While he lauded trusteeship as "ideal at this stage for Indochina," he questioned if it was "within the realm of practical politics" as "it would be most certain to be opposed and obstructed" by France and Great Britain. The "only logical proposition for Indo-China," Langdon argued, was a period of tutelage under continued French rule. Reflecting American confidence in its abilities to reform both French colonialism and Vietnamese society, Langdon suggested the "commanding position" of the United States ought to make it possible to impose "certain conditions" on the French "to obtain for Annamites some substantial political rights." Gauss, the U.S. ambassador in Chunking, shared Langdon's views, telling Washington the time had come "to formulate a clear and definite policy" for the making of postcolonial Vietnam.[29]

With Roosevelt's death in April 1945 came the end of the U.S. advocacy of international trusteeship in Vietnam. When Harry S. Truman moved into the Oval Office, he undoubtedly knew little, if anything, of American postwar planning on Vietnam. Confronted by a host of more pressing issues, Truman only nominally oversaw two decisions that severely limited U.S. ability to influence immediate postwar developments in Vietnam. In May, Truman offered no opposition to State Department assurances to France that the United States recognized French sovereignty over Indochina. In July, at the Potsdam Conference, Truman endorsed the expansion of the British-led Southeast Asia Command's (SEAC) borders. Northern Vietnam remained in the American-dominated China theater, but Vietnamese territory south of the sixteenth parallel became the responsibility of SEAC that was sympathetic to French efforts to regain control of Indochina in the postwar period. By early September, French troops had joined British forces in occupying Sàigòn and accepting the surrender of Japan.

Despite the U.S. decision to move away from trusteeship, a number of contemporary French and British observers viewed U.S. support for the French return to Indochina with caution, remaining uneasy about future American intentions in Vietnam. While the European powers were right to be skeptical of a fundamental transformation in U.S. thinking about Vietnam, their lingering suspicions should not obscure the critical commonalities that united American and European perceptions toward Vietnam. Much of the existing scholarship on trusteeship minimizes or ignores those similarities. Along with viewing trusteeship as Roosevelt's personal crusade, these works often ruefully render it as a lost opportunity for acting on U.S. historical identification with the principle of self-determination.[30] The few departures from this tack, which depict trusteeship as an example of a peculiarly American manifestation of empire, also remain bounded by an exceptionalist explanatory framework for wartime U.S. policy in Vietnam.[31] But whether mourning the declension of U.S. anticolonial ideals or recovering a suppressed empire with uniquely American values and forms, these works emphasize essential U.S. differences from European colonial norms and the historical novelty of an American approach to colonialism. Like the policy makers they analyze, they do not pause to critically interrogate the contradictions in U.S. self-conceptions as an anticolonial power. Nor do they explore the revealing ways in which American discourse on colonized peoples closely followed that of most European powers.

The central place of time in American thinking about trusteeship for Vietnam is particularly revealing of the shared Euro-American norms out of which U.S. policy arose as well as how it would complicate relations with the French and the Vietnamese after 1945. Whether posed as the almost half-century of U.S. colonial rule in the Philippines or the quarter-century of trusteeship envisioned for Vietnam, the virtually unanimous perception among wartime American policy makers of the necessity for an exceedingly long period of tutelage in U.S. political, social, and cultural models signaled an underlying certainty of the vast chasm that separated the stasis of backward Vietnam from the dynamism of the United States. The conscious ordering of time in plans for trusteeship in Vietnam—premised on a gradual, unilinear, and progressive path to human development—sought to provide a temporal framework to guide the Vietnamese toward political and social change in the American image. By attempting to engineer the processes of change in Vietnam through the manipulation of the meaning and passage of time, trusteeship represented a variation, rather than a sharp departure, from the hierarchical conceptions of racial difference and the exercise of power at the heart of European colonialism.[32] In this sense, European suspicions about U.S. intentions in Vietnam might be seen not so much as fears that a crusading U.S. anticolonialism sought to overturn the colonial order but as a more nationalistic reaction against the emergence of a powerful rival who sought to challenge Europeans' own efforts to control colonial time and space.

Significantly, however, the temporal order embedded in trusteeship was also an effort to retard the passage of time, indicating doubts that lurked beneath the supreme confidence through which American and Europeans appeared to approach the colonial project. The compression of time was an essential element in the dual character of the conceptions of modernity that animated Euro-American understandings of their own societies and those they encountered in the colonized world. On the one hand, the embrace of modernity reflected assurance of the universal and enduring virtues of contemporary Western society. On the other hand, the telescoping of time, an inevitable result of the competitive and speculative rhythms of capitalism that accompanied the rise of modernity, also produced an overwhelming fear of fragmentation, transience, and chaotic change.[33] This prevailing sensibility was reinforced for both American and European policy makers of the World War II era, whose historical experience was shaped by two world wars, the rise of fascism, and the worldwide economic depression.

The palpable doubts and fears over what the uncontrolled acceleration of time could produce framed the temporal order that informed U.S. plans for trusteeship in Vietnam. The dislocations of World War II quickened the pace toward decolonization in Vietnam and much of the colonized world, producing a sense among both the colonizers and the colonized of time rushing forward. For both the French and the Americans, the quickening pace of change was viewed with alarm. If the French would have preferred to arrest completely the temporal movement toward decolonization, U.S. plans for trusteeship, with the twenty-year timetable for Vietnamese independence, were also profoundly conservative. Emblematic of the fears on which the faith in modernity rested, trusteeship aimed to retard the passage of time in order to wrest control over temporality and reassert the centrality of rational, orderly, and gradually progressive paths to Vietnam's future development.

With the movement away from trusteeship, and the related notions of colonial commissions and charters, Americans abandoned their efforts to manipulate so closely the processes of change in Vietnam. Moreover, the accelerating movement toward decolonization in Vietnam made an extended period of tutelage in advance of independence moot. Ironically, the Vietnamese revolutionaries who joined Hồ in proclaiming Vietnam free of French colonial rule in 1945 enthusiastically embraced the modernist conception of quickening time. But the American vision of postcolonial Vietnam that emerged during the World War II period remained an essential starting point for U.S. attitudes toward Vietnam in the postwar period.

Like their counterparts during World War II, America policy makers after the 1945 period seldom paused to explicate the premises that lay behind their perceptions of the Vietnamese and the role they believed U.S. models should play in the construction of a new political community in Vietnam. Nor were these ideas ever fundamentally challenged. Americans continued to classify and define the Vietnamese in a way that signaled U.S. power and superiority. At the same time, the growing American sense of mission to remake Vietnamese society in its own image continued to join U.S. policy in Vietnam to the broader Euro-American project to transform the immutable, stagnant, and primitive "Oriental."

As the Cold War came to dominate American policy, the idiom of modernization rather than cultural hierarchies informed U.S. discourse toward the postcolonial world, including Vietnam. In its conceptual underpinnings, however, modernization theory reflected many of the central assumptions of the racialized cultural hierarchies that had shaped U.S. efforts to identify and manipulate social change in non-Western societies throughout the century, including a sharp distinction between the "backward" and the "modern" and the insistence that "stagnant societies" ought to move in a gradual, linear path toward the universal evolutionary endpoint represented by the United States.[34]

The significance of these ideas in mediating and framing the Cold War imperatives that brought Vietnam to a central position for U.S. foreign policy in the 1960s is perhaps best revealed in Lyndon B. Johnson's thinking about Vietnam at the time of his decision to send U.S. ground troops to South Vietnam. Johnson's attitude toward the Vietnamese was derisive, as his often-expressed sense of North Vietnam as a "piss-ant" nation or "a raggedy-ass little fourth-rate country" suggests.[35] But for Johnson, the escalating war in Vietnam held meanings beyond the need for Soviet containment. In a key speech on, Vietnam delivered at Johns Hopkins University in April 1965, Johnson coupled his expression of U.S. resolve against communism with an offer of $1 billion to support an immense project under the auspices of the United Nations to build dams along the Mekong River in Thailand, Laos, Cambodia, and Vietnam to foster regional economic development, a project Johnson believed could include Hồ's government. "The vast Mekong River," Johnson said in the speech, "can provide food and water and power on a scale to dwarf even our own TVA."[36]

The connection Johnson made to the New Deal Tennessee Valley Authority, a project one scholar of Johnson's policy in Vietnam aptly terms the internal colonization of a backward America, suggests that the interconnections between U.S. models of development and their universal applicability continued to exert a powerful hold on America's imagined Vietnam.[37] As Johnson said after the speech, "I want to leave the footprints of America on Vietnam. I want them to say when the Americans come, this is what they leave—schools, not long cigars. We're going to turn the Mekong into a Tennessee Valley. . . . Old Hồ can't turn me down."[38]

# 13

# The United States and Southeast Asia in an Era of Decolonization, 1945–1965

*Robert J. McMahon*

The end of the imperial era and the concomitant rise of the so-called Third World unquestionably rank among the central, defining features of modern world history. In no corner of the globe, of course, did the twin processes of decolonization and national and regional transformation proceed with greater violence, turmoil, and upheaval than in Southeast Asia. These processes both shaped and were in turn shaped by another of the modern epoch's central, defining features: the geopolitical and ideological battle for global power and influence waged between the United States and the Soviet Union. The so-called Cold War not only coincided temporally with the epic struggles for freedom that erupted across the Third World in the wake of World War II, but inevitably shaped the temper, pace, and ultimate outcome of those struggles as well. Nowhere, of course, more powerfully than in Southeast Asia. Scholars of modern Southeast Asia, whether their specializations lie in the realms of politics, culture, economy, foreign relations, or social and intellectual history, must grapple, either directly or indirectly, with these structural forces that have exerted so profound an imprint on the region's states and societies. This chapter examines in broad-brush fashion the role played by the United States in the evolution of post–World War II Southeast Asia. How important was the United States to the region's evolution? What difference, in the end, did its active involvement in regional affairs make?

During the two crucial, formative decades bracketed by the end of the Pacific war in August 1945 and the introduction of American ground forces into South Vietnam in March 1965, the United States emerged as the dominant external power in the region, far eclipsing the former European colonial masters. Top U.S. political leaders, diplomats, military strategists, and intelligence experts reached virtual unanimity during those years about the vital importance of the Southeast Asian region to the protection and furtherance of fundamental national interests. They sought, accordingly, to promote political stability and economic recovery throughout the region, while simultaneously laboring both to inoculate the area's regimes and peoples against the communist virus and to gain their alignment with the West in the Cold War.

U.S. officials saw Southeast Asia as a critical international battleground in which the stakes appeared extraordinarily high. Paul H. Nitze, head of the State Department's Policy Planning Staff, baldly asserted in early 1952 that the "loss of Southeast Asia would present an unacceptable threat to [the] position of [the] U.S., both in [the] Far East and world-wide."[1] The region's "loss" to the communists, insisted State Department Soviet expert Charles Bohlen, would exert so profound an impact on the overall balance of world power that were it to occur, "we would have lost the Cold War."[2] Secretary of State Dean Acheson, in equally alarmist fashion, confided to British foreign secretary Anthony Eden, in mid-1952, that "we are lost if we lose Southeast Asia without a fight"; the Western powers, consequently, "must do what we can to save Southeast Asia."[3] The views of U.S. officials emerged from a set of generalized fears concerning both the communist threat and the prospect of global economic stagnation. While the strategic and economic explanatory frameworks that have long dominated the historical and social science literature about American Cold War foreign policy may hold true, they themselves are not entirely sufficient interpretive categories for explicating American actions in post–World War II Southeast Asia. The more diffuse realms of culture and ideology, including deep-seated racialist attitudes and convictions about presumed racial hierarchies, must be added to the mix if we are to achieve a fuller and more nuanced appreciation of the complexities of the American–Southeast Asian encounter.

Several key, guiding questions will give shape and form to the ensuing analysis: Why did Southeast Asia became so important to the United States? Why were American fears about regional trends so intense, so alarmist, and at the same time so exaggerated? What did the United States actually seek to achieve in Southeast Asia, and through what means? And why, for all its exertions, commitments, and massive reservoirs of military and economic power, did Washington policy makers achieve so few of their stated goals?

It might be useful, from the outset, simply to ponder the breathtaking magnitude of the changes that swept Southeast Asia and impelled the concomitant transformation of the U.S. role in the region during this twenty-year period. As the Pacific war hurtled toward its fiery close in the early days of August 1945, only Thailand among Southeast Asian territories possessed an independent, indigenous government. And Thailand's independence had been severely curtailed and compromised first by the Europeans and then by the Japanese. Independence for most of the region's other territories, despite the dreams and plans of Hồ Chí Minh, Sukarno, Aung San, and other aspiring nation-builders, and despite the cynical last-minute promises of the embattled Japanese, seemed but a distant prospect. Still laboring under the harsh yoke of the Japanese occupation, in many cases economically and physically devastated from the combined weight of Tokyo's imperium and the Pacific war, Southeast Asian polities and peoples longed for a respite from the death, destruction, dislocation, and suffering that the anvil of war and occupation had brought them. To what extent, though, could they now be the principal agents of their own destiny?

The Japanese advance had, to be sure, irrevocably shattered the myth and mystique of both Western invincibility and white racial superiority. Perhaps no event proved more telling in that regard than the surrender of the British garrison in Singapore on February 15, 1942, to a numerically inferior force of Japanese attackers. It ranked as "the greatest disaster in our history," lamented British prime minister Winston Churchill. "The British Empire in the Far East depended on prestige," observed one Australian diplomat at the time. "This prestige has been completely shattered." Yet, what would take the place of the Western colonial order? At the end of the war, the United States seemed unlikely to take too direct and forceful of a role in Southeast Asia. Its prime interests lay elsewhere; the administration of Franklin D. Roosevelt, moreover, had promised an early grant of formal independence to the Philippines, its lone possession in the region, presaging a possible reduction in America's regional involvement.

A Southeast Asian Rip Van Winkle who had gone to bed at the time of the Hiroshima and Nagasaki atomic bomb blasts only to reawaken in 1965 would have been flabbergasted by the region's metamorphosis. Independent nation-states had by then, of course, replaced virtually all of the old colonial regimes. Few vestiges of French or Dutch influence remained, and British strength, though still significant in the Malaysian territories, had receded entirely from Burma and was plainly on the wane everywhere else. The dramatic eclipse of European power and the ascendancy of indigenous nationalist movements and governments would doubtless have topped the list of astonishing changes observed by our awakening friend. Yet, he surely would have noted another tectonic shift in the local landscape as well: the pervasive presence and influence of the United States—of American soldiers, diplomats, businessmen, technical advisers, and development experts, and of American dollars, arms, goods, ideas, culture, and more. This latter-day Rip Van Winkle could hardly have failed to recognize the surging American military involvement in the region—not just in South Vietnam, where a major land war was brewing, and over North Vietnam, where the United States had just inaugurated a punishing air war, but in Thailand and Laos as well, where U.S. military and intelligence personnel threatened to overrun these countries, and in the Philippines, where the United States had constructed the largest air and naval bases in the entire Pacific region.

If measuring and accounting for change over time remains one of the historian's chief responsibilities, then surely the twenty-year period that our metaphorical visitor slumbered through—and that we will be investigating with all the advantages conferred by hindsight—offers interpretive challenges aplenty.

Any explanation for the dramatic expansion of American interests and involvement in Southeast Asia after 1945 must begin with the transformative impact of World War II on U.S. thinking and planning. The Roosevelt and Truman administrations were determined to mold a new world order out of the wreckage of history's most costly conflict, a world order that would ensure the long-term security of the United States and would establish a more open, vibrant, and depression-proof global economic system. Although never as central to overall U.S. plans as Western Europe and Northeast Asia, the Southeast Asian region was, nonetheless, quite important to those plans in several distinct respects. The United States intended to maintain a strong military posture throughout the Pacific, which, first of all, necessitated the maintenance of extensive military bases and air transit rights in the Philippines and elsewhere. American planners also recognized the important contribution that Southeast Asian oil, rubber, tin, and other key resources could make to world economic recovery and growth. In addition, Roosevelt and Truman administration officials sought to effect a gradual and orderly devolution of political authority from Western colonists to moderate, local nationalists. That policy aim, first publicized in the context of Roosevelt's vaguely formulated trusteeship scheme, derived from the American belief that only the progressive evolution toward eventual native self-government could defuse the tensions endemic to imperial rule and thus keep the area peaceful, stable, and productive over the long term.

The Truman administration's chief initiatives of the early postwar years— its formal transfer of sovereignty to an independent Philippines government, its quiet entreaties to the European colonial powers to follow suit, its discouragement of violence as a solution to the colonial problem, its decision to retain huge naval and air bases in the Philippines, its efforts to help negotiate peaceful resolutions of local political conflicts in Indonesia and Indochina, and its efforts to spark regional economic recovery through programs of economic and technical assistance—all aimed at the development of an orderly, peaceful, and productive Southeast Asia. Washington's civilian and military decision makers were convinced that the United States needed to use its power actively, constructively, and imaginatively in Southeast Asia as elsewhere, in order to help sculpt the kind of world most conducive to American security and commercial interests. These policy priorities almost certainly meant that the United States would assume a far more active role in postwar Southeast Asia than it ever had in the prewar period, even after divesting itself of its Philippine colony. That would have been the case even if the Soviet Union had not existed. Yet, without the intensifying Cold War of the late 1940s and the heightened insecurities and fears it generated, it is highly unlikely that the United States would have carved its own empire out of the rapidly decolonizing Southeast Asia.[4]

Probably no question stemming from the stunning transformation in America's regional role has divided scholarly experts more than the relative weight that should be assigned to economic interests, on the one hand, versus strategic variables, on the other.[5] As I have argued elsewhere, the economic and strategic foundations of U.S. policy were so closely interrelated that they are best understood as mutually reinforcing phenomena. Southeast Asia's growing importance from the late 1940s onward sprang both from its perceived vulnerability to communism and from the value of its resources and markets to the economic rehabilitation of Western Europe and Japan. Put another way, the region became vital to the United States because of its salience to the global containment strategy and because of its importance in the building of a vibrant, American-led, world capitalist system.

But material and strategic factors, either alone or in combination, cannot fully account for the dramatically increased levels of U.S. involvement in Southeast Asia during these years. Political variables, stemming especially from the vagaries of America's two-party system and the incessant partisan competition for advantage and votes that marked Cold War America, must be added to the interpretive mix. Throughout the 1950s and 1960s, political considerations frequently reinforced the material and strategic factors that were propelling the United States toward a more active, interventionist posture in Southeast Asia. The initial U.S. aid commitment to the French in Indochina, it bears remembering, came in early 1950, a time in which Harry S Truman was being savagely assaulted by Republican critics in Congress for having "lost" China. The embattled president's determination to protect his exposed political flank by drawing the line against further communist advances somewhere in Asia plainly influenced his decision to reverse previous policy and to begin providing direct aid to the French. Significantly, the initial aid dollars Truman approved for French Indochina came from a fund created to contain communism within the "the general area of China," a legislative pot of money established by many of the same congressional Republicans who were vilifying the Democratic chief executive for failing to prevent Mao Tse-tung's triumph.[6] Dwight D. Eisenhower, John F. Kennedy, and Lyndon B. Johnson proved equally attuned to the treacherous Cold War domestic environment; they were each haunted by similar fears about the dire political consequences of appearing weak or indecisive in the face of communist challenges. Referring specifically to Vietnam, Kennedy confided to a journalist friend early in his presidency, "I can't give up a piece of territory like that to the Communists and get the American people to reelect me."[7]

Similarly, Johnson worried, according to political adviser Jack Valenti, that Republicans and conservative Democrats together would have "torn him to pieces" had he failed to hold the line against communism in Southeast Asia.[8]

The fixation of American policy makers with the psychological underpinnings of power, best captured by the frequently invoked concept of credibility, also pushed Washington to assume greater obligations in Southeast Asia. Locked in what it viewed as a life-and-death struggle with an inexorably expansionist Soviet Union, the United States felt compelled to demonstrate not just its power, but its resolution and reliability, to deter adversaries, reassure allies, and rally to its side fence-straddling neutrals. If it failed to do so, the Soviet Union, China, and local communist revolutionary movements would view the United States as a paper tiger and thus be emboldened—the dreaded Munich syndrome. Aggression would spread, according to this nightmare-inducing calculus; the proverbial dominoes would fall: alliances would crack; America's friends would lose faith in the power and promises of their superpower patron; and the nonaligned would tilt toward the Soviet bloc, convinced that historical momentum lay there and not with the West.[9]

The credibility fixation, so prominently featured in most leading accounts of the Johnson administration's descent into war in Vietnam, influenced virtually every major Southeast Asian commitment undertaken by the United States throughout this period. Certainly, the decision to form the Southeast Asia Treaty Organization (SEATO) in 1954 makes little sense if one leaves out the underlying psychological calculus. Secretary of State John Foster Dulles appreciated the criticisms directed toward the SEATO concept from the skeptical British and from his own joint chiefs of staff, each of whom pointed to the inadequacy of local forces for any major military action. Dulles countered, however, that SEATO's prime value lay in the powerful signal that it sent about America's firm commitment to the region. Hence, the very existence of SEATO, no matter how weak it might be in terms of actual forces on the ground, could serve as a deterrent to Chinese aggression; it could, at the same time, give heart and hope to the region's struggling noncommunist nations. The United States, Dulles told Eisenhower, needed "to take account of political factors, to give the Thai people, the Burmese, and the Malayans some hope that their area would not simply be overrun and occupied until China was destroyed, in order to keep them on our side."[10]

The abiding need to demonstrate strength, determination, and reliability, for the sake of enemies, friends, and the uncommitted alike, thus also governed the shape and extent of U.S. commitments in post–World War II Southeast Asia. Economic interests, geostrategy, and politics, in whatever combination one assembles them, offer incomplete explanations for how a 1959 State Department report could depict sparsely populated, landlocked

Laos as "a front line in the Cold War."[11] They could not explain why, two years later, the Kennedy administration would describe the crisis in Laos as "a symbolic test of intentions, wills and strengths between the major powers of the West and the Communist Bloc."[12] Or for how, even more fundamentally, the United States came to equate the survival of the Sàigòn regime with the security of the entire free world.

The symbolic imperatives that so elevated the perceived stakes involved for the United States in Southeast Asia frequently dovetailed with and reinforced more tangible interests, as did the political variables mentioned earlier. Yet, these forces need to be disaggregated for analytic purposes. Credibility, as an analytic category, belongs more appropriately to the ideational realm—the realm of beliefs, ideas, values, and fears—than to the realm of interests. It is rooted in the murky terrain of perception and cognition. Essentially, only other states can validate the credibility of any power's words or actions. To be credible—to deter or to reassure successfully—means that others will believe your threats and your promises and act accordingly. For a state to establish its resolve effectively, it must thus influence the perceptions and beliefs of other states.[13] America's generalized credibility obsession had as much or more to do with its rapidly multiplying commitments in postwar Southeast Asia as did the value its strategists placed on the region's intrinsic importance. There is also something peculiarly American about the preoccupation with the credibility of power—and with the excessive fear of external dangers and search for complete security so closely associated with it.

Calculations about one's credibility are culturally bound, it bears emphasizing, as are threat assessments. At the root of credibility lies fear: fear about dangers lurking in the international environment, fear about the intentions (and capabilities) of adversaries and potential adversaries, fear about the fragility of one's alliances, and fear about one's own limitations and vulnerabilities. For those who might object that such fears were actually quite reasonable, or at least prudent, in view of the highly unsettled nature of the Cold War system and the insatiable appetites of Moscow and Beijing, it might be useful to compare American perceptions with those of its North Atlantic Treaty Organization alliance partners. They did not, for the most part, view Southeast Asia either as a critical Cold War battleground or as a symbolic test of U.S. power and will. From the early 1950s up through the Vietnam War, America's closest Cold War allies parted company with Washington in their assessments of China's intentions in the region, in their judgments about the dangers posed to free world security by the Pathet Lao, Viet Cong, and North Vietnamese, and in their broader appreciation of Southeast Asia's relevance to the overall balance of world power.

European allies, and the Canadians and Japanese as well, proved generally sympathetic to the anti-interventionist advice and neutralization proposals pertaining to Indochina that French president Charles de Gaulle put forward in the early 1960s. They tended to view Southeast Asia as peripheral to Western security, downplayed the existence of the presumed Chinese regional threat that so exercised the Americans, and disparaged the relevance of a Sàigòn regime mired in corruption and incompetence to the overall position of the West in the ongoing Cold War. They mocked, though rarely in public, the American effort to make Sàigòn synonymous with Berlin.[14]

An unusually candid exchange between Secretary of State Dean Rusk and French ambassador Herve Alphand, in July 1964, well captures the chasm that separated American and European views regarding South Vietnam's symbolic importance. "To us," Rusk told his French interlocutor, "the defense of South Vietnam has the same significance as the defense of Berlin." Alphand vehemently dismissed the validity of such a comparison. The stakes in Europe were "enormous," the French diplomatic countered, and "the loss of Berlin would shake the foundations of Western security." If South Vietnam were lost, on the other hand, he observed dismissively, not much would be lost. Rusk parried that U.S. guarantees to protect Berlin would lose their credibility if the United States were to pull out of South Vietnam. "It was all part of the same struggle to prevent an extension of Communist influence," he insisted. Alphand would have none of it; he stressed that any negotiated settlement in Vietnam would naturally contain its own set of guarantees and hence would not have the effect of weakening Western confidence in U.S. guarantees elsewhere.[15]

That the apocalyptic fears underlying the massive U.S. escalation in Indochina were not generally shared by America's most valued allies—nations also committed to the containment of communism, nations on the very same side of the Cold War divide—points again to the importance of culture and ideology in any holistic interpretation of American involvement in postwar Southeast Asia. Nations apprehend external developments not in some purely objective, detached analytical fashion, but rather through a series of filters, filters laminated by the prejudices, hopes, fears, insecurities, and historical baggage particular to individual societies. To recognize that Americans saw the Cold War, and Southeast Asia's role in the Cold War, in a starkly different manner than did most of their alliance partners should hardly surprise us. Despite a deep reservoir of shared values and interests, Europeans were not Americans. They did not apprehend dangers or opportunities in a similar manner, nor did they vest the Cold War with the same degree of moral-ideological meaning as did their friends on the other side of the Atlantic.

Scholars have of late begun to pay increased attention to this dimension of American foreign policy. In his introduction to a recent collection of essays on the Cold War, the Norwegian historian Odd Arne Westad correctly identifies "the increasing willingness to take ideas and beliefs seriously as causal factors" as one of the hallmarks of recent scholarship.[16] In the same collection, Melvyn P. Leffler, whose own impressive and influential work has emphasized the centrality of strategic variables in U.S. Cold War decision making, concedes that he previously "understated the role of ideology" by conceiving it "too narrowly." Ideology, he now recognizes, "shaped perceptions of threat, the selection of friends, the assessment of opportunities, and the understanding of what was happening within the international system itself."[17] Anders Stephanson, in the same volume, goes so far as to label the Cold War an American ideological project. "Amidst the present triumphalism," he provocatively suggests, "one might ask . . . what it was about the United States and its self-conception that made the Cold War a natural way of being toward the world, why indeed the Cold War turned out to be the American way."[18]

The work of Michael H. Hunt, whose pioneering 1987 book *Ideology and U.S. Foreign Policy* calls much needed attention to the powerful influence exerted by beliefs, ideas, values, and fears throughout the two-century history of American foreign relations, remains highly suggestive on these larger issues. Hunt posits three core ideas that governed the American engagement with the wider world from the foundation of the republic through the Cold War era: a commitment to freedom, a fear of revolution, and a belief in racial hierarchies among peoples and nations.[19]

Each of these three core ideas bear direct relevance to our understanding of U.S. actions in postwar Southeast Asia. I have already emphasized the importance of the fear-based element of Hunt's triptych, as revealed especially by America's credibility fixation—in its various guises. Another source of that anxiety did, indeed, spring from long-standing American worries about the instability, chaos, and threats to life, property, and investment climates invariably unleashed by revolutionary movements. The uncertainties posed by a region in the throes of sweeping socioeconomic turmoil, revolutionary ferment, and anticolonial, often anti-Western, insurgencies clearly unsettled an American elite that had a long established preference for gradual, evolutionary change. That so many Southeast Asian nationalists looked for advice, aid, and inspiration to the Soviet Union and China, revolutionary states whose own universalizing ideology of Marxism-Leninism stood as the mocking mirror opposite of America's, induced further apprehension within policy-making circles.

Another deeply rooted ideological principle also conditioned the American encounter with the external world: a commitment to freedom, at home and overseas. Embedded at the very heart of American foreign policy, before and after the Cold War, was a Manichean differentiation between freedom and tyranny, between good and evil. That morally tinged view of world affairs merged with a national self-conception of the United States as the beacon for and savior of the globe's freedom-loving peoples to produce a powerful sense of self-righteousness among Americans. Its commitment to freedom stood as the ultimate justification for America's entry into World War II, after all, and for its vigorous prosecution of the Cold War. That commitment found expression in the Atlantic Charter's sweeping promise to "respect the right of all peoples to choose the form of government under which they will live," as well as in NSC 68's dire warnings about the brutal suppression of freedom sure to follow in any new territories falling under the sway of the Kremlin's godless tyrants.[20]

U.S. leaders typically linked the survival of freedom at home with the preservation of freedom abroad. "If communism is allowed to absorb the free nations," warned Truman at the height of the Cold War, "then we would be isolated from our sources of supplies and detached from our friends. Then we would have to take defense measures which might really bankrupt our economy, and change our way of life so that we couldn't recognize it as American any longer."[21] Secretary of State Acheson likewise identified the overriding U.S. foreign policy challenge as deriving from the need "to foster an environment in which our national life and individual freedom can survive and prosper."[22] Or, as the editors of the popular periodical *Saturday Evening Post* put it, the United States had "to reconstitute civilized life and decent political and economic relations in the world, if we want those conditions to continue here at home."[23]

That this genuine, deeply felt commitment to freedom rarely led to the unequivocal embrace of the independence movements that crested in postwar Southeast Asia has often perplexed scholars. Some have posited a dichotomy between idealism and realism in American policy making, one of the hoariest of diplomatic history's clichés about the United States; others have highlighted what they see as the rank hypocrisy and cynicism revealed by America's public support for a self-determination that it rarely backed without serious reservations; still others have dismissed the importance of ideas entirely, contending that they served merely as a convenient mask that helped obscure the "real" material forces driving policy. An appreciation for ideas as causal factors in their own right provides a more satisfactory explanation for the waffling and seemingly inconsistent U.S. response to decolonization in Southeast Asia. Ideologies are complex, not simple; they frequently harbor conflicting and contested sentiments. In the "policy agendas and cognitive frameworks" of American leaders, argues Hunt, freedom has been the central, pivotal notion. Americans have seen themselves as exemplars and champions of a universal, progressive principle applicable abroad no less than at home. That Americans might repeatedly argue over how to understand that principle and by extension how to give proper expression to their collective identity in domestic and foreign policy does not negate the point about freedom's importance. To the contrary, it indicates that freedom was a central point of reference and that whoever could impose their definition gained the power to mobilize national sentiment and thus to create political support.[24]

But that element of American ideology frequently clashed, throughout the decolonization era, with the equally powerful antirevolutionary current that was also embedded in the U.S. belief system. Americans "saw revolutionary outbreaks as a kind of disease that could spread," Hunt notes, "sickening societies and deranging civilized values associated with the family, private property, religion and individual freedom."[25]

The third core conviction of American ideology, a belief in racial hierarchies, joined with the fear of revolution to further temper the commitment to freedom. Hunt, once again, puts this as well and as bluntly as anyone, "Americans found it easy to distinguish the civilized from the barbarian, the advanced from the backward. . . . They confidently arrayed themselves and other peoples along that continuum according to their estimate of their cultural achievements and its close correlate, skin colour."[26] Roosevelt's fixation with the "yellow peril" and his reflexive condescension toward people of color is well known, as is Truman's regular use of the crudest of racial epithets and stereotypes. How could such deep-seated attitudes about the limitations and incapacities of nonwhite peoples fail to influence U.S. policy toward decolonizing Southeast Asia?

Mark Philip Bradley makes a strong case for how much such attitudes did matter. The American response to the August 1945 revolution in Vietnam and the emergence in its wake of a fledgling, indigenous regime, he observes, "remained bounded by the hierarchical notions of Vietnamese incapacities for self-government and claims of the superiority of U.S. models for postwar Vietnamese development that had become almost axiomatic to U.S. conceptions of postcolonial Vietnam." A May 1945 memorandum from Office of Strategic Services analyst James R. Withrow, cited by Bradley, vividly captures prevailing American convictions about the inferiority of the Vietnamese—and other Southeast Asians. Psychological operations in Vietnam "would be a wasted effort" due to the innate incapacities of the indigenous population, he insisted:

> The natives . . . cannot be inspired to resistance by an ideological appeal. They are apathetic as to who rules them, nationalistic movements to the contrary notwithstanding. What nationalist agitation there is, has been instigated by individuals seeking mainly to serve their self-interests rather than those of their countrymen. . . . An Annamite's services are at the dis-

posal of him who pays the best. . . . There is no sense of solidarity among the natives, and hence no sense of nationalism. They are in consequence always divided and thus subject to foreign rule. . . . The natives . . . are naturally lazy. . . . Such a background of life-long habits of indolence, is another obstacle to zeal for a cause.[27]

The wartime assessments of Indonesians by Walter Foote, a long-serving U.S. consul, were cut from the same racialist cloth. "The natives of the Netherlands Indies," he reported confidently in June 1942, "are most definitely not ready for independence. That condition is fifty or seventy-five years in the future." He elaborated on this analysis two years later in a report to General Douglas MacArthur, assuring the American commander that Indonesian political parties were too small to have any influence or importance during the reoccupation period, "The reason for this was that the natives were docile, peaceful, contented, and apathetic towards politics. They were sociable, fun loving, and witty, but exhibited little or no interest in political affairs. This is easily understood when it is realized that the natives of the East Indies, practically without exception, are polite, mild, docile, friendly, and possess a sense of humor somewhat akin to our own."[28]

By way of illustration, Foote pointed out that he had had the same servants for nearly fifteen years and "found them to be rather proud, brave, loyal, ready to accept just reproof calmly, but highly resentful of a personal injustice." He was convinced that the news of the first landing of troops in the Indies "will spread like wild fire and will be the signal of jubilation."[29] Convictions regarding the limited capacity of Southeast Asians to exercise the responsibilities of self-government thus joined with a fear of revolutionary excess and instability to circumscribe the American commitment to nationalist bids for independence. Nor did such attitudes disappear after independence became a reality in each of the region's territories. Quite to the contrary, a tendency to disparage the capabilities of newly independent regimes, even those of friendly, allied states, such as Thailand, the Philippines, and South Vietnam, continued to mark American relations with the emerging nation-states of postcolonial Southeast Asia. To offer but one telling example, John Melby, the State Department officer in charge of Philippine affairs, urged in 1950 that the United States assume "direct, if camouflaged" supervision over Filipino finances. Such control was necessary, he quipped, with a people who "are only one generation out of the tree tops."[30]

By the 1950s and 1960s, the language of development theory—equally condescending and paternalistic, if less blatantly racist—carried forward these long-established views about race-based hierarchies among nations. The combination of a vigorous civil rights movement at home and the emergence of scores of newly independent regimes across Asia, Africa, and the Middle

East made the framing of such hierarchies in explicitly racial terms increasingly untenable. The old race-based differentiation was thus recast along developmental, cultural lines; nations were now ranked according to their progress along the continuum of a modernist ideal, an ideal defined by the norms of the Western, industrialized nations. "Not surprisingly," notes Hunt, "the resulting rankings were strikingly similar to the ones assigned two centuries earlier by race-conscious ancestors."[31] Anglo-Americans came first once again, followed by Europeans, with the nonwhite peoples of the Third World occupying the bottom rungs of the developmental ladder. These views mattered in numerous ways, big and small, in the interactions between Americans and Southeast Asians throughout this period. The condescension and paternalism so frequently displayed by Americans in their dealings with Southeast Asians, a problem exacerbated by vast power disparities, not only made genuine cooperation and mutuality exceedingly difficult to establish, but also bred resentment among those on the receiving end of such attitudes. How could American officials patronize their South Vietnamese allies, privately disparaging their leaders as "clowns" and venal incompetents, and then work together toward common goals?[32] How could Southeast Asians fail to detect, and resent, such underlying prejudices? The formation of the Association of Southeast Asian Nations in August 1967 stands as a historic regional watershed in numerous respects, not the least because it represents a fledgling effort on the part of indigenous states to create a indigenous regional order— one liberated from the suffocating, paternalistic embrace of the Americans.

The rapidly multiplying commitments that Americans made in the region during the 1945–1965 period stemmed primarily from an interrelated set of strategic and economic interests that were illuminated by the ongoing Cold War. Those interests together elevated Southeast Asia to a diplomatic priority of the first order by the late 1940s. Yet, those interests, albeit essential to any appreciation of U.S. attitudes and actions, cannot fully explain the extent of U.S. involvement in regional affairs or the depth of the fears on which that involvement was based. Politics, culture, and ideology, I have suggested, must be added to the interpretive mix. Interests and ideas cannot so easily be separated. The importance that American strategists came to attach to Southeast Asian developments and to the area's international orientation derived not from some clearheaded, objective reading of the external environment, but from a highly subjective reading. That reading was conditioned by the hopes, dreams, fears, biases, and collective memories of a particular society with its own particular cultural values, historical experiences, and deeply held beliefs. There is, in short, something peculiarly and particularly American about the way in which U.S. leaders apprehended dangers and identified interests and opportunities in postwar Southeast Asia.

# 14

# John Foster Dulles and Decolonization in Southeast Asia

*Ronald W. Pruessen*

Decolonization was an issue that figured prominently in John Foster Dulles's career as an American foreign policy maker—and Dulles was important to the course of decolonization in turn.

On the one hand, Dulles saw himself as grappling with a volatile world during his years as Dwight D. Eisenhower's secretary of state and the fate of traditional empires seemed to him to be a key source of turmoil. He had, however, actually begun contemplating the significance of imperialism more than three decades before—and the extended nature of his intellectual engagement makes his thoughts of great value in understanding the essence of his worldview.

On the other hand, Dulles's status as a top-level leader of the world's most powerful state made him a key player in the important 1950s' phase of the decolonization process. This was especially true in Southeast Asia. There were no Americans more important than the secretary of state in shaping Washington policies toward the crises and developments that unfolded in Indochina, Indonesia, the Philippines, Thailand, and the South China Sea (among others)—nor any who would have been more influential in determining U.S. strategy concerning other powerful players in the region (the European colonial states, the Soviet Union, the People's Republic of China, and Japan). The gamut of Dulles's authority, in fact—encompassing virtually every Southeast Asian issue of his time—only increases the degree of his impact.

If the symbiotic relationship between Dulles and decolonization was striking, it was also complex. Like many American leaders of the post-1945 era—and not a few Europeans and Asians as well—he harbored essentially ambivalent views concerning imperialism. Although he was sometimes aware of the unresolved nature of his perspective, his policy preferences were still conflicted. As a result, he very much contributed to shaping a U.S. posture that could be—or could appear to be—erratic and confused.

There was a zigzag pattern to Dulles's approach to Southeast Asian decolonization—with at least three relatively distinct facets discernible as he moved through the post-1945 era:

1. At first glance, there would have seemed no question concerning his determination to move energetically toward the dismantling of old European empires and/or to prevent their reestablishment on the ashes of Japan's Greater East Asia Co-prosperity Sphere counterpart. Dulles vigorously articulated the kind of anticolonial ideas that were quite common among his countrymen both during and after World War II.
2. Although he could be quite explicit about taming historic European proclivities, however, the future secretary of state also made it clear that he was perfectly ready to work with once and future allies to shape a reformed world order. Cold War calculations as well as non–Cold War or pre–Cold War concerns generated an early and steady willingness to provide a real measure of American support, for instance, to the French in Indochina, the Dutch in Indonesia, and the British in Malaya.
3. But yet another bend in Dulles's intellectual path is also evident: If he was ready to work with transatlantic partners in Southeast Asia, there were also distinct limits to this predisposition and flexibility. Like American leaders who plotted the boundaries of U.S. policy concerning the Dutch East Indies in the 1940s, for example, Dulles worked with Eisenhower to calibrate the nature and scale of what they deemed appropriate support.

It is tempting to refer to the three stages of Dulles's thinking concerning decolonization—instead of facets—but there really is no neat chronological pattern to his intellectual peregrinations. He never actually left any component of these views fully behind. Specific moments and cases could bring any or all of the facets of his perspective to the fore even as he neared the end of his life and career in 1958–1959.

**Anticolonial Impulses**

Dulles shared the almost visceral anticolonial views that were common among Americans—both well before and then during the 1950s. Although the articulation of these views was activated by developments and crises around the world, Southeast Asia certainly provided regular prompts.

In his first extended discussions with British foreign secretary Lord Salisbury, for example, Eisenhower's recently installed secretary of state voiced sentiments that would surface almost countless times over the next six years. Dulles spoke about developments in Egypt, in particular, but he delivered a message that had clear, broad relevance:

> He said that some Americans had the impression that the British attitude towards the Arab States and Egypt in particular were reverting to the old "Western superiority" cult and to the view that the way to deal with such peoples was to be stern and firm with them and to deliver a well-placed kick when they made difficulties. He pointed out that Great Britain had had more experience in the Middle East than had the United States, but the latter were now to some extent involved there . . . [because] United States financial and economic help would be required. . . . They recognised their fallibility and British experience, and while they were willing to be convinced to the contrary, they felt that such an attitude could not succeed and would create anti-Western feelings in the Middle East which would affect us all.[1]

Less than a year later, in May 1954, Dulles's frustration with Washington's transatlantic partners led to his unburdening himself in an executive session of the Senate Foreign Relations Committee—and on this occasion it was the crisis in Indochina that generated his remarks:

> We face a very, very fundamental problem. Historically we are traditionally alined [sic] with the British and the French and the Europeans. We are called Europeans in much of the world. . . . These are the countries which have been primarily the colonial nations. We still have that tag attached to them. Wherever we go in the world, if we work in cooperation with the British and the French, we are tarred by the same brush. In fact, to some extent now, there is a disposition on the part of the Communists not to bother to talk about the British and French any more. They count them off. They concentrate their attacks upon us.[2]

Dulles's anticolonial views had both gut-level and intellectual sources, as may have been the case with other American leaders. At the most basic level, where certain political or ideological perspectives are absorbed through a surrounding culture's rituals and educational system, he was certainly sensitive to his own country's history—in this case, of course, the way in which its very origins were linked with a revolutionary struggle against a great empire of modern times. Specific experiences in Dulles's adult life then led him to shape these instinctive sentiments in certain ways. Eisenhower's secretary of state was greatly influenced, for example, by the leader under whom he had experienced his first period of government service: Woodrow Wilson. The young Dulles (then a rising Wall Street lawyer) had been drawn to Washington in 1917 by his uncle Robert Lansing. He had served on the War Trade Board and as an economic adviser at the Paris Peace Conference—and, unlike his uncle, he had remained a lifelong admirer of the charismatic Wilson. Dulles was impressed by the president's dramatic vision of a peaceful postwar world, very much including Wilson's conviction that the dangerous imperial behavior of the Old World required reforms that the New World was ready and able to conceptualize. Over the years, Dulles explicitly referred to the "mandate system" of the League of Nations as one initiative that had never been allowed to fulfill its real potential for helping to make the international arena a safer and more stable environment.[3]

A Wilsonian tilt to Dulles's worldview was significantly reinforced by the prolonged economic crises of the 1930s. His post–Great War legal career had specialized in work for international banks and corporations, bringing with it a firm dedication to the liberal "Open Door" principles that Wilson had also held dear. Under the pressure of the Great Depression, Dulles saw a freer global economic environment—with respect to both trade and investment—as a greater and greater necessity. Imperial reform became a particular concern in this context. He wrote regularly in the mid and late 1930s of the need to create "a world which is elastic and fluid in its organization." For instance, why could there not be international agreements to maintain "national monetary units in some reasonably stable relationship to each other"? Why not some "substantial removal of barriers to the exchange of goods"? And, "When we move on to those nations which are less highly developed, and particularly when we consider colonial areas, a much more ambitious program is practical. . . . There would seem to be no insuperable obstacle to opening up vast areas of the world through the application of the principles of the 'mandate' system as proposed by President Wilson."[4]

The outbreak of World War II and the eventual involvement of the United States powerfully knit Dulles's reform convictions together. He became a highly energized advocate for a Wilsonian program designed to give a new postwar era a hope of enjoying more than very temporary peace. As leader of a group called the Commission on a Just and Durable Peace, for example, he invested an enormous amount of time in mobilizing support among liberal American Protestants for an explicitly Wilsonian agenda. A new and improved international organization was a high priority, as was a move toward freer "interstate commerce." So, too, was a reform of traditional imperialism. During a 1942 London meeting with Anthony Eden and Colonial Secretary Lord Cranborne (Lord Salisbury after 1947), Dulles offered the pointed advice that "[w]hat you have got to do is have some of your important people say that from now on we are going to have a new deal and open up the door to these colonies and start off on a new basis."[5]

## Second Thoughts

In the postwar era that so concerned him in the early 1940s, however, Dulles revealed a clear readiness to define concepts like a "new deal" for colonies in a very moderate fashion. His rhetoric regularly suggested more dramatic impulses than his actual policy calculations and choices. In Southeast Asia, for example, sharp continuing critiques of European plans and ambitions in no way prevented a significant investment of American resources in the support of those very plans and ambitions. The course of the decolonization process in Indochina, Indonesia, Malaya, and elsewhere would almost certainly have been very different if Dulles and other Washington leaders had honed policies that were closer to their anticolonial principles.

Why did Dulles (and others) trim anticolonial sails to become significant de facto partners of the European powers in Southeast Asia (and elsewhere)? A traditional answer to this question would begin and end with reference to the transformative power of the Cold War. While this remains an important component of the story, however, it would actually be more accurate to nest it within a sequence of explanatory factors in which it turns out to be neither first nor last. Initial emphasis should be placed, in this modified conceptualization, on the core conviction of many American leaders of the 1940s and 1950s that the United States required at least relatively potent allies or partners if the multiple problems of the post–World War II and post–Great Depression era were to be solved.

Dulles was certainly a whole-hearted believer in the fundamental significance of transatlantic partnerships, for example. In the realm of business and banking, he had helped to build and manage relationships between Americans and Europeans for almost four decades by the time he became Eisenhower's secretary of state—and this facet of his experience and identity proved to be a strong bond between him and the former North Atlantic Treaty Organization (NATO) chief. The Eisenhower-Dulles team, that is, placed transatlantic collaboration at the heart of their "New Look" grand strategy. Although primary attention was once paid to the nuclear weapons features of the New Look, it has long been clear that the pronouncement of what came to be called the "massive retaliation" doctrine was just one component of a multifaceted reconceptualization of strategy—a reconceptualization designed to deal with the very real (if unappealing) limits to American power in a troubled international arena. The wealth, idealism, and energy of the United States were all very great after 1945—especially in comparison to the resources of other countries—but pragmatic leaders recognized that they were simply not great enough to match the problems of the era.[6] Close working relationships with key Europeans—old partners in two world wars, after all—proved to be especially important as a result. And when some of the most troubling problems of the post-1945 era developed in precisely those Third World areas where the very same European partners had significant resources and experience, then the stage was set for a serious modification of American anticolonial impulses.

What post–World War II challenges were so profound as to be beyond the abilities of the United States to solve on its own? Two problems—or perhaps more accurately, two complex sets of problems—can be identified as particularly relevant to Dulles's approach to the course of decolonization in Southeast Asia: first, the Cold War, and second, the reconstruction of a healthy world economy. Both problems were of enormous significance in the minds of policy makers like Dulles and were actually linked in all kinds of ways beyond this—with the existence of each greatly compounding the difficulty of solving the other. Separate and distinctive characteristics should nevertheless be recognized. Not the least, for instance, it is important to appreciate the way economic reconstruction would have been a major concern—and a major problem—for Dulles and others if the Cold War had never begun.

The Cold War did begin, of course, and the postwar future of Southeast Asia was quickly seen to have relevance to it. By 1950, after five years of primary attention to European issues, Dulles began to speak more regularly about a possible shift in communist tactics—a shift undertaken in response to successful American initiatives like the Marshall Plan and NATO. In a Seattle speech, for example, he said:

> Twenty five years ago Stalin, looking at the colonial situation, said that it offered the best chance of overthrowing the West. "The road to victory of the revolution in the West lies through the revolutionary alliance with the liberation movement of the colonies and dependent countries." He noted the economic value of the colonies to the Western countries and saw that violent revolution would not only take away that economic value, but involve the colonial countries in costly and futile struggles that would exhaust them.[7]

Dulles quickly became particularly concerned about the Asian front of this wide-ranging challenge, pushed by a troubling sequence of events that began with the establishment of the People's Republic of China and proceeded to the outbreak of war on the Korea Peninsula, steadily worsening developments in Indochina, and yet other difficulties. By the time he assumed leadership of the State Department, he had a vision that was both wide ranging and sharply etched. As he put it in a mid-1953 conversation with Syngman Rhee, for example:

[T]he United States must take a broad view as the leader in the world struggle against communism. The Secretary explained the general strategic position in the Far East which required holding a position anchored in the north in Korea, which swung through the offshore island chain through Japan, Formosa, and the Philippines, to Indo-China at the other end. If that arc can be held and sufficient pressures developed against the communists, it might be possible eventually to overthrow communist control of the mainland. However, if any part of that strategic position is lost, the whole position will go under.[8]

Such a perspective remained with Dulles throughout his years as secretary of state—at least as one important factor in his policy-making deliberations concerning Asian affairs. It is a thoroughly familiar component of his thinking concerning the Indochina conundrum, of course, and was at the core of his calculations during two duels at the brink with Beijing over the fate of Nationalist-held islands in the Taiwan Strait.[9] Still somewhat less well known is the complex plotting of U.S. policy concerning what were seen as disturbing developments in Indonesia in 1957–1958—which generated regular additional glimpses of the Cold War tilt in Dulles's analysis. Testifying to the House Foreign Affairs Committee, he referred to his

> fear that the trend of the Sukarno Government may be to put Communists in control there. . . . We would be happy to see non-Communist elements who are really in a majority there, the Moslem elements, the non-Communist parties, exert a greater influence in the affairs of Indonesia than has been the case in the past, where Sukarno has moved toward this so-called "guided democracy" theory which is a nice sounding name for what I fear would end up to be Communist despotism.[10]

Dulles's Cold War concerns and calculations clearly had a significant impact on his approach to decolonization. On the one hand, he was very conscious of the fact that the material and psychological well-being of traditional European partners would be affected by the course and pace of imperial reform—and, thereby, the ability of those partners to resist communist dangers within their home environment. On the other hand, healthier transatlantic partners would also be able to play a vital role in avoiding the threats facing their former colonies. A readiness to modify the biting nature of anticolonial criticisms of Britain, France, and the Netherlands was one result, but this was rapidly and significantly complemented by the provision of substantial American aid in support of European programs for regions like Southeast Asia. Washington's—and Dulles's—readiness to cover fully half of the costs of the French campaign in Indochina is the most familiar example.[11]

But Dulles's anticolonial instincts were modified for other reasons as well. His Cold War policies, in fact, developed in the context—or against the backdrop—of a yet more sweeping set of concerns prompted by the wars and the depression that preceded conflict with Moscow and the "international communist conspiracy." Dulles's anxieties regarding the profound dangers of economic and political dislocation would all by themselves have prompted a tempered calibration of policies toward old European partners and colonial regions in turmoil. The sweeping reform proposals he articulated during and immediately after World War II are telling in this respect. He was anxious to build support for a Wilsonian program, he argued, because the end of a major conflict would inevitably bring "a critical and difficult period" for "an unsettled world." There were regular litanies of potential problems, like the one offered in April 1946, "Asia, Africa, and South America are lacking in healthy societies. Most of Continental Europe is in postwar demoralization, accentuated by indecisive and incoherent attitudes toward Germany. The capitalistic centers, notably the British Empire and the United States, have developed some major defects. One of these is imperialism, with its by-product of racial intolerance. Another is the failure to maintain steady production and employment."[12]

Overviews of this kind were always used to launch an injunction: If future wars and depressions were to be prevented, such problems would have to be solved. "We are at the beginning of a long and difficult negotiation which will involve the structure of the post-war world," Dulles wrote, and it was important to avoid historical patterns that had always seen war and economic crisis being perpetuated through short-sighted behavior. "This time we must break the cycle. We have what may be mankind's last chance."[13]

Dulles's long career as a lawyer for major banks and corporations with a heavy international cast to their business led him to be particularly sensitive to the problems inherent in the reconstruction of a healthy world economy—though he would always and accurately have located this feature of his interests in the context of a concern for avoiding future wars as well. The inclination very much affected the evolution of his thoughts concerning Southeast Asia. Here, he followed a path charted by any number of policy makers during the late 1940s. Both Democrats and Republicans came to see what had been the relatively unfamiliar terrain of Southeast Asia as having great economic importance, by way of an increasing appreciation for the historic role of the region's rich raw materials and market opportunities. As Dean Acheson explained to a congressional committee in 1949, European industries had long used the resources of colonial territories to produce manufactured goods sold around the world, which had "kept the economies going in South America, Southeast Asia, in India, in the Middle East and everywhere." Related, if not identical, patterns needed to be re-created in the post–World War II era. On the one hand, this would allow Europeans to enjoy continuing access to the raw materials that would fuel industries and generate dollar revenues to off-set serious trade deficits with the United States. As Harry S. Truman put it at one point, the protection and integration of regions like Southeast Asia were "the other side of the medal of Western European recovery." On the other hand, the region's raw materials and markets would also be of enormous potential value to a Japan struggling to recover from the devastation of World War II, with the defeated enemy's rehabilitation and reintegration into the global economy identified as high priorities.[14]

Since Dulles had long emphasized the vital need to reconstruct an international economy shattered by depression and war, it is not at all surprising that he quickly came to share 1940s' calculations concerning Southeast Asia's potential role. Indeed, he very much helped to push the thinking of the Truman administration in this direction—through his important role as a bipartisan participant in the design of the Marshall Plan and, even more, his special 1950–1952 responsibility for the negotiation of the Japanese Peace Treaty.[15]

Dulles saw the peace settlement with Japan, in particular, as a major tool for addressing trade, currency, and investment issues in the broad Asia-Pacific region. Summarizing his sense of priorities on one occasion, for example, he said "one of the things we must try to do is to help create in that part of the world, Asia and the Pacific, economic health. . . . A greater degree of economic health . . . is a thing which is perhaps most of all wanted in that part of the world."[16] Among the other policy impulses that emerged from this goal was a strong interest in building bridges between Japan and Southeast Asia. While peace treaty negotiations were underway, for example, Dulles tried to persuade Tokyo leaders that they would be wise to accept substantial reparations obligations toward former enemies and victims in the region—since payments would be used to purchase Japanese goods in a way that would establish longer-term trade patterns. This was still a theme of Washington-Tokyo discussions during Dulles's years as secretary of state. In a November 1954 meeting with Shigeru Yoshida, the prime minister referred to Japan's readiness "to use reparations to help rebuild Southeast Asia and develop wider markets there for themselves and other nations." For his part, Dulles repeated his well-known desire "to work in cooperation with Japan and other countries to build expanding economies in South and Southeast Asia."[17]

Some months later, he made a related point to the Senate Foreign Relations Committee. Southeast Asia's raw materials were a "fabulous potential wealth" of great significance to Japan and the United States, "We feel Japan has a very important economic problem and one that can best be solved by their relations with other Asian countries rather than by a situation where the United States has to take vast quantities of Japanese goods that we may not want."[18]

Dulles's quite typically American emphasis on the importance of Southeast Asian raw materials and markets for Japan and Europe suggests an overall perspective with a distinctively hierarchical character—one that is important to recognize if his worldview and his impact on Southeast Asia are to be fully understood. Over several decades, Eisenhower's secretary of state had developed a wide-ranging Wilsonian vision of international reform in which different states and regions played varying roles. In essence, Dulles believed the United States needed to play the key role of global manager. This would be necessary if a deeply historic cycle of war and depression were to be broken and if the twentieth century were to be allowed to witness the belated birth of what he once referred to as "a world-wide commonwealth of peace."[19] This role was required whether the focus was on Cold War dangers or more traditional political economy concerns—or the frequent combination of the two. In the former case, massive military power and global reach made it logical for the United States to serve as the "general staff."[20] In the latter case, unique American economic power (and needs) dictated a sense of special responsibilities.

Under U.S. leadership, there was little question that Dulles saw an essentially "junior partner" role for relatively more powerful states, that is, Japan and traditional allies in Western Europe, and an even lesser status for those yet weaker. He was sensitive to the burgeoning ambitions of the peoples and states of what he thought of as the "less developed" regions, and he was clearly ready to think about reforms that would move them toward greater independence and satisfaction. Both Dulles's practice and conceptualization, however, limited the degree of change and placed the needs of areas like Southeast Asia in a subordinate position. This had been true in earlier years (when an "Open Door" to colonial territories was supposed to ease the impact of the Great Depression on industrialized states) and it remained true in the 1950s (when primary attention to the safety and economic health of Britain, France, the Netherlands, and Japan trimmed the actions that might have been more proportionate to anticolonial sentiment).

It deserves mention here that one source of Dulles's hierarchical vision of global management was his sense that the leaders and populations of colonial and formerly colonial territories would generally require a long period of tutelage and experience before an effective role in international affairs could be anticipated. This was certainly evident in his private comments on Southeast Asian developments. In an early 1954 testimony to a closed-door meeting of the Senate Foreign Relations Committee, for example, he followed a discussion of problems with French policy in Indochina by nonetheless suggesting that "the principle difficulty in the way of achieving independence there is the lack of political maturity on the part of the people themselves, and their inability to make up their own minds as to what they want."[21] A year later, he reported to the same group on his recent meeting with Burma's U Nu, "He and his government are young people. They think they know all the answers. They run about pretty freely consorting with Chou En-lai and Nehru and others, and while they are eager to maintain their independence, I think they are rather naïve about how they can do it."[22] And near the end of his tenure as secretary of state, he had a conversation with Belgian foreign minister Pierre Wigny that twinned his ongoing convictions concerning Southeast Asia with reassuring words concerning his understanding of Brussels' problems in the Congo:

> [A]lthough the US believed in the basic proposition that "governments derive their just powers from the consent of the governed," this did not mean that wholly untrained people could exercise these powers until they were prepared to assume them. We recognized that the process of making people capable of self-government was a slow and difficult one. . . . We believed that the governing elements should be educated, moral, and self-disciplined and that much time is required to achieve this degree of preparation. He recalled that the United States had spent 50 years preparing the Philippines for independence and there were times we believed that that had perhaps not been long enough.[23]

**Third Thoughts**

Ironically, the sense of superiority that permeated Dulles's attitudes toward colonial and recently independent peoples could be turned against those very Europeans who would have shared his assumptions. If Europeans made useful partners for dealing with the post-1945 problems of areas like Asia and Africa, that is, they were partners who regularly fell short of American expectations and requirements. In the end, Dulles's perception of the United States as the predominant global manager could lead him (and other American leaders, to be sure) to a further twist in his analytical and policy-making road: Anticolonial convictions could be tempered by a sense of the need to keep Europe strong both at home and in Asia and Africa—but if European behavior seemed to compound the perceived problems of Asia and Africa, then it would be necessary to maneuver around them or even replace them in the end. In essence, this was an intellectual progression that involved moving from "Great Power" calculations to "hegemonic" conclusions.

Indochina in the mid-1950s provides dramatic examples of this route, of course, with Dulles's chagrin concerning both France and Great Britain powerfully contributing to the fateful Eisenhower administration decision to have the United States play an essentially unilateral role. The secretary of state—and the president—was prodded by multiple dissatisfactions with transatlantic partners. On the one hand, Dulles had long had doubts about the wisdom of French policies. Problems reached a critical pass in the spring of 1954, at the time of the Điện Biên Phủ debacle and the Geneva Conference, and a sense of confidence regarding the prospect of an effective partnership with Paris never really recovered after that. A May 1954 list of "defects" in French policies suggests Dulles's step-by-step move toward more independent action:

> The first was that they had not given any adequate assurance of independence to the Associated States of Vietnam, Laos, and Cambodia, and without that there was not the spirit on the part of the people locally to engage in the struggle nor were the conditions such as facilitate participation in the struggle by outside countries.
> Second was they had no adequate provisions for the training and recruitment of the native forces.
> The third was they had no well thought out military program for a period of time.
> The fourth was that because of the impoverished position of the French treasury, they were trying to economize on Indochina.[24]

Although French policies were bad enough, their negative impact was compounded by British behavior. As Paris's ability to maintain a military effort in Indochina waned in the spring of 1954—in spite of massive U.S. economic aid—Eisenhower and Dulles devised a plan to mobilize international support for the anticommunist struggle. Dubbed "United Action," the hope was that a coalition of European, Southeast Asian, and Pacific partners would give Hànội, Moscow, and Beijing pause either before or during what Washington viewed as the dangerous Geneva Conference. British support was seen as crucial for this effort—since, among other things, Foreign Secretary Eden was likely to play an important role in Geneva—but American leaders never succeeded in roping London into the United Action plan. By mid-May, Eisenhower was furious, "[I]t was incomprehensible to him that the British should be acting as they were," the president said. "He suggested that possibly in a further letter to Churchill dealing with the latter's prospective visit some strong note might be injected implying that the Churchill Government was really promoting a second Munich."[25] Dulles sometimes overmatched the president's anger, displaying on one occasion what one observer called "almost pathological rage" against the uncooperative British and French. "Nobody was supporting the US," he snapped at Eden over lunch, "nobody has said a word to defend [us] against Chou En-lai's attacks; the alliance was nearly at an end; Asia was lost; France finished; etc. . . . When the chips were down," the Europeans had revealed "a pathetic spectacle of drifting without any agreed policy or purpose."[26]

The outgrowth of mid-1954's frustrations, of course, was an increasing American determination to forge Indochina policies less dependent on transatlantic allies: Washington kept itself at arm's length from the Geneva Accords, proceeded to build the Southeast Asia Treaty Organization, and step by step replaced the French as the key external actor in Vietnam. Although horrendous consequences would flow from these policies, Eisenhower and Dulles took them in the belief that they were steps in the right direction—and that the American ability to control the situation would actually be strengthened if there was less dependence on Europeans. When the United Action failed to come together in May 1954, for example, Dulles suggested that work with Australia, New Zealand, the Philippines, and other countries might be a more productive route:

> [W]e might conceivably go ahead without the active participation of the United Kingdom. I pointed out that while this had its grave disadvantages in indicating a certain breach, there were perhaps greater disadvantages in a situation where we were obviously subject to UK veto, which in turn was in Asian matters largely subject to Indian veto, which in turn was largely subject to Chinese Communist veto. Thereby a chain was forged which tended to make us impotent. . . .
> The President agreed to this fully.[27]

Nor was this preoccupation with being subject to the "veto" of a whole string of states a prickly and temporary reaction to the pressures of a difficult moment. From 1954 on, Dulles and Eisenhower regularly opted for policies that separated the United States—sometimes bitterly—from the allies who were said to be important partners. In addition to replacing France in Indochina, for example, Washington charted a distinctly independent course with respect to the People's Republic of China. Although European leaders expressed vigorous doubts about the significance of several tiny Nationalist-held islands in the Taiwan Strait, Dulles forged to the nuclear brink in 1954–1955 and 1958 in order to deter what he believed was a potential Beijing appetite for aggression—aggression that might be directed, in particular, toward Southeast Asia.[28] It is perhaps not surprising that Washington would set its own course on issues or crises it considered of truly major significance, even if this meant paying less heed than rhetoric and prevailing logic would have suggested to the need for partners. The future of Indochina and China's role in Asia were certainly matters of such high import as far as Dulles and Eisenhower were concerned—as were the Middle Eastern developments that generated an even more notable split with allies during the Suez Crisis. In fact, though, American policy makers could opt for more unilateral behavior in situations that generated far fewer headline alarums. For example, Dulles's extended micromanaging of complex U.S. efforts to deal with perceived problems in Indonesia in 1957–1958 absorbed great energy and substantial resources.[29]

What gradually emerged in the Washington of the 1950s, in essence, was a conceptualization of the broad Asia-Pacific region as a distinctively American sphere of influence. Faced with problematic behavior by traditional allies in Indochina in 1954, for example, both the president and the secretary of state articulated a readiness to act more independently than previous rhetoric and policy explorations had suggested. A situation in which "all our allies desert us and none will stand with us" would create a "different story" and the need for "a different consideration," Eisenhower said at one point: the bottom line was that the United States would go its own way if need be in order "to keep the Pacific as an American lake."[30] (The phraseology here was related to Dulles's "agonizing reappraisal" speech some months earlier, when doubts about French acceptance of the European Defense Community had led to one of the first of the Eisenhower administration's warnings concerning the potential implications of allied behavior— or nonbehavior.) For his part, Dulles proposed using a famous unilateral American declaration of an earlier era as a model for working through 1954's transatlantic morass regarding Indochina. He told the president, "I had in mind saying in a paraphrase of the Monroe address that the freedom of Southeast Asia was important from the standpoint of our peace, security, and happiness, and that we could not look upon the loss to Communism of that area with indifference."[31]

Not surprisingly, American efforts to manage regions like Southeast Asia in a forceful, unilateral fashion prompted resistance and protests. Allies and supposed partners from Western Europe to Japan found much to displease them and many moments in which they would not feel able to cooperate— even if resistance sometimes took the form of "passive aggression." Dulles may have been furious during the 1954 Geneva Conference, for example, but so was Eden, "[A]ll the Americans want to do is replace the French and run Indo-China themselves," he snapped to his private secretary. "They want to replace us in Egypt too. They want to run the world."[32] To his credit, Dulles was conscious of this resentment. In the aftermath of the especially explosive Suez Crisis, for example, he ruminated with the president in revealing words:

[W]e must bear in mind that some of our friends felt that they were having to bear the brunt of our present policies. In this connection, I referred to [Syngman] Rhee, Chiang [Kai-shek], the Dutch in Indonesia, the French in Indochina, the British, French and Israelis in the Middle East, and the Hungarians. All of them at one time or another felt that they were being sacrificed to our policies. I mentioned that while we did not seek it, we in fact did tend by our anti-colonial policies gradually to replace British, French and Dutch interests in what had been their particular spheres and that there was a tendency on the part of these colonial countries to attribute this motivation to us.[33]

Awareness did not translate into a readiness to seriously compromise what he considered sound American policies, however. If valued allies would not provide enthusiastic support—and if leaders or populations in Southeast Asia mounted vigorous resistance as well—then Dulles was prepared to incur both costs as the unavoidable price of great power and responsibility.

# 15

# Between SEATO and ASEAN

## The United States and the Regional Organization of Southeast Asia

### Kai Dreisbach

[T]he Association represents the collective will of the nations of South-East Asia to bind themselves together in friendship and cooperation and, through joint efforts and sacrifices, secure for their peoples and for posterity the blessings of peace, freedom and prosperity.

*—Bangkok Declaration (The ASEAN Declaration), 1967*

International regionalism as defined by Joseph S. Nye "in the descriptive sense is the formation of interstate associations or groupings on the basis of regions."[1] It is based on cooperation among states that share common objectives and interests—economic, political, cultural, or social. But regional cooperation rarely takes place in a vacuum—the definition of these common objectives and interests is usually influenced by extraregional forces, such as the great political and economic powers of the world and their global politics.[2] Against this background, it is the goal of this chapter to explore the significance of the concept of regional cooperation for American Southeast Asian policy as well as the interaction between U.S. policy and regional initiatives taken by the noncommunist countries of Southeast Asia themselves.

In the aftermath of World War II, Washington was stuck between the interests of its European allies, who attempted to reestablish the prewar colonial order and expectations of Southeast Asian liberation movements. In spite of the American stance against colonialism, the U.S. policy toward the region was often significantly shaped by considerations relating to the European colonial powers. Moreover, decolonization was regarded as having the potential to bring to power independence movements hostile to Western capitalism. In short, there seemed to be at least a symbiotic relationship between social transformation in the Third World and the interests of the Soviet state. A March 1949 Policy Planning Staff paper stated, "Nationalism, both political and economic, is the dominant issue in all SEA countries. . . . It is now clear that SEA as a region has become the target of a coordinated offensive plainly directed by the Kremlin."[3]

To counter this perceived threat of a loss of influence in the Third World, many of the U.S. policies in the post–World War II period were formulated with a view to containment. After the communist takeover in China in 1949, containment became the central objective of U.S. Asian policy. Suddenly, the conflicts of independence and self-rule in Southeast Asia gained significance for the global distribution of power and influence.[4] At this point, U.S. policy makers tried to find ways to prevent communist expansion into regions like Southeast Asia, thus calling for an evaluation of American policy toward Asia. As early as February 1949, the U.S. ambassador to China in a telegram to Secretary of State Dean Acheson warned that "the effective containment of Soviet expansion-through-Communism requires in Asia [a] new approach with appropriate implementation not so much in terms of money or munition but in convincingly dramatized ideas."[5]

At that time, policy makers in Washington began the discussion of concepts of regional cooperation in Southeast Asia. A March 1949 Policy Planning Staff paper emphasized the limits of bilateral actions to reduce communist influence in Southeast Asia:

> It is our continuing objective to encourage the SEA region to develop in harmony with the Atlantic Community and the rest of the Free World.
>
> Conversely, it is also our objective to contain and steadily reduce Kremlin influence in the region. Because there is a slight hope of our achieving either of these objectives through a policy limited to unilateral actions with the individual SEA countries, we should adopt a wider concept—multilateral collaboration, primarily with certain British Commonwealth countries and the Philippines, in approaching SEA as a region.[6]

At the same time, the U.S. Congress, through the Foreign Military Assistance Act of 1949, called for "the creation by the free countries and the free peoples of the Far East of a joint organization . . . to establish a program of self-help and mutual cooperation."[7] In the face of anticolonial and anti-Western feelings in Southeast Asia, however, the administration of Harry S. Truman believed that an active American role in organizing regional cooperation had to be avoided. Thus, in March 1949 the State Department's Policy Planning Staff developed a strategy that would eventually become the basis for future U.S. policy concerning the regional organization of Southeast Asia:

> We should avoid at the outset urging an area organization. . . . Only as a pragmatic and desirable basis for more intimate association appears, should we encourage the area to move step by step toward formal organization. If

Asian leaders prematurely precipitate an area organization, we should not give the impression of attempting to thwart such a move but should go along with them while exerting a cautiously moderating influence. . . .

In order to minimize suggestions of American imperialist intervention, we should encourage the Indians, Filipinos and other Asian states to take the public lead in the political matters. Our role should be the offering of discreet support and guidance. . . .

We should seek vigorously to develop the economic interdependence between SEA, as a supplier of raw materials, and Japan, western Europe and India, as suppliers of finished goods.[8]

It is interesting to note that the paper called for regional cooperation but rejected the creation of organizational structures. There is also no word about American participation in already existing multilateral organizations like the Economic Commission for Asia and the Far East (ECAFE).[9] Although the United States was one of the founding members of that organization, policy makers in Washington mistrusted ECAFE, claiming, in the words of W. Walton Butterworth, the director of the Office of Far Eastern Affairs, that the organization "far from proving a useful instrument to the creation of regionalism in Southeast Asia, had, because of the presence of the Russians, been virtually useless."[10] Moreover, U.S. policy in Asia, unlike in Europe, neither promoted a military alliance like the North Atlantic Treaty Organization (NATO), nor did it foster multilateral aid packages like the Marshall Plan. In September 1949, Butterworth remarked, "We had been obliged to discourage the members of ECAFE in their efforts to lay the foundations for a Marshall Plan for Asia, not only because a Marshall Plan for Asia was in itself impractical but because we felt that the Asiatic states should make increased efforts to solve their own economic problems."[11]

Finally, it is interesting to have a closer look at the language of the Policy Planning Staff paper. Officially, the document called for regional initiatives to be taken by the governments of the Southeast Asian states themselves, while the U.S. role was described by expressions like "moderating influence" or "discreet support and guidance." This, of course, meant that unofficially the United States intended to keep a decisive influence on the shaping of any regional blueprint in Southeast Asia. It was therefore not surprising that the U.S. government distrusted solely Asian initiatives like the 1947 Asians Relations Conference or the 1949 New Delhi Conference.[12]

One of the most outspoken proponents of the regionalization of Asia was Philippine president Elpidio Quirino. In view of the communist takeover in China, Quirino suggested the formation of a Pacific military alliance, a so-called Pacific Pact. Chiang Kai-chek, the leader of the Kuomintang, and Syngnam Rhee, the South Korean president, supported the initiative, but most of the other Asian states rejected the idea of any kind of cooperation with National China and South Korea. In response, Quirino decided to facilitate a conference in the Philippine city of Baguio without the participation of either Chiang or Rhee. Thailand, Indonesia, India, Pakistan, Ceylon, and Australia accepted the invitation and on May 26, 1950, the Baguio Conference opened. The participants talked about social, economic, and cultural matters, but refrained from discussions of military cooperation.[13]

The United States' reception of the idea of a Pacific Pact was mixed. On the one hand, policy makers in Washington feared that Asian governments expected the United States to join such a military alliance (even though no corresponding public request was ever made)—a commitment that in 1949–1950 Washington was not yet willing to make.[14] On the other hand, regional initiatives fit into Washington's concept of strengthening the coherence of the Western bloc. Thus, a report by the National Security Council (NSC) stated, "The United States should make known its sympathy with the efforts of Asian leaders to form regional associations of non-Communist states of the various Asian areas, and if in due course associations eventuate, the United States should be prepared, if invited, to assist such associations to fulfill their purposes under conditions which would be to our interest."[15]

Finally, in the wake of the outbreak of the Korean War in June 1950 and a major Việt Minh offensive against the French in September 1950, the Truman administration decided to alter the course of its Asian policy and to play a more active role in the regional organization of noncommunist Southeast Asia. Although the forces of nationalism, the voices against colonialism, the opposition to the Cold War, and the growing popularity of nonaligned foreign policy prevented the United States to openly create and promote a regional organization in Asia, Washington discreetly set up regional collective defense mechanisms wherever possible.

The first of these was the Australia, New Zealand, and United States (ANZUS) Treaty, founded in San Francisco in 1951.[16] Washington had initially planned to include the Philippines in the agreement, but later decided this would not correspond with U.S. security interests.[17] For Washington, the ANZUS Treaty was one of the instruments of containment, but for Australia and New Zealand it was a safeguard against the possible reemergence of Japan as a military threat.[18] Although none of the signatory states was part of Southeast Asia, the formation of ANZUS as a collective security organization with the participation of the United States had direct relevance for developments in the region. The organization, however, was not meant to be limited only to Australia and New Zealand. Instead, Washington expected the two countries to assist the execution of U.S. containment policy in Southeast Asia.[19] Furthermore, ANZUS was the first U.S. treaty commitment for a multilateral military engagement in the Asia-Pacific region. In this respect, it was a prelude to direct American involvement in Asian regionalism, which would manifest itself in the creation of the Southeast Asia Treaty Organization (SEATO).

For the time being, the Truman administration was not willing to further extend American security commitments in Southeast Asia.[20] The idea of a regional security pact for Southeast Asia was kept alive, however, by Thailand and the Philippines and especially by the British government, who was angered by its exclusion from ANZUS. Washington had argued that a British, and a possible French, participation in ANZUS would strengthen the impression of the alliance being "a white man's arrangement for the mutual safety of white countries."[21] However, the actual reason for Washington's rejection of Britain and France joining ANZUS was the United States' unwillingness to give security commitments to those countries' colonies in Malaya and Indochina. As John Foster Dulles stated before the Senate Foreign Relations Committee in 1954, this decision had been made as early as 1950, "At that time our military people were strongly opposed to bringing Indochina or Malaya into the scope of our responsibilities in that part of the world, so it had been decided to exclude France and the United Kingdom from any pact that we made."[22]

The American position changed decisively when the administration of Dwight D. Eisenhower assumed office. The new administration was far more willing than its predecessor to commit itself militarily on the Southeast Asian mainland.[23] When in January 1954, six months after the end of the Korean War, the fighting between the Việt Minh and the French in Indochina reached a climactic point, President Eisenhower approved an NSC study that called for a coordinated approach to the defense of noncommunist Southeast Asia and recognized "that the initiative in regional defense measures must come from the governments of the area."[24] Eisenhower also appointed a special committee to study the possible course of action for the United States in Southeast Asia. The committee submitted its report in April 1954. One of the recommendations read as follows:

> It should be U.S. policy to develop within the UN Charter a Far Eastern regional arrangement subscribed and underwritten by the major European powers with interests in the Pacific.
>
> Full accomplishment of such an arrangement can only be developed in the long term and should therefore be preceded by the development, through indigenous sources, of regional and cultural agreements between the several Southeast Asian countries and later with Japan. Such agreements could take a form similar to that of the OEEC in Europe. . . .

Upon the basis of such agreements, the US should actively but unobtrusively seek their expansion into mutual defense agreements and should for this purpose be prepared to underwrite such agreements with military and economic aid and should be willing to become a signatory to such agreements upon invitation.[25]

The recommendation is significant for two reasons. First, it called for regional cooperation in cultural affairs as a basis for potential future military cooperation. Thus, it already referred to the concept of regionalism that was to be realized later in the form of the Association of Southeast Asian Nations (ASEAN). And second, the committee report for the first time explicitly recommended the creation of a regional security pact.

Within the U.S. administration, Secretary of State Dulles took the lead in promoting a regional military organization. As late as January 1954, he had rejected an extension of American security commitments to Southeast Asia, "The United States should not assume formal commitments which overstrain its present capabilities and give rise to military expectations we could not fulfill."[26] But in the wake of the French defeat at Điện Biên Phủ in May 1954, Dulles and British foreign minister Anthony Eden now declared their countries' willingness "to take part, with the other countries principally concerned, in an examination of the possibility of establishing a collective defense . . . to assure the peace, security and freedom of Southeast Asia and the Western Pacific."[27] Dulles proposed to establish a working group to discuss the formation of a formal collective security treaty, but Eden refused to jeopardize the ongoing Geneva Conference by opening negotiations for such a pact.[28] Finally, President Eisenhower announced to move ahead without the British.[29] London countered with a suggestion to form a security pact either as a nonaggression Locarno-type arrangement or alternatively as a NATO-like military alliance. Washington rejected both concepts on the basis that a Locarno-type arrangement was considered to offer too little, while a NATO-type commitment would demand too much:

There is a fundamental difference in the Western European situation which led to the development of NATO and the contemporary situation in the Far East. The difficulties which handicapped efforts to develop NATO were serious enough but hardly approach the complexity of obstacles which appeared in the Far East situation: Asian nationalism and anti-colonialism; neutralism . . . ; the elements of tensions which exist between the free countries of the Far East; and the Chinese influence.[30]

Ultimately, an agreement between Washington and London was reached to invite Thailand, the Philippines, Indonesia, Burma, Australia, New Zealand,

India, Pakistan, Ceylon, and France to a conference to discuss a collective security strategy for Southeast Asia. Burma, Indonesia, India, and Ceylon referred to their policies of nonalignment, thus refusing to participate in the proposed conference. On September 6, 1954, representatives from the United States, Great Britain, France, Australia, New Zealand, Thailand, the Philippines, and Pakistan met in Manila to discuss the formation of a regional military alliance for Southeast Asia. While the United States proposed to define the alliance's objective as protection against communist aggression, the other participants preferred a broader phrasing. Finally, the U.S. delegation agreed to a more general wording but in a supplementary communiqué declared that Washington still regarded "aggression" as "communist aggression."[31] On September 8, the Southeast Asia Collective Defense Treaty (also known as the Manila Treaty) was signed. It was intended to prevent the expansion of communism by the threat of collective retaliatory measures by the signatory parties, but unlike the NATO pact, it did not obligate one member to assist another in the case of military threat.[32] A secret supplement extended the treaty's provisions to Cambodia and Laos and "the free territory under the jurisdiction of the State of [South] Vietnam."

The Eisenhower administration regarded the Manila Treaty as an integral part of its Southeast Asian policy. The treaty with its general provisions did not force Washington into binding commitments to its allies and it gave the United States justification for a military intervention in Southeast Asia, which was especially significant in view of the deteriorating situation in Indochina.[33] Thus, Secretary of State Dulles described the primary benefit of the Manila Treaty as "[to] prevent Communism from rushing on into the Pacific area, where it would seriously threaten the defense of the United States."[34]

A year later, the signatory parties of the Manila Treaty founded SEATO in Bangkok. Rather than a Southeast Asian regional grouping, SEATO may be more appropriately characterized as a component of a worldwide system of anticommunist military alliances under American leadership.[35] Consequently, the Soviet Union and its allies, as well as other noncommunist states of the region, primarily Indonesia, denounced the organization as a "club of white colonial powers."[36] Moreover, the member countries' support for SEATO was half-hearted at best. Thus, Washington's aspiration to create an effective military alliance to meet communist aggression in Southeast Asia had failed.[37]

In view of the apparent failure of the SEATO concept, the Eisenhower administration decided to modify its foreign policy strategy in Southeast Asia. Policy makers in Washington started to put more emphasis on economic development and cooperation—but this new approach did not represent a break from American containment policy:

The principal U.S. objectives in supporting the development of an expanded Asian economic program would be to:

(a) strengthen the economies of . . . the free countries of Asia and thus facilitate their governments' efforts to achieve greater political and economic stability;

(b) encourage greater regional cohesion and cooperation, thereby increasing the ability of these countries to resist both overt Communist aggression and Communist attempts to subvert and gain control by non-military means;

(c) engender an Asian desire for continuing association with the West in general, and the U.S. in particular.[38]

In this context, American policy makers merely agreed on what economic strategies they did not want to pursue. "While avoiding any suggestion that what we had in mind was a Marshall Plan for Asia, we did feel that an economic plan which would have a psychological effect somewhat similar to that of the Marshall Plan in Europe was needed—something which would really arouse the interest and enthusiasm of free Asians and constitute a setback to the communists."[39]

Then, in early 1955 President Eisenhower called for the establishment of an Asian development fund "with adequate latitude to meet changing circumstances and to take advantage of constructive opportunities."[40] On July 8, 1955, the U.S. Congress approved the establishment of a President's Fund for Asian Economic Development as part of the Mutual Security Act of 1955. Originally, $200 million was approved. Later on, this amount was reduced to $100 million to be spent for both bilateral as well as multilateral projects until June 30, 1958.[41]

At the same time, policy makers in Washington unveiled a policy approach directed to Southeast Asia as a whole. "Whether in the field of economic assistance, or that of trade, or of private investment, our policies and programs have been designed in terms of the relationship between the United States and the particular country in question, rather than in terms of the relationship of the Asian countries with each other, or of Southeast Asia as a whole. . . . That period is passing."[42] Now, members of the U.S. executive branch discussed concepts for an organizational structure for Southeast Asian regionalism—"the prompt organization of an economic grouping by the maximum number of free Asian states," as the NSC in a draft proposal had already demanded in November 1954.[43] Some U.S. policy makers suggested an organization along the lines of the Organization for European Economic Cooperation (OEEC),[44] others proposed the founding of an Asian development bank, and yet more favored a conversion of the Colombo Plan into a multilateral organization.[45] The latter proposal had the advantage that most

Southeast Asian states, but not China, were already members of the Colombo Plan. Thus, Deputy Undersecretary of State Robert Murphy demanded that "because of the nature of its membership and objectives, the Consultative Committee for Economic Development in South and Southeast Asia (Colombo Plan) should be developed into the kind of regional organization which will accomplish the desired objectives."[46] On the other hand, many American policy makers regarded the plan as "a group which is socialist in influence, and British in background."[47] Moreover, the U.S. government feared that, because of limited American influence within a multilateral framework like the Colombo Plan, Congress might not be willing to approve the funding for the plan's extension to a formal regional organization.[48]

Agreement on the conversion of the Colombo Plan into a regional organization could not be reached, but the discussion about a regional economic organization had fostered the understanding for the significance of economic development and cooperation, which were now regarded "in the long run, as important to the security of the free world as the military measures we have taken."[49] Furthermore, the Eisenhower administration was now determined to leave the initiative for the development of regional cooperation schemes to the governments of the Southeast Asian states, "Encourage the countries of Southeast Asia to cooperate closely with each other on a basis of mutual aid and support, and support indigenous efforts to develop regional associations as long as they do not weaken SEATO or the spirit of resistance to Communism."[50]

Finally, in January 1959 the Malayan prime minister Tunku Abdul Rahman proposed an agreement—the so-called South East Asia Friendship and Economic Treaty (SEAFET)—among Malaya, Thailand, the Philippines, Burma, Indonesia, South Vietnam, Cambodia, and Laos to foster the cultural, social, and economic ties among those states. The agreement was not "intended to form a political bloc of any kind or a confederation of South East Asian countries, or to establish an anti-Western or an anti-Communist bloc. . . . The proposed cooperation . . . is not in any way connected with SEATO or other defence arrangements."[51] In July 1960, the Malayan prime minister announced that Thailand and the Philippines expressed the most interest in his proposal for regional cooperation.[52] Negotiations intensified between the three governments and in late summer of 1960 they announced their intention to create a formal regional organization named the Association of South East Asian States.[53] Attempts to convince Indonesia to join the proposed grouping failed because Jakarta distrusted the perceived pro-Western orientation of the three other potential member states.[54] Finally, on July 31, 1961, Thailand, Malaya, and the Philippines founded a regional organization now named the Association of Southeast Asia (ASA).[55]

ASA was the first regional grouping based on an exclusively Southeast Asian initiative. The new association was intended to offer an alternative approach to security than that provided by military alliances. Its underlying rationale was that economic progress provided the foundation for political stability and the best guarantee for political independence.[56] The Soviet Union and China denounced ASA as a "misguided military bloc," while Jakarta simply announced that the "Indonesian Government wishes them well."[57] The reaction in the United States was more positive—the *New York Times* commented on the Southeast Asian regional initiative:

> If the new organization crystallizes in a permanent and effective form, it should be able to perform a useful, though restricted, role. Southeast Asian countries . . . have now reached a stage both politically and economically that warrants increased mutual relationships of all kinds. One of the purposes of the new grouping will be to try to get better income for the raw materials they produce. . . . This as well as the other aims of the new organization should be accepted with sympathy by the United States.[58]

With its focus on economic development, the formation of ASA did, in effect, fit into the Kennedy administration's foreign policy strategy toward the Third World. John F. Kennedy was convinced that the United States could only win the struggle against communism in Asia if economic and social reforms were put into effect on that continent.[59] Therefore, to a certain extent, the United States welcomed ASA as an engine for economic progress leading to the strengthening of the noncommunist countries of the region. Moreover, it corresponded with American demands that the countries of Southeast Asia should take the initiative in fostering regional cooperation.[60] The neutralist outlook of ASA, however, prevented Washington from becoming too enthusiastic about the association's objectives.

Besides, Washington was preoccupied with developments in Vietnam and Laos. Discussions within the American executive branch regarding the crisis in Laos centered around the value and future role of SEATO. While the State Department demanded the continuing existence of SEATO,[61] several members of the executive branch advocated the dissolution of the organization in favor of bilateral security agreements with the Asian member states.[62] Ultimately, the administration decided not to dissolve SEATO. In addition, the question of regional cooperation in Southeast Asia was almost completely ignored until the summer of 1963.

On July 31, 1963, the heads of state of Malaya, Indonesia, and the Philippines—the Tunku Abdul Rahman, Sukarno, and Diosdado Macapagal—announced the launch of a new regional organization for Southeast Asia called

Maphilindo.[63] This organization proved to be a short-lived experiment amid conflicting goals. Unlike ASA, Maphilindo, with its focus on economic progress, was an experiment in conflict resolution.[64] The organization was launched to settle the disputes surrounding the proposed formation of a Greater Malaysia, which envisaged the amalgamation of Malaya, Singapore, North Borneo, Brunei, and Sarawak into a single state. It broke down when the Federation of Malaysia was eventually established on September 16, 1963, and Indonesia and the Philippines both refused to recognize the legitimacy of the new state.[65] The Philippines reaffirmed its claim on North Borneo and Indonesia resumed its konfrontasi campaign against Malaysia. Those political tensions not only resulted in the failure of Maphilindo, but also caused a stalemate in ASA, which lasted for about three years.

The Kennedy administration appeared to have given some encouragement to Maphilindo mainly because it was hoped that it would help "Indonesia to steer the forces of its nationalism into constructive channels, to turn toward economic development and towards picking up some of the responsibility for peace and security in the region."[66] The United States had hoped that Maphilindo would reduce the danger of Indonesia, the most populous Southeast Asian country, turning communist. After the breakdown of Maphilindo, the United States tried to mediate between Indonesia and the Philippines on one side and Malaysia on the other. In January 1964, Kennedy's successor Lyndon B. Johnson sent Attorney General Robert Kennedy on a mediating mission to Southeast Asia. Contrary to expectations in Jakarta, Kennedy was not disposed to put pressure on Kuala Lumpur. Moreover, the United States showed an extreme lack of enthusiasm over the Philippine claim to North Borneo, which only served to divide the loyalties of nations already aligned with the West. The American standpoint demonstrated Washington's unwillingness to allow noncommunist countries to drift apart because of "minor" differences.[67]

Then, in 1964 a reformulation of U.S. policy toward the regional organization of Southeast Asia became apparent. As the war in Vietnam escalated and American involvement was contested at home, President Johnson took the lead in developing an alternative approach to U.S. policy in Southeast Asia. As vice president, he had already suggested a new, economically based evaluation of U.S. foreign policy priorities in that region. In a secret report to President Kennedy following a trip to Southeast Asia in 1961, Johnson had written, "In large measure, the greatest danger Southeast Asia offers to nations like the United States is not the momentary threat of communism itself, rather that danger stems from hunger, ignorance, poverty and disease. We must, whatever strategies we evolve, keep these enemies the point of our attack."[68] Johnson clearly regarded the promotion of regional economic cooperation as an essential part of the American strategy of containment. In the face of the Southeast Asian states' self-blockade, the president took the initiative to revive the idea of regional cooperation in that part of the world. In a speech at Johns Hopkins University in April 1965, Johnson declared:

> Neither independence nor human dignity will ever be won . . . by arms alone. It also requires the work of peace. The American people have helped generously in past times in these works. Now there must be a much more massive effort to improve the life of man in that conflict-torn corner of our world.
>
> The first step [to improve life in Southeast Asia] is for the countries of Southeast Asia to associate themselves in a greatly expanded cooperative effort for development. . . .
>
> For our part I will ask the Congress to join in a billion-dollar American investment in this effort as it is underway. . . .
>
> So I will very shortly name a special team of outstanding, patriotic, and distinguished Americans to inaugurate our participation in these programs. This team will be headed by Mr. Eugene Black, the very able former President of the World Bank.[69]

U.S. financial support was intended to be part of a multilateral development program for Southeast Asia. First, American policy makers favored the creation of a new regional organization, a so-called Southeast Asia Development Association that was supposed to be either an affiliate organization or an independent organization cooperating with ECAFE in order "to detach it from U.S. South Vietnam policy."[70] As a member of the NSC staff wrote, "[The Southeast Asia Development Association] must not be conceived of as simply one more device to 'stop Communism' or 'contain China'; it must not be regarded or treated as a creature or special client of the U.S. This means that to the maximum extent possible, the concept must appear to be an Asian initiative and be Asian in character."[71] Consequently, the new organization would have been open to all states, thus consisting of "regional (recipient) and non-regional (donor) members."[72]

The plans for the creation of a new regional organization never materialized, but they provided the impetus for American participation in two further regional cooperative projects in Southeast Asia. The first one was the Mekong River Project, which allowed for an internationally financed cooperation among North and South Vietnam, Laos, Cambodia, and Thailand for the development of the Mekong. The second was the founding of an Asian development bank, which would provide investment loans and expertise for development projects. It was believed in Washington that a regional bank would help to create conditions conductive to the promotion of stability and maintenance of noncommunist, pro-Western regimes.[73] Thus, President Johnson announced the appointment of former World Bank president Eugene R. Black to head a special commission to prepare American participation in a multilateral aid program for Southeast Asia and the founding of an Asian development bank. Black was able to convince the Southeast Asian governments of the bank's potential benefits and at the same time persuade the Japanese government to increase its contributions to the bank.[74] Finally, in December 1965 twenty-one states (including the United States) signed the charter of the Asian Development Bank (ADB) with headquarters in Manila. The Soviet Union and its allies refrained from joining the ADB, complaining that the United States and Japan had more votes in the bank's bodies than all the developing nations put together.[75]

Encouraged by the large participation of Asian countries in the ADB project, Johnson, in his State of the Union Address in 1966, asked the developing countries to create regional organizations of their own and promised American support for those ventures.[76] In this context, the first regional organization to receive the attention of the U.S. government was the Asian and Pacific Council (ASPAC), which was founded in Seoul in 1966. ASPAC was the brainchild of President Park Chung Hee of South Korea. An openly anticommunist organization, its objective was "greater cooperation and solidarity among the free Asian and Pacific countries in their efforts to safeguard their national independence against communist aggression or infiltration."[77] Except for Malaysia, all member states[78] had formal security relationships with the United States, either on a bilateral basis and/or by means of membership in SEATO or ANZUS. But it was exactly its strong anticommunist stance that limited ASPAC's potential to become a successful regional grouping. Anticommunism alone did not provide a sufficient foundation for cooperation. Besides, the largest state of the region, Indonesia, refused to join ASPAC, continuing instead to pursue its policy of nonalignment.[79]

The Johnson administration continued to search for ways to build a regional organization, that, in the president's words, "would not look like just a collection of our own satellites."[80] Washington again turned its attention to ASA and in a joint declaration made in Washington in March 1966 Vice President Hubert Humphrey and Thai prime minister Thanom Kittakachorn announced

> that the war in Southeast Asia must be waged on two fronts simultaneously—
> the military front and the struggle to improve the social, economic and
> physical well-being of the people. . . .
> It was agreed that organizations such as the Association of Southeast
> Asia could play a valuable role in fostering new cooperative institutions

and stimulating the ideas that would make dramatic economic transformations possible.[81]

Secretary of State Dean Rusk expressed a similar viewpoint in a news conference in October 1966, "We will see substantial advantage in the development among the Asian nations themselves of systematic machinery for consultation on political problems."[82] Additionally, Johnson used every opportunity during his Asian tour in October and November 1966 to refer to the advantages of regional cooperation.[83]

The final impetus for the further regional organization of Southeast Asia, however, came from within the region itself. In November 1965, Philippine president Macapagal had lost the presidential election in Manila against Ferdinand Marcos, who immediately tried to ease tensions with Malaysia. Shortly thereafter, President Sukarno was overthrown by a coup d'état in March 1966. His successor, General Suharto, ended the Indonesian policy of konfrontasi toward Malaysia. During this period of détente, the foreign ministers of Indonesia and Thailand, Adam Malik and Thanat Khoman, respectively, took the initiative in promoting the formation of a new regional organization. After several rounds of negotiations, Malik announced in June 1966 the willingness of the governments of Indonesia, Thailand, Malaysia, and the Philippines to form a new regional organization called the South East Asian Association for Regional Cooperation.[84] But it was to take yet another year until differences of opinion and tensions between the potential member states had been eased. A series of bilateral meetings between the foreign ministers of the Southeast Asian states in the first half of 1967 finally paved the way for the formation of a new regional organization: ASEAN. ASEAN was founded in Bangkok on August 8, 1967, by Thailand, Indonesia, Malaysia, the Philippines, and Singapore.[85]

The Bangkok Declaration, the founding document of ASEAN, represents a careful melding of purposes and statements of ASA and Maphilindo. In the preamble to the declaration, the five signatory parties declared "that the countries of South-East Asia share a primary responsibility for strengthening the economic and social stability of the region and ensuring their peaceful and progressive national development, and that they are determined to ensure their stability and security from external interference in any form or manifestation in order to preserve their national identities in accordance with the ideals and aspirations of their peoples." They also confirmed "that all foreign bases are temporary and remain only with the expressed concurrence of the countries concerned and are not intended to be used directly or indirectly to subvert the national independence and freedom of States in the area or prejudice the orderly processes of their national development."[86]

It is interesting to note the distinctive correspondence of these phrases within the text of the Manila Accord and the Manila Declaration, the basic documents of Maphilindo.[87] This has to be seen as a concession to Indonesia, whose basic foreign policy principles of neutrality and autonomy in security affairs had not changed in spite of the overthrow of Sukarno.[88]

On the other hand, Thailand, Malaysia, and the Philippines pressed for the representation of ASA's principles in the ASEAN Declaration. Thus, the main part of the Bangkok Declaration with its focus on economic, cultural, and social cooperation is almost identical with the ASA Declaration of 1961.[89] Indonesia could claim that a new organization had been formed, while ASA leaders could say that ASEAN was merely an extension of ASA.[90]

In the beginning, the objectives of ASEAN were officially limited to economic and cultural affairs; political cooperation was not mentioned as one of the new organization's goals. Nevertheless, political considerations had played a major role in the formation of ASEAN. Against the background of the Vietnam War, ASEAN was regarded as a safeguard against communist expansion. Thailand in particular viewed the new organization as a security guarantee in case of an American withdrawal from Southeast Asia. Indonesia on the contrary saw its participation in ASEAN as an opportunity to realize its ideals for a new regional order in Southeast Asia. Malaysia interpreted the Bangkok Declaration as the final recognition of its state and national borders by Indonesia and the Philippines. Manila on the other hand regarded its participation in the new regional organization as a way to reduce Philippine dependence on the United States, while Singapore viewed its accession to ASEAN as a step toward equal recognition by its larger neighbors.[91]

The U.S. government voiced its support for the new organization but tried to avoid the impression of a close American association with ASEAN.[92] Walt W. Rostow, President Johnson's national security adviser, characterized the American approach to Southeast Asian regionalism by saying, "It means that the United States increasingly will lead from the middle, not from the front."[93] And Vice President Humphrey, on a trip to Southeast Asia in November 1967, stressed "the importance of the regional cooperation undertaken by the countries of Southeast Asia in the fields of economic and social development."[94]

In view of the deteriorating situation in Vietnam, however, American policy makers were well aware of ASEAN's importance for U.S. security interests in the region. Certain phrases in the Bangkok Declaration—such as the reference to "joint endeavors in the spirit of equality and partnership to strengthen the foundations for a prosperous and peaceful Southeast Asia" and the statement "that they [the member states of ASEAN] are determined to ensure their stability and security from external interference in any form"—could have been perceived as an open door for future military association. Therefore,

Washington tended to link ASEAN to the question of military security and hoped that the grouping would take on a military role. This indicates that the United States' views on ASEAN did not represent a sharp break from the containment policy, but rather the outgrowth of a more sophisticated understanding of the requirements for and constraints on that policy.[95] When those hopes did not materialize, the United States increasingly cast doubts on the viability and effectiveness of ASEAN. Until at least the end of the Vietnam War, American relations with ASEAN consisted mainly of moral and verbal support for the idea of regional cooperation without a corresponding willingness to treat the five countries as a group in any other than a symbolic way.

But contrary to possible expectations on behalf of the United States, ASEAN did not fall apart. Instead, a series of deep political tremors, including the Guam Doctrine, the American withdrawal from Vietnam, and the communist victory there, forced the governments of the ASEAN states to intensify their cooperative efforts. At the same time, the United States needed to replace its now totally discredited deterrence policy in Southeast Asia with a new focus. It was the Carter administration that finally formulated a new American policy toward a region torn by decades of warfare but poised to take off economically. The new approach was based on the recognition that the process of regional cooperation in Southeast Asia had gained a momentum of its own and that ASEAN had become an independent and effective force in international politics.[96] ASEAN proved to become the most successful regional organization outside of Europe as well as a collective focus within the foreign policy formation of the United States toward Asia.

# 16

## Parable of Seeds

### The Green Revolution in the Modernizing Imagination

*Nick Cullather*

In 1898, the followers of an eccentric sect known as the British Israelites tunneled into the tombs of the ancient Irish kings at Tara in what turned out to be a fruitless hunt for the Ark of the Covenant. According to historian Hubert Butler, the story of what the British Israelites had done at Tara was widely known sixty years later, a cautionary tale about the urgency of protecting Ireland's heritage from the shovels of English fanatics. But when Butler chose to research the incident by consulting an eyewitness—his elderly cousin, Synolda French—he found the story more durable than any of its parts. "Tell me, cousin Synolda," he ventured, "about the band of British Israelites who excavated the mound at Tara." "Well, there wasn't any band," came the reply, "but just one young student, and he was not a British Israelite and he didn't excavate the mound." Apart from that, she assured him, it was all true.[1]

A researcher looking into the history of the Green Revolution finds it difficult to escape the ghost of Synolda French. As an episode in the history of economic development, the Green Revolution is as real as the Marshall Plan, as famous, as praised, and as vilified. No history of modern Asia, or indeed, of the twentieth-century world, would be complete without reference to it.[2] It was internationally acknowledged by the awarding of the 1970 Nobel Peace Prize to Norman Borlaug, the best known of the Green Revolutionaries. It has been the subject of congressional hearings, scores of books, film documentaries, and (perhaps the surest indication that an event is real) several fictionalizations, including a magical realist Vietnam War novel and a recent episode of the television series *The West Wing*.[3]

On the show, the president of the United States (played by Martin Sheen) asks one of his aides if he had ever read Paul Erlich's *The Population Bomb*. "Erlich said it was a fantasy that India would ever feed itself," the president continues without waiting for an answer. "Then Norman Borlaug comes along with the dwarf wheat. It was an agricultural revolution that was credited with saving one billion lives."[4] American magazines are in the grip of Borlaug fever. *Reason* and *The Atlantic Monthly* have recently proclaimed him as the man who has "saved more lives than any other person who ever lived."[5] Advocates of plant biotechnology are among the most enthusiastic commemorators of the Green Revolution, which they invoke as a precedent for the coming revolution in genetically altered grains.[6] Sheen's encapsulation contains the main ingredients of the story they all tell: the Malthusian crisis, which made famine inevitable by 1965; Asian nations, especially India, helpless in the path of the fourth horseman; and then the appearance, in the nick of time, of Borlaug and other American scientists bearing a miracle of technology, seeds for dwarf rice and dwarf wheat that multiplied the yield of Asian fields by two- or threefold. In 1968, the Philippines declared self-sufficiency in rice, and India, Indonesia, South Vietnam, Pakistan, and Malaysia each predicted that the era of food scarcity was at an end.

Probe any one of these elements, however, and one soon encounters doubting eyewitnesses, fuzzy math, and contradictory understandings of causation. There was no shortage of skeptics at the Green Revolution's moment of triumph. Calling it a "cruel joke," William C. Paddock explained in 1970 that the revolution's supposed success could be accounted for by improving weather, price subsidies (which depressed consumption), and the opening of new lands.[7] The Central Intelligence Agency (CIA), that omniscient eyewitness, was inclined to agree. The latest declassified reports are from 1972, and at that point the agency felt the jury was out on whether the new seeds had produced any effect on yields. Observing that three successive good monsoons had improved harvests throughout Asia, the agency noted that dwarf wheat and rice accounted for only a small portion of the total crop.[8] The CIA was also aware that the country reporting the most dramatic turnaround, the Philippines, was systematically faking statistics.[9] Claims about "miracle" seeds encountered substantial public cynicism in Asia, as well. When India's harvest declined in 1972 owing to a drought, the State Department noted that New Delhi had to "defend the reality of the green revolution" against widespread disbelief.[10]

These doubts would be easier to dismiss were they not echoed by the scientists responsible for the Green Revolution, many of whom believed a media frenzy distorted their message. Forrest F. Hill, the agronomist and Ford Foundation grant slinger who created the International Rice Research Institute (IRRI) in the Philippines that bred the dwarf rice IR-8, believed the story owed much to luck and television, "Then you ran into two severe drought years in the Indian subcontinent in 1965 and '66 and just at that time it looked as though you were set for starvations on a major scale, out came IR-8, so that you not only had a new variety, but you went on TV with it and the 'miracle rice' fairy tale had been born."[11]

Aggregate or per capita production figures fail to provide hard evidence of an agricultural miracle. No spike is visible on the charts at or about 1967. Instead, the late 1960s and 1970s continue a consistent upward trend in food crop yields beginning in 1945.[12] India, the Philippines, Sri Lanka, and other new nations shifted production away from colonial export crops (tea, sugar, and rubber) toward domestically consumed foods, supporting the transition with investments in agricultural research, irrigation, and fertilizer production. These evolutionary changes, rather than the seed revolution, account for the bulk of the change. Even in the area of seed breeding, Borlaug's specialty, local research institutes contributed many of the most widely used varieties. American scientists built on (exploited?) their discoveries, continuing research interrupted by war and the collapse of colonialism. IR-8, for instance, was the result of a cross between an Indonesian variety developed by a Dutch breeder in the 1930s and another variety developed about the same time by Japanese breeders working in Taiwan.[13] It was, in other words, a botanical expression of the imperial succession sealed by the U.S. victory in World War II.[14]

Apart from these deviations from the heroic narrative, there are also the objections posed by theory. Any attempt to verify the Green Revolution saga runs into the towering figure of Amartya Sen, Nobel laureate in economics, known as the "Mother Theresa of Economics" in his native India, where a dessert is named in his honor.[15] Unquestionably the preeminent development economist working today, Sen has made his principal contribution in the study of the causes of famines, among them India's Bihar famine of 1967, the one the Green Revolution supposedly averted. Challenging Thomas Malthus, he contends that the availability of food is a distant and minor link in the chain of causation. Famine results from a "massive social failure," compounded by unemployment, a catastrophic loss of buying power, and gender inequality amid a breakdown of public mechanisms (e.g., the media and the state) capable of coordinating a response.[16] The cure for famine, he insists, is not more food but more freedom. In the case of the Bihar famine, he blames the antiquated Famine Codes and misleading press reports rather than either a surplus of population or a shortage of food.

To recapitulate: the American scientists were not the only ones providing the seeds, the seeds may not have produced the bumper crops, the bumper crops did not avert a Malthusian crisis, and there was no Malthusian crisis. Apart from that, it was all true. In this case and most others, it may be sensible to resist the impulse to debunk history; as Butler discovered, myths invariably outlast their debunkers. There is another reason as well: false turns, missing characters, phony figures, and plot fabrications aside, this story is true. The intensification of Asian agriculture that occurred in the 1960s and

1970s propelled the massive urbanization and industrialization of the 1980s and 1990s, changing the shape of the economies, and consequently the politics, of South and Southeast Asia. The real question is why we choose to sum up the history of these momentous developments in a fable of magic beans and scientific wizards from over the sea. Even more surprisingly, Americans, Europeans, and Asians tell largely the same story, a version standardized not through a process of discursive hegemony, I will argue, but by a kind of transnational collaboration.

The origins of the Green Revolution legend lie in a momentary alignment of Asian, American, and transnational narratives of modernization. In 1958, just four years after his famous "Dams Are the Temples of Modern India" speech, Jawaharlal Nehru was talking about limits. In words that might have been taken from *The Ugly American* (then a best seller in the United States), he decried "the 'disease of gigantism.' We want to show that we can build big dams and do big things. [But] it is . . . the small irrigation projects, the small industries, and the small plants for electric power, which will change the face of the country."[17] The beginning of the Development Decade marked the passing of the high modernist euphoria that inspired Point IV and the planned city of Chandigarh. Asian and American planners, however, recalibrated their expectations for different reasons: In the states along China's southern boundary, nationalist modernization's urban/industrial bias was beginning to yield political liabilities in the form of a stagnating agricultural sector, restive peasants, and high and unstable food prices. In each of the states most identified with the Green Revolution in its opening stages—India, the Philippines, and Pakistan—an infant industrial sector suffered from its dependency on dwindling revenues from agricultural exports.

In the Philippines, the economic crisis coincided with the rise of President Ferdinand Marcos and a generation of Harvard-trained planners known as the "technocrats." Marcos's Nacionalista Party ran in 1965 on the slogan "Progress Is a Grain of Rice."[18] His predecessor, Diosdado Macapagal, had been dogged by sporadic rice panics induced by the weakness of the peso and consequent fluctuations in the price of imported rice. During the campaign, Marcos promised an all-out effort to achieve national self-sufficiency in rice by 1970.[19] A similar promise had been made by Macapagal four years earlier (as well as by his predecessor), but Marcos showed unusual resourcefulness in making his prophesy come true, or at least appear to come true. He took an interest in the newly established institute funded by the Rockefeller and Ford Foundations, and began pressuring the IRRI to allow government research stations to begin reproducing one of the IRRI's new dwarf strains. With some misgivings, the scientists allowed experimental releases of one of its more promising varieties, IR-8.[20]

In late July 1966, the IRRI found itself at the center of a media whirlwind. "Miracle Rice," the title of a cover story in the *Philippines Free Press,* the national magazine, gave a name to a new phenomenon touted by Marcos officials as the answer to the country's food problem. Press accounts promised three- to tenfold increases in yields without any increased effort or investment:[21] "The miracle is lodged in the grain itself—a built-in productivity."[22] That this was decidedly not true was what made IR-8 attractive to the technocrats and to the American aid officials who jumped on the miracle rice bandwagon. IR-8 required artificial fertilizers as well as pesticides and carefully controlled irrigation. Its short stature allowed mechanical harvesting. The Agency for International Development (AID) began distributing IR-8 in a package with Atlas and Esso farm chemicals, while another leading manufacturer, Caltex, built a nationwide distribution network.[23] The technocrats knew that reliance on these "inputs" afforded opportunities to impose a real solution to the rice crisis by extending government control over this unruly sector of the economy. Marcos set up a coordinating council directed by Rafael Salas to direct the supply of seed, chemicals, loans, and machinery, enabling the government to control prices and supply at every step of cultivation. "Even if it wasn't such a spectacular producer," Salas believed, "one would advocate pushing miracle rice culture if only to train the Filipino farmer into thinking in terms of techniques, machines, fertilizers, schedules, and experiments."[24] An American AID official affirmed that creating "an American time pressure culture" was essential to the program. "If people do not accept discipline," he observed, "we cannot progress."[25]

Bountiful harvests could always be produced another way: through fraud. The Marcos administration, which first claimed self-sufficiency in 1968, maintained the illusion well into the 1970s through the simple device of exporting small quantities amid great fanfare while secretly importing tons of rice from Hong Kong and faking the figures.[26] To explain the Philippines' historic, if imaginary, transformation, Marcos's publicity agents wrote the early drafts of the Green Revolution legend. "Coming at the precise moment in history when the Philippines' growing population was forcing the country steadily and surely into a maelstrom of hunger," a spokesman elaborated, "the development of miracle rice marks a turning point which may not only arrest this possibility, but makes possible a complete reversal toward self-sufficiency."[27] Marcos has a deserved reputation as a fabulist, but in this case he was far from unique. American advisers noted that South Vietnamese "service chiefs were ordered, often somewhat arbitrarily, to raise yield figures, lower consumption figures, or decrease estimate of drought damage" to the new seeds.[28] Academic researchers discovered that figures on the acreage planted with dwarf varieties were inflated by 300 percent in southern India and 500 percent in East Pakistan (Bangladesh).[29] Dwarf seeds were often planted in strips along roads to create a Potemkin Green Revolution for traveling dignitaries.

The occurrence of fraud hardly detracts from the reality of the achievement: plenty of anecdotal evidence suggests that yields did go up, farmers did adopt the new techniques in large numbers, and chemicals, machines, and irrigation were applied more widely (it's all true!). The pattern of falsification was designed to inspire public and international confidence in the new government agromonopolies and to stabilize food prices by persuading the markets that the transformation that was occurring had actually occurred already and was irreversible. A Bangladeshi rural development officer explained in 1978 that "in hopes of keeping the price [of rice] down the government predicted a much larger crop than there was. We junior officials meet each other, we talk about the use of statistics, we know what is going on. Last week I attempted to explain my concern to a senior man visiting from Dhaka. He would not hear of it. Politely he told me it was none of my business."[30]

The exposure of the fabrication in the mid to late 1970s did not erase the impression created by the original announcement. History's hand had been compressed. Gradual diffusion of technologies, infrastructure, and practices, a process unfolding over decades from the 1950s through the 1970s, had been made to appear as a single historical event that occurred in the late 1960s in the context of other events: a population crisis, a famine, the election of Marcos or Indira Gandhi, and the introduction of the dwarf seeds.[31]

If the seeds fulfilled prophecies of abundance in Asia, in the United States they came in answer to a prophecy of famine. Since the triumph of Adam Smith in the early national period, the United States has been relatively unhaunted by the specter of Parson Malthus. In the late nineteenth century, Malthusian ideas gained a foothold through their association with evolutionism, and a marginal scientific field, ecology, worked to substantiate a presumed relationship between populations and resources. The American birth control movement, in contrast with its European counterparts, emphasized voluntary motherhood and eugenic arguments over issues of population control until after World War II. The geopolitical interpretation of the causes of war, which emphasized competition for scarce resources, and Hiroshima-induced misgivings about the inevitability of progress laid the groundwork for the first postwar Malthusian panic in 1948. The appearance of two best sellers, Fairfield Osborne's *Our Plundered Planet* and William Vogt's *Road to Survival,* in the same year marked the beginning of the popular ecology movement. Under the sponsorship of the Atomic Energy Commission, ecology gained prominence and respectability, while the Rockefeller and Ford

Foundations supported research in the related fields of demography and "human ecology," a field positing the existence of an endangered equilibrium between human populations and available resources, particularly food.[32]

While the new population control movement enjoyed elite financing and support, its influence on the sciences and national policy remained limited. Vogt and Osborne were belittled in the national press, and Elvin Stakman, the president of the American Association for the Advancement of Science, assured the *New York Times* that an ongoing agricultural revolution would provide an "answer to the gloomy Malthusian prophets of doom."[33] In the biological sciences, the concept of a "balance of nature," endangered or otherwise, had fallen into disrepute and ecologists struggled with indifferent success to identify smaller microbalances, a concept that came to be called an ecosystem.[34] Demand-side economists, led by John Maynard Keynes, contended that insufficient population growth was a primary cause of economic stagnation. "One cannot repress the thought," an American economist wrote in 1939, "that perhaps the whole Industrial Revolution . . . has been . . . largely induced by the unparalleled rise in population."[35] President Harry S. Truman's Point IV program contained no uncertainty about the capacity for underdeveloped areas to achieve growth without limits. Writing in 1954, Max F. Millikan and Walt W. Rostow expected development policy to deliver "a sustained increase in production per head, which gives or promises to give a higher real income to every free world citizen."[36]

President Dwight D. Eisenhower considered population control an untouchable issue, but modernization theory provided a point of entrance for neo-Malthusian ideas. In the heady days of Point IV, the very breadth of the technology gap between rich and poor nations was optimistically taken as evidence that a simple transference of tools and methods would induce profound social and economic effects. Within a few years, it was clear that cultural and structural barriers made modernization a more complicated transaction.[37] The government turned to social scientists, funding institutes dedicated to generating theories and studies useful to policy planners. Early studies, such as Millikan and Rostow's, sought to identify techniques and map out a process of economic growth emphasizing the primacy of capital accumulation, but later monographs suggested the existence of barriers—perhaps even an absolute barrier—to what development could achieve.

In 1958, demographer Ansley J. Coale and development economist Edgar M. Hoover produced a seminal study of India that set the terms of debate for the next decade.[38] Applying the new technique of economic modeling, Coale and Hoover contended that a high rate of population growth would erase capital accumulation by saddling economies with dependents too young to work and forcing investment into health and education instead of growth-oriented sectors. The study modified Malthus in two ways: by emphasizing population rates rather than absolute numbers, and by identifying capital rather than food as the critical scarcity. In the hands of policy makers, however, the study was used to assert the existence of a "food-population balance" essential to economic growth. It should be noted here that the Coale and Hoover model has since been rejected by economists, who found in the 1970s and 1980s that some of its main assumptions were flawed. Population growth, particularly in Asia, resulted from declining death rates, not high birth rates, so the proportion of dependents was not as high or as unproductive as Coale and Hoover guessed. Large populations also create compensating economies of scale. A National Academy of Sciences review of the literature in 1986 concluded that the net effect of population on economic growth was unknown and probably could not be determined.[39] Coale and Hoover's thesis was incorporated in the Draper Committee's 1959 report on foreign assistance programs, which provided the basis for the Kennedy administration's aid reorganization and the creation of AID.[40] The Draper report found that "too rapidly growing population in many underdeveloped countries was largely offsetting our economic aid."[41] Poor nations were simply consuming economic assistance in the form of imported food.

Food was emerging as a primary front in the Cold War struggle for hearts and minds. After Soviet engineers and heavy industry entered the development game in 1958, the United States began emphasizing agriculture as the distinguishing feature of free world success. The Chinese famine of 1961 and failed Soviet harvests allowed American farm surpluses to be presented as fruits of a gentler modernization process. "Wherever Communism goes, hunger follows," Secretary of State Dean Rusk alleged in 1962. "Communist China is today in the grip of a vast and terrible famine, which in turn has led to stagnation and decline of industry. There is hunger in North Vietnam."[42] The conflict in the latter nation was depicted in the American press as a war about rice. Rice "is precisely what makes underpopulated, rice-rich, easy going South Vietnam—hardly anyone bothers to plant two crops there—such a tempting target for North Vietnam."[43] The Coale and Hoover findings suggested, however, that a galloping population increase would soon overtake any American lead in food production.

Population control found an important ally in the director of the UN Food and Agriculture Organization, Binay R. Sen, whose office overlooked the headquarters of the antibirth control resistance. Sen "kept hammering on these chilling statistics. . . . Mankind was approaching the crisis predicted in 1798 by Malthus, and, with the division of wealth broadly coinciding with the division of color, the rich nations of the West were living uncomfortably close to something like a white man's 1789."[44] In 1963, Sen brought his campaign to Washington in the form of a World Food Congress that featured a keynote by Arnold Toynbee on the perils of unrestricted population growth.[45] President John F. Kennedy then took the podium and issued a prophetic response. Calling for a "scientific revolution which may well rival, in its social consequences, the industrial revolution," he declared that "the key to a permanent solution to world hunger is the transfer of technology to food deficit nations."[46] In true New Frontier style, he endorsed the strategy already adopted by the Ford and Rockefeller Foundations by predicting imminent, history-making success.

In 1963, Borlaug had just received his first invitation to visit India's research stations and IRRI was just beginning its breeding program, but the broad sketch of the drama they were about to perform had already been written. The next Asian famine was sure to be taken as a fulfillment of neo-Malthusian forecasts. The next advance in agricultural practice would be regarded as the revolutionary breakthrough. Well, perhaps not quite any advance. Fertilizer lacked a certain telegenic quality, and as for irrigation, "water is an odd subject," a Ford Foundation official observed, "seeds can be created, displayed, and held in the hand; water is dispersed and elusive and slides out of sight."[47] There was another reason why dwarf seeds were recognized, before they had produced a discernible payoff, as the pivotal technology. Modernization theory again supplied the narrative frame.

There is a strange and unremarked intersection in the histories of modernization theory and aerial bombardment. Several of the leading postwar figures in theoretical economics, including Rostow, Charles P. Kindleberger, and Carl Kaysen, served in the Economic Warfare Division of the London embassy as bombing targeters. There, they debated how best to dismantle the German economy from the air, whether the whole system had to be taken down together or if there might be specific points—a ball-bearing factory or a refinery—that could be removed, bringing the entire war machine to a halt.[48] Development theory, which proceeded from the assumption economies could be created by dropping in ingredients, oscillated, as the targeteers had, between a "systems" approach and a "bottleneck" approach. Beginning in 1949 with a disappointing search for breakthrough techniques, modernization theorists had fallen in line behind a systems approach known as "balanced" development, which saddled aid officials with the formidable task of coordinating the simultaneous advance of all social and economic sectors. The approach explained the pattern of failure witnessed over the previous decade, but it afforded little hope for anything less than a new Marshall Plan. The pendulum, however, would swing the other way in the 1960s.

A massive Ford Foundation/Social Science Research Council inquiry into the sources of economic development begun in 1955 postulated that in previous modernizing revolutions a single ingredient, an "epochal innovation" (such as the steam engine or internal combustion) had propelled historical and economic transformation.[49] Albert O. Hirschman, writing in 1958, suggested that the technological trigger could be something as ordinary as a rice seed. Rejecting balanced development, he argued that a disruptive technology, an "inducement mechanism," could stir unused talent and capital into activity. Like an atomic pile, underdeveloped societies would undergo a "chain of disequilibria" as energy was released from the breaking of traditional bonds.[50] John P. Lewis, former head of the India AID mission, told Congress in 1969 that Hirschman had written the history of the Green Revolution in advance. "He taught many of us to realize that this is the way you expect successful development to happen. When it succeeds, you get a thrust, one sector moves ahead, and it begins to create effective pulls on the laggards."[51] Lester Brown, a Department of Agriculture economist, explained that farmers who discarded customary practices would assert control of their environment in other ways, demanding schools, roads, birth control, and new political arrangements. Change would percolate upward from the rice roots, until "peasant farmers are drawn into the mainstream of modern economic life."[52]

Like Marcos's technocrats, American modernizers prized miracle seeds less for what they did for farming than for what they did to the farmer, and the whole society of which the farmer was a part. The Green Revolution was understood and criticized then, and is so today, not as simply an agricultural innovation, but as an economic, political, environmental, and moral transformation, as Modernization itself. This is why the seeds were imagined to have the power to end poverty and war,[53] and why the introduction of improved rice and wheat varieties is an unnoticed occurrence in the history of North America and Europe (although, of course, they grow there, too) but is recorded as a seminal event in the history of Asia.[54] This is also why critics, from Al Gore to Prince Charles, remember the Green Revolution as the moment when Asians forsook their traditional, sacred bond to the earth.[55]

The modernizers' prophecies came to pass in 1966. On January 20, speaking in Independence, Missouri, President Lyndon B. Johnson announced that "the position of the United States is clear. We will give our help and support to nations which make their own decisions to insure an effective balance between the number of their people and the food they have to eat."[56] The short-tether policy, as it came to be called, treated each country as a human ecosystem, with each government responsible for maintaining a supposedly natural balance between food and population. Johnson responded to the Bihar famine by dispatching 5.1 million tons of wheat, one-fifth of the American crop, to Calcutta.[57] He imposed short-tether policies to compel New Delhi to adopt self-help measures—including dwarf seeds—that it had in fact already been adopted, thereby alienating the Gandhi government and allowing future generations of critics to claim that the Green Revolution had been forced on India by Washington and the World Bank.[58] On October 25, amid the furor over IR-8, Johnson stood next to Marcos in an experimental IRRI rice field in Los Baños, Philippines, and praised the inventors of miracle rice. He spoke of a "divine anger" that made miracles happen, "There is an anger that cannot tolerate hunger, disease, illiteracy, and injustice in the world. And it becomes divine anger when it is translated into the practical work of healing and teaching."[59]

If the Green Revolution makes for problematic history, as parable it retains considerable power to motivate and instruct. Within its apologue, modernization is no longer an impersonal, historic force but an exchange of gifts, with all of the possibilities for compassion, reciprocation, and betrayal inherent in such an act. Having a triumphant example of the application of science and altruism to a world problem may not be a bad thing, even if the example is less than completely triumphant, scientific, or altruistic. Michael Ignatieff remarks on the disappearance of moral narratives, "the stories we tell that make sense of distant places and explain why we should get involved in their plight."[60] The white man's burden and the domino theory each carried a flawed sense of obligation that bound people in the safe, wealthy areas of the world to people in the poor, dangerous zones. Globalization contains no such terms of engagement, which may be why we hold so tightly to the few myths of heroic internationalism that we have.

# 17

## Afterword

### The Limits of Decolonization

*Wang Gungwu*

It may be said that the previous chapters are rich and meaty and not easy to digest. Using the word "meaty" gives me the chance to refer to animals and birds in my comments. For indeed they are the images that the chapters have conjured up in my mind. Most of the chapters remind me of the imperial British lion's final survey of its distant terrain and the American eagle's perspective of what was happening down there among those scurrying around, undeveloped if not unwashed. These two splendid images remind me of the deep and immediate fear of the Soviet bear's embrace and the longer-term threat of the Chinese dragon's reach. What is less obvious is the local Southeast Asian worm's eye view, or what Southeast Asians might prefer, the image of the *pelanduk*, that legendary mouse deer who could always outwit its larger enemies.

The book's subject is decolonization and transformation in Southeast Asia. What is striking is the way the two words, decolonization and transformation, have been directly linked. That really affects at least four major issues worthy of consideration: First, what did the metropolitan decolonizers, and their local elitist modernizers who abetted them, really want? Second, what did those who found themselves decolonized actually get? Third, in what ways were the former colonial powers transformed? And, finally, how differently did the changes transform the successor nation-states after these powers went home? One might follow these with many more questions, but I shall leave it at that. The whole thing is complicated enough already. In fact, I will not try to deal with all the questions I have asked. Like the chapters represented in this volume, I shall talk more about decolonization and less about transformation.

It is rare to have so many different uses of the idea of decolonization appearing in one book. Reading these juxtaposed ideas has been a mind-stretching experience for me. I have personally lived through the decades of decolonization at several levels, and read most of the writings at the time by decolonizers from both sides, that is, by the colonial officials and their political masters and also by the anticolonial nationalists of various hues. The set of actors and actions with which I was familiar were fairly sharply focused on their goal: the replacement of a foreign regime by one that was locally based. The means of achieving that end, however, were varied. They ranged from violence and revolution involving ordinary people, to negotiations among political elites, and to the idea that the colonial rulers were, for whatever reason and to whatever degree, preparing the colonized for independence. I confess to being nostalgic for the time when the word was so much easier to comprehend and explain.

Let me get back to the British lion's survey of its realm. Several chapters show how skillfully the British postponed the inevitable for several years, and how hard they tried to create some sort of virtual empire for at least their businessmen. They had been left to take care of Southeast Asia while the Americans concentrated on Japan and East Asia. It was obvious that the colonial powers of Southeast Asia were differently situated after the ravages of World War II. The British were in a stronger position to restore their prewar authority than were the French and the Dutch. The Americans had promised independence to the Philippines and returned in time to dot the i's and cross the t's. The Japanese occupation of the whole region shook the respect and fear that locals had of European power, but its own forced withdrawal from Korea and Taiwan reminded everyone that not all colonial powers were European. China's reemergence as a potential power was strengthened by its national reunification under the Chinese Communist Party and that added a new dimension to the struggles the former colonial powers and their nationalist successors would have to face.

What does arouse wonder was the British concern for continuities even as their power waned, and their efforts to set up more rational arrangements for themselves for the long haul were impressive. They certainly did seem to know what to do, even if the flesh was now weak. In those early years, decolonization did look like it was going to be a linear process, a story that might have had a sad beginning, but was about to have a happy ending.

Like all fairy tales, it turned out that the ending was too simple. No one was happy for long, whether they were the colonizers or the colonized. For both sides, the hardest part began after one flag came down and another went up. The British lion had to admit that it was tired and old and the young and vigorous American eagle was expected to come to the rescue. The full and excellent chapters in this book that describe the eagle's predicaments have been fascinating to read. And I am amazed by the immense amount of work on the impact of decolonization on the metropolitan countries themselves, notably on Britain and France.

Of particular interest is the recent renewal of interest in the Vietnam syndrome for the United States and its allies in Europe and in the region. This reminds us what a traumatic experience that was for American politics and public opinion. To have Robert J. McMahon and Mark Philip Bradley give us their latest thoughts on how it all happened and what hopes had led the United States to intervene in the region to the extent it did, is a treat. Their accounts of the assumptions that lie beneath the plans for the new nation-states that it wanted to see created and strengthened add an extra dimension to what we know about the work the other powers had left unfinished. Although some of these assumptions were known at the time, the depth of feeling, of misreading, and even of ignorance that they display suggest that probably all great powers that reach out too far too quickly necessarily expose themselves to such risks. But was that really decolonization? Was it the first phase of a new kind of virtual empire?

Or was that something else again? Does the story of American intervention and commitment not overlap with something that should belong to another story, that of the anticommunist Cold War, of keeping the Soviet bear away and containing the Chinese dragon? Some overlaps in history are to be expected. The question is, when do the overlaps become really part of a different story? This matter of thematic overlap is, of course, also apparent in several of the other chapters. Take the example of foreign investment that could well be presented as part of the story of capitalist stimulation and expansion. Similarly, could the issue of Green Revolution mythmaking be a new phase in informal empire-building, whether consciously embarked on or not, in order to secure American strategic interests? I wonder how much it really helps to include them as aspects of decolonization.

I do think that it is useful for scholars of decolonization to consider all the factors that had helped to bring it about. My worry is that the word "decolonization" might be overworked and made to do too much. It was a complex enough historical phenomenon, and the ramifications were great for all concerned even when it primarily meant what it started out as: the replacement of a foreign regime by one that was locally based. Although this is an unrealistic hope now, we still need to pause to ask if we should stretch the meaning of the word "decolonization" too far in all directions.

This, of course, reflects my own bias. I am more used to the word being looked at from the worm's eye view, that is, in the eyes of those nationalist leaders who inherited state power and set out to transform themselves by building new nations. It soon became clear that building nations out of the fragmented pieces left behind was difficult, especially in the cold hard world divided by ideology and great economic disparities. Even the leaders who were not worms but thought of themselves as clever *pelanduks* began to wonder how decolonized their countries really were. New words were soon invented to describe the continuing battle for true independence or sovereignty, for example, words like the more euphemistic "developing" and "modernizing"; the blunter and ruder words like "dependency" and "puppet state"; and the ideological abstractions like "neocolonial" and "postcolonial," "postmodern" and "Orientalist," among many others. These words, used largely to acknowledge the imperfect power transference that had occurred, convey the sense of frustration that accompanied new responsibilities.

Of course, some of these words had helped the new leaders stay in power, others had assisted them in creating stable and prosperous sovereign states, and others had provided excuses as to why their countries were not doing better. Yet others had enabled opposition groups, alternate leaders, the military, and the revolutionaries to change the regimes and try and start again. Some of these developments could be brought under the rubric of a "continuing decolonization," one that had been given a long fuse and could blow up any time, one that might be seen as a state of uncertainty that could be drawn out for a long time. It could even be made to appear that decolonization has no boundaries and might never end. Almost everything could be made to appear to have something to do with the fact that decolonization had not been fully achieved. But I am not sure how far and long we should let that same word take us. There must be a cutoff point when we say that there is now a new beast, something that might have notched up victory as a new nation-state, marked the final corruption of the national leadership, recorded failure of the legal and political system, or triggered a popular rebellion or revolution. Then a new story can begin.

I agree that there could be, for historians, a long view of the phenomenon of decolonization and a shorter one that focuses on the specific events that led to and accompanied the actual transfer of power. For the latter, the periods concerned are easier to identify and there is considerable agreement as to what events are significant. For the long view, it might be argued that colonialism carried the seeds of its destruction from the day it was imposed on local peoples. Certainly, there is much historical evidence to show that no such rule by force could endure for long, especially when they were long-distance naval-based empires. But I am not persuaded that the hopeless resistance to colonialism in the early stages were anything more than discrete problems of regime failure or social decay and disunity in the face of a superior alien power. I don't believe we should talk about decolonization until we can say that the local reactions against colonial rule had begun to persuade the colonial rulers to think of how and when they would have to leave and go home. So the long view for Southeast Asia, while it may vary from territory to territory, would not be much earlier than the 1930s (with the possible exception of the United States in the Philippines). For most, the story only began after 1941. Certainly, the 1930s are relevant and, of course, several countries like Malaysia, Singapore, and the Indochina states carry the story into the 1960s and the 1970s. Beyond that, the problems of these new states must be new ones that the word "decolonization" is too weak to support.

In the end, I have to admit that it has been easier for me to recognize the beast when I read the excellent chapters on French Indochina and British Malaya or Malaysia. Here, I am on more familiar ground. There was enough going on within the conventional framework that we historians have yet to examine. The sterling work of Nicholas Tarling and his Singapore and Malaysian colleagues, who have searched assiduously to tell more of the British decolonizing story or to tell the story better, is not only assuring, but it also warns us of how much there is to be done.

Karl Hack's stimulating chapter suggests that we may now know enough to be able to reexamine the theories and approaches offered so far for the phenomenon. This is an attractive idea. He says, "What is needed is a model that can hyperlink the various imperial, globalization, colonial records, radical, counterinsurgency, diplomatic, and nationalist strands into a coherent account." I am less sure of that. My concern is that this ambitious plan could lead us back to seeing almost everything as having something to do with decolonization, even to the point where the British Empire may be seen as never truly being decolonized and its imperial shadow was subsumed seamlessly by the far greater reach of American global power. I do not deny that it is possible to make everything seem connected to everything else, but I am uneasy as to what this would do to the model that is actually made to stretch that far.

The fact is that every major historical phenomenon can be shown to have relationships with other important contemporary events. A holistic effort to get the narrative right is commendable, but to speak of an inclusive model runs the risk of merging so many factors into the frame that it collapses because of its own weight. Recently, I questioned Hack about using the original meaning of the word "colon" to show that "decolonization" in that sense could lead us to some kind of ethnic cleansing of all colonizers. He asked me to be more explicit. Let me say that I have real difficulties with not distinguishing colonists, or colonizers, from various kinds of immigrants. If there is to be no clear distinction, then an ancient and powerful phenomenon like migration gets drawn anachronistically into the modern problem of decolonization. If the word is used so broadly, then almost any kind of people movement or settlement would be in danger of being included under the decolonization umbrella.

I found it interesting to see how many chapters dealt with the connection between decolonization and international relations. This operates at two levels at least. In the context of the rivalry between the colonial powers themselves before or during decolonization, there had to be great power relations. There, decolonization had weakened the old colonizing powers and changed the international relationships. Several chapters touch on this for Britain and France and show that the decolonization phenomenon was a subset of the larger international structure.

For the former colonies, after they had become legally new nation-states, international conventions brought them into the world of nations and each then began to have its own place in the framework. This was for them obviously a very different international relations, more like a beginner's kind. I wish there was more discussion in this book about these newly transformed states, how they dealt with the transition stages, their self-discovery of their weaknesses, their automatic Third World status, the need to take sides or stay "neutralist," and their efforts to know their place in the deadly games played by the powerful countries with which they had to deal. This is an area closest to the reality of decolonization for the decolonized. But it is not clear whether decolonization has had much impact on the international realities in the region. More likely, it is the new international power relations that shaped the way the decolonized were made to fit into the globalized world.

Here, I return to the importance of the chapters on the United States. They remind us of the trend since the 1970s of revising the history of U.S. judgments, intentions, and plans for the region to emphasize their Machiavellian side against the idealistic, even altruistic, rhetoric that some American leaders used. That is commendable history writing. What strikes me is that the American role in the international relations of the region is much greater than anything that the word "decolonization" can conjure up. It is no accident that the best work in the international relations field had once come from the writings of the theorists and practitioners of the British Empire, and that this work came to be dominated by the U.S. perspective after that great colonizing power had weakened during World War II. This is particularly true of East and Southeast Asia. Thus, I believe that decolonization did little for our understanding of international relations. On the contrary, it was the actions of the Americans within the framework that they had come to dominate that shaped the later progress of decolonization. I believe that once this fact is better understood, then we can usefully distinguish between what decolonization did for transformation in Southeast Asia and what transformations actually occurred because a restructured international architecture had transcended the heritage of decolonization.

# Notes

## Chapter 1

1. W. David McIntyre, *British Decolonization, 1946–1997*. New York: St. Martin's, 1998, pp. 79, 89, 95.

2. Charles-Robert Ageron, *La décolonisation française*. Paris: Armand Colin, 1991.

3. H. W. van den Doel, *Afscheid van Indië: De val van het Nederlandse imperium in Azië*. Amsterdam: Prometheus, 2001.

4. The phrase is Norman Angell, "The New Imperialism and the Old Nationalism." *International Affairs* 10, no. 1 (1931): 70.

5. See Paul Doumer, *Situation de l'Indo-Chine*. Hànôi: Schneider, 1902; and Herbert Ingram Priestley, *France Overseas: A Study of Modern Imperialism*. New York: Appleton-Century, 1938, pp. 228–229. Discussing a later advocate of *mise en valeur*, Albert Sarraut, the historian D. Bruce Marshall writes of the policy, "It did not seek primarily to create self-sustaining economic growth or to promote the emergence of politically independent states. . . . Instead, its aim was to tie the colonies and France together in a cooperative program of economic and social expansion." See D. Bruce Marshall, *The French Colonial Myth and Constitution-Making in the Fourth Republic*. New Haven, Conn.: Yale University Press, 1973, p. 44.

6. Sir Frederick John Dealtry Lugard, "The Basis of the Claim for Colonies." *International Affairs* 15 (January–February 1936): 3.

7. Quoted in Lugard, "Basis of the Claim for Colonies," p. 16.

8. Dame Rachel Crowdy, "The Humanitarian Activities of the League of Nations." *Journal of the Royal Institute of International Affairs* 5 (1926): 153–169. The author was chief of the Opium and Social Questions Section of the League of Nations. See also Kenneth Robinson, *The Dilemmas of Trusteeship: Aspects of British Colonial Policy between the Wars*. London: Oxford University Press, 1965; William Roger Louis, *Imperialism at Bay, 1941–45: The United States and the Decolonization of the British Empire*. Oxford: Clarendon, 1977, especially chapter 5; and Royal Institute of International Affairs, *The Colonial Problem*. London: Oxford University Press, 1937, p. 112, citing Lord Sydney Haldane Olivier, *White Capital and Coloured Labour*. 2nd ed. London: Woolf, 1929, chapters 4, 24.

9. Joop de Jong, *De waaier van het fortuin: De Nederlanders in Azië en de Indonesische archipel, 1595–1950*. Den Haag: Sdu Uitgevers, 1998, p. 22. The Dutch "ethical policy" is discussed in chapters 22 and 23.

10. Jacobus A. A. van Doorn, *Indische lessen: Nederland en de koloniale ervaring*. Amsterdam: Bert Bakker, 1995, p. 38. The quotation appears on p. 34 and is taken

from H. H. van Kol, "Ontwerp-program voor de Nederlandsche Koloniale Politiek." *De Nieuwe Tijd* 6 (1901): 199.

11. Kenneth Robinson, *The Dilemmas of Trusteeship: Aspects of British Colonial Policy between the Wars.* London: Oxford University Press, 1965, p. 31, citing House of Commons, Hansard, 30 July 1919, 2174.

12. Sir Frederick John Dealtry Lugard, *The Dual Mandate in British Tropical Africa.* Edinburgh: Blackwood, 1926, p. 617.

13. The quotation is found in Sir Bernard H. Bourdillon, "Colonial Development and Welfare." *International Affairs* 20 (1944): 372–373.

14. Gilbert Meynier, "La France coloniale de 1914 à 1931." Pt. 2. In *Histoire de la France coloniale, 1914–1990,* ed. Jacques Thobie et al. Paris: Armand Colin, 1990, p. 133; see also Guy Pervillé, *De l'Empire français à la decolonisation.* Paris: Hachette Livre, 1993, p. 62.

15. The quotation is from Albert Sarraut's *La mise en valeur des colonies françaises.* Paris: Payot, 1923, as cited in Raymond F. Betts, *Decolonization.* London: Routledge, 1998, p. 12. For a discussion of the response to Sarraut's projects in Indochina, see Patrice Morlat, *La repression coloniale au Vietnam (1908–1940).* Paris: L'Harmattan, 1990, chapter 5.

16. This formulation appears in Lugard, "Basis of the Claim for Colonies," p. 10.

17. Angell, "New Imperialism and the Old Nationalism," p. 69.

18. Cited in Lugard, "Basis of the Claim for Colonies," p. 10.

19. The journal of the Royal Colonial Institute bore this title.

20. Lugard, "Basis of the Claim for Colonies," p. 10.

21. Cited in Lugard, "Basis of the Claim for Colonies," p. 11.

22. Paul Bernard, *Le Problème économique Indochinois.* Paris: Nouvelle Éditions Latines, 1934, pp. 28, 32–35, 106–107, 150–151; Martin J. Murray, *The Development of Capitalism in Colonial Indochina, 1870–1940.* Berkeley: University of California Press, 1980, pp. 197–198; and Pervillé, *De l'Empire français à la decolonisation,* pp. 63–64.

23. Pervillé, *De l'Empire français à la decolonisation,* p. 73.

24. Daniel Hémery, *Révolutionnaires Vietnamiens et pouvoir colonial en Indochine.* Paris: François Maspero, 1975, p. 303.

25. Hémery, *Révolutionnaires Vietnamiens et pouvoir colonial en Indochine,* p. 309; Catherine Coquery-Vidrovitch, "La colonisation française, 1931–1939." Pt. 3. In *Histoire de la France coloniale, 1914–1990,* ed. Jacques Thobie et al., Paris: Armand Colin, 1990, pp. 260–263; and Pervillé, *De l'Empire français à la decolonisation,* p. 77.

26. De Jong, *De waaier van het fortuin,* p. 510; and Anne Booth, *The Indonesian Economy in the Nineteenth and Twentieth Centuries: A History of Missed Opportunities.* Houndmills: Macmillan, 1998, pp. 218–231.

27. George H. C. Hart, "The Netherlands Indies and Her Neighbors." *Pacific Affairs* 16, no. 1 (March 1943): 27.

28. Hart, "Netherlands Indies and Her Neighbors," p. 28.

29. For a discussion of the importance of the Atlantic Charter for colonial affairs, see Louis, *Imperialism at Bay,* chapter 6. The quoted material appears on pp. 129–130. L. S. Amery, a staunch defender of the British Empire, stated in 1942 that "smashing Hitler is only a means to the essential end of preserving the British Empire and all it stands for in the world." See Louis, *Imperialism at Bay,* p. 33, citing Amery to Cranborne, 26 August 1942, CO 825/35/55104.

30. Prime Minister Winston Churchill, 9 September 1941, House of Commons, Hansard Parliamentary Debates, vol. 372, cols 67–69, printed as Document 9 in Andrew N. Porter and A. J. Stockwell, *Introduction to British Imperial Policy and Decolonization, 1938–64.* Houndmills: Macmillan, 1987, p. 105.

31. William Roger Louis, *Imperialism at Bay. The United States and the Decolonization of the British Empire.* New York: Oxford University Press, 1978, p. 132.

32. Keith Jeffery, "The Second World War." In *The Oxford History of the British Empire.* Vol. 4, *The Twentieth Century,* ed. Judith M. Brown and William Roger Louis. Oxford: Oxford University Press, 1999, p. 325.

33. Porter and Stockwell, *British Imperial Policy and Decolonization,* p. 27.

34. Charles-Robert Ageron, "De l'Empire á la dislocation de l'Union française (1939–1956)." Pt. 2. In *Histoire de la France coloniale, 1914–1990,* ed. Jacques Thobie et al. Paris: Armand Colin, 1990, pp. 318–320; see also Pervillé, *De l'Empire français à la decolonisation,* p. 85.

35. Quoted in Gaston Rueff, "Postwar Problems of French Indo-China: Social and Political Aspects." *Pacific Affairs* 18, no. 3 (September 1945): 229. Rueff was a member of the French Colonial Institute.

36. Charles André Julien, "From the French Empire to the French Union." *International Affairs* 26 (1950): 492–493.

37. Pierre-Olivier Lapie, "The New Colonial Policy of France." In *Foreign Affairs* 23, no. 1 (October 1944): 105. Lapie was a member of the Chamber of Deputies, and from 1940 to 1942 had been the governor of Chad.

38. Pervillé, *De l'Empire français à la decolonisation,* p. 101.

39. Cees Fasseur, *Indischgasten.* Amsterdam: Bert Bakker, 1997, p. 254. W. F. Wertheim, a young official in the Indies when de Jonge made this remark, later described it as "immortal, and in the eyes of some, immortally ridiculous." See Remco Meijer, *Oost Indisch doof: Het Nederlandse debat over de dekolonisatie van Indonesië.* Amsterdam: Bert Bakker, 1995, p. 154.

40. Van Doorn, *Indische lessen,* p. 23, citing the report of the Colonial Congress of the Dutch Social Democratic Workers Party in 1930, and Ch. G. Cramer, *Onze koloniale politiek.* Amsterdam: Partijbestuur der SDAP, 1930.

41. Sejarah Nasional Indonesia untok SMA, *Indonesian National History for Upper Middle School.* Vol. 3. Jakarta: Balai Pustaka, 1987, p. 41. This textbook, issued by the state publishing body, is based on an officially sanctioned six-volume history of Indonesia entitled *Sejarah Nasional Indonesia,* published in 1975.

42. This discussion of the Visman commission is based on Jan Otto Marius Broek, "Indonesia and the Netherlands." (Review Article). *Pacific Affairs* 16, no. 3 (September 1943): 329–338. Later Dutch commentators tend to treat the Visman commission as unimportant. De Jong notes that this "Commission to study constitutional reforms" convened after it had been made clear that no discussion of reforms could take place until after the war and was restricted to identifying Indonesian political demands. See de Jong, *De waaier van het fortuin,* pp. 559–560. Van den Doel notes that the commission downplayed the nationalist movement, and saw the local people as farmers who were incapable of understanding larger political affairs. See Doel, *Afscheid van Indië,* pp. 59–60. The author of one Indonesian school textbook remarks dryly that the commission report accurately reflected the views of those Indonesian who wished to retain ties with the Netherlands. See I. Wayan Badrika, *Sejarah National Indonesia dan Umum untuk SMU Kelas 2.* Vol. 2. Jakarta: Penerbit Erlangga, 2000, p. 184.

43. Broek, "Indonesia and the Netherlands," p. 338. The queen's talk was delivered on December 7, 1942.

44. Broek, "Indonesia and the Netherlands," p. 329.

45. See Louis, *Imperialism at Bay,* pp. 29–30; and de Jong, *De waaier van het fortuin,* p. 573.

46. *Burma's New Order Plan.* Rangoon: Bureau of State Printing Presses, Burma, 1944, p. 25.

47. *Burma Home Service,* 22 August 1944, cited in W. S. Desai, "The Activities of the Mahabama Asi Ayone." NARA RG226 Entry 16 134105.

48. Peter Gordon Gowing, *Muslim Filipinos: Heritage and Horizon.* Quezon City: New Day, 1979, p. 176.

49. Sukarno's Pancasila speech appears in Roger M. Smith, ed., *Southeast Asia: Documents of Political Development and Change.* Ithaca, N.Y.: Cornell University Press, 1974, pp. 174–182.

50. Chapter 11 of the charter; see also Rupert Emerson, *From Empire to Nation: The Rise of Self-Assertion of Asian and African Peoples.* Cambridge, Mass.: Harvard University Press, 1960, p. 35.

51. Emerson, *From Empire to Nation,* pp. 308–309.

52. Raymond Kennedy, "Dutch Charter for the Indies." *Pacific Affairs* 16, no. 2 (June 1943): 220; see also appendix 4 in the Royal Institute of International Affairs' volume on *The Colonial Problem,* p. 387.

53. Kennedy, "Dutch Charter for the Indies," p. 219.

54. Hart, "Netherlands Indies and Her Neighbors," pp. 23–24. Unwisely from a debating standpoint, Hart argued for a union of the Netherlands and the Netherlands Indies on the grounds that the Dutch and Indonesians had "notable traits of character in common," but opposed a union involving Filipinos and Indonesians because they were so different, prompting Kennedy to ask: "Have the Dutch some hidden Oriental cultural traits of which we have not yet heard?" See Kennedy, "Dutch Charter for the Indies," p. 219.

55. Hart, "Netherlands Indies and her Neighbors," pp. 25–26.

56. Donald Anthony Low, *Eclipse of Empire.* Cambridge: Cambridge University Press, 1991, p. 34.

57. Low, *Eclipse of Empire,* p. 34; see also Ide Anak Agung Gde Agung, *Dari Negara Indonesia Timur ke Republik Indonesia Serikat.* Yogyakarta: Gadjah Mada University Press, 1985. Doel compares French initiatives in Indochina and the so-called Bảo Đại solution with the Dutch situation in Indonesia, drawing a parallel between Norodom Sihanouk's assertion of a Cambodian identity separate from the rest of Indochina, and the creation of the states of East Indonesia and Pasundan (in West Java). See Doel, *Afscheid van Indië,* pp. 352–355.

58. For example, see Ruth T. McVey, "The Beamtenstaat in Indonesia." In *Interpreting Indonesian Politics: Thirteen Contributions to the Debate,* ed. Benedict Anderson and Audrey Kahin. Ithaca, N.Y.: Cornell Modern Indonesia Project, Interim Reports Series no. 62, 1982.

59. Louis, *Imperialism at Bay,* pp. 567–569.

60. William Roger Louis, "The Dissolution of the British Empire." In *The Oxford History of the British Empire.* Vol. 4, *The Twentieth Century,* ed. Judith M. Brown and William Roger Louis. Oxford: Oxford University Press, 1999, p. 332.

61. See Universities Historical Research Centre, *The 1947 Constitution and the Nationalities.* Vol. 1. Yangon: Universities Historical Research Centre and Inwa

Publishing House, 1999; Josef Silverstein, *Burmese Politics: The Dilemma of National Unity.* New Brunswick, N.J.: Rutgers University Press, 1980; and Burma, Frontier Areas Committee of Enquiry, *Report Presented to H. M. Government in the United Kingdom and the Government of Burma.* Maymyo, 24 April 1947, parts 1 and 2.

62. Charles-Robert Ageron, "La décolonisation au regard de la France." Pt. 5. In *Histoire de la France coloniale, 1914–1990,* ed. Jacques Thobie et al. Paris: Armand Colin, 1990, pp. 449–450.

63. Julien, "From the French Empire to the French Union." *International Affairs* 26 (1950): 492–493.

64. Julien, "From the French Empire to the French Union," pp. 494–495.

65. Ageron, "La decolonisation au regard de la France," p. 412.

66. Julien, "From the French Empire to the French Union," p. 498.

67. Louis, *Imperialism at Bay,* p. 552.

68. Ageron, *La decolonisation française,* pp. 81–93.

69. Marilyn Young, *The Vietnam Wars, 1945–1990.* New York: HarperCollins, 1991, p. 38.

70. Raymond Kennedy, "Dutch Plan for the Indies." *Far Eastern Survey* 15, no. 7 (April 1946): 97–102.

71. Robert J. McMahon, *Colonialism and Cold War: The United States and the Struggle for Indonesian Independence, 1945–49.* Ithaca, N.Y.: Cornell University Press, 1981, p. 304.

72. Low, *Eclipse of Empire,* p. 35. Low suggests that the French "were all but united in believing that the retention of their empire was vital to the restoration of their gravely damaged position as a great power in the world," but the cited survey data suggests that this was not the view of the public at large.

73. Ageron, "La décolonisation au regard de la France," p. 413.

74. Ageron, "La décolonisation au regard de la France," p. 412.

75. See the preface to Louis, *Imperialism at Bay,* p. x.

## Chapter 2

1. Gerhard L. Weinberg, *A World at War: A Global History of World War II.* Cambridge: Cambridge University Press, 1994; and Christopher Thorne, *The Limits of Foreign Policy: The West, the League and the Far Eastern Crisis of 1931–1933.* London: Hamilton, 1972, pp. 396–397.

2. Recent research has expanded much in comparison to the standard volume: Alexander Dallin, *Deutsche Herrschaft in Rußland, 1941–1945: Eine Studie über Besatzungspolitik.* Düsseldorf: Droste, 1958; Mechthild Rössler and Sabine Schleiermacher, eds., *Der "Generalplan Ost": Hauptlinien der nationalsozialistischen Planungs- und Vernichtungspolitik.* Berlin: Akademie-Verlag, 1993; and Czeslaw Madajcyk, ed., *Vom Generalplan Ost zum Generalsiedlungsplan.* München: Saur, 1994.

3. Jost Dülffer, "Kolonialismus ohne Kolonien: Deutsche Kolonialpläne 1938." In *Machtbewußtsein in Deutschland am Vorabend des Zweiten Weltkrieges,* ed. Franz Knipping and Klaus-Jürgen Müller. Paderborn: Schöningh, 1984, p. 269; and Klaus Hildebrand, *Vom Reich zum Weltreich. Hitler, NSDAP und koloniale Frage, 1919–1945.* München: Fink, 1969.

4. Andreas Hillgruber, *Hitlers Strategie: Politik und Kriegführung, 1940–1941.* Frankfurt am Main: Bernard and Graefe, 1965, pp. 242–254; and Michael Salewski,

*Die deutsche Seekriegsleitung, 1935–1945.* Vol. 2. Frankfurt am Main: Bernard and Graefe, 1975.

5. Magnus Brechtken, *"Madagaskar für die Juden": Antisemitische Idee und politische Praxis, 1885–1945.* München: Oldenbourg, 1997; compare the documentation of German worldwide naval planning in Michael Salewski, ed., *Die deutsche Seekriegsleitung, 1935–1945.* Vol. 3, *Documents.* Frankfurt am Main: Bernard and Graefe, 1973.

6. John W. Dower, *War without Mercy: Race and Power in the Pacific War.* New York: Pantheon, 1986, p. 273.

7. Joyce C. Lebra (ed.), *Japan's Greater East Asia Co-prosperity Sphere in World War II: Selected Readings and Documents.* Kuala Lumpur: Oxford University Press, 1975, p. 92.

8. Lebra (ed.), *Japan's Greater East Asia Co-prosperity Sphere,* p. 93; and Bernd Martin, *Deutschland und Japan im Zweiten Weltkrieg: Vom Angriff auf Pearl Harbor bis zur deutschen Kapitulation.* Göttingen: Musterschmidt, 1969, pp. 199–205.

9. Peter Duus, Ramon H. Myers, and Marc R. Peattie, eds., *Japanese Wartime Experience, 1931–1945.* Princeton, N.J.: Princeton University Press, 1996, p. xxvi; Evelyn Colbert, *Southeast Asia in International Politics, 1941–1956.* Ithaca, N.Y.: Cornell University Press, 1977, pp. 54–60; Saburo Ienaga, *Japan's Last War: World War II and the Japanese, 1931–1945.* Oxford: Blackwell, 1979, pp. 153–180; Akira Iriye, *Power and Culture: The Japanese-American War, 1941–1945.* Cambridge, Mass.: Harvard University Press, 1981, pp. 36–95; and William G. Beasley, *Japanese Imperialism, 1894–1945.* Oxford: Oxford University Press 1987, pp. 233–250.

10. Martin Broszat and Ladislaus Hory, *Der kroatische Ustaschastaat, 1941–1945.* Stuttgart: Deutsche Verlagsanstalt, 1964; and Holm Sundhaussen, *Wirtschaftsgeschichte Kroatiens im nationalsozialistischen Großraum, 1941–1945.* Stuttgart: Deutsche Verlagsanstalt, 1983.

11. "Joint Declaration of Japan, Germany and Italy about India and Arabia," quoted in Bernd Martin, *Deutschland und Japan im Zweiten Weltkrieg: Vom Angriff auf Pearl Harbor bis zur deutschen Kapitulation.* Göttingen: Musterschmidt Verlag, 1969, doc. no. 9, 238f.; see also Bernd Philipp Schröder, *Deutschland und der Mittlere Osten im Zweiten Weltkrieg.* Göttingen: Musterschmidt Verlag 1975.

12. E. Bruce Reynolds, "Anomaly or Model? Independent Thailand's Role in Japan's Asian Strategy, 1941–1943." In *Japanese Wartime Experience, 1931–1945,* ed. Peter Duus, Ramon H. Myers, and Marc R. Peattie. Princeton, N.J.: Princeton University Press, 1996, pp. 243–273; Nigel Brailey, "Thailand, Japanese Pan-Asianism and the Greater East Asia Co-prosperity Sphere." In *From Pearl Harbor to Hiroshima: The Second World War in Asia and the Pacific, 1941–1945,* ed. Saki Dockrill. Basingstoke: Macmillan, 1994, pp. 119–134; and Dietmar Rothermund, *Delhi, 15 August 1947: Das Ende kolonialer Herrschaft.* München: DTV, 1998, pp. 52–86.

13. Ken'ichi Goto, "Cooperation, Submission, and Resistance of Indigenuous Elites of South-East Asia in the Wartime Empire." In *Japanese Wartime Experience, 1931–1945,* ed. Peter Duus, Ramon H. Myers, and Marc R. Peattie. Princeton, N.J.: Princeton University Press, 1996, pp. 286–290; and Louis Allen and David Steeds, "Burma: The Longest War, 1941–45." In *From Pearl Harbor to Hiroshima: The Second World War in Asia and the Pacific, 1941–1945,* ed. Saki Dockrill. Basingstoke: Macmillan, 1994, pp. 109–118.

14. See Bruce M. Lockhart, chapter 4, in this volume.

15. Friedrich Bernhardt, *Die "Kollaboration" asiatischer Völker mit der japanischen*

*Besatzungsmacht im Zweiten Weltkrieg als Glied im Dekolonisationsprozeß.* Hamburg: Institut für Asienkunde, 1971, pp. 37, 41ff.

16. Goto, "Cooperation, Submission, and Resistance," pp. 274–303.

17. Rudolf von Albertini, *Dekolonisation: Die Diskussion über Verwaltung und Zukunft der Kolonien, 1919–1960.* Köln: Westdt: Verl., 1966, pp. 232–244; and Bernhardt, *Die "Kollaboration" asiatischer Völker,* p. 62.

18. Wenzhao Tao, "The China Theatre and the Pacific War." In *From Pearl Harbor to Hiroshima: The Second World War in Asia and the Pacific, 1941–1945,* ed. Saki Dockrill. Basingstoke: Macmillan, 1994, pp. 134–152; and Ienaga, *Japan's Last War,* pp. 75–86.

19. Johannes H. Voigt, *Indien im Zweiten Weltkrieg.* Stuttgart: Dt. Verl.-Anst., 1978, p. 166f.; Milan Hauner, *India in Axis Strategy: Germany, Japan, and Indian Nationalists in the Second World War.* Stuttgart: Klett-Cotta, 1981; Bernd Martin, "Die Verselbständigung der Dritten Welt: Der Prozeß der Entkolonisierung am Beispiel Indiens." *Saeculum* 34, no. 2 (1983): 165–186; and Dennis Merrill, "The Ironies of History: The United States and the Decolonization of India." In *The United States and Decolonization: Power and Freedom,* ed. David Ryan and Victor Pungong. Basingstoke: Macmillan, 2000, pp. 102–120.

20. Voigt, *Indien im Zweiten Weltkrieg,* p. 205.

21. Voigt, *Indien im Zweiten Weltkrieg,* p. 250ff.

22. Sisir K. Bose, Alexander Werth, and S. A. Ayer, *A Beacon across Asia: A Biography of Subhas Chandra Bose.* New Delhi: Orient Longman, 1973, p. 318.

23. Goto, "Cooperation, Submission, and Resistance," p. 277.

24. Bose, *A Beacon across Asia,* p. 288.

25. Richard Overy, *Why the Allies Won.* New York: Norton, 1997.

26. Christopher Thorne, *Allies of a Kind: The United States, Britain and the War against Japan, 1941–1945.* Oxford: Oxford University Press, 1978, pp. 7–8.

27. David Reynolds, *Britannia Overruled: British Policy and World Power in the Twentieth Century.* New York: Longman, 1991, p. 164.

28. *The Economist,* 21 March 1942, pp. 386–387, cited in Albertini, *Dekolonisation,* p. 189.

29. Albertini, *Dekolonisation,* pp. 206ff.

30. Albertini, *Dekolonisation,* pp. 414ff.

31. Charles-Robert Ageron and Marc Michel, eds., *L'Afrique noire française: l'heure des Indépendances.* Paris: CNRS, 1992 (especially the contributions by Myron Echenberg, Bernard Lanne, Pierre Guillen, and C. Akpo and V. Joly).

32. Albertini, *Dekolonisation,* pp. 419–437.

33. Albertini, *Dekolonisation,* p. 437.

34. Gerhard Thomas Mollin, *Die USA und der Kolonialismus: Amerika als Partner und Nachfolger der belgischen Macht in Afrika, 1939–1965.* Berlin: Akad.-Verl., 1996, pp. 101–102, 129.

35. Lodewijk de Jong, *Het Koninkrijk der Nederlanden in de Tweede Wereldoorlog.* Pt. 9.1, *Nederlands-Indie III.* 's-Gravenhage: Staatsuitgeverij, 1986, pp. 363–492 and passim; and Robert J. McMahon, *Colonialism and Cold War: The United States and the Struggle for Indonesian Independence, 1945–49.* Ithaca, N.Y.: Cornell University Press 1981, pp. 74–113.

36. John Darwin, *Britain and Decolonization: The Retreat from Empire in the Post-war World.* Basingstoke: Macmillan, 1988; Jürgen Osterhammel, "Spätkolonialismus und Dekolonisation." *Neue Politische Literatur* 37 (1992): 408–409f.

37. William Roger Louis and Ronald Robinson, "The Imperialism of Decolonization." *Journal of Imperial and Commonwealth History* 22 (1994): 462–511; and R. F. Holland, "The Imperial Factor in British Strategies form Attlee to McMillan, 1945–63." *Journal of Imperial and Commonwealth History* 12 (1984): 165–186.

38. Paul Orders, "'Adjusting to a New Period in World History': Franklin Roosevelt and the European Colonialism." In *The United States and Decolonization: Power and Freedom*, ed. David Ryan and Victor Pungong. Basingstoke: Macmillan, 2000, pp. 63–84; Victor Pungong, "The United States and the International Trusteeship System." In *The United States and Decolonization: Power and Freedom*, ed. David Ryan and Victor Pungong. Basingstoke: Macmillan, 2000, pp. 85–101; Gerry R. Hess, *The United States' Emergence as a Southeast Asian Power, 1940–1950*. New York: Columbia University Press, 1987; and Cary Fraser, "Understanding American Policy towards the Decolonization of European Empires, 1945–64." *Diplomacy and Statecraft* 3, no. 1 (1992): 105–125.

## Chapter 3

1. A. R. Miller, "American Investments in the Far East." *Far Eastern Survey* 19, no. 9 (1950): 88.

2. J. Thomas Lindblad, *Foreign Investment in Southeast Asia in the Twentieth Century.* London: Macmillan, 1998, pp. 34–36.

3. Marc Frey, "Creations of Sovereignty and the Waning of Influence: Southeast Asian-European Relations after Formal Decolonization." In *Europe-Southeast Asia in the Contemporary World: Mutual Images and Reflections 1940s-1960s,* ed. Franz Knipping and Suthiphand Chonchirdsin. Baden-Baden: Nomos, 2000, pp. 5–20; J. Thomas Lindblad, "The Political Economy of Realignment in Indonesia during the Sukarno Period." In *Europe-Southeast Asia in the Contemporary World: Mutual Images and Reflections 1940s-1960s,* ed. Piyanart Bunnag, Franz Knipping, and Sud Chonchirdsin. Baden-Baden: Nomos, 1999, pp. 149–171; and Thee Kian Wie, "Economic Policies in Indonesia during the Period 1950–1965, in Particular with Respect to Foreign Investment." In *Historical Foundations of a National Economy in Indonesia,* ed. J. Thomas Lindblad. Amsterdam: North-Holland, 1996.

4. Benjamin Higgins, "Indonesia's Development Plan and Problems." *Pacific Affairs* 29 (1956): 107–125; and Anne Booth, *The Indonesian Economy in the Nineteenth and Twentieth Centuries: A History of Missed Opportunities.* London: Macmillan, 1998, pp. 70–72.

5. R.F. Emery, "Agricultural Production Trends and Problems in Indonesia," *Far Eastern Survey* 29, no. 8, (1960): 113–120.

6. Sumitro Djojohadikusumo, "Economic Aspects of the Indonesian Struggle." *United Asia* 1 (1948–1949): 428–431.

7. Booth, *Indonesian Economy,* pp. 61–65.

8. Justus M. van der Kroef, "Minority Problems in Indonesia." *Far Eastern Survey* 24, no. 9 (1955): 129–133, and no. 11, 165–171.

9. Higgins, "Indonesia's Development Plan and Problems," pp. 107–125; and Benjamin Higgins, "Indonesia's Five Year Plan." *Far Eastern Survey* 25, no. 7 (1956): 122–123.

10. Justus M. van der Kroef, "Indonesia's Economic Future." *Pacific Affairs* 32 (1959): 46–72.

11. G. J. Pauker, "Indonesia's Eight-Year Development Plan." *Pacific Affairs* 34 (1961): 130.

12. Audrey Gladys Donnithorne, "Western Business in Indonesia Today." *Pacific Affairs* 27 (1954): 36, 38.

13. van der Kroef, "Minority Problems in Indonesia"; and Justus M. van der Kroef, "Indonesia's Economic Difficulties." *Far Eastern Survey* 24, no. 2 (1955): 17–24.

14. Justus M. van der Kroef, "Instability in Indonesia." *Far Eastern Survey* 26, no. 4 (1957): 49–62.

15. van der Kroef, "Instability in Indonesia," pp. 49–62.

16. Frey, "Creations of Sovereignty," p. 18n50.

17. Lindblad, *Foreign Investment in Southeast Asia,* p. 14.

18. Miller, "American Investments in the Far East," p. 83.

19. H. Meijer, "Den Haag-Djakarta: De Nederlands-Indonesische betrekkingen, 1950–1962." Ph.D. diss., University of Utrecht, 1994, pp. 648–654; see also details in Frey, "Creations of Sovereignty and the Waning of Influence," p. 16n45.

20. Meijer, *Den Haag-Djakarta,* p. 529.

21. James Warren Gould, *Americans in Sumatra.* The Hague: Nijhoff, 1961, p. 79.

22. John Wong, *ASEAN Economies in Perspective: A Comparative Study of Indonesia, Malaysia, the Philippines, Singapore and Thailand.* London: Macmillan, 1979, pp. 176–177.

23. For more information on this, see J. Thomas Lindblad, "Political and Economic Integration in Newly Independent Indonesia." Paper presented at Sixteenth Conference of the International Association of Historians of Asia, Kota Kinabalu, Sabah, Malaysia, July 27–31, 2000.

24. See Yoshihara Kunio, *The Nation and Economic Growth: The Philippines and Thailand.* Kuala Lumpur: Oxford University Press, 1994.

25. Benjamin Higgins, "Development Problems in the Philippines: A Comparison with Indonesia." *Far Eastern Survey* 26, no. 11 (1957): 161–169.

26. Pierre van der Eng, "Assessing Economic Growth and Standards of Living in Asia, 1870–1990." In *The Evolving Structure of the East Asian Economic System since 1700: A Comparative Analysis,* ed. A. J. H. Latham and Heita Kawakatsu. Milan: Università Bocconi, 1994, p. 102.

27. M. Cuaderno, "The Bell Trade Act and the Philippine Economy." *Pacific Affairs* 25 (1952): 323–333.

28. Frank H. Golay, "Consequences of the Philippine Trade Act." *Pacific Affairs* 28 (1955): 53–70.

29. Lindblad, *Foreign Investment in Southeast Asia,* p. 102.

30. Frank H. Golay, "Entrepreneurship and Economic Development in the Philippines." *Far Eastern Survey* 29, no. 6 (1960): 81–86.

31. Frank H. Golay et al., *Underdevelopment and Economic Nationalism in Southeast Asia.* Ithaca, N.Y.: Cornell University Press, 1969, p. 91.

32. Golay et al., *Underdevelopment and Economic Nationalism,* p. 91.

33. Lindblad, *Foreign Investment in Southeast Asia,* p. 14; Miller, "American Investments in the Far East," p. 83; and Golay et al., *Underdevelopment and Economic Nationalism,* pp. 92–93.

34. M. Tsuda et al., *The Impact of TNCs in the Philippines.* Vol. 2. Quezon City: University of Philippines Law Centre, 1978, pp. 30–34.

35. Golay et al., *Underdevelopment and Economic Nationalism,* pp. 92–93.

36. Figure 3.1; and Golay et al., *Underdevelopment and Economic Nationalism,* pp. 106–107.

37. Tsuda et al., *Impact of TNCs in the Philippines,* summary report.

38. N. J. White, *Business, Government and the End of Empire: Malaya, 1942–1957.* Kuala Lumpur: Oxford University Press, 1996, pp. 296–297.

39. van der Eng, "Assessing Economic Growth," p. 102.

40. Golay et al., *Underdevelopment and Economic Nationalism,* p. 352.

41. John H. Drabble, *An Economic History of Malaysia, c. 1800–1990: The Transition to Modern Economic Growth.* London: Macmillan, 2000, pp. 186–189.

42. David Lim, *Economic Growth and Development in West Malaysia, 1947–1970.* Kuala Lumpur: Oxford University Press, 1973, pp. 261–265.

43. Golay et al., *Underdevelopment and Economic Nationalism.*

44. Cited by T. N. Harper, *The End of Empire and the Making of Malaya.* Cambridge: Cambridge University Press, 1999, p. 248.

45. White, *Business, Government and the End of Empire,* pp. 119–122.

46. Harper, *End of Empire,* pp. 199–204.

47. Lindblad, *Foreign Investment in Southeast Asia,* p. 14.

48. Junid Saham, *British Industrial Investment in Malaysia, 1963–1971.* Kuala Lumpur: Oxford University Press, 1980, p. 34; and Wong, *ASEAN Economies in Perspective,* pp. 176–177.

49. See Anne Booth, "The Economic Development of Southeast Asia, 1870–1985." In *Exploring Southeast Asia's Economic Past (Australian Economic History Review* 31), ed. Graeme Donald Snooks and Jonathan J. Pincus. Canberra: Australian National University, 1991, p. 21.

50. Figure 3.2.

51. Frey, "Creations of Sovereignty," p. 38.

52. Figure 3.3; and Saham, *British Industrial Investment,* pp. 24–25.

53. Saham, *British Industrial Investment,* pp. 120, 232.

54. Drabble, *Economic History of Malaysia,* pp. 244–245.

55. Cited by Frey, "Creations of Sovereignty," p. 39n124.

56. Some reference should be made of the situation in Singapore after it left, or was invited to leave, the federation in 1965. An extremely liberal climate for foreign investment was created from the beginning, in acknowledgment of the essential function of multinationals in the Singapore strategy for economic growth. Annual gross capital formation doubled in volume between the years 1960–1966 and 1967–1969, with foreign capital providing 11 percent of the total in the latter period. This contribution was eventually to rise to 25 percent. See W. G. Huff, *The Economic Growth of Singapore: Trade and Development in the Twentieth Century.* Cambridge: Cambridge University Press, 1994, p. 338. In the decolonization of Singapore, there was no place for a choice between assertion of national identity and attracting foreign capital.

## Chapter 4

1. Sihanouk's reign formally ended in 1955 with his abdication in favor of his father, though he of course continued to dominate Cambodian politics as prince rather than king.

2. Quoted in Bruce M. Lockhart, *The End of the Vietnamese Monarchy.* New Haven, Conn.: Yale Council on Southeast Asian Studies, 1993, p. 151; chapter 8 covers the final months of the war. For more detailed accounts, see David Marr, *Vietnam*

*1945: The Quest for Power.* Berkeley: University of California Press, 1995; and Vu Ngu Chieu, *The Other Side of the 1945 Vietnamese Revolution: The Empire of Viet-Nam (3–8/1945)/Phía bên kia cuộc cách mạng 1945: Đế Quốc Việt Nam (3–8/1945).* Houston, Tex.: Tủ Sách Văn Hoá, 1996.

3. See Bảo Đại, *Dragon d'Annam.* Paris: Plon, 1980, pp. 127–153; the story of Hồ's proposal is on pp. 150–151. See also Philippe Devillers, *L'histoire du Vietnam de 1940 à 1952.* Paris: Éditions du Seuil, 1952, pp. 216–217. The Indochinese federation proposal was shelved in early 1947. See Stephen Lyne, "The French Socialist Party and the Indochina War, 1944–1954." Ph.D. diss., Stanford University, 1965, p. 169. Detailed accounts of 1945–1946 include Stein Tønnesson, *The Outbreak of War in Indochina 1946.* Oslo: International Peace Research Institute, 1982; Phạm Khắc Hoè, *Từ triều đình Huế đến chiến khu Việt Bắc* (From the Huế Court to the Việt Bắc Resistance Zone). 4th ed. Hồ Chí Minh City: NXB Trẻ, 1996; Philippe Devillers, *Paris Saigon Hanoi: Les archives de la guerre 1944–1947.* Paris: Éditions Gallimard/ Julliard, 1988; and Martin Shipway, *The Road to War: France and Vietnam, 1944–1947.* Providence, R.I.: Berghahn, 1996.

4. On Bảo Đại's mission to China, see Bảo Đại, *Dragon d'Annam,* pp. 152–161; and Nghiêm Kế Tổ, *Việt Nam máu lửa* (Vietnam in Blood and Fire). Sàigòn: Mai Linh, 1954, pp. 93–97. Bảo Đại says that Hồ requested that he head the delegation in his capacity as supreme counselor to negotiate with Chiang Kai-shek. Tổ, an anticommunist nationalist leader who was part of the delegation, says that Bảo Đại was only allowed to accompany the group as a tourist, implying that Hồ did not want to give him greater responsibilities. See also the discussion in Daniel Grandclément, *Bao Daï ou les derniers jours de l'Empire d'Annam.* Paris: JC Lattès, 1997, pp. 220–226. Hồ supposedly wanted to split the Chinese and French by attempting to purchase arms from the Guomindang government.

5. Grandclément discusses plans for the crown prince (*Bao Daï,* pp. 231, 285–286) and Vinh San (pp. 231–236). On the latter, see also Lockhart, *End of the Vietnamese Monarchy,* pp. 162–165. Although several published French sources have attributed considerable importance to the plan for a "Vinh San solution," archival sources suggest that de Gaulle's enthusiasm was not shared by most policy makers.

6. Devillers traces the evolution of French policy with numerous citations from archival documents. See Devillers, *Paris Saigon Hanoi,* pp. 89 (d'Argenlieu, September 1945 and Pignon, October 1946), 234, 238, 337–343 (d'Argenlieu, late 1946 to early 1947). Although d'Argenlieu was the highest-ranking (and most criticized) French official in Indochina during this period, Christopher Goscha (personal communication) emphasizes the importance of Pignon's role behind the scenes. On Pignon's role, see Lucien Bodard, *La guerre d'Indochine: L'Enlisement.* Paris: Gallimard, 1963, pp. 196–198; and Devillers, *Paris Saigon Hanoi,* pp. 367–369.

7. Lê Văn Hiến, *Nhật ký của một bộtrưởng* (Diary of a Minister). Vol. 2. Đànăng: NXB Đànăng, 1995, p. 45. Bảo Đại's account of the 1947–1949 period is in Bảo Đại, *Dragon d'Annam,* pp. 161–186. A detailed study of the Hong Kong period is Nguyễn Khac Ngữ, *Các đảng phái quốc gia lưu vong 1946–1950: Hội Nghị Hương Cảng 9–9–1947* (Nationalist Parties in Exile 1946–1950: The Hong Kong Congress of 9 September 1947). Montréal: Tủ sách Nghiên cứu Sử Địa, 1991. American diplomatic documents are also a helpful source. See *Foreign Relations of the United States (FRUS), 1947.* Vol. 6, *The Far East.* Washington, D.C.: U.S. Government Printing Office, 1972.

8. Thailand was the first Asian country to recognize the three Indochina states (in March 1950), and this only after intense lobbying by American diplomats and a split

in the cabinet that precipitated the resignation of Foreign Minister Pote Sarasin. For U.S. lobbying efforts in January and February 1950, see *FRUS, 1950.* Vol. 6, *East Asia and the Pacific.* Washington, D.C.: U.S. Government Printing Office, 1976, pp. 694–768 and passim; and Bangkok's decision is in Telegram 190, Ambassador Stanton to Secretary of State, 1 March 1950, *FRUS, 1950.* Vol. 6, pp. 747–748.

9. Stanley Karnow, *Vietnam: A History.* New York: Viking, 1983. One source claims that Bảo Đại valued Xuân mainly for his skill at concealing the former emperor's "amours délicates" under the guise of political outings. See Lucien Bodard, *La guerre d'Indochine: L'Humiliation.* Paris: Gallimard, 1965, p. 252.

10. Bodard, *La guerre d'Indochine: L'Humiliation,* pp. 199–200.

11. A good overview of these years can be found in Ellen Hammer, *The Struggle for Indochina 1940–1955: Vietnam and the French Experience.* 3rd ed. Stanford, Calif.: Stanford University Press, 1966; and Devillers, *L'histoire du Vietnam;* see also Bảo Đại, *Dragon d'Annam,* and Tô, *Việt Nam máu lửa,* both of which emphasize the former emperor's role. Political developments are chronicled in detail in the successive volumes of the *FRUS.* For accounts of the referendum, see *FRUS, 1955–1957.* Vol. 1, *Vietnam.* Washington, D.C.: U.S. Government Printing Office 1985, pp. 565–595 and passim. The conversation between Bảo Đại and Diệm is in Bảo Đại's, *Dragon d'Annam,* p. 328. According to Bảo Đại's account, he made Diệm swear in front of a crucifix that he would defend Vietnam "against the Communists and, if necessary, against the French" (p. 329).

12. The comment on "easing out" Bảo Đại is in Ambassador Dillon to Department of State, 27 July 1954, in *FRUS, 1952–1954.* Vol. 13, *Indochina.* Washington, D.C.: U.S. Government Printing Office, 1982, pt. 2, p. 1881. The U.S. ambassador to France is referring to remarks by Guy La Chambre, the minister for the Associated States. The one high-ranking French leader who seems to have seen any real usefulness in Bảo Đại was Prime Minister Pierre Mendès-France, who still felt that there was a certain amount of "prestige" to be derived from his "legitimacy" even while concurring that he should stay in France. See Dillon to Department of State, 23 October 1954, in *FRUS, 1952–1954.* Vol. 13, pp. 2165–2166. On the reversal of the French position (articulated by Commissioner-General Paul Ély), see Special Representative Collins to Department of State, 28 March 1955, in *FRUS, 1955–1957.* Vol. 1, pp. 151–154, and subsequent documents in the same volume. A good overview of this period from the French perspective is in Georges Chaffard, *Indochine dix ans d'indépendance.* Paris: Calmann-Lévy, 1964.

13. American criticisms of Bảo Đại's ties to the Bình Xuyên, expressed to him in person, are in Chargé Achilles to Department of State, 1 March 1955, *FRUS, 1955–1957.* Vol. 1, pp. 97–99; Collins to Department of State, 5 May 1955, *FRUS, 1955–1957.* Vol. 1, pp. 364–365.

14. Ambassador Reinhardt to Department of State, 25 October 1955, *FRUS, 1955–1957.* Vol. 1, p. 566. On efforts to dissuade Diệm from the referendum, see Dulles to Embassy in Vietnam, 1 July 1955, *FRUS, 1955–1957.* Vol. 1, p. 474; and Reinhardt to Department of State, 5 July and 29 September 1955, *FRUS, 1955–1957.* Vol. 1, pp. 476, 547–548. Reinhardt's detailed postmortem on the referendum, dated 29 November 1955, is Document 278, pp. 589–594.

15. There was a rather ironic episode in late 1952 when French Associated States Minister Jean Letourneau apparently commented to Bảo Đại on the active role that his Cambodian counterpart took in both political and military affairs. Nguyễn Đệ, who often spoke and acted on the former emperor's behalf, remarked sarcastically to

the American ambassador that the Vietnamese would "see through any theatrically-arranged mil[itary] campaign appearances" like those of Sihanouk and that Bảo Đại could not afford to "lose face" or to "impair [his] role" as a "symbol" by engaging in "unconvincing public tours and occasional graspings of the reins of gov[ernmen]t." See Ambassador Heath to Department of State, *FRUS, 1952–1954.* Vol. 13, pt. 1, pp. 284–285. Heath observed that "Letourneau was well advised" to bring up Sihanouk's "activity" to Bảo Đại, but that he himself was "not too sanguine" about the prospects of "stirring [the latter] to greater activity." When Sihanouk embarked on his "royal crusade" the following year, Bảo Đại expressed to Heath strong criticisms of this initiative, clearly still remembering Letourneau's implication that he compared unfavorably to the Cambodian monarch. See Heath to Department of State, 26 June 1953, *FRUS, 1952–1954.* Vol. 13, pt. 1, pp. 620–621.

16. Good summaries of these developments can be found in David Chandler, *The Tragedy of Cambodian History.* New Haven, Conn.: Yale University Press, 1991, pp. 15–28; Milton Osborne, *Sihanouk: Prince of Light, Prince of Darkness.* St. Leonards, Australia: Allen and Unwin, 1994, chapter 4; and Paul Huard, "La rentrée politique de la France au Cambodge (octobre 1945–janvier 1946)." In *Les chemins de la décolonisation de l'empire colonial français,* ed. Charles-Robert Ageron. Paris: Éditions du CNRS, 1986. Huard represented the French during the first months after their return.

17. See the eyewitness account of these events in Huard, "La rentrée politique." Huard emphasizes the important role of Monireth, along with Khim Tith, a former officer in the French army.

18. This agreement is summarized in Landon to Sec. of State, n.d., *FRUS, 1946.* Vol. 8, *The Far East.* Washington, D.C.: U.S. Government Printing Office, 1971, pp. 20–21. Sihanouk says the modus vivendi was "forced" on his government, and it was clearly much less significant for him than later agreements. See Sihanouk, *L'action de S.M. Norodom Sihanouk pour l'indépendance du Cambodge, 1941–1955.* Phnom Penh: Réalités Cambodgiennes magazine, 1959, p. 6. Huard also notes that Sihanouk was not satisfied with the agreement, particularly the fact that France would be responsible for the kingdom's defense. See Huard, "La rentrée politique," p. 229.

19. Osborne, *Sihanouk,* chapter 5; and Chandler, *Tragedy of Cambodian History,* pp. 28–65. The December 1948 proclamation and the ceremony on that occasion are reported in Consul-General Abbott to Secretary of State, 23 December 1948, *FRUS, 1948.* Vol 6, p. 55. A summary of the 1949 treaty is in Abbott to Secretary of State, 26 November 1949, *FRUS, 1949.* Vol. 7, *The Far East and Australasia.* Washington, D.C.: U.S. Government Printing Office, 1976, pp. 99–100. For a discussion on the treaty, see Sihanouk, *L'action de S.M. Norodom Sihanouk,* pp. 10–15. Abbott pointed out that the Franco-Cambodian Agreement, unlike the Élysée Agreements signed earlier that year for Vietnam, explicitly abrogated the nineteenth-century treaties with France.

20. The best study of resistance movements during this period is Ben Kiernan, *How Pol Pot Came to Power.* London: Verso, 1985.

21. Osborne, *Sihanouk,* chapter 6; and Chandler, *Tragedy of Cambodian History,* pp. 65–72. Sihanouk's own account of his "crusade," with copious documentation, can be found in Sihanouk, *L'action de S.M. Norodom Sihanouk;* and in Gouvernement Royal du Cambodge, *Livre jaune sur les revendications de l'indépendance du Cambodge (depuis le 5 Mars 1953).* Phnom Penh: Gouvernement Royal du Cambodge, 1953.

22. David K. Wyatt, ed., *Iron Man of Laos: Prince Phetsarath Ratanavongsa.* 2nd ed. Trans. John B. Murdoch. Ithaca, N.Y.: Cornell Southeast Asia Program, 1988, pp. xiii-xiv.

23. Sources differ as to just when Souphanouvong arrived in Laos. According to two recent accounts published in the Lao People's Democratic Republic, he reached Savannakhet in early September, a full month before the formation of the Lao Issara government. See Duangxay Luangphasi, *Sam bulut lek haeng meuang Tha Khaek* (The Three Iron Men of Thakhek). Vientiane: Khana Kammakan Lao pheua Santhipap Lok Samakkhi lae Mitthaphap kap Pasasat, 1993, p. 33; and Thongsa Sainhavongkhamdi et al., *Pavatsat Lao* (History of Laos). Vol. 3. Vientiane: Ministry of Education and Sports and Social Science Research Institute, 1989, p. 162. Conversely, Trần Văn Dinh, a Vietnamese military officer who escorted the prince, says they arrived on October 7. See Trần Văn Dinh, "The Birth of the Pathet Lao Army." In *Laos: War and Revolution,* ed. Nina S. Adams and Alfred W. McCoy. New York: Harper Colophon, 1970, p. 427. Sila Vilavong, recounting the events of 1945–1946 from the perspective of a Lao Issara associate of Phetsarath, says that when the first Issara cabinet was drawn up on October 8, Souphanouvong was "still in Vietnam at the time." See Sila Vilavong, *Pavatsat van thi 12 tula 1945* (The History of 12 October 1945). Vientiane: Pakpassak Kanphim, 1975, p. 17. The October date would seem to be correct, and I have argued elsewhere that the purported September return represents a conscious attempt to bring the prince onto the Lao political stage earlier than he actually appeared on it. See also Bruce M. Lockhart, "Narrating 1945 in Lao Historiography." In *Contesting Visions of the Lao Past: Lao Historiography at the Crossroads,* ed. Christopher Goscha and Søren Ivarsson. Richmond, Surrey: Curzon, forthcoming.

24. Detailed accounts of this period based on French archives are in Geoffrey Gunn, *Political Struggles in Laos (1930–1954).* Bangkok: Editions Duang Kamol, 1988; and Jean Deuve, *Le Laos 1945–1949: Contribution à l'histoire du mouvement Lao Issala.* Montpellier: Université Paul-Valéry, 2000. For a good summary, see Martin Stuart-Fox, *A History of Laos.* Cambridge: Cambridge University Press, 1999. A book that purports to be Phetsarath's memoirs has been translated and published in Wyatt, *Iron Man of Laos.* For a detailed study of the Lao Issara government's short existence, see Vilavong, *Pavatsat van thi 12.* On Souphanouvong, see Duangxay Luangphasi, *Sam bulut lek;* and Duangxay Luangphasi, *Autobiography of Prince Souphanouvong.* Kuala Lumpur: Malaysia Mining Corporation Berhad, n.d. The Lao People's Revolutionary Party gives its own version of these events in Sainhavongkhamdi et al., *Pavatsat Lao,* pp. 144–223.

25. For a summary of these developments, see Gunn, *Political Struggles,* pp. 173–180. An observer's account of one round of national elections (1951) is in Chargé Gullion to Secretary of State, 11 September 1951, *FRUS, 1951.* Vol. 6, p. 493. The texts of the 1947 constitution and the 1949 Franco-Lao convention are in Katay D. Sasorith, *Le Laos: Son évolution politique; Sa place dans l'Union française.* Paris: Éditions Berger-Levrault, 1953, pp. 98–110, 117–126, respectively.

26. For a discussion on the breakup of the Lao Issara government-in-exile, see MacAlister Brown and Joseph Zasloff, *Apprentice Revolutionaries: The Communist Movement in Laos, 1930–1985.* Stanford, Calif.: Hoover Institution Press, 1986, chapter 4. For a translation of the polemical correspondence between Souphanouvong and Katay Don Sasorith, the moderate future prime minister, see Brown and Zasloff, *Apprentice Revolutionaries,* appendix D. Katay reproduces the October 1949 decree

dissolving that government, along with a newspaper commentary that he wrote at the time. See Katay, *Le Laos,* pp. 130–140.

27. On the possibility of his replacing the king, see Minister Stanton to Secretary of State, 7 January 1947, *FRUS, 1947.* Vol. 6, p. 57. American suspicions are voiced in "Probable Developments in South Vietnam, Laos, and Cambodia through July 1956," National Intelligence Estimate NIE 63–7–54, dated 23 November 1954, *FRUS, 1952–1954.* Vol. 13, pt. 2, p. 2298. Earlier that year, the American chargé d'affaires in Sàigòn had expressed the view that Phetsarath's return "would be welcome if he agreed [to] behave and act for good of Laos, instead of fight [the] ruling family" and that he "could easily become Prime Minister." See Chargé McClintock to Department of State, 19 June 1954, *FRUS, 1952–1954.* Vol. 13, pt. 2, p. 1722. For a discussion of French and Vietnamese initiatives in Phetsarath's direction, see Christopher E. Goscha, "Le contexte asiatique de la guerre franco-vietnamienne: Réseaux, relations et économie." Ph.D. thesis, École Pratique des Hautes Études, Partie laotienne, chapters 1–3 and passim. I am grateful to Goscha for providing me with a copy of his very important work.

28. Gunn, *Political Struggles,* provides a detailed though somewhat fragmented account of the 1946–1954 period. Goscha, "Contexte asiatique," has a more thorough narrative, mainly emphasizing the revolutionary side. My observation on the crown prince's importance is based on his prominence in American diplomatic reports through 1955, where he figures more or less on an equal basis with Souvanna Phouma. It is ironic that although Phetsarath was long perceived as Savang's main rival, it was ultimately the former's brother (Souvanna Phouma) who overshadowed Savang politically and another brother (Souphanouvong) who (presumably) acquiesced to his incarceration by the revolutionary government in a prison camp in the late 1970s; Savang Vatthana and his queen eventually died in captivity.

29. In a conversation with the U.S. secretary of state in September, French foreign minister Robert Schuman affirmed that "at the present time the three infant governments were incapable of succeeding alone" and that "the presence of the French Army and French technical advisers was indispensable to the emergence of truly nationalist and independent states in Indochina." France, he added, "intended to be most liberal in dealing with these governments so that gradually they could attain an increasing degree of independence." This conversation is included in Memorandum by Mr. James L. O'Sullivan, of the (State Dept.) Division of Southeast Asian Affairs, on Preliminary Talks As to Indochina, 28 September 1949, *FRUS, 1949.* Vol. 7, p. 87. One French scholar, writing in 1952, believed that the Pau Conference of mid-1950, which hashed out the preliminary framework for the Associated States, signaled "the loss of Indochina as we had conceived of it in 1939 or even in 1945–46." See Paul Mus, *Viêt-Nam sociologie d'une guerre.* Paris: Éditions du Seuil, 1952, p. 65.

30. In January 1952, Minister Letourneau could comfortably inform an American visitor that "despite French efforts [to] give independence to [the] Vietnamese, [they] were incapable of independence" and that if the French withdrew their forces, "[the] Vietminh [would] be in control in two days." See Ambassador Bruce to Department of State, 15 January 1952, *FRUS, 1952–1954.* Vol. 13, pt. 1, p. 16. It must be acknowledged that Letourneau's pessimism was at least partially rooted in an all too realistic assessment of the weaknesses of Båo Đại and his government. See the record of his conversation with the American ambassador to Vietnam later that year in Heath to Department of State, 6 November 1952, *FRUS, 1952–1954.* Vol. 13, pt. 1, pp. 272–275.

31. Neo Lao Itsala can be translated as "Free Lao Front." "Itsala" and "Issara" are two different transcriptions of the same Lao word; Phetsarath's organization is normally spelled with the latter variant, and the distinction will be maintained here to avoid confusion between the two movements.

32. Goscha discusses the strengths and weaknesses of Souphanouvong's position in Goscha, "Contexte asiatique." Partie laotienne, pp. 14–15, 16–19.

33. Kiernan, *How Pol Pot*, makes extensive use of French archival documents, but his focus is the rebels rather than the ruler. Sihanouk's views can be found in his various memoirs, notably Sihanouk, *L'Indochine vue de Pekin: Entretiens avec Jean Lacouture*. Paris: Editions du Seuil, 1972; Sihanouk, *L'action de S.M. Norodom Sihanouk;* and Gouvernement Royal du Cambodge, *Livre jaune sur les revendications.* More skeptical views of Sihanouk's crusade are in Osborne, *Sihanouk;* and Martin Herz, *A Short History of Cambodia from the Days of Angkor to the Present.* New York: Praeger, 1958.

34. Devillers quotes archival documents that show that in 1946 Paris was indeed concerned about the possible impact of events in Vietnam on Cambodia and Laos but that d'Argenlieu gave his reassurance that there were no "solid grounds for uncertainty as to the future" of the French presence in the latter two countries. See Devillers, *Paris Saigon Hanoi,* pp. 164–165, 185.

35. This seems to have been the general view of American diplomats as well, as reflected in the documents published in the *FRUS*. Sihanouk received little American sympathy for his "crusade," however, as the United States felt it was ill timed and would weaken the struggle against communism in Cambodia. Sihanouk later complained about this "incompréhension anglo-saxonne" on the part of the United States and the United Kingdom in Sihanouk, *L'action de S.M. Norodom Sihanouk,* pp. 66–68.

36. As in Cambodia and Laos, France maintained a fairly strong presence in South Vietnam until 1975 through cultural and educational institutions. Even in these areas, though, French influence among the Vietnamese was more effectively supplanted by the United States than was the case for the other two countries.

37. I have studied this topic in detail in Lockhart, *End of the Vietnamese Monarchy,* see especially chapter 10.

38. Lockhart, *End of the Vietnamese Monarchy,* p. 174; see also Bruce to Secretary of State, 2 June 1949, *FRUS, 1949.* Vol. 7, p. 35; and Bruce to Secretary of State, 16 March 1951, *FRUS, 1951.* Vol. 6, p. 401.

39. Bảo Đại, *Dragon d'Annam,* pp. 192 (Bollaert), 198 (abdication and restoration). Bảo Đại said that his abdication was actually not "forced" but that the Việt Minh failed to live up to the expectations he had when he turned over power to them (p. 198). Devillers suggests that he ultimately decided to be "head of state" rather than "emperor" because he had not forgotten that his abdication was "the most popular act of his lifetime." See Devillers, *L'histoire du Vietnam,* p. 445n7.

40. Quoted in Bảo Đại, *Dragon d'Annam,* p. 289. Bảo Đại's comment on his legitimacy is on p. 207. De Lattre's public remarks quoted here were rather more favorable than his private characterization of Bảo Đại earlier that year, when he had shouted at a high-ranking Vietnamese official that the head of state was "a rotten scum [who] goes on shacking up with his whores instead of visiting my soldiers in Tonkin." See Lucien Bodard, *La guerre d'Indochine: L'Aventure.* Paris: Gallimard, 1967, pp. 302–304. Although Bodard's entire account is very critical of de Lattre, whom he calls "le roi Jean"("King John"), this outburst from a general whose troops were bearing the

brunt of the fighting is not at all implausible. Grandclément, though generally sympathetic to Bảo Đại, trenchantly observes that while de Lattre lost a son fighting in Vietnam, the royal family remained in France and did not even allow the crown prince to enlist. See Grandclément, *Bao Daï,* p. 314.

41. Heath to Department of State, 18 November 1952, *FRUS, 1952–1954.* Vol. 13, pt. 1, p. 286. This conversation is somewhat odd given that technically speaking, the State of Vietnam was not a "monarchy." I take it to mean that Bảo Đại was afraid that Letourneau and the others wished to remove him from the scene entirely, which would break any ties between the Vietnamese government and the former ruling dynasty. He told Heath that "it was all one to him what the form of gov[ernmen]t was. He was willing to get out as he had in 1945. All he sought was the good and the will of the country."

42. Quoted in Mus, *Viêt-Nam sociologie d'une guerre,* p. 68.

43. Bodard, *La guerre d'Indochine: L'Enlisement,* p. 173; and Bảo Đại, *Dragon d'Annam,* p. 259.

44. The bonds holding together the State of Vietnam remained fragile throughout its existence, despite the periodic "rallying" of various elements. At the time of the Geneva Conference, when the political situation in Sàigòn was deteriorating as rapidly as the military situation in Điện Biên Phủ, a former prime minister commented to an American diplomat that the public pronouncements of loyalty by various groups had very little meaning. These people, he said, made pilgrimages to Paris or the Riviera, where Bảo Đại was then staying, "and they all agree that they prefer bright weather to rainy weather. This is then proclaimed as new evidence of union around Bảo Đại. Furthermore, they get [a] free trip to France." See McClintock to Department of State, 12 May 1954, *FRUS, 1952–1954.* Vol. 13, pt. 2, p. 1544.

45. Consul Sturm to Department of State, 10 June 1952, *FRUS, 1952–1954.* Vol. 13, pt. 1, p. 178. Sturm noted that he himself reserved judgment on the accuracy of these views but affirmed that they were widespread. One perennial problem was that many of the leaders were southerners with little or no popularity north of the Mekong Delta. Tâm, for example, was "anathema in Tonkin," where he was "considered [a] Fr[ench] puppet, 'cop' and sadist," as well as an "indifferent administrator" (p. 177); the latter was presumably the more serious flaw in a prime minister.

46. Bảo Đại believed that "contrary to what one might think, even with French citizenship Cochinchinese have maintained a deep respect for the [Nguyễn] dynasty," partially because it was a tradition of that ruling family (including himself) to take southern women as consorts. See Bảo Đại, *Dragon d'Annam,* p. 201. However, even Grandclément, his sympathetic biographer, notes the tepid welcome he received in Sàigòn. See Grandclément, *Bao Daï,* pp. 310–311.

47. In his memoirs, Bảo Đại says that he was very much attached to his home in Ban Mê Thuột and that because of its proximity to the Lao and Cambodian borders, he could "keep an eye on all of southern Indochina." See Bảo Đại, *Dragon d'Annam,* p. 263. On the issue of the palace, see his remarks cited in Heath to Secretary of State, 5 January 1951, *FRUS, 1951.* Vol. 6, p. 339. Bodard, who had no particular sympathy for the Vietnamese of any political stripe, observes that the building "is the symbol of sovereignty" and that "its occupants are the true masters." See Bodard, *La guerre d'Indochine: L'Enlisement,* pp. 192–193.

48. Goscha, "Contexte asiatique." Partie laotienne, chapter 3, pp. 20–22, chapter 5, pp. 1–2, Partie cambodgienne, chapter 3, p. 12. Goscha is citing captured ICP documents discussing strategies for the Lao and Cambodian revolutions.

49. This point is mentioned by Mus, *Viêt-Nam sociologie d'une guerre*, pp. 33–34, 78–79.

50. Ellen Hammer, "The Bao Dai Experiment." *Pacific Affairs* 23, no. 1 (1950): 46. A Vietnamese national army, for example, was only established in 1951.

51. Mus, *Viêt-Nam sociologie d'une guerre*, p. 367.

52. This issue is discussed in more detail in Lockhart, "Narrating 1945 in Lao Historiography." A separate Lao People's Party (Phak Pasason Lao) was not founded until 1955, four years after the final dissolution of the ICP and the establishment of separate Vietnamese and Cambodian People's Parties.

53. On these events, see Goscha, "Contexte asiatique." Partie cambodgienne, chapter 3, pp. 19–22, Partie laotienne, chapter 5, pp. 6–7.

54. Goscha, "Contexte asiatique," analyzes in detail the challenges facing the Vietnamese in trying to create rival Cambodian and Lao "states."

55. Lockhart, *End of the Vietnamese Monarchy*, chapter 10, especially pp. 187–193. Mus comments that the French had a false perception of the Vietnamese monarchy as being sacred in and of itself and failed to understand the extent to which its potency depended on its position within the broader cosmology of Vietnamese society. He also notes that d'Argenlieu's successor, Bollaert, initially advocated returning to a system whereby Bảo Đại's authority would be "mainly religious," with most of the political power in French hands. See Mus, *Viêt-Nam sociologie d'une guerre*, pp. 287, 58.

56. Lockhart, *End of the Vietnamese Monarchy*, pp. 18–27.

## Chapter 5

1. Hugues Tertrais, *La Piastre et le Fusil: Le Coût de la guerre d'Indochine, 1945–1954*. Paris: Comité pour l'histoire économique et financière de la France, Ministère de l'Économie, des Finances et de l'Industrie, 2002; and Hugues Tertrais, "France Facing Indochina: Images and Misunderstandings." In *Europe–Southeast Asia in the Contemporary World: Mutual Images and Reflections, 1940s-1960s*, ed. Piyanart Bunnag, Franz Knipping, and Sud Chonchirdsin. Baden-Baden: Nomos Verlagsgesellschaft, 2000, pp. 41–50.

2. Fonds du Commissariat général au Plan, série 80 AJ, carton 12, French National Archives, Paris.

3. Daniel Hémery, "Asie du Sud-Est 1945: vers un nouvel impérialisme colonial? Le projet indochinois de la France au lendemain de la seconde guerre mondiale." In *L'ère des décolonisations*, ed. Charles-Robert Ageron and Marc Michel. Paris: Karthala, 1995.

4. March 6, 1946, Hồ-Sainteny Agreement; Dalat Conference, April 19–May 11, 1946; and Fontainebleau Conference, July 6–August 8, 1946.

5. On Bảo Đại, see Bruce M. Lockhart, chapter 4, in this volume.

6. 14 January 1947 Memorandum, Mayer Papers, 363 AP 31, French National Archives, Paris.

7. 23 July 1947 Valluy Instruction, cited in G. Bodinier, *Indochine, 1947*. Château de Vincennes: Service Historique de l'Armée de Terre, 1989, p. 303.

8. Actes définissant les rapports des États associés du Vietnam, du Cambodge et du Laos avec la France, Notes et études documentaires no. 1295, *La Documentation française*, 14 March 1950.

9. Conclusions of the Revers Mission in Indochina, from May 11 to June 21,

1949, Archives Militaires, Ministère de la Défense, Revers Papers, 1 K 331, Château de Vincennes, Service Historique de l'Armée de Terre (SHAT).

10. French Ministry of Finance, Boxes 33545 and 33546, Archives Économiques et Financières (AEF), Fonds Trésor.

11. Hugues Tertrais, "The Associated States Experience (Indochina, 1950–1954)." In *Europe and Southeast Asia in the Contemporary World: Mutual Influences and Comparisons,* ed. Franz Knipping, Piyanart Bunnag, and Vimolvan Phatharodom. Baden-Baden: Nomos Verlagsgesellschaft, 1999, pp. 205–210.

12. See the extensive documentation in French Ministries of National Defence, série 14 H, SHAT; and French Ministry of Finance, AEF, Fonds Trésor.

13. Note of the Asia Department regarding American assistance to Indochina, January 25, 1951, Fonds Asie-Océanie, Indochine (AO/IC), Box 264, Ministère des Affaires étrangères (MAE), Paris.

14. Hugues Tertrais, "America Takes over Vietnam, the French View." *Itinerario* 22 (1998): 51–59.

15. "Military Aid to Indochina," 1 February 1950, in *Foreign Relations of the United States, 1950.* Vol. 6, *East Asia and the Pacific.* Washington, D.C.: U.S. Government Printing Office, 1976, pp. 711–715.

16. Telegram of 22 March 1950, AO/IC, Box 262, MAE.

17. Letter by Léon Pignon to the French Minister of Foreign Affairs, 21 March 1951, AO/IC, Box 262, MAE.

18. French Ministry of Finance, Boxes 43915 and 43916, AEF, Fonds Trésor

19. *Wall Street Journal,* 11 August 1953.

20. Mayer Papers, 363 AP 24.

21. General Leclerc Mission in Indochina Report, 8 January 1947, Leclerc Papers, 1 K 239, SHAT.

22. 23 July 1947 Valluy Instruction, cited in Bodinier, *Indochine,* p. 303.

23. *Le Monde,* 13–14 March 1949; see also Lucien Bodard, *La guerre d'Indochine. I. L'enlisement.* Paris: Gallimard, 1963.

24. Pleven Papers, 560 AP 55, French National Archives, Paris.

## Chapter 6

1. Throughout the text, I refer to the Dutch colony, until February 1948 officially called the Netherlands East Indies, as Indonesia. Until 1942, the capital's name was Batavia when it changed to Djakarta. The Indonesians continued to call it Djakarta, while the returning Dutch renamed the city in 1945 according to the old name. That changed officially in 1950. Today, it is spelled Jakarta. Throughout the text, I refer to the city as Batavia/Jakarta.

2. See Paul H. Kratoska, chapter 1, in this volume. See also Bernhard Dahm, "Der Dekolonisierungsprozess Indonesiens: Endogene und exogene Faktoren." In *Das Ende der Kolonialreiche: Dekolonisation und die Politik der Großmächte,* ed. Wolfgang Mommsen. Frankfurt am Main: Fischer, 1990, pp. 67–88; John Darwin, *Britain and Decolonization: The Retreat from Empire in the Post-war World.* Basingstoke: Macmillan, 1988, pp. 23–25; and Jürgen Osterhammel, "Spätkolonialismus und Dekolonisation." In *Neue Politische Literatur* 37 (1992): 404–426.

3. Audrey R. Kahin, *Rebellion to Integration: West Sumatra and the Indonesian Polity, 1926–1998.* Amsterdam: Amsterdam University Press, 1999, p. 153; George McTurnan Kahin, *Nationalism and Revolution in Indonesia.* Ithaca, N.Y.: Cornell

University Press, 1952; Jan Pluvier, *South-East Asia from Colonialism to Independence*. Kuala Lumpur: Oxford University Press 1974, p. 487; and Anthony Reid, *The Indonesian National Revolution, 1945–1950*. Hawthorn, Australia: Longman, 1974, p. 170.

4. H. W. van den Doel, *Afscheid van Indië: De val van het Nederlandse imperium in Azië*. Amsterdam: Prometheus, 2001, pp. 371–382; C. Fasseur, *De weg naar het paradijs en andere Indische geschiedenissen*. Amsterdam: Bert Bakker, 1995, p. 250; Lodewijk de Jong, *Het Koninkrijk der Nederlanden in de tweede Wereldoorlog, 1939–1945*. Vol. 12. Pt. 2. 's-Gravenhage: SDU-Uitgeverij, 1988, p. 1069; and Yong Mun Cheong, *H. J. van Mook and Indonesian Independence: A Study of His Role in Dutch-Indonesian Relations, 1945–48*. The Hague: Nijhoff, 1982, p. 197.

5. P. J. Drooglever, "Dekolonisatie in twintig delen: Een persoonlijke impressie." In *De leeuw en de banteng: Bijdragen aan het congres over de Nederlands-Indonesische betrekkingen 1945–1950*, ed. P. J. Drooglever and M. J. B. Schouten. Den Haag: Instituut voor Nederlandse Geschiedenis, 1997, pp. 273–282; J. J. P. de Jong, *Diplomatie of strijd: Een analyse van het Nederlands beleid tegenover de Indonesische Revolutie, 1945–1947*. Meppel: Boom, 1988, pp. 423–425; and J. J. P. de Jong, "The Netherlands, Great Britain and the Indonesian Revolution, 1945–1950." In *Unspoken Allies: Anglo-Dutch Relations since 1780*, ed. Nigel Ashton and Duco Hellema. Amsterdam: Amsterdam University Press, 2001, pp. 179–202.

6. Frances Gouda with Thijs Brocades Zaalberg, *American Visions of the Netherlands East Indies/Indonesia: U.S. Foreign Policy and Indonesian Nationalism, 1920–1949*. Amsterdam: Amsterdam University Press, 2002, 297f.; Gerlof D. Homan, "The Netherlands, the United States and the Indonesian Question, 1948." *Journal of Contemporary History* 25 (1990): 123–141; and Robert J. McMahon, *Colonialism and Cold War: The United States and the Struggle for Indonesian Independence, 1945–49*. Ithaca, N.Y.: Cornell University Press, 1981, p. 304; see also Cees Wiebes and Bert Zeeman, "United States 'Big Stick' Diplomacy: The Netherlands between Decolonization and Alignment, 1945–1949." *International History Review* 14 (1992): 45–70.

7. Stein Tønnesson, "Filling the Power Vacuum: 1945 in French Indochina, the Netherlands East Indies and British Malaya." In *Imperial Policy and Southeast Asian Nationalism, 1930–1957*, ed. Hans Antlöv and Stein Tønnesson. London: Curzon, 1995, pp. 110–143, in particular pp. 115–118, 122. On the Japanese occupation, see Theodore Friend, *The Blue-Eyed Enemy: Japan against the West in Java and Luzon, 1942–1945*. Princeton, N.J.: Princeton University Press, 1988, pp. 105–120, 211–239; Shigeru Sato, *War, Nationalism and Peasants: Java under the Japanese Occupation*. St. Leonards, Australia: Allen and Unwin, 1994; and Nicholas Tarling, *The Japanese Occupation of Southeast Asia, 1941–1945*. Honolulu: University of Hawaii Press, 2001, pp. 95–100, 174–192, 226–231.

8. On economic developments, see J. Thomas Lindblad, chapter 3, in this volume; see also Twang Peck Yang, *The Chinese Business Élite in Indonesia and the Transition to Independence, 1940–1950*. Kuala Lumpur: Oxford University Press, 1998, pp. 150–316.

9. Benedict Anderson, *Java in a Time of Revolution: Occupation and Resistance, 1944–1946*. Ithaca, N.Y.: Cornell University Press, 1972, p. 1; William H. Frederick, *Visions and Heat: The Making of the Indonesian Revolution*. Athens: Ohio University Press, 1989, pp. 186–193; and Reid, *Indonesian National Revolution*, pp. 25–39.

10. Lambert Giebels, *Soekarno. Nederlandsch onderdaan: Eeen biographie, 1901–1950*. Amsterdam: Bert Bakker, 1999, pp. 375–404.

11. Minutes by G. E. J. Gent on Dutch views on colonialism, 12 June 1942, in *British Documents on the End of Empire,* Series B, 3 vols., Parts 1–3, *Malaya,* ed. A.J. Stockwell. London: HMSO, 1995, vol. 1, 8f.; Anthony Eden to Oliver Stanley, January 1944, Foreign Office (FO) 371/41726, Public Record Office (PRO), London; and Minutes of a meeting of the Dutch council of war, 10 August 1945, in *Officiële Bescheiden Betreffende de Nederlands-Indonesische Betrekkingen, 1945–1950 (NIB).* Vol. 1. Ed. S. L. van der Wal, P. J. Drooglever, and M. J. B. Schouten. 's-Gravenhage: SUV, 1971–1996, pp. 2–9.

12. Memorandum of a Conversation at the Department of State between James C. Dunn and Alexander Loudon, the Dutch ambassador, and Hubertus van Mook, 10 January 1944, National Archives (hereafter NA), Record Group (hereafterRG) 59, 856D.01/122; and "Principles Governing Arrangements for Civil Administration and Jurisdiction in Netherlands Territory in the Southwest Pacific Area," 10 December 1944, NA, RG 59, 711.56D119/12–1044.

13. The American intelligence outfit Office of Strategic Services reported Dutch plans to assassinate Sukarno and Hatta. See General William H. Donovan to Harry S Truman, 26 September 1945, Harry S Truman Library (HSTL), Independence, Missouri, Harry S Truman Papers, Miscellaneous White House Central Files, Rose Convoy File, Box 15.

14. Van Mook to Mountbatten, 3 September 1945, in *NIB.* Vol. 1, pp. 82–86; and Ch. O. van der Plas to van Mook, 18 September 1945, in *NIB.* Vol. 1, pp. 121–130.

15. Van Mook to Embassy London, 29 September 1945, in *NIB.* Vol. 1, 190f.; and Sukarno to Mountbatten, 30 September 1945, in *NIB.* Vol. 1, pp. 202–206.

16. On November 1, 1945, the Republican government issued a statement in which it recognized the need for Western, and especially Dutch, technical assistance and capital. The original text is printed in *Documenta Historica, Sedjarah dokumenten dari pertumbuhan dan perdjuangan negara Republik Indonesia,* ed. Osman Raliby. Jakarta: Bulan-Bintang, 1953, 525ff. Quoted in *NIB.* Vol. 3, p. 565. For a corresponding view, see W. MacMahon Ball, the Australian political representative in Batavia/Jakarta, to Department of External Affairs, 12 November 1945, in *Documents on Australian Foreign Policy, 1937–49.* Vol. 8, *1945,* ed. W. J. Hudson and Wendy Way. Canberra: Australian Government Publishing Service, 1989, 598f.

17. Bernhard Dahm, *Sukarnos Kampf um die Indonesiens Unabhängigkeit: Werdegang und Ideen eines asiatischen Nationalisten.* Frankfurt am Main: Metzner Verlag, 1966, pp. 255–266; and Nugroho Notosusanto, *The National Struggle and the Armed Forces in Indonesia.* Jakarta: Department of Defense and Security, Centre for Armed Forces History, 1980, 17f.

18. C. E. L. Helfrich to J. M. de Booy, minister of the navy, 2 December 1945, in *NIB.* Vol. 2, pp. 266–272.

19. J. B. D. Derksen and J. Tinbergen, "Berekeningen over de economische beteekenis van Nederlandsch-Indië voor Nederland." In *Maandschrift van het Centraal Bureau voor de Statistiek* 40 (1945): 210–216; see also van den Doel, *Afscheid van Indië,* pp. 81–124.

20. Hatta to Christison, 9 November 1945, in *NIB.* Vol. 2, pp. 11–14.

21. See Nicholas Tarling, chapter 8, in this volume; see also Tilman Remme, *Britain and Regional Cooperation in South-East Asia, 1945–49.* London: Routledge, 1995, pp. 27–53; and Rolf Tanner, *"A Strong Showing": Britain's Struggle for Power and Influence in Southeast Asia, 1942–1950.* Stuttgart: Steiner, 1994, pp. 90–109.

22. See Mark Philip Bradley, chapter 12, and Robert J. McMahon, chapter 13, in

this volume; see also McMahon, *Colonialism and Cold War,* pp. 74–113; and "An Estimate of Conditions in Asia and the Pacific at the Close of the War in the Far East and the Objectives and Policies of the United States," 22 June 1945, in *Foreign Relations of the United States* [*FRUS*], *1945.* Vol. 6, *The British Commonwealth, the Far East.* Washington, D.C.: U.S. Government Printing Office, 1969, pp. 556–580.

23. J. H. A. Logemann to van Mook, 13 October 1945, in *NIB.* Vol. 2, p. 351; and van Mook to Logemann, 31 October 1945, in *NIB.* Vol. 2, 489f.

24. Logemann to van Mook, 25 October 1945, in *NIB.* Vol. 1, 437f.; and Minutes of a meeting of the council of war, 12 November 1945, in *NIB.* Vol. 2, pp. 42–50.

25. See the chapter by Paul Kratoska; see also McMahon, *Colonialism and Cold War,* 63–65; and Christopher Thorne, *Allies of a Kind: The United States, Britain and the War against Japan, 1941–1945.* London: Hamish Hamilton, 1978, p. 219.

26. H. J. van Mook, *The Stakes of Democracy in South-East Asia.* London: Allen and Unwin, 1950, 180f.

27. Speech by Logemann, 16 October 1945, in *NIB.* Vol. 1, pp. 577–588; Proclamation by the Netherlands East Indies Government, 6 November 1945, in *NIB.* Vol. 1, pp. 588–590; Logemann to cabinet, 24 December 1945, in *NIB.* Vol. 2, pp. 422–425; and Minutes of a meeting at Chequers, 27 December 1945, in *NIB.* Vol. 2, pp. 453–469.

28. Van Mook to Embassy London, 29 September 1945, in *NIB.* Vol. 1, 190f.; van Mook to Prime Minister Willem Schermerhorn, 21 December 1945, in *NIB.* Vol. 2, pp. 394–397; Minutes of a meeting of the cabinet, 21 December 1945, in *NIB.* Vol. 2, pp. 397–403; and H. F. C. Walsh, British Consul-General, to Foreign Office, 8 November 1945, in *NIB.* Vol. 1, 570f. On van Mook's paternalism, see Cheong, *Van Mook and Indonesian Independence;* and Reid, *Indonesian National Revolution,* p. 105.

29. Doel, *Afscheid van Indië,* p. 143.

30. Van Mook to J. A. Jonkman, Minister of Overseas Territories, 10, 20, and 25 July 1946, in *NIB.* Vol. 4, 627f., and vol. 5, 45f., 84f.

31. Intelligence Service to van Mook, 14 July 1946, in *NIB.* Vol. 4, pp. 652–657.

32. Mountbatten to Cabinet Office, 9 August 1946, Colonial Office (CO) 537/1924, PRO; and "South East Asia: Work of the Special Commission during 1946," Lord Killearn to Ernest Bevin, 12 April 1947, despatch no. 119 from Lord Killearn to Mr. Bevin, *British Documents on the End of Empire,* Series B, 3 vols., Parts 1–3, *Malaya,* ed. Anthony J. Stockwell. London: HMSO, 1995, vol. 1, pp. 307–318; see also Karl Hack, *Defense and Decolonisation: Britain, Malaya and Singapore, 1941–1968.* Richmond, Surrey: Curzon, 2001, p. 61.

33. van den Doel, *Afscheid van Indië,* pp. 184–193; and McMahon, *Colonialism and Cold War,* 133f.

34. Jonkman to van Mook, 15 August 1946, in *NIB.* Vol. 5, 227f.

35. van den Doel, *Afscheid van Indië,* p. 213.

36. Dean Acheson to Walter A. Foote, 3 April 1947, *FRUS, 1947.* Vol. 6, *The British Commonwealth, the Far East.* Washington, D.C.: U.S. Government Printing Office, 1969, p. 912.

37. Quoted in van Mook to P. J. Koets, 5 April 1947, in *NIB.* Vol. 8, p. 117.

38. Minutes of a meeting of the Council for War, 6 March 1946, in *NIB.* Vol. 3, pp. 500–507; Van Mook to Jonkman, 2 September 1946, in *NIB.* Vol. 5, pp. 288–290; Spoor to Prime Minister L. J. M. Beel, 21 December 1946, in *NIB.* Vol. 6, pp. 611–

632; Minutes of a Meeting of the Council for War, 21 January 1947, in *NIB*. Vol. 7, pp. 117–141; Note by the chief of the general staff of the army, H. J. Kruls, to minister of war, A. H. J. L. Fiévez, 9 April 1947, in *NIB*. Vol. 8, pp. 148–151; and Report by Idenburg on his tour to Jogjakarta, 31 May 1947, in *NIB*. Vol. 9, pp. 110–135.

39. This concept draws on Edward Said, *Orientalism*. New York: Pantheon, 1978.

40. Alan K. Henrikson states that "[m]ental maps are taken to mean an ordered but continually adapting structure of the mind—alternatively conceivable as a process—by reference to which a person acquires, codes stores, recalls, reorganizes, and applies information about his or her environment." See Alan K. Henrikson, "Mental Maps." In *Explaining the History of American Foreign Relations*, ed. Michael H. Hogan and Thomas G. Paterson. New York: Cambridge University Press, 1991, p. 177.

41. C. Smit, ed., *Het dagboek van Schermerhorn*. Utrecht: Wolters-Noordhoff, 1970, 167f., quoted in de Jong, "The Netherlands, Great Britain, and the Indonesian Revolution," p. 195.

42. Note by the chief of the general staff in the Netherlands East Indies, D. C. Burman van Vreeden, 28 March 1946, in *NIB*. Vol. 3, pp. 672–678; J. Herman van Roijen to W. F. L. count van Byland, 27 April 1946, in *NIB*. Vol. 4, p. 182; and Jonkman to van Mook, 4 October 1946, in *NIB*. Vol. 5, p. 485. The mobilization of a comparatively large number of young Dutchmen just one year after the end of the war in Europe caused widespread discontent among the draftees. In October 1946, an embarkation call caused a temporary 30 percent desertion rate.

43. See van Byland to van Roijen, 9 March 1946, in *NIB*. Vol. 3, 524f.; and W. S. B. Lacy to F. P. Graham, "US Policy on the Sale or Transfer of Arms and Munitions to the Government of NEI," 13 October 1947, NA, RG 59, Lot 54 D 190, Box 11.

44. P. Lieftinck to Beel, 18 April 1947, in *NIB*. Vol. 8, pp. 313–319.

45. Minutes of a meeting with Prime Minister Beel in Batavia, 15 May 1947, in *NIB*. Vol. 8, pp. 695–700; and Minutes of a meeting of the council of ministers, 28 May 1947, in *NIB*. Vol. 9, pp. 63–73.

46. Note by H. van Vredenburch, 3 June 1947, in *NIB*. Vol. 9, pp. 204–206

47. Mook to Jonkman, 11 August 1947, in *NIB*. Vol. 10, pp. 326–328. During the offensive, the number of Dutch casualties was comparatively low. Until August 4, 84 had been killed and 206 wounded. See also Petra M. Groen, "Militant Response: The Dutch Use of Military Force and the Decolonization of the Dutch East Indies, 1945–50." *Journal of Imperial and Commonwealth History* 21 (1993): 30–44.

48. Mook to Beel and Jonkman, 29 July 1947, in *NIB*. Vol. 10, pp. 106–108; and Spoor to Kruls, 6 August 1947, in *NIB*. Vol. 10, pp. 253–254.

49. Minutes of a meeting of the cabinet, 13 August 1947, in *NIB*. Vol. 10, pp. 380–384; and Mook to Jonkman, 14 August 1947, in *NIB*. Vol. 10, pp. 385–389.

50. Editorial Note, *FRUS, 1947*. Vol. 6, p. 1003.

51. Because of security interests, the Australian government was an early supporter of Indonesian independence. In public, there was also a lot of sympathy for the nationalist struggle. For instance, see H. V. Evatt to N. J. O Makin, 23 November 1945, in *Documents on Australian Foreign Policy*. Vol. 8, pp. 635–638.

52. Idenburg to Jonkman, 11 August 1947, in *NIB*. Vol. 10, pp. 335–337.

53. McMahon, *Colonialism and Cold War*, pp. 183–192.

54. Doel, *Afscheid van Indië*, pp. 270–302.

55. See also Bradley, chapter 12, in this volume.

56. Graham to State Department, 27 December 1947, *FRUS, 1947*. Vol. 6, pp.

1094–1096; Robert A. Lovett to Graham, 31 December 1947, *FRUS, 1947.* Vol. 6, pp. 1099–1101; and McMahon, *Colonialism and Cold War,* pp. 203–205.

57. Reid, *Indonesian National Revolution,* pp. 129–131.

58. Central Intelligence Agency, "The Prospects for a United States of Indonesia," 4 June 1948, ORE 26–48, HSTL, Truman Papers, President's Secretary's File, Intelligence File, Box 255.

59. van den Doel, *Afscheid van Indië,* pp. 296f., 301.

60. The Republican view of Musso as an agent of Moscow and an enemy of the Indonesian Republic is revealed in documents the Dutch seized in December 1948. See also Minutes of a meeting on the reorganization of the armed forces, 31 August 1948, in *NIB.* Vol. 16, pp. 712–715.

61. Gouda, *American Visions,* pp. 275–280; McMahon, *Colonialism and Cold War,* pp. 242–243; Reid, *Indonesian National Revolution,* pp. 136–147; and Ulf Sundhaussen, *The Road to Power: Indonesian Military Politics, 1945–1967.* Kuala Lumpur: Oxford University Press, 1982, p. 40.

62. Reid, *Indonesian National Revolution,* p. 147.

63. Beel to E. M. J. A. Sassen, Minister of Overseas Territories, 20 September 1948, in *NIB.* Vol. 15, pp. 140–142.

64. E. N. van Kleffens, ambassador to the United States, to Dirk U. Stikker, minister of foreign affairs, 20 September 1948, in *NIB.* Vol. 15, p. 161.

65. John Morgan to H. Freeman Matthews, 7 August 1947, NA, RG 59, 856D.00/2–847; and Charles Reed to Benninghoff, 27 August 1948, NA, RG 59, 856D.00/8–2748; see also McMahon, *Colonialism and Cold War,* pp. 206–250.

66. H. J. Manschot, financial adviser to the Netherlands Indies Government, to minister without portfolio, L. Götzen, and chief financial officer, A. Treep, 29 September 1948, in *NIB.* Vol. 15, p. 260; van Kleffens an Stikker, 6 October 1948, in *NIB.* Vol. 15, 352f., 354f.; Sassen to van Mook, 7 October 1948, in *NIB.* Vol. 15, 371f.; and T. Elink Schuurman to Sassen, 11 October 1948, in *NIB.* Vol. 15, pp. 405–407

67. Kennan to Lovett and Acheson, 17 December 1948, NA, RG 59, Lot 64 D 563, Box 18, Folder Indonesia.

68. Sassen to van Roijen, 11 October 1948, in *NIB.* Vol. 15, pp. 422–424; Spoor to Kruls, 12 October 1948, in *NIB.* Vol. 15, pp. 429–431; and Notes by Stikker on his travel to Indonesia, 11 October 1948, in *NIB.* Vol. 15, pp. 639–643.

69. Beel to Sassen, 20 December 1948, in *NIB.* Vol. 16, p. 251.

70. Minutes of a meeting of the cabinet, 13 and 15 December 1948, in *NIB.* Vol. 16, pp. 114–119, 157–169; and Paul Hoffman to van Kleffens, 22 December 1948, in *NIB.* Vol. 16, 299f.

71. Van Kleffens to Stikker, 30 December 1948, in *NIB.* Vol. 16, pp. 432–440; Stikker to Cabinet, 14 January 1949, in *NIB.* Vol. 17, pp. 30–38; and CIA Intelligence Memorandum 113, "Consequences of Dutch 'police action' in Indonesia," 4 January 1949, HSTL, Truman Papers, National Security Council Files, CIA File, Daily Digest-March 1951, Intelligence Memos, January 1950–January 1951, Box 1.

72. Minutes of a meeting of the cabinet, 3 January 1949, in *NIB.* Vol. 16, pp. 502–507.

73. McMahon, *Colonialism and Cold War,* p. 273.

74. Van der Plas to Beel, 22 January 1949, in *NIB.* Vol. 17, pp. 178–180; Ide Anak Agung Gde Agung, Prime Minister of East Indonesia, to M. van der Goes van Naters, 22 January 1949, in *NIB.* Vol. 17, pp. 183–186; and Beel to H. J. van Maarseveen, Minister of Overseas Territories, 7 March 1949, in *NIB.* Vol. 18, pp. 53–56.

75. van den Doel, *Afscheid van Indië,* p. 336; and Ted Schouten, *Dwaalsporen. Oorlogsmisdaden in Nederlands-Indië.* Zutphen, the Netherlands: Alpha, 1995, p. 174.

76. Van Kleffens, the ambassador in the United States, regarded a "radical left-wing" White House as the source of all the problems. See van Kleffens to Stikker, 10 March 1949, in *NIB.* Vol. 18, p. 114; see also Memorandum of a Conversation between Acheson and Stikker, 31 March 1949, *FRUS, 1949.* Vol. 4, *Western Europe.* Washington, D.C.: U.S. Government Printing Office, 1975, pp. 258–261; see also Pierre van der Eng, "Marshall Aid As a Catalyst in the Decolonization of Indonesia, 1947–49." *Journal of Southeast Asian Studies* 19 (1988): 335–352.

77. van den Doel, *Afscheid van Indië,* p. 346.

78. Executive Committee of the "Vereeniging grooter Nederland actie ter bevordering van Nederlansche volksplantingen op Nieuw-Guinea" to van Mook, 11 March 1946, in *NIB.* Vol. 3, pp. 543–544; Minutes of a meeting of van Maarseveen with officials, 27 June 1949, in *NIB.* Vol. 19, pp. 172–175; and Jongejan, director of the business association of the Netherlands East Indies, to Götzen, 5 September 1949, in *NIB.* Vol. 19, pp. 697–698.

79. Ide Anak Agung Gde Agung, *Twenty Years Indonesian Foreign Policy, 1945–1965.* The Hague: Mouton, 1973, pp. 289–312; Evan Luard, *A History of the United Nations.* Vol. 2, *The Age of Decolonization, 1955–1965.* London: Macmillan, 1989, pp. 327–347; and Hans Meijer, *Den Haag-Djakarta: De Nederlands-Indonesische Betrekkingen, 1950–1962.* Utrecht: Het Spectrum, 1994.

## Chapter 7

1. This is not to deny the complex and uneven formation of "regional" relationships, nor prewar use of the term "*Südostasien*" by German scholars. See Amitav Acharya, *The Quest for Identity: International Relations of Southeast Asia.* Singapore: Oxford University Press, 2000; and *Southeast Asian Journal of Social Science* 27, no. 1 (1999), special edition on "Reconceptualizing Southeast Asia."

2. For 1949–1950, see William J. Duiker, *U.S. Containment Policy and the Conflict in Indochina.* Stanford, Calif.: Stanford University Press, 1994, pp. 61–90; Andrew Rotter, *The Path to Vietnam: Origins of the American Commitment to Southeast Asia.* Ithaca, N.Y.: Cornell University Press, 1989; and Karl Hack, *Defence and Decolonisation in Southeast Asia: Britain, Malaya and Singapore, 1941–1968.* London: Curzon, 2001, pp. 64–69.

3. Hack, *Defence and Decolonisation,* pp. 14–18, 56–69.

4. William G. Beasley, *Japanese Imperialism, 1894–1945.* Oxford: Clarendon, 1987; Ramon H. Myers and Mark R. Peattie, eds., *The Japanese Colonial Empire, 1895–1945.* Princeton, N.J.: Princeton University Press, 1984; and Mark R. Peattie, "The Japanese Empire, 1895–1945." In *Cambridge History of Japan,* ed. Peter Duus. Cambridge: Cambridge University Press, 1988, pp. 217–270.

5. Anthony Reid, "A Saucer Model of Southeast Asian Identity." *Southeast Asian Journal of Social Science* 27, no. 1 (1999): 17–18.

6. Albert Lau, *The Malayan Union Experiment.* Oxford: Oxford University Press, 1991; Hack, *Defence and Decolonisation,* p. 9; and *British Documents on the End of Empire.* Series B. 3 vols. Parts 1–3, *Malaya,* Anthony J. Stockwell, ed. London: HMSO, 1995, vol. 1, pp. li-lii, "1942 is the clearest turning point in the history of British Malaya: before that date policy was based on the belief in indefinite rule; afterwards the premise became that of eventual self-government."

7. For the feeling of the Japanese movement as almost one more, natural factor in a stream of Asian ferment, stretching from India to Japan, see U Maung Maung, *Burma and General Ne Win*. Rangoon: Religious Affairs Department Press, 1969, pp. 62–92. Already by 1939 the thakins' Dobama Asiayone was not alone in having links to paramilitary style organizations, such as the Letyon Tat (Army of the People), and the Rangoon University Students' Thanmani (Steel Corps).

8. A classic example of the complications was Britain's recognition, in early 1950, of the French-supported and Bảo Đại-led State of Vietnam. Other Asian powers Britain hoped to court could not but frown on such a move. See Nicholas Tarling, *Britain, Southeast Asia and the Onset of the Cold War, 1945–1950*. Cambridge: Cambridge University Press, 1998, pp. 315–412; and for the background on Britain's regional planning, see Tilman Remme, *Britain and Regional Cooperation in South-East Asia, 1945–49*. London: Routledge, 1995, especially pp. 133–216.

9. Hack, *Defence and Decolonisation*, pp. 35–50.

10. This tension was entrenched in British notions of the "dual mandate" of development and protection, often by combining British control of central levers with traditional rule via a collaborative if not "traditional" elite. Sir Frank Swettenham expressed this well in an 1896 speech, which stressed Britain's need to develop Malaya through immigration, while bettering the Malays. See Paul Kratoska, ed., *Honorable Intentions: Talks on the British Empire in South-East Asia Delivered at the Royal Colonial Institute, 1874–1928*. Singapore: Oxford University Press, 1983, pp. 170–211.

11. This developmental attitude avoids naive Hobson-Lenin type assumptions that · imperial policy makers responded to groups of companies or structural needs to export surplus capital, but acknowledges the "economic" element of imperial demands for standardization, bureaucratization, building larger units, and so on. This is my interpretation of K. Sinclair, "Hobson and Lenin in Johore." *Modern Asian Studies* 1 (1967): 335–352. For the Malay states, see also Jagjit Sing Sidhu, *Administration in the Federated Malay States, 1896–1920*. Kuala Lumpur: Oxford University Press, 1980.

12. For a recent survey of this "cleansing of anti-Japanese" Chinese in 1942, see Kevin Blackburn, "The Collective Memory of the Sook Ching Massacre and the Creation of the Civilian War Memorial of Singapore." *Journal of the Malayan Branch of the Royal Asiatic Society* 73, no. 2 (2000): 71–90.

13. Paul Kratoska, *The Japanese Occupation of Malaya, 1941–1945*. London: Allen and Unwin, 1998; P. Lim Pui Huen and Diana Wong, *War and Memory in Malaysia and Singapore*. Singapore: Institute of Southeast Asian Studies, 2000; and Alfred McCoy, ed., *Southeast Asia under Japanese Occupation*. New Haven, Conn.: Yale University Press, 1980.

14. Ritchie Ovendale, *The English-Speaking Alliance: Britain, the United States, the Dominions and the Cold War, 1945–51*. London: Allen and Unwin, 1985, pp. 145–184.

15. Ronald Hyam, "The Dynamics of British Imperial Policy, 1763–1963." *Journal of Imperial and Commonwealth History* 27, no. 2 (1999): 45. Even without the Cold War, however, Britain aimed at fostering good relations between successor elites and itself, rather than the West in general. It remained ambivalent about American interest in British colonies, including Malaya.

16. John Gallagher, *The Decline, Revival and Fall of the British Empire*. Cambridge: Cambridge University Press, 1982; and John Darwin, "Imperialism in De-

cline? British Imperial Policy Between the Wars." *Historical Journal* 23, no. 3 (1980): 657–679.

17. David Reynolds, *Britannia Overruled: British Policy and World Power in the Twentieth Century.* New York: Longman, 1991, pp. 173–174, 298–304; and John Darwin, *Britain and Decolonisation: The Retreat from Empire in the Post-war World.* Basingstoke: Macmillan, 1988, pp. 304–307.

18. Put another way, Britain saw itself managing the orderly, slow, emergence of a postcolonial Asian Third World of sovereign, democratic, free-trading nation-states, cognizant of Britain's experience and goodwill, if not exactly susceptible to outright British leadership. See Nicholas Tarling, *The Fall of Imperial Britain in South-East Asia.* Oxford: Oxford University Press, 1995, pp. 1–2, 197–207. Tarling's *Britain, Southeast Asia and the Onset of the Cold War* concentrates on Foreign Office documents that reinforce this general line of thought.

19. Karl Hack, "'Iron Claws on Malaya': The Historiography of the Malayan Emergency." *Journal of Southeast Asian Studies* 30, no. 1 (March 1999): 99–125. On the need to write the Emergency as a conflict between competing British and communist narratives, see also Karl Hack, "Corpses, Prisoners of War, and Captured Documents: British and Communist Narratives of the Malayan Emergency, and the Dynamics of Intelligence Transformation." In *The Clandestine Cold War in Asia, 1945–65,* ed. Richard Aldrich. London: Frank Cass, 2000, pp. 211–241.

20. Hack, *Defence and Decolonisation,* pp. 83–95. The fact that the plan had been aborted in 1941 in no way dissuaded Prime Minister Winston Churchill from relying on it again in 1951.

21. Marc Ferro points out that "decolonization" and "colonization" should not always be thought of as chronologically sequential, both coming together in cases such as Burma/Myanmar. A case could be made for seeing both as two sides of one process, that of the integration of areas "peripheral" to a global economy. See Marc Ferro, *Colonization: A Global History.* London: Routledge, 1997, p. ix.

22. Takashi Shirashi's notion of interwar Indonesia as in motion, learning, and struggling to translate Western forms of organization might be seen in this context of "decolonization" as mastering "discourses," whether for anticolonial purposes or, as with Raden Kartini, for modernization per se. Were Budi Utomo and the Indian National Congress initially aimed at increasing such transference, becoming anticolonial as they perceived unnecessary obstruction relative to their potential? See Takashi Shirashi, *An Age in Motion: Popular Radicalism in Java, 1912–1926.* Ithaca, N.Y.: Cornell Southeast Asia Program, 1990. Is the predominant use of "discourse" too narrowly cultural and/or too problematically reliant on literary sources of dubious representativeness to realize the concept's full potential? Are concepts such as "Orientalism" too one-sidedly fixated on Western stereotyping and representation, at the expense of questions about practical Asian attempts to learn, adapt, and challenge to discourses? See Edward Said, *Culture and Imperialism.* New York: Vintage, 1993.

23. In this vein, Chris Dixon's *South East Asia in the World Economy* (Cambridge: Cambridge University Press, 1991) should perhaps be seen as one of the classics of regional imperialism and decolonization.

24. For the latter, see Auguste Pavie, *Pavie Mission Exploration Work, Laos, Cambodia, Siam, Yunnan, and Vietnam.* Trans. Walter E. J. Tips. The Pavie Mission Indochina Papers, 1879–1895. Bangkok: White Lotus, 1999.

25. For Peter J. Cain and Anthony G. Hopkins, decolonization involved territories gaining access to, and the ability to handle independently, a variety of sources of

financial services and investment. See Peter J. Cain and Anthony G. Hopkins, *British Imperialism: Crisis and Deconstruction, 1914–1990.* London: Longman, 1993, pp. 300–315, especially 308–313; see also Tarling, *Fall of Imperial Britain.*

26. John A. Gallagher and Ronald E. Robinson, "The Imperialism of Free Trade." *Economic History Review* 6, no. 2 (1953): 1–15; and Ronald E. Robinson, "Non-European Foundations of European Imperialism: Sketch for a Theory of Collaboration." In *Studies in the Theory of Imperialism,* ed. Richard Owen and Bob Sutcliffe. London: Longman, 1972, pp. 117–140. For the "official mind," see John Gallagher, Ronald E. Robinson, and Alice Denny, *Africa and the Victorians: The Official Mind of Imperialism.* London: Macmillan, 1961. The supremacy of "geopolitics" in the official mind comes in Ronald Hyam, "The Primacy of Geopolitics: The Dynamics of British Imperial Policy, 1763–1963." *Journal of Imperial and Commonwealth Politics* 27, no. 2 (1999): 27–52. He posits two levels, metropolitan and non-European. The non-European provides pressures and initiatives, often because of economic or nationalist pressure. The metropolis then takes the decisions based on geopolitical considerations, with the "man on the spot" acting as a telegraph relay or link. This would be more convincing for decolonization if, say, Brunei had had any strategic significance or bases in Kenya were scuttled in the face of accelerating decolonization.

27. W. David McIntyre, *The Imperial Frontier in the Tropics, 1865–75.* London: Macmillan, 1967, pp. 200–206.

28. Andrew Porter, *European Imperialism, 1860–1914.* London: Macmillan, 1994; and Peter J. Cain and Anthony G. Hopkins, *British Imperialism: Innovation and Expansion, 1688–1914.* London: Longman, 1991, pp. 5–17. For a very sensible article on what Vladimir Lenin meant, see A. M. Eckstein, "Is There a 'Hobson-Lenin Thesis' on Late Nineteenth-Century Colonial Expansion?" *Economic History Review* 44, no. 2 (1991): 297–318.

29. The same held true of decolonization, with London being very anxious to defend general interests, such as Malaya's dollar earnings or Hong Kong's economic value, but often being disdainful of businessmen individually. See Nicholas White, *Business, Government, and the End of Empire: Malaya, 1942–1957.* Kuala Lumpur: Oxford University Press, 1996; John Darwin, "Decolonisation and the End of Empire." *Oxford History of the British Empire.* Vol. 5, *Historiography,* ed. Robin Winks. Oxford: Oxford University Press, 1999, pp. 545–546; Hyam, "Primacy of Geopolitics"; and Raymond E. Dumett, ed., *Gentlemanly Capitalism and British Imperialism: The New Debate on Empire.* London: Longman, 1999.

30. Jeffrey Pickering stresses the conjunction between "external shock" and internal coalitional changes. See Jeffrey Pickering, *Britain's Withdrawal from East of Suez: The Politics of Retrenchment.* London: Macmillan, 1998, pp. 150–176.

31. For Kuala Lumpur and the Chinese power brokers, see J. M. Gullick, *A History of Kuala Lumpur, 1855–1939.* Selangor: Journal of the Malaysian Branch of the Royal Asiatic Society, 2000. Though these had their parallels in Malacca, the sheer numbers and power of Chinese organization changed things.

32. The term is from, and the issues are discussed economically and skillfully, in Richard Aldrich, *The Key to the South: Britain, the United States, and Thailand during the Approach of the Pacific War, 1929–1942.* Kuala Lumpur: Oxford University Press, 1993, pp. 1–24.

33. Historians of decolonization, for instance, rarely cite works such as Fred W. Riggs, *Thailand: The Modernization of a Bureaucratic Polity.* Honolulu: East-West Center, 1966.

34. Hack, *Defence and Decolonisation*, pp. 193–195; and Duiker, *U.S. Containment Policy*, pp. 194–248. True to type, the latter calls the pages on Diệm, "Experiment in Nation-Building," yet talks mainly of high politics and strategic hamlets, which concern security structures, political management, and state-building, but not "nation-building."

35. Michael Adas, *Machines As Measures of Men: Science, Technology, and Ideologies of Western Dominance*. Ithaca, N.Y.: Cornell University Press, 1989; and Michael E. Latham, *Modernization As Ideology: American Social Science and "Nation-Building" in the Kennedy Era*. Chapel Hill: University of North Carolina Press, 2000.

36. John W. Cell, "Colonial Rule." In *The Oxford History of the British Empire*. Vol. 4, *The Twentieth Century*, ed. Judith M. Brown and William Roger Louis. Oxford: Oxford University Press, 1999, pp. 232–254.

37. Clive Trocki, *Opium, Empire and the Global Political Economy: A Study of the Asian Opium Trade, 1750–1950*. London: Routledge, 1999; Donald Nonini, *British Colonial Rule and the Resistance of the Malay Peasantry, 1900–1957*. New Haven, Conn.: Yale University Southeast Asian Studies, 1992; Li Dun Jen, *British Malaya: An Economic Analysis*. Kuala Lumpur: INSAN, 1992; and Lenore Manderson, *Sickness and the State: Health and Illness in Colonial Malaya, 1870–1940*. Cambridge: Cambridge University Press, 1996.

38. For instance, see Christine B. N. Chin, *In Service and Servitude: Foreign Female Domestic Workers and the Malaysian "Modernity" Project*. New York: Columbia University Press, 1993.

39. Jan Aart Scholte, "The International Construction of Indonesia Nationhood, 1930–1950." In *Imperial Policy and Southeast Asian Nationalism, 1930–1957*, ed. Hans Antlöv and Stein Tønnesson. London: Curzon, 1995, pp. 191–226; and Elsbeth Locher-Scholten, "Dutch Expansion in the Indonesian Archipelago around 1900 and the Imperialism Debate." *Journal of Southeast Asian Studies* 25, no. 1 (1994): 91–111.

40. Ben Batson and Paul Kratoska, "Nationalism and Modernist Reform." In *The Cambridge History of Southeast Asia*. Vol. 2. Pt. 2. Ed. Nicholas Tarling. Cambridge: Cambridge University Press, 1992, pp. 249–324; and Anthony J. Stockwell, "Imperialism and Nationalism in Southeast Asia." In *Oxford History of the British Empire*. Vol. 4, *The Twentieth Century*, ed. Judith M. Brown and William Roger Louis. Oxford: Oxford University Press, 1999, pp. 465–489.

41. Hugh Tinker, in including Burma in "South Asia," writes that "Pakistan, India, Bangladesh, Burma and Ceylon . . . have much in common; all find their origins in the ancient Indic civilisation" and together they formed "the British Empire bloc in Indian Ocean which was at the heart of that worldwide empire." See Hugh Tinker, *South Asia: A Short History*. Honolulu: University of Hawaii Press, 1990, p. xi

42. Stockwell, "Imperialism and Nationalism in Southeast Asia," pp. 465–489.

43. From different angles there are U Maung Maung, *Burmese Nationalist Movements, 1940–1948*. Edinburgh: Kiscadale, 1989; and Hugh Tinker, ed., *Burma: The Struggle for Independence, 1944–1948*. London: HMSO, 1983–1984.

44. Hack, *Defence and Decolonisation*, pp. 43–49, 57–60. The four were the Malayan Union colony, Sarawak, North Borneo, and Singapore. Of these, only Singapore had formally had colonial status before, as part of the Straits Settlements colony.

45. See Cabinet meeting, 31 December 1946, minute 4, Public Record Office, London, Cab128/CM(46)106, discussing whether to announce Britain would leave

India by a set date, as done on February 20, 1947. In the discussion, it was suggested that since departure was "inevitable," Britain should ride the tide in order to "claim credit" that could be cashed in for influence.

46. See Lau, *Malayan Union Experiment;* and Anthony J. Stockwell, *British Policy and Malay Politics during the Malayan Union Experiment, 1942–1948.* Kuala Lumpur: Journal of the Malayan Branch of the Royal Asiatic Society, 1979.

47. Hack, *Defence and Decolonisation,* pp. 137–138, 243–245.

48. See especially Ronald Robinson, "The Non-European Foundations of European Imperialism." In *Studies in the Theory of Imperialism,* ed. Richard Owen and Bob Sutcliffe. London: Longman, 1972, pp. 117–140. For the idea of "disimperialism," with elites in empire and metropolis simultaneously losing interest in continuing empire, see Robert F. Holland, *European Decolonisation, 1918–1981.* Basingstoke: Macmillan, 1985.

49. Hack, *Defence and Decolonisation,* pp. 131–142, 243–245, 275–276.

50. R. H. W. Reece, *The Name of Brooke: The End of White Raja Rule in Sarawak.* Kuala Lumpur: Oxford University Press, 1982; Vernon L. Porritt, *British Colonial Rule in Sarawak, 1946–1963.* Kuala Lumpur: Oxford University Press, 1997; and Chin Ung-Ho, *Chinese Politics in Sarawak: A Study of the Sarawak United People's Party.* Kuala Lumpur: Oxford University Press, 1996.

51. Greg Poulgrain, *The Genesis of Konfrontasi: Malaysia, Brunei, Indonesia, 1945–1965.* London: Hurst, 1998, pp. 87–111, 206–230.

52. Clive Christie, *A Modern History of Southeast Asia: Decolonisation, Nationalism and Separatism.* London: Tauris, 1996, pp. 28–52.

53. Anthony C. Milner, "Colonial Records History: British Malaya." *Kajian Malaysia* 4, no. 2 (December 1986): 1–18; and Yeo Kim Wah, "The Milner Version of History—A Rider." *Kajian Malaysia* 5, no. 1 (June 1987): 1–28. For a restatement of the periphery against the official mind, see D. Throup, "The Historiography of Decolonisation." *Institute of Commonwealth Studies Paper* (January 1991): 3, 4, 17–18.

54. A. B. Shamsul, *From British to Bumiputera Rule: Local Politics and Rural Development in Peninsular Malaysia.* Singapore: Institute of Southeast Asian Studies, 1986; Nonini, *British Colonial Rule;* and Loh Kok Wah, *Beyond the Tin Mines: Coolies, Squatters and New Villagers in the Kinta Valley, Malaysia, c. 1880–1980.* Singapore: Oxford University Press, 1988.

55. Tan Liok Ee, *The Rhetoric of Bangsa and Minzu: Community and Nation in Tension—The Malay Peninsula, 1900–1955.* Melbourne: Monash University, 1988; W. R. Roff, *The Origins of Malay Nationalism.* Kuala Lumpur: Oxford University Press, 1994; Ariffin Omar, *Bangsa Melayu: Malay Concepts of Democracy and Community, 1945–1950.* Oxford: Oxford University Press, 1993; and Anthony C. Milner, *The Invention of Politics in Colonial Malaya: Contesting Nationalism and the Expansion of the Public Sphere.* Cambridge: Cambridge University Press, 1994. On publishing in the 1950s, see Khoo Khay Kim, *Malay Society: Transformation and Democratisation.* Petaling Jaya, Malaysia: Pelanduk, 1995, pp. 280–303; and for changing Malay politics, see Cheah Boon Kheng, "The Erosion of Ideological Hegemony and Royal Power and the Rise of Postwar Malay Nationalism, 1945–46." *Journal of Southeast Asian Studies* 19, no. 1 (March 1988): 1–27.

56. Cheah Boon Kheng, *Red Star over Malaya: Resistance and Social Conflict during and after the Japanese Occupation, 1941–1946.* Singapore: Singapore University Press, 1983. For a summary of Malaysian writing on these issues, see Cheah

Boon Kheng, "Writing Indigenous History in Malaya: A Survey on Approaches and Problems." *Crossroads* 10, no. 2 (1996): 49–52.

57. Tim Harper, *The End of Empire and the Making of Malaya.* Cambridge: Cambridge University Press, 1999, pp. 274–307.

58. Hack, *Defence and Decolonisation,* p. 5.

59. Harper, *End of Empire,* pp. 142–143.

60. Hack, *Defence and Decolonisation,* pp. 1–5.

61. Anthony Short gives a subtle survey of this, highlighting Admiral Lord Louis Mountbatten's directive of June 2, 1945, that no one should suffer for "political opinions honestly held" even if anti-British, so that Aung San's troops could take part in the Rangoon victory parade in Japanese uniforms. See Anthony Short, "Pictures at an Exhibition." In *Imperial Policy and Southeast Asian Nationalism, 1930–1957,* ed. Hans Antlöv and Stein Tønnesson. London: Curzon, 1995, pp. 15–33

62. For the argument that once broad British strategy was set the micromanagement of local politics and of maneuvering for the best collaborators, to channel their actions, or in the face of effective nationalist challenge, to concede in the hope of postcolonial credit, often predominated in British minds, see Hack, *Defence and Decolonisation,* pp. 131–132, 139–143, 240.

63. See Mark Curtis, *The Ambiguities of Power: British Foreign Policy since 1945.* London: Zed, 1995, pp. 1–50, 56–65; Malcolm Caldwell and Mohamed Amin, eds., *Malaya: The Making of a Neo-Colony.* Nottingham: Bertrant Russell Peace Foundation for Spokesman Books, 1977; Frank Furedi, *Colonial Wars and the Politics of Third World Nationalism.* London: Tauris, 1994; and Michael R. Stenson, "The Malayan Union and the Historians." *Journal of Southeast Asian History* 10, no. 2 (1969): 344–354. Poulgrain argues that British Petroleum Malaya helped shape policy in favor of a compliant sultan and against the less reliable Partai Rakyat Brunei. See Poulgrain, *Genesis of Konfrontasi.* For a Marxist account, see Nonini, *British Colonial Rule;* Stenson, "Malayan Union and the Historians," pp. 344–354; Michael R. Stenson, *The 1948 Communist Revolt in Malaya: A Note on Historical Sources and Interpretation.* Singapore: Institute of Southeast Asian Studies, 1970; Michael R. Stenson, *Industrial Conflict in Malaya: Prelude to the Communist Revolt of 1948.* Oxford: Oxford University Press, 1971; and Cheah Boon Kheng, *The Masked Comrades: A Study of the Communist United Front in Malaya, 1945–48.* Singapore: Times Books International, 1979. Police support of capitalists included enforcing trespass laws to exclude unionists from estates and breaking up pickets and demonstrations.

64. Hack, *Defence and Decolonisation,* p. 3; see also Anthony J. Stockwell, "Malaya: The Making of a Neo-Colony." In *Managing the Business of Empire: Essays in Honor of David Fieldhouse,* ed. Peter Burroughs and Anthony J. Stockwell. London: Cass, 1998, pp. 138–156; Nonini, *British Colonial Rule,* pp. 143–165; and Harper, *End of Empire,* p.363.

65. Hack, *Defence and Decolonisation,* pp. 277–278, 293n27; and Albert Lau, *A Moment of Anguish: Singapore in Malaysia and the Politics of Disengagement.* Singapore: Times Books International, 1998.

66. Hack, *Defence and Decolonisation,* pp. 234–243.

67. John Darwin, "Imperialism in Decline? British Imperial Policy between the Wars." *Historical Journal* 23, no. 3 (1980): 657–679; and John Darwin, "Decolonisation and the End of Empire." *Oxford History of the British Empire.* Vol. 5, *Historiography,* ed. Robin Winks. Oxford: Oxford University Press, 1999, pp. 545–546.

68. *British Documents on the End of Empire.* Series B, 3 vols., Parts 1–3, *Malaya,* Anthony J. Stockwell, ed. London: HMSO, 1995, vol. 3, p. 189.

69. For this withdrawal process and its impact on Singapore, see Malcolm Murfett et al., *Between Two Oceans: A Military History of Singapore from First Settlement to Final British Withdrawal.* Oxford: Oxford University Press, 1999, pp. 306–330.

70. Hack, *Defence and Decolonisation,* pp. 272–298; John Baylis, "'Greenwoodery' and British Defence Policy." *International Affairs* 62, no. 3 (1986): 443–457; Reynolds, *Britannia Overruled,* pp. 163–169, 227–230; and John Darwin, *Britain and Decolonisation: The Retreat from Empire in the Post-war World.* London: Macmillan, 1988, p. 294.

71. Darwin, *Britain and Decolonisation,* p. 7.

72. Anthony Reid, preface to *The Quest for Identity: International Relations of Southeast Asia,* by Amitav Acharya. Singapore: Oxford University Press, 2000, p. v.

73. Wilson to Johnson, 15 January 1968, Prem13/1999, Public Record Office.

74. Quoted in Ritchie Ovendale, ed., *British Defence Policy since 1945.* Manchester: Manchester University Press, 1994, p. 144.

75. Chin Kin Wah, *The Defence of Malaysia and Singapore: The Transformation of a Security System, 1957–1971.* Cambridge: Cambridge University Press, 1983.

76. Marc Ferro, *Colonization: A Global History.* London: Routledge, 1997, p. 1, see also chapter 1.

77. For the Emergency origins, see Harper, *Malaya and the End of Empire,* see especially pp. 94–148.

78. The issue of the Chinese as outsiders is examined in Daniel Chirot and Anthony Reid, eds., *Essential Outsiders: Chinese and Jews in the Modern Transformation of Southeast Asia and Central Europe.* Seattle: University of Washington Press, 1997. This fails, however, to differentiate between countries where the Chinese position as a small minority was analogous to Europe's Jews, such as in Indonesia, and where there were large-scale nineteenth-century settlers replicating language, clan, and religious organizations, such as in Singapore.

79. Christie works through some of this "unfinished" decolonization. See Christie, *Modern History of Southeast Asia.* His approach hints at a regional "decolonization" that involves permutations from modus vivendi to racial violence and jihad, right through to the current events in East Timor, West Papua, and Maluku.

## Chapter 8

1. Theodore Friend, *Between Two Empires: The Ordeal of the Philippines, 1929–1946.* New Haven, Conn.: Yale University Press, 1965, p. 170.

2. Report by the Chancellor of the Duchy of Lancaster, 29 October 1941, WP (41) 286, Cabinet Office (hereafter CAB) 66/20, Public Record Office (PRO), London.

3. Anita Inder Singh, *The Limits of British Influence: South Asia and the Anglo-American Relationship, 1947–1956.* London: Pinter, 1993, p. 33.

4. H. F. C. Walsh, Foreign Secretary, 26 March 1942, Foreign Office (hereafter FO) 371/31751 (F4969/90/61), PRO.

5. Telegram, 27 June 1946, 1097, FO 371/53799 (F9648/1/61), PRO.

6. FE (O) (46) 52, 16 April 1946, enclosing draft memorandum, "British Foreign Policy in the Far East," 31 December 1945, CAB 134/280, PRO.

7. Christopher Thorne, *The Issue of War: The Far Eastern War—States and Societies, 1941–1945.* London: Unwin, 1986, p. 134.

8. Angus Madisson, "Dutch Income in and from Indonesia, 1700–1938." *Modern Asian Studies* 23, no. 4 (1989): 645–670.

9. Thomas A. August, "Colonial Policy and Propaganda: The Popularization of the 'Idee Coloniale' in France, 1919–1939." Ph.D. thesis, University of Madison-Wisconsin, 1978, p. 68.

10. Oey Hong Lee, *War and Diplomacy in Indonesia, 1945–1950.* Townsville: James Cook University, 1981, p. 77n.

11. Thomas Henry Silcock, *The Commonwealth Economy in Southeast Asia.* Durham, N.C.: Duke University Press, 1959, pp. 78–79.

12. D. Bruce Marshall, *The French Colonial Myth and Constitution-Making in the Fourth Republic.* New Haven, Conn.: Yale University Press, 1973, p. 106.

13. Telegram, 8 May 1947, 1087, FO 371/63591 (F6393/45/62), PRO.

14. Telegram, 20 May, 273, FO 371/63593 (6905/45/62), PRO.

15. Minute by Frank Roberts, 18 December 1947, FO 371/63629 (F16665/45/62), PRO.

16. Minutes, 21 December 1946, n.d., FO 371/53969 (F18076/8/61), PRO.

17. Christopher M. Andrew and Alexander Sydney Kanya-Forstner, *France Overseas: The Great War and the Climax of French Imperial Expansion.* London: Thames and Hudson, 1981, p. 246.

18. Minute, 18 November 1946, FO 371/54046 (F16726/1109/61), PRO.

19. Minute, 7 January 1947, FO 371/63547 (F1969/1969/61), PRO.

20. Minutes, 27 April, 17 May 1948, FO 371/69689 (F5922/286/61), PRO.

21. PMM (48) 3rd, 12 October 1948, CAB 133/88, PRO.

22. FE (O) (48), 8th, 4 December 1948, CAB 134/285, PRO.

23. FE (O) (48) 34 Revise, 10 December 1948, CAB 134/285, PRO.

24. Nicholas Mansergh, ed., *Documents and Speeches on British Commonwealth Affairs, 1931–1952.* London: Oxford University Press, 1953, p. 1179.

25. Telegram, 31 January 1949, X197, DO [Dominion Office] 35/2858, PRO.

26. M. J. MacDonald/M. E. Dening, 15 March 1949, FO 371/76031 (F5016/1072/61), PRO.

27. Dening, 4 April 1949, FO 371/76031 (F2191/1072/61), PRO.

28. Minute, 21 April 1949, FO 371/76032 (F5863/1072/61), PRO.

29. Minutes of a meeting with Mr. MacDonald and Sir A. Nye, 24 May 1949, FO 371/76034 (F8338/1075/61), PRO.

30. FMM (50) 2nd, 9 January 1950, CAB 133/78, PRO.

31. FMM (50) 8th, 12 January, CAB 133/78, PRO.

32. Telegram, 20 December 1948, 1803, FO 371/69547 (F177714/33/10), PRO.

33. Graves/Dening, 16 April 1949, FO 371/76023 (F5743/1023/61), PRO.

34. CM (49) 62nd, 27 October, CAB 128/16, PRO.

35. Peter Lowe, *The Origins of the Korean War.* London: Longman, 1986, p. 177; and Anthony Farrar-Hockley, *The British Part in the Korean War.* Vol. 1. London: HMSO, 1990, pp. 107, 110.

36. CP (50) 200, 30 August 1950, CAB 129/41, PRO.

37. CP (50) 200, 30 August 1950, CAB 129/41, PRO.

38. Anthony Farrar-Hockley, *The British Part in the Korean War.* Vol. 2. London: HMSO, 1990, p. 85.

39. Frank Farudi, "Creating a Breathing Space: The Political Management of Colonial Emergencies." In *Emergencies and Disorder in the European Empires after 1945,* ed. Robert Holland. London: Cass, 1994, pp. 96, 104.

40. MacDonald/ Eden, 9 June 1952, 34, FO 371/101012 (FB 1041/102), PRO.

41. Minute, 3 May 1951, FO 371/93028 (FZ 1071/1), PRO.

42. Minute, 20 October 1951, FO 371/93028 (FZ 1071/4), PRO.

43. Minute, 20 October 1951, FO 371/93028 (FZ 1071/4), PRO.

44. Brief for Foreign Secretary, 3 November 1951, FO 371/939028 (FZ 1071/3), PRO.

45. Memorandum, 5 December 1952, FO 371/105179 (F1022/1), PRO.

46. Telegram, 19 April 1954, 1696, FO 371/112053 (DF1071/238), PRO.

47. Minute, 18 September 1954, FO 371/111888 (D1074/663), PRO.

48. Minute, 25 November 1954, FO 371/111893 (D1074/762), PRO.

## Chapter 9

1. Mohamed Noordin Sopiee, *From Malayan Union to Singapore*. Kuala Lumpur: Penerbit Universiti Malaya, 1974, pp. 125–128.

2. See Mohamed Noordin Sopiee, "The Advocacy of Malaysia—Before 1961." *Modern Asian Studies* 7, no. 4 (1973): 717–732.

3. Tunku Abdul Rahman, "Formation of Malaysia: The Trend towards Merger Cannot be Reversed," 2 March 1975. In *Looking Back: Monday Musings and Memories,* by Tunku Abdul Rahman Putra. Kuala Lumpur: Pustaka Antara, 1977, p. 77.

4. David Marshall, *Singapore's Struggle for Nationhood, 1945–1959*. Singapore: University Education Press, 1971, p. 12; and Record of Conversation between Australian Secretary of State and Lim Yew Hock (Chief Minister), 30–31 October 1957, in A1838/318, 3024/1/7, PT 1, Australian National Archives.

5. For a summary of such views, see Anthony J. Stockwell, "Malaysia: The Making of a Neo-Colony?" *Journal of Imperial and Commonwealth History* 26, no. 2 (1998): 141.

6. Stockwell, "Malaysia," p. 152.

7. Stockwell, "Malaysia," p. 152.

8. Karl Hack, *Defence and Decolonisation in Southeast Asia: Britain, Malaya and Singapore, 1941–1968.* London: Curzon, 2001, p. 275; see also Matthew Jones, "Creating Malaysia: Singapore Security, the Borneo Territories, and the Contours of British Policy, 1961–63." *Journal of Imperial and Commonwealth History* 28, no. 2 (2000): 85–109.

9. This was clearly the view of policy makers in London as well as the men on the ground—the governors, high commissioners, and military commanders. For instance, see the memoirs of Robert Noel Turner, a senior civil servant who served in the Borneo Territories in the 1950s. Robert Noel Turner, "From the Depths of My Memories." MSS. Brit. Emp.S. 454, Rhodes House Library, Oxford.

10. Quoted in John Drysdale, *Singapore: Struggle for Success*. Singapore: Times Books International, 1984, p. 259.

11. See Nicholas Tarling, "'Some Rather Nebulous Capacity': Lord Killearn's Appointment in Southeast Asia." *Modern Asian Studies* 20, no. 3 (1986): 559.

12. [Malaya]: minute by J. J. Paskin on the question of closer constitutional association between the Federation of Malaya and Singapore, 10 December 1952, in David Goldsworthy, ed., *British Documents on the End of Empire*. Series A. Vol. 3, *The Conservative Government and the End of Empire, 1951–1957, Part II: Politics and Administration.* London: HMSO, 1994, p. 377.

13. Greg Poulgrain, *The Genesis of Konfrontasi: Malaysia, Brunei, Indonesia, 1945–65*. London: Hurst, 1998.

14. For a discussion of British foreign policy to Malaya in the late 1950s, see Archana Sharma, *British Policy towards Malaysia, 1957–67*. London: Sangam, 1993, pp. 55–61.

15. Malcolm MacDonald was commissioner-general from 1949 to 1952. See Sopiee, *From Malayan Union to Singapore Separation*, p. 128.

16. White Paper on Detachment of Singapore from Straits Settlements, Cmd. 6274, January 1946.

17. Paper on "Greater Malaysia," n.d., Dominion Office (DO) 169/247, Public Record Office (PRO), London.

18. Paper on "Greater Malaysia," DO 169/247, PRO.

19. "Proposals for a Wider Association between the British Borneo Territories, Singapore and the Federation of Malaya," n.d., Colonial Office (CO) 1030/980, PRO.

20. "Proposals for a Wider Association between the British Borneo Territories, Singapore and the Federation of Malaya," CO 1030/980, PRO.

21. Record of conversation between the Australian Commissioner in Singapore, Mr. R. L. Harry and Sir Robert Scott, 26 July 1957, in A1838/318, Singapore Relations with the UK, item 3024/11/51, PT 1.

22. Papers of William Goode, Box 5, File 5, Rhodes House Library.

23. Notes of the Future of Borneo Territories, n.d., CO 1030/977, PRO.

24. "Proposals for a Wider Association between the British Borneo Territories, Singapore and the Federation of Malaya," CO 1030/980, PRO.

25. The Papers of Sir William Goode, Box 4, File 5, Rhodes House Library, Oxford University.

26. Turner, "From the Depths of My Memory."

27. "Background to the Greater Malaysia Plan," a report by M. J. Moynihan, deputy UK High Commissioner to Malaya, 20 October 1961, Prime Minister's Files (PREM) 11/3422, PRO.

28. Note to Prime Minister, "Singapore, the Malayan Federation and the Borneo Territories," 17 April 1961, PREM 11/3418, PRO.

29. Memorandum by the Secretary of State for the Colonies on "Possibility of an Association of the British Borneo Territories with the Federation of Malaya and the State of Singapore," to the Colonial Policy Committee, April 1961, DO 169/25, PRO.

30. "Possibility of an Association of the British Borneo Territories with the Federation of Malaya and the State of Singapore," a memorandum submitted by the Secretary of State for the Colonies, April 1961, to Cabinet Colonial Policy, CPC (61), DO 169/25, PRO.

31. Lord Selkirk, United Kingdom Commissioner General for Southeast Asia to Iain Mcleod, 27 June 1961, PREM 11/3418, PRO.

32. Report of Joint Planning Staff, 19 June 1961, DO 169/25, PRO.

33. Chiefs of Staff Committee Meeting, "Military Implications of Establishing Malaysia without Singapore and Possibly without Brunei," n.d., DO 160/221, PRO.

34. Han Fook Kwang, Warren Fernandez, and Sumiko Tan, *Lee Kuan Yew: The Man and His Ideas*. Singapore: Singapore Press Holding, 1998.

35. Economic Relations between Singapore and Malaya, n.d., CO 1030/972, PRO.

36. Proceedings of the Singapore Legislative Assembly, *Legislative Assembly Debates: Official Report 1955–1965*, 8 October 1958, col. 804.

37. "An Assessment of the Present Situation and the Future Outlook in Singapore,"

Department of External Affairs, Canberra, 20 August 1957, "Singapore—Internal Affairs," A1838/318, item 3024/1/7, PT 1.

38. Han, Fernandez, and Tan, *Lee Kuan Yew,* p. 70.

39. Han, Fernandez, and Tan, *Lee Kuan Yew,* p. 280

40. Lee Kuan Yew, speaking in the Singapore Legislative Assembly, *Legislative Assembly Debates: Official Report 1955–1965,* 30 July 1963, col. 301.

41. M. J. Moynihan, to Commonwealth Relations Office, 12 October 1961, DO 169/30, PRO; and the Tunku's speech in Parliament on 16 October 1961, as given to the press.

42. Draft brief for Prime Minister's Conference, 13 February 1961, CO 1030/978, PRO.

43. Proposals for a Wider Association between the British Borneo Territories, Singapore and the Federation of Malaya, n.d., CO 1030/980, PRO.

44. *Straits Times,* 25 September 1960.

45. Paper on the future on the Federation of Malaya, Singapore and the Borneo Territories, n.d., CO 1030/979, PRO.

46. Paper on the future on the Federation of Malaya, Singapore and the Borneo Territories, CO 1030/979, PRO.

47. Note of a meeting between UK delegation and Singapore delegation on Internal Security Council, which took place on Saturday, as enclosed in Acting UK Commissioner, Singapore, to Secretary of State, Colonial Office, 28 June 1960, no. 256, CO 1030/977, PRO.

48. Selkirk to Secretary of State, CO, 2 May 1961, no. 135, CO 1030/979, PRO.

49. Note of a meeting between UK delegation and Singapore delegation on Internal Security Council, 28 June 1960, no. 256, CO 1030/977, PRO.

50. Note of a meeting between UK delegation and Singapore delegation on Internal Security Council, 28 June 1960, no. 256, CO 1030/977, PRO.

51. Lee Kuan Yew, National Day Rally Address at the Padang, on 3 June 1961.

52. Tunku Abdul Rahman to Commonwealth Relations Office (CRO), 16 August 1961, PREM 11/3418, PRO.

53. Although the Tunku had effectively developed a form of interracial cooperation with which he was able to win independence from the British and maintain the government of the federation, he and his Malay ministers had always maintained that the interests of the Malays were paramount and would never agree to anything that would result in the political subordination of the Malay race. See A. J. Brown, Kuala Lumpur, to Bailly, CRO, 13 July 1961, DO 169/10, PRO.

54. British High Commissioner in the Federation of Malaya to the Secretary of State for Commonwealth Relations, "Federation of Malaya: Background to the Greater Malaysia Plan," 20 October 1961, DO 169/30, PRO; see also note of meeting in Colonial Office on "Relations between the Federation of Malaya and Singapore," 26 July 1960, CO 1030/972, PRO.

55. Selkirk to Mcleod, 27 June 1961, PREM 11/3418, PRO.

56. Note by Moynihan on Malaysia, 12 October 1961, DO 169/30, PRO.

57. The Future of the Borneo Territories, n.d., CO 1030/977, PRO.

58. "Malayan Attitude to 'Grand Design' and Singapore," A. J. Brown, High Commissioner's Office, Kuala Lumpur, to Bailly, CRO, 13 July 1961, DO 169/10, PRO.

59. "Malayan Attitude to 'Grand Design' and Singapore," Brown to Bailly, 13 July 1961, DO 169/10, PRO.

60. Note by Colonial Office for Cabinet Committee on Greater Malaysia: Draft Brief for Minister on Race in the Borneo Territories, 7 November 1961, CO 1030/1003, PRO.

61. Tory to Sandys, 1 December 1960, CO 1030/978, PRO.

62. "Malayan Attitude to 'Grand Design' and Singapore," Brown to Bailly, 13 July 1961, DO 169/10, PRO.

63. Memorandum no. 1020, Critchley to Secretary, Department of External Affairs, 14 July 1960, A1838/333, item 3006/10/4, PT 1.

64. Critchley to Secretary, Department of External Affairs, on his private conversation with Razak, n.d., A/1838/280, item 3027/2/1, PT 1.

65. Record of Conversation between Lee Kuan Yew and P. B. C. Moore, United Kingdom Commission in Singapore, 28 April 1961, DO 169/25, PRO.

66. Sopiee, *From Malayan Union to Singapore Separation,* p. 138.

67. British High Commissioner in the Federation of Malaya to the Secretary of State for Commonwealth Relations, "Federation of Malaya: Background to the Greater Malaysia Plan," 20 October 1961, DO 169/30, PRO.

68. Reported in telegram from British Commission in Kuala Lumpur to Commonwealth Relations Office, 6 November 1961, DO 169/30, PRO.

69. KL to CRO, 6 November 1961, DO 169/30, PRO.

70. Selkirk to Macmillan, telegram 49, 3 October 1961, PREM 11/3422, PRO.

## Chapter 10

1. Richard Stubbs, *Hearts and Minds in Guerrilla Warfare: The Malayan Emergency, 1948–1960.* Singapore: Oxford University Press, 1993, p. 250; Harry Miller, *Jungle War in Malaya: The Campaign against Communism, 1948–60.* London: Arthur Barker, 1972, pp. 75–76; and Donald Mackay, *The Malayan Emergency, 1948–60: The Domino That Stood.* London: Brassey's, 1997, p. 152.

2. Thomas R. Mockaitis, *British Counterinsurgency, 1919–1960.* London: Macmillan, 1990.

3. Richard Clutterbuck, *Riot and Revolution in Singapore and Malaya, 1945–1963.* London: Faber and Faber, 1973; and Anthony Short, *The Communist Insurrection in Malaya, 1948–60.* London: Mueller, 1975, pp. 502–503.

4. Robert Thompson, *Defeating Communist Insurgency: Lessons from Malaya and Vietnam.* London: Chatto and Windus, 1966, pp. 50–58; and Mockaitis, *British Counterinsurgency.*

5. John Coates, *Suppressing Insurgency: An Analysis of the Malayan Emergency, 1948–1954.* Boulder: Westview, 1992, pp. 143–169.

6. Karl Hack, "'Iron Claws on Malaya': The Historiography of the Malayan Emergency." *Journal of Southeast Asian Studies* 30, no. 1 (1999): 99–125.

7. Leon Comber, *13 May 1969: A Historical Survey of Sino-Malay Relations.* Singapore: Brash, 1988, p. xvi; Anthony Short, "The Malayan Emergency." In *Regular Armies and Insurgency,* ed. Ronald Haycock. London: Croom Helm, 1979, p. 64; Stubbs, *Hearts and Minds in Guerrilla Warfare,* p. 250; and Brian Crozier, *Southeast Asia in Turmoil.* Harmondsworth: Pelican, 1966, pp. 74–75.

8. Coates, *Suppressing Insurgency,* p. 186; Mackay, *Malayan Emergency,* pp. 140, 147–148; and Charles Townshend, *Britain's Civil Wars: Counterinsurgency in the Twentieth Century.* London: Faber and Faber, 1976, p. 164.

9. This is not the place to go into the details of the structure of the relationship

between the MCP and the MRLA, nor how the MRLA evolved from the wartime Malayan People's Anti-Japanese Army (MPAJA). Suffice to say that the party—as on the Maoist model—retained control of its armed wing through a network of political commissars at the regiment, company, and platoon levels. Short refers to the MPAJA as "largely the MCP in battle-dress." See Anthony Short, "Communism and the Emergency." In *Malaysia: A Survey,* ed. Wang Gungwu. London: Pall Mall, 1965, p. 151.

10. Virtually the only detailed and enduring study of MCP terrorist motivations and surrender behavior has been Lucien W. Pye, *Guerrilla Communism in Malaya: Its Social and Political Meaning.* Princeton, N.J.: Princeton University Press, 1956. Pye, an American scholar, interviewed sixty SEPs in 1952–1953. His analysis does not extend to the final years of the Emergency.

11. Short, *Communist Insurrection,* p. 492.

12. For instance, see Khong Kim Hoong, *Merdeka! British Rule and the Struggle for Independence in Malaya, 1945–57.* Kuala Lumpur: Institute for Social Analysis, 1984; Stubbs, *Hearts and Minds,* pp. 201–224; and Mackay, *Malayan Emergency,* pp. 141–148.

13. Meeting between the Tunku Abdul Rahman and Chin Peng, in Sir D. MacGillivray to Mr. Lennox-Boyd, 25 October 1955, and "Federation of Malaya," Chin Peng, 31 October 1955, in *British Documents on the End of Empire,* Series B, 3 vols., Parts 1–3, *Malaya,* ed. Anthony J. Stockwell. London: HMSO, 1995, vol. 3., Docs. 378, 381; CO 1030/27, Inward Tel. 669 from High Commissioner Federation of Malaya (HCFM) to Secretary of State for the Colonies (SSC), 29 October 1955; MacGillivray to Sir John Martin, 1 December 1955; and Inward Tel. 778 from HCFM to SSC, 9 December 1955.

14. "The present day situation and duties of the Malayan Communist Party" note by Mr. Strachey for the Cabinet Malaya Committee commenting on a captured MCP document, 12 May 1950, in *British Documents on the End of Empire,* Series B, 3 vols., Parts 1–3, *Malaya,* ed. Anthony J. Stockwell. London: HMSO, 1995, vol. 2, Doc. 215.

15. Rhodes House, Oxford (RHO), W. J. Watts Papers, MSS.Ind.Ocn.s.320, David Gray, Acting Secretary for Chinese Affairs, Federation of Malaya to W. J. Watts, 17 December 1951; see also David Gray, "The Chinese Problem in the Federation of Malaya," July 1952.

16. WO 291/1781, P. B. Humphrey, "A Study of the Reasons for Entering the Jungle within a Group of Surrendered Chinese Terrorists," ORS (PW) 8/54, 17 June 1954; WO 291/1764, P. B. Humphrey, "A Preliminary Study of Entry Behaviour among Chinese Communist Terrorists in Malaya," ORS (PW) 2/53, June 1953; and WO 291/1699, D. F. Bayly-Pike, "Interrogation of 112 Surrendered Communist Terrorists in 1955," ORUFE 4/56, May 1956.

17. RHO, W. L. Blythe Papers, MSS.Ind.Ocn.s.116, Blythe's notes on a draft manuscript by Victor Purcell called "The Chinese in Malaya," due to be published by Oxford University Press, dated March 1949; Frank Brewer, *The Chinese Problem in the Federation of Malaya.* Kuala Lumpur: Government Printer, 1955, p. 7; and RHO, Watts Papers, Gray, "The Chinese Problem in the Federation of Malaya." Brewer and Gray were senior Chinese affairs officers during the Emergency.

18. RHO, *End of Empire Papers (EEP)*, MSS.Brit.Emp.s.527, Tunku Abdul Rahman interview transcript, n.d.

19. RHO, *EEP,* Sir Michael Hogan interview transcript, n.d.

20. RHO, John C. Litton Papers, MSS.Ind.Ocn.s.113, John Litton, circular letter, 30 November 1951.

21. RHO, Watts Papers, Watts to A. D. C. Peterson, 24 March 1953.

22. RHO, Watts Papers, Gray to Watts, 17 December 1951. For the English-educated core of the MCA, see also T. N. Harper, *The End of Empire and the Making of Malaya.* Cambridge: Cambridge University Press, 1999, pp. 169–171.

23. RHO, Heussler Papers, Blythe note, 12 September 1948; and Blythe to Heussler, 26 November 1970.

24. Heng Pek Koon, *Chinese Politics in Malaysia: A History of the Malaysian Chinese Association.* Singapore: Oxford University Press, 1988, p. 129. For the contrary views, see Francis Loh Kok Wah's review of Heng in the *Journal of Southeast Asian Studies* 22, no. 1 (1991): 200–201; and Stubbs, *Hearts and Minds,* pp. 203–204.

25. Institute of Southeast Asian Studies (ISEAS), Tan Cheng Lock Papers, TCL.11.5, "Tan Chin Siong" to Dato Tan Cheng Lock, 18 May 1950; and RHO, Blythe Papers, R. N. Broome, "Communism in Malaya: Background to the Fighting," 1949.

26. RHO, *EEP,* C. C. Too interview transcripts, August 1981.

27. ISEAS, TCL.11.5, "Tan" to Tan Cheng Lock, 18 May 1950; RHO, Blythe Papers, Broome, "Communism in Malaya"; and WO 291/1509, also F. H. Lakin, "Psychological Warfare Research: Its Role in the Cold War," AORG Report 5/56, n.d.

28. WO 291/1781, P. B. Humphrey, "A Study of the Reasons for Entering the Jungle"; and WO 291/1764, P. B. Humphrey, "A Preliminary Study of Entry Behaviour."

29. WO 291/1764, P. B. Humphrey, "A Preliminary Study of Entry Behaviour"; and WO 291/1781, P. B. Humphrey, "A Study of the Reasons for Entering the Jungle," 17 June 1954; see also Pye, *Guerrilla Communism,* p. 190.

30. WO 291/1783, F. H. Lakin and Mrs. G. J. Humphrey, "A Study of Surrenders in Malaya during January 1949–June 1954," ORS (PW) 11/54, July 1954; and WO 291/1798, Mrs. A. D. C. Peterson, "Immediate Interrogation of Surrendered Enemy Personnel," ORS (PW) 7/53, n.d.

31. *Communist Banditry in Malaya: The Emergency June 1948–Dec 1949.* Kuala Lumpur: Department of Public Relations, 1950, pp. 59–60; and National Army Museum (NAM), 7410–29–1, "Talking Points for H.E.'s Farewell Visits on 29th and 30th April 1954."

32. RHO, A. E. Young Papers, MSS.Brit.Emp.s.486, Box 1, "Short History of the Emergency," 21 October 1952.

33. Judith Strauch, *Chinese Village Politics in the Malaysian State.* Cambridge, Mass.: Harvard University Press, 1981, p. 65. For a detailed analysis of the 1951 directives, see Karl Hack, "British Intelligence and Counter-insurgency in the Era of Decolonisation: The Example of Malaya." *Intelligence and National Security* 14, no. 2 (1999): 143.

34. C. C. Too, "Psychological Warfare and Some Aspects of the Psychology of the People in Southeast Asia in Areas Where Communist Insurrection Is Likely to Arise." Transcript of a speech at the U.S. Army Command and General Staff College, Fort Leavenworth, Kansas, 15 October 1962. In author's possession.

35. Kumar Ramakrishna, *Emergency Propaganda: The Winning of Malayan Hearts and Minds, 1948–1958.* Richmond, Surrey: Curzon, 2002, p. 60.

36. Chinese affairs officers lamented that following the abolition of the Protectorate in 1945, Chinese consuls extended their hold over the Malayan Chinese middle classes while the MCP gained control of the Chinese proletariat. See RHO, Frank

Brewer Papers, MSS.Ind.Ocn.s.306, Box 1, "The Chinese Protectorate and the Chinese Affairs Department," October 1954.

37. RHO, Watts Papers, Watts to SCA, FM, 7 January 1952.

38. RHO, Watts Papers, Gray to Watts, 17 December 1951; Blythe Papers, W. L. Blythe, "The Significance of Chinese Triad Societies in Malaya," 16 March 1949; and CO 537/4751, "Present Attitude of the Chinese Population," 11 April 1949.

39. RHO, Watts Papers, Gray to Watts, 17 December 1951. On December 12, 1948, troops from the Scots Guards shot dead twenty-four Chinese at Batang Kali village in Selangor in questionable circumstances. Firsthand accounts of the incident by two women, Ching Yoong and Wong Foo Moi, both interviewed by Granada Television in 1981, are found in RHO, *End of Empire Papers*. A comprehensive discussion of the Emergency Regulations and their effects, including on Chinese sentiments toward government, is found in R. D. Rhenick Jr., "The Emergency Regulations of Malaya: Causes and Effect." *Journal of Southeast Asian History* 6, no. 2 (1965): 1–39; see also *Detention and Deportation during the Emergency in the Federation of Malaya*. Kuala Lumpur: Government Press, 1953, p. 14; and CO 1022/165, W. A. Muller to H. Fraser, 22 December 1951.

40. ISEAS, TCL.3.271, Memorandum to the Right Honourable Oliver Lyttelton, Secretary of State for the Colonies, by an MCA Delegation headed by Dato Tan Cheng Lock at King's House, Kuala Lumpur, 2 December 1951.

41. Coates, *Suppressing Insurgency,* pp. 109–142; and John Cloake, *Templer: Tiger of Malaya.* London: Harrap 1985.

42. RHO, W. C. S. Corry interview transcript, MSS.Ind.Ocn.s.215, n.d.; and NAM, 7410–29–1, "Speech by H.E. the High Commissioner to F. M. S. Chamber of Commerce," 25 April 1952.

43. NAM, 7410–29–1, "Address by H.E. the High Commissioner to Division III officers at Selangor Badminton Hall, Kuala Lumpur," 30 October 1952.

44. RHO, Young Papers, Box 3, "Malaya," May 1967.

45. RHO, Young Papers, Box 2, draft article for *New York Herald Tribune,* 6 May 1953; MSS.Brit.Emp.s.525, Prof. Max Beloff's interview with Oliver Lyttelton, 27 February 1970; and 59 WO 291/1781, P. B. Humphrey, "A Study of Reasons for Entering the Jungle," 17 June 1954.

46. RHO, Lyttelton interview; and NAM, 7410–29–1, "H.C.'s Speech at the First Meeting of the 6th Session, Legislative Council, 18 March 1953."

47. Liddell Hart Centre for Military Archives, King's College, London, General Sir Hugh Charles Stockwell Papers, Lieutenant-Colonel W. Walker, CO 1/6th Gurkha Rifles, to Colonel C. Graham, CO Gurkha Brigade, 12 July 1952.

48. CO 967/181, A. D. C. Peterson, "Report and Recommendations on the Organisation of Information Services in the Federation of Malaya," 20 August 1952.

49. NAM, 7410–29–1, "A New Year Message from the H.C. to all Public Servants, 1 Jan. 1953"; and NAM, 7410–29–1, "H.C.'s Speech at the First Meeting of the 6th Session, Legislative Council, 18 March 1953."

50. C. M. Turnbull, correspondence with the author, 31 July 1997.

51. *Detention and Deportation,* p. 8.

52. CO 1022/132, Extract from "Federation of Malaya Saving No. 79, 18 Jan. 1954"; and Extract from "Federation of Malaya Administrative Report for January 1953."

53. Ramakrishna, *Emergency Propaganda,* pp. 138–139.

54. For details of the Tanjong Malim affair, see Short, *Communist Insurrection,* pp. 340–341.

55. RHO, *EEP,* G. Madoc interview transcript, August 1981; and A. D. C. Peterson to the *Listener,* 14 August 1969.

56. CO 1022/58, Extract from "High Commissioner's Budget Speech to Federation of Malaya Legislative Council, 25 Nov. 1953"; and 75 NAM, 7410–29–1, "High Commissioner's Press Conference: Replies to Written Questions," 26 May 1954.

57. Lieutenant-General Harold Briggs, as director of operations between April 1950 and November 1951, had drawn up the blueprint for counterinsurgency operations in Malaya, popularly known as the Briggs Plan. The operational thrust of the plan, implemented from June 1950 onward by newly formalized war executive committees at the state and district levels, was to deny the MRLA access to their squatter supply networks through resettlement of the rural Chinese into defended Resettlement Areas (later New Villages). This was intended to flush the starving terrorists out of their jungle lairs and into the rifle sights of Security Force patrols operating on the jungle fringe. Meanwhile, the police would prevent infiltration into the populated areas. While squatters were resettled, estate workers and miners were more usually regrouped or more closely settled into defended compact locales within estates and mines. Altogether, about 1.2 million rural folk were resettled or regrouped. For details of the Briggs Plan, resettlement, and regrouping, see Stubbs, *Hearts and Minds,* pp. 198–200.

58. CO 1022/30, Extract from "Federation of Malaya Administrative Report for January 1953"; and NAM, 7410–29–1, "H.E.'s Speech Opening the Connaught Bridge Power Station," 26 March 1953.

59. CO 1022/29, Extract from "Federation of Malaya Saving No. 470, 16 March 1953"; see also Stubbs, *Hearts and Minds,* pp. 234–235.

60. RHO, *EEP,* transcript of an interview with John Davis, August 1981.

61. Ramakrishna, *Emergency Propaganda,* pp. 129–130.

62. T. N. Harper, "The Colonial Inheritance: State and Society in Colonial Malaya, 1945–57." Ph.D. diss., Cambridge University, 1991, pp. 249–252.

63. J. L. M. Gorrie, interview with the author, 16 January 1998. Gorrie was an MCS officer during the Emergency; and Datin Jean Marshall, interview with the author, 21 January 1998. Marshall worked as a Red Cross administrator.

64. Dato Mubin Sheppard, *Taman Budiman: Memoirs of an Unorthodox Civil Servant.* Kuala Lumpur: Heinemann, 1979, pp. 218–221.

65. Hack, "British Intelligence," pp. 132–133.

66. *Federation of Malaya Annual Report 1956.* London: HMSO, 1957, p. 451; and 90 AIR 23/8697, AVM V. E. Hancock, "Ninth Report of the Royal Air Force Operations in Malaya: 1 Jan. 1957 to 31 Dec. 1957."

67. For a detailed description of central cooking in Broga, Selangor, see M. Sheppard, "Riceless Reds." *Malaya: Journal of the British Association of Malaya* (January 1957): 25–27.

68. Tartan Rock was the largest operation of its kind at the time, and it was promoted by the Combined Emergency Planning Staff as a model for future operations. See Department of Information Weekly News Summary (WNS) week ending (w.e.) 1 December 1956; and RHO, C. H. F. Blake Papers, MSS.Ind.Ocn.s.276, "Minutes of the 237th Formal Meeting of the Operations Sub-committee of Perak SWEC, held in the Combined Operations Room, Ipoh, on Tuesday, 30th July 1957, at 10.00 A.M."

69. CO 1030/10, Director of Operations, "Review of the Emergency Situation in Malaya at the end of 1954," 10 January 1955; and WNS, w.e. 7 May 1955.

70. WO 291/1787, P. B. Humphrey, "Some Statistics Relating to Communist Terrorist Recruitment in Malaya," ORS (PW) 16/54, 21 December 1954.

71. WNS, w.e. 26 March 1955, 9 April 1955; WNS, w.e. 16 April 1955, 25 June 1955; and WNS, w.e. 26 November 1955.

72. *The Communist Threat to the Federation of Malaya.* Kuala Lumpur: Government Printer, 1959, pp. 19–30.

73. WO 291/1792, F. H. Lakin, "A Review of Recent Trends in Surrender Behaviour," ORS (PW) 6/55, 17 March 1955; see also CO 1030/22, Major Wynford, "Review of Surrender Behaviour from 1951 to February 1955, with particular reference to the period July 1954 to February 1955," 4 May 1955.

74. WO 291/1786, F. H. Lakin and G. J. Humphrey, "A Study of Surrenders amongst Communist Terrorists in Malaya, June to November 1954," ORS (PW) 15/54, 18 November 1954; WO 291/1718, D. F. Bayly-Pike, "Surrender Rate," ORUFE 3/55, 1 November 1955; and WO 291/1699, D. F. Bayly-Pike, "Interrogation of 112 Surrendered Terrorists," May 1956.

75. WO 291/1788, F. H. Lakin, "Some Effects of International Affairs on Communist Terrorists in Malaya," ORS (PW) 17/54, 7 December 1954.

76. WO 291/1699, D. F. Bayly-Pike, "Interrogation of 112 Surrendered Terrorists," May 1956.

77. CO 1030/10, Director of Operations, "Review of the Emergency Situation in Malaya at the end of 1956," 12 February 1957 (hereafter DOR 1956).

78. National Archives of Singapore (NAS), DIS 116/57, "Information Services Monthly Reports," June and November 1957.

79. SB, 29 August 1957.

80. Richard Clutterbuck, correspondence with the author, 22 July 1997.

81. CO 1030/10, DOR 1956, 12 February 1957.

82. WO 291/1781, P. B. Humphrey, "A Study of the Reasons for Entering the Jungle," 17 June 1954.

83. ISEAS, TCL.11.5, "Tan' to Dato Tan Cheng Lock," 18 May 1950; and J. N. McHugh, "Psychological, or Political Warfare in Malaya." Pt. 2. *Journal of the Historical Society, University of Malaya* 5 (1966–1967): 89.

84. CO 537/7255, Hugh Carleton Greene, "Report on Emergency Information Services, September 1950–September 1951," 14 September 1951. Greene—brother of the novelist Graham—had been a BBC German editor during the war.

85. CO 1022/49, Inward Tel. 595 from HCFM to SSC, 12 May 1952. Taiping had been set up in November 1949, the SOVF in May 1953, and Kemendore in March 1954.

86. Ramakrishna, *Emergency Propaganda,* p. 191

87. In 1981, Too recalled that it took several years for government to build up its credibility in the eyes of the terrorists. See RHO, *EEP,* Too interview transcripts.

88. WNS, w.e. 25 June 1955.

89. Liddell Hart Centre for Military Archives, King's College, London, Major-General Dennis Edmund Blaquiere Talbot Papers, Lieutenant-General Geoffrey Bourne, Director of Operations on behalf of High Commissioner Federation of Malaya, "Declaration of Amnesty," 9 September 1955.

90. CO 1030/10, Director of Operations, "Review of the Emergency Situation in Malaya at the end of 1955," January 1956; and WNS, w.e. 11 Feb. 1956.

91. "Report by the chief minister of the Federation of Malaya on the Baling talks: draft summary by Tunku Abdul Rahman on the verbatim record, CO 1030/30, ff 3–16, 29 Dec. 1955," in *British Documents on the End of Empire*, Series B, 3 vols., Parts 1–3, *Malaya*, ed. Anthony J. Stockwell, vol. 3, Doc. 391.

92. CO 1030/10, DOR 1956.

93. SB, 11 and 18 September 1957.

94. SB, 13 November and 25 December 1957.

95. AIR 23/8697, Hancock Report 1957.

96. SB, 18 and 25 December 1957; and Hancock Report 1957, AIR 23/8697.

97. Ramakrishna, *Emergency Propaganda*, p. 201.

98. AIR 23/8698, AVM V. E. Hancock, "Tenth Report on the Royal Air Force Operations in Malaya, 1 Jan. 1958–31 Dec. 1958."

99. Notes of a Talk by Chin Peng, 18 June 1998, London; and Aloysius Chin, *The Communist Party of Malaya: The Inside Story.* Kuala Lumpur: Vinpress, 1995, pp. 50–51.

100. Chin, *Communist Party of Malaya*, pp. 50–52; Miller, *Jungle War in Malaya*, p. 198; and Noel Barber, *The War of the Running Dogs: Malaya 1948–1960.* London: Arrow 1989, p. 320.

## Chapter 11

1. John Darwin, *Britain and Decolonisation: The Retreat from Empire in the Post-war World.* London: Macmillan, 1988, pp. 17–18.

2. Ord to Kimberley, 8 October 1868, CO 273/22 no. 203, cited in Edwin Lee, *The British As Rulers: Governing Multiracial Singapore, 1867–1914.* Singapore: Singapore University Press, 1991, p. 32.

3. Lee, *British As Rulers*, p. 47.

4. Lee, *British As Rulers*, p. 30.

5. Stephen Leong, "The Chinese in Malaya and China's Politics 1895–1911." *Journal of the Malaysian Branch of the Royal Asiatic Society* 50, no. 2 (1977): 7–24.

6. See C. F. Yong, *Tan Kah-kee: The Making of an Overseas Chinese Legend.* Singapore: Oxford University Press, 1987, p. 141.

7. Radin Soenarno, "Malay Nationalism, 1900–1945." *Journal of Southeast Asian History* 1, no. 1 (March 1960): 5.

8. W. Roff, *The Origins of Malay Nationalism.* Kuala Lumpur: University of Malaya Press, 1967, p. 32.

9. Jawi Peranakan (local-born Muslims) were the offspring of southern Indian Muslim and Malay Unions. According to Roff, "Malay journalism, like book publication in Malay, owes its origins very largely to locally born Indian Muslims in Singapore or, to be more exact, to the community known as 'Jawi Peranakan.'" In the 1901 census, there were only 919 Arabs in Singapore. See Roff, *Origins of Malay Nationalism*, pp. 40, 48.

10. Roff, *Origins of Malay Nationalism*, pp. 58, 81.

11. Rajeswary Ampalavanar, *The Indian Minority and Political Change in Malaya, 1945–1957.* Kuala Lumpur: Oxford University Press, 1981, p. 2.

12. Government of India to Indian Secretary, 14 July 1941, CO 717/145, no. 51574/1, Public Record Office (PRO), London.

13. Suresh Kumar, "Singapore Indian Association, 1923–1941." Academic Exercise, Department of History, National University of Singapore, 1995, p.17.

14. *Free Press,* 3 March 1923, cited in Kumar, "Singapore Indian Association," pp. 1, 9.

15. Visandakumari Nair, "Tamils Reform Association, Singapore (1932–1961)." Academic Exercise, Department of History, National University of Singapore, 1972, pp. 6–7. Its founders included Nagalingam Nundaliar, a Ceylon Tamil and a wealthy merchant, India-born G. Sarangapany, a journalist, and A. C. Suppiah and Damodaran Pillai, both merchants.

16. Nair, "Tamils Reform Association," p. 42.

17. See A. D. Smith, introduction to *Nationalist Movements.* London: Macmillan, 1976.

18. Zheng Liren, "Overseas Chinese Nationalism in British Malaya, 1894–1941." Ph.D. diss., Cornell University, 1997, pp. 191–224.

19. Kumar, "Singapore Indian Association," pp. 8, 11, 31–32, 44.

20. Chua Ai Lin, "Negotiating National Identity: The English-Speaking Domiciled Communities in Singapore, 1930–1941." Master's thesis, National University of Singapore, 2001, p. 66.

21. Roff, *Origins of Malay Nationalism,* pp. 191–192.

22. Abdul Majid b. Zainuddin, *The Malays of Malaya, by One of Them.* Singapore: Malaya Publishing House, 1928, pp. 94–95.

23. See Khoo Kay Kim, "The Beginning of Political Extremism in Malaya, 1915–1935." Ph.D. diss., University of Malaya, 1973.

24. Report by Inspector-General, CO 717/145, no. 51574/1, PRO.

25. Cited in C. F. Yong and R. B. Mckenna, "The Kuomintang Movement in Malaya and Singapore, 1912–1925." *Journal of Southeast Asian Studies* 12, no. 1 (March 1981): 129, 132. The May 30 incident arose from labor disputes engineered by the communists in Shanghai against the Naigai Wata Kaisha's cotton mills beginning in February 1925. After the Japanese foreman opened fire against the strikers, wounding ten and killing one of them, anti-Japanese and anti-imperialist demonstrations broke out, culminating in the massive mass rally of May 30 that was attended by some ten thousand Chinese. At the Lousa Police Station in Shanghai's International Settlement, a large and angry crowd of protestors was fired at by Chinese and Sikh constables. Four demonstrators were killed instantly and eight others subsequently died of their wounds. Protests soon spread to other Chinese cities and the movement soon took an antiforeigners turn. See C. Martin Wilbur, *The Nationalist Revolution in China, 1923–1928.* Cambridge: Cambridge University Press, 1983, p. 23.

26. M. Musso, "How Great Britain Is Ruling the Malayan Countries." *Eastern and Colonial Bulletin* (December 1929): 15, cited in Gene Z. Hanrahan, *The Communist Struggle in Malaya.* Kuala Lumpur: Oxford University Press, 1979, p. 34.

27. Ban Kah Choon notes that by the mid-1920s, the Special Branch had already put in place "a highly sophisticated and extensive intelligence coverage" that was "astonishingly comprehensive" and gave it "a special perspective and knowledge of events and personalities." He adds, "Most of its actions had become by the mid-1930s almost surgical in the precision with which it detected and removed subversives." See Ban Kah Choon, *Absent History: The Untold Story of Special Branch Operations in Singapore, 1915–1942.* Singapore: SNP Media Asia, 2001, pp. 80, 156.

28. See Akashi Yoji, "Lai Teck, Secretary General of the Malayan Communist Party, 1939–1947." *Journal of the South Seas Society* 49 (1994); and Ban, *Absent History,* pp. 80, 98.

29. S. W. Jones (Deputy Governor) to M. MacDonald, 30 March 1940, CO 273/

662, no. 50336, Pt. 1, PRO; see also Yeo Kim Wah, "The Communist Challenge in the Malayan Labour Scene, September 1936–March 1937." *Journal of the Malaysian Branch of the Royal Asiatic Society* 64, no. 2 (1976): 36–79; and M. R. Stenson, *Industrial Conflict in Malaya: Prelude to the Communist Revolt of 1948.* Kuala Lumpur: Oxford University Press, 1970, p. 23.

30. Director, Special Branch, Malayan Combined Intelligence Summary (MCIS) no. 4 (1940), in CO273/662, no. 50336, Pt. 1, PRO.

31. S. Thomas to M. MacDonald, 2 May 1940, CO 273/662, no. 50336, Pt. 1, PRO.

32. Director, Special Branch, MCIS, no. 4 (1940), in CO 273/662, no. 50336, Pt. 1, PRO.

33. Director, Special Branch, MCIS, no. 7, July 1937, War Office (WO) 106/5701, PRO, cited in C. F. Yong, *The Origins of Malayan Communism.* Singapore: South Seas Society, 1997, p. 203.

34. Extract of letter in CO 273/662, no. 50336, Pt. 1, PRO.

35. Director, Special Branch, MCIS no. 4 (1940), co 273/662, no. 50336, Pt. 1, PRO.

36. S. Thomas to M. MacDonald, 9 April 1940, CO 273/662, no. 50336, PRO.

37. Chua, "Negotiating National Identity," pp. 109, 114. It was only in 1924 that the Legislative Council included Unofficials, but it still was without an Unofficial majority. An Asian was made a member of the Executive Council only in 1932.

38. Quoted in B. Montgomery, *Shenton of Singapore, Governor and Prisoner of War.* Singapore: Leo Cooper, 1984, p. 189; see also S. L. Falk, *Seventy Days to Singapore: The Malayan Campaign, 1941–1942.* London: Robert Hale, 1975; and Alfred W. McCoy, ed., *Southeast Asia under Japanese Occupation.* New Haven, Conn.: Yale University, Southeast Asia Studies, 1980, pp. 1–4.

39. See Albert Lau, "Some Conceptual Issues in the Study of Contemporary South East Asian History." *Journal of the History Society* (1987–1988): 16–20.

40. Lee Kuan Yew, *The Singapore Story: Memoirs of Lee Kuan Yew.* London: Prentice Hall, 1998, p. 53.

41. Ang Hwee Suan, ed., *Dialogues with S. Rajaratnam: Former Senior Minister in the Prime Minister's Office.* Singapore: Shin Min Daily New, 1991, p. iii.

42. Said Zahari, *Dark Clouds at Dawn: A Political Memoir.* Kuala Lumpur: INSAN, 2001, p. 27.

43. Fong Sip Chee, *The PAP Story: The Pioneering Years.* Singapore: Times Periodicals, 1980, p. 9.

44. Cheah Boon Kheng, *Red Star over Malaya: Resistance and Social Conflict during and after the Japanese Occupation, 1941–1946.* Singapore: Singapore University Press, 1983, pp. 46–47.

45. Tan Chin Tuan, who was a municipal commissioner and also a member of the China Relief Fund Committee and Passive Defence Council, for instance, escaped to Batavia and then Australia. See Grace Loh, Goh Chor Boon, and Tan Teng Lang, *Building Bridges, Carving Niches: An Enduring Legacy.* Singapore: Oxford University Press, 2000, p. 56.

46. Cheah, *Red Star over Malaya,* p. 54.

47. See Nalini M. Pillai, "Subhas Chandra Bose in Singapore, 1943–1946." Academic Exercise, Department of History, National University of Singapore, 1995. Bose apparently had made a good and lasting impression among Indians who attended his mass rallies and listened to his "magnetic speeches" (pp. 30, 49).

48. Ampalavanar, *Indian Minority and Political Change in Malaya*, p. 8.

49. According to the *Utusan Melayu* report of February 12, 1946, the Singapore MNP branch was established on February 3, 1946. See Elinah Abdullah, "Malay Political Activities in Singapore, 1945–1959." Academic Exercise, Department of History, National University of Singapore, 1992, p. 20.

50. Ahmad Boestamam, who was one of the founding leaders of the MNP, wrote that there was "no doubt that our group was deeply influenced by the independent struggle of Indonesia headed by Soekarno and Hatta. In other words, [we] wanted the Malay Nationalist Party to become like the Partai Nasionalis Indonesia, led by Soekarno and Hatta." See Ahmad Boestamam, *Carving the Path to the Summit.* Athens, Ohio: Ohio University Press, 1979, p. 25; see also Angus McIntyre, "The Greater Indonesia Idea of Nationalism in Malaya and Indonesia." *Modern Asian Studies* 1, no. 7 (1973): 75–83.

51. The organizations associated with the MNP included the Angkatan Pemuda Insaf (API; Generation of Aware Youth), formed in February 1946, the Angkatan Wanita Sedar (AWAS; Generation of Awakened Women), formed in December 1946, Pusat Tenaga Rakyat (PUTERA; Center of People's Power), established in February 1947, Barisan Anak (BARA; Children's Front), and Barisan Tani Sa-Malaya (All Malaya Peasant Front). The Malayan Security Service noted ominously that the "abbreviations of API, AWAS and BARA meant 'Fire,' 'Beware,' and 'Glowing Embers' respectively." See *Malayan Security Service Political Intelligence Journal,* 31 December 1947, p. 230; see also Abdullah, "Malay Political Activities in Singapore," p. 21.

52. *Malayan Security Service Political Intelligence Journal,* 31 October 1946, p. 1.

53. According to the *Utusan Melayu* of May 10, 1947, some eighty-four Malay associations were in the PUTERA; cited in Abdullah, "Malay Political Activities in Singapore," p. 25; see also Albert Lau, *The Malayan Union Controversy, 1942–1948.* Singapore: Oxford University Press, 1991, pp. 212–219, 254.

54. Abdullah, "Malay Political Activities in Singapore," p. 27. Similar branches in Malaya had been outlawed since July 1947.

55. *Utusan Melayu* of May 11, 1950, cited in Abdullah, "Malay Political Activities in Singapore," p. 35.

56. Cheah, *Red Star over Malaya,* p. 54.

57. Yeo Kim Wah, "Joining the Communist Underground: The Conversion of English-Educated Radicals to Communism in Singapore, June 1948–January 1951." *Journal of the Malaysian Branch of the Royal Asiatic Society* 67, no. 1 (1994): 29–59.

58. For discussion of the outbreak of the Malayan Emergency, see Kumar Ramakrishna, chapter 10, in this volume; see also Anthony Short, *The Communist Insurrection in Malaya, 1948–60.* London: Frederick Muller, 1975; and Richard Stubbs, *Hearts and Minds in Guerrilla Warfare: The Malayan Emergency, 1948–1960.* Singapore: Oxford University Press, 1989.

59. For the Progressive Party, see Yeo Kim Wah, *Political Development in Singapore, 1945–1955.* Singapore: Singapore University Press, 1973, pp. 98–105.

60. Cited in Ang, *Dialogues with S. Rajaratnam,* p. iii.

61. Under the plan, the Straits Settlements would be dismantled, and Penang and Malacca would join the nine Malay states in a constitutional union in mainland Malaya. Britain's purpose was to make Malaya more united and more defensible to fulfil British objectives in the postwar world. Singapore was excluded for a variety of reasons, but chiefly because the British feared that its inclusion would tilt the racial

balance in favor of the Chinese and make the scheme unacceptable to the Malays. See Lau, *Malayan Union Controversy,* pp. 282–284.

62. W. E. Willmott, "The Emergence of Nationalism." In *Management of Success: The Moulding of Modern Singapore,* ed. Kernial Singh Sandhu and Paul Wheatley. Singapore: ISEAS, 1989, p. 584.

63. Speech by Lee Kuan Yew to the Guild of Nanyang University Graduates, 6 November 1960, cited in Han Fook Kwang, Warren Fernandez, and Sumiko Tan, *Lee Kuan Yew: The Man and His Ideas.* Singapore: Times Editions, 1997, p. 67.

64. Lee Kuan Yew, *The Battle for Merger.* Singapore: Government Printing Office, 1961, p. 5; Mohamed Noordin Sopiee, *From Malayan Union to Singapore Separation.* Kuala Lumpur: Penerbit Univesiti Malaya, 1976, p. 113–115; and Albert Lau, "The Colonial Office and the Singapore Merdeka Mission, 23 April to 15 May 1956." *Journal of the South Seas Society* 49 (1994): 109–111.

65. Lau, *Malayan Union Controversy,* pp. 276–278.

66. The UMNO was inaugurated formally on May 11, 1946, to spearhead the anti-Malayan Union struggle. See Anthony J. Stockwell, *British Policy and Malay Politics during the Malayan Union Experiment, 1942–1948.* Kuala Lumpur: Malaysian Branch of the Royal Asiatic Society Monograph no. 8, 1979, pp. 64–72.

67. Black to Lennox-Boyd, 6 December 1955, CO 1030/290, no. 20, PRO. This point is argued in James Low Choon Sai, "Kept in Position: The Labour Front–Alliance Government of Chief Minister David Marshall in Singapore, April 1955–June 1956." Master's thesis, National University of Singapore, 2000.

68. Lau, "Colonial Office and the Singapore Merdeka Mission," pp. 104–117.

69. Thomas Lloyd to Saville Garner, 9 April 1956, CO 1030/120, no. 157, PRO.

70. David Marshall, "Singapore's Struggle for Nationhood, 1955–1959." *Journal of Southeast Asian Studies* 1, no. 2 (September 1970): 104.

71. Proceedings of the Singapore Legislative Assembly, *Legislative Assembly Debates Official Report 1955–1965,* 4 October 1956, col. 318.

72. T. J. S. George, *Lee Kuan Yew's Singapore.* London: Andre Deutsch, 1973, pp. 163–164. Thomas J. Bellows notes that "[f]or at least twelve months before the May 1959 elections, Goode had maintained close contact with Lee Kuan Yew." See Thomas J. Bellows, *The People's Action Party of Singapore: Emergence of a Dominant Party System.* New Haven, Conn.: Yale University Southeast Asia Studies, 1970, p. 35.

## Chapter 12

1. For the existing scholarship on Roosevelt's plans for trusteeship in Indochina, see Lloyd Gardner, *Approaching Dien Bien Phu.* New York: Norton, 1988, pp. 21–53; Gary R. Hess, "Franklin Roosevelt and Indochina." *Journal of American History* 59, no. 2 (September 1972): 353–368; Gary R. Hess, *The United States' Emergence As a Southeast Asian Power, 1940–1950.* New York: Columbia University Press, 1987, pp. 47–158; Walter LaFeber, "Roosevelt, Churchill and Indochina: 1942–1945." *American Historical Review* 80, no. 5 (December 1975): 1277–1295; and Christopher Thorne, "Indochina and Anglo-American Relations, 1942–1945." *Pacific Historical Review* 45, no. 1 (February 1976): 73–96.

2. The most important analysis of the place of racialized cultural hierarchies in American thinking is George W. Stocking Jr., *Victorian Anthropology.* New York: The Free Press, 1987.

3. Edward W. Said, *Orientalism.* New York: Vintage, 1979; and Edward W. Said, *Culture and Imperialism.* New York: Knopf, 1993.

4. Minutes of the Pacific War Council, 21 July 1943, Folder: "Naval Aide's Files, Pacific War #2," Box 168, Map Room File, Franklin D. Roosevelt Papers As President, 1941–1945, Franklin D. Roosevelt Library, Hyde Park, New York.

5. Elliott Roosevelt, *As He Saw It.* New York: Duell Sloan and Pearce, 1946, p. 115; Roosevelt–Stalin–Churchill Meeting, 28 November 1943, *Foreign Relations of the United States (FRUS), The Conferences at Cairo and Tehran,* 1943. Washington, D.C.: U.S. Government Printing Office, 1961, p. 485.

6. Minutes of the Pacific War Council, 23 May 1942. The recollections of participants in the May 1954 Princeton Seminar, which gathered together wartime and Cold War policy makers, also suggest that Roosevelt's critique of French rule in Vietnam was less an attack on colonialism than on France's inadequacies as a colonial power. See Transcript of 15 May 1954, Folder Title: "Reading Copy III: Princeton Seminars May 15–16, 1954 (Folder 2)," Box 84, Papers of Dean Acheson, Harry S Truman Library, Independence, Missouri: Reel 5, Track 1, Page 8.

7. Minutes of the Pacific War Council, 17 March 1943; see also Edward R. Stettinius Jr., *Roosevelt and the Russians.* Garden City, N.Y.: Doubleday, 1949, p. 237; and Roosevelt, *As He Saw It,* pp. 115, 165, 251.

8. Roosevelt-Stalin Meeting, 8 February 1945, *FRUS, The Conferences at Malta and Yalta, 1945.* Washington, D.C.: U.S. Government Printing Office, 1955, p. 770.

9. Roosevelt-Stalin Meeting, 28 November 1943, *FRUS, The Conferences at Cairo and Tehran, 1943.* Washington, D.C.: U.S. Government Printing Office, 1961, p. 485.

10. Glenn Anthony May, *Social Engineering in the Philippines: The Aims, Execution and Impact of American Colonial Policy, 1900–1913.* Westport, Conn.: Greenwood, 1980, p. xvii.

11. Vincete L. Rafael, "White Love: Surveillance and Nationalist Resistance in the U.S. Colonization of the Philippines." In *Cultures of United States Imperialism,* ed. Amy Kaplan and Donald E. Pease. Durham, N.C.: Duke University Press, 1993, p. 216; see also Michael Salman, "The United States and the End of Slavery in the Philippines, 1898–1914: A Study of Imperialism, Ideology and Nationalism." Ph.D. diss., Stanford University, 1993, pp. 605–617.

12. Biographical information on Kenneth P. Landon is contained in *Biographic Register of the Department of State: September 1, 1944.* Washington, D.C.: U.S. Government Printing Office, n.d., p. 125. Landon's wife, Margaret, is the author of *Anna and the King,* which served as the basis of the Broadway musical *The King and I.* Amry Vandenbosch's best-known work was *The Dutch East Indies: Its Government, Problems and Politics.* Grand Rapids, Mich.: Eerdmans, 1933. Melvin King's critiques of French colonialism emerge in *Morocco As a French Economic Venture.* New York: Appleton-Century, 1937. Isaiah Bowman's writings on Africa reflected the framework of racialized cultural hierarchies that animated American perceptions of Vietnam; on Bowman, see Thomas Borstelmann, *Apartheid's Reluctant Uncle: The United States and Southern Africa in the Early Cold War.* New York: Oxford University Press, 1993, p. 11.

13. T Minutes, 56, 11 November 1943; T Minutes 55, 5 November 1943; Indochina: Political and Economic Problems (T-398); and Subcommittee on Territorial Problems, Division of Political Studies, Box 59, Records of the Advisory Committee on

Post-War Foreign Policy (Harley Notter Files, 1939–1945), Record Group 59, U.S. National Archives, Washington, D.C.

14. T Minutes 56, 11 November 1943; and T Minutes 55, 5 November 1943.

15. T Minutes 56, 11 November 1943. Prevailing skepticism of Vietnamese ability to immediately undertake self-government is also reflected in a November 2, 1943, memo from John Carter Vincent, assistant chief of the Division of Far Eastern Affairs, to Assistant Secretary of State Berle. Vincent argued that the Vietnamese were "capable of self-government" only after a postwar administration had trained them to assume "the responsibilities of self-government." The memo was initialed by Joseph W. Ballantine, chief of the Division of Far Eastern Affairs and a member of the subcommittee. See Memo from Vincent to Berle, 2 November 1943, *FRUS, 1943, China.* Washington, D.C.: U.S. Government Printing Office, 1957, p. 886.

16. Indo-China: Political and Economic Factors (T-398), 2 November 1943; and T Minutes 56, 11 November 1943.

17. Indo-China: Political and Economic Factors (T-398), 2 November 1943.

18. "Draft Outline of an International Trusteeship Government for Indochina," CAC-114, 13 March 1944, Box 109, Notter Files.

19. CAC Document 89, 1 March 1944, Box 109; and T Minutes 56, 11 November 1943, Notter Files.

20. Gauss to Secretary of State, 31 December 1942, 851G.00/81; and Gauss to Secretary of State, 23 December 1943, 851G.00/95, Box 5065, State Department Decimal Files, Record Group 59.

21. Gauss to Secretary of State, 23 December 1943, 851G.00/95.

22. "Outline of MO Objectives and Operations in Indo-China," n.d.; "Indo-China MO Mission," 30 October 1943; and "Indo-China-MO Unit," 13 December 1943, Folder #1864, Box #138, Entry #139, Records of the Office of Strategic Services, Record Group 226, U.S. National Archives, Washington, D.C.

23. Memo from R. P. Leonard to Harley C. Stevens, 16 May 1944; "Propaganda and the War in Indo-China," n.d.; "Comments re Memorandum of Mr. Leonard," 23 May 1944; and Memo from Harold C. Faxon to Betty MacDonald, 17 November 1944, Folder #1863, Box #138, Entry #139, Record Group 226.

24. "Determining a Policy for MO Operations in Indochina," n.d., Folder #1863, Box #138, Entry #139, Record Group 226.

25. "Suggestions for Leaflets to French Indo China," 7 December 1944, Folder #1863, Box #138, Entry #139, Record Group 226.

26. "Suggestions for Leaflets to French Indo China," 7 December 1944, Folder #1863, Box #138, Entry #139, Record Group 226, emphasis in original.

27. "Political Conditions in Indo-China," William J. Powell, OWI Air Liason, Kunming, 28 August 1944, 851G.00/9–944, Folder 273, Box 35, Entry 35, Record Group 226.

28. Langdon to Secretary of State, 9 September 1944, 851G.00/9–944; Memorandum of Conversation, 9 September 1944, 851G.00/9–944; and Langdon to Secretary of State, 20 September 1944, 851G.00/9–2044.

29. "Indo-China Question," William R. Langdon, 3 August 1944, 851G.00/8–344, and Gauss to Secretary of State, 26 July 1944, 851G.00/7–2644.

30. Robert J. McMahon has most recently made this argument in his *The Limits of Empire: The United States and Southeast Asia since World War II.* New York: Columbia University Press, 1999, pp. 9–13, 28, but it is more fully developed in Hess, *United States' Emergence,* pp. 47–158. Similar interpretations emerge in two broader ac-

counts of U.S. wartime attitudes toward decolonization. See Warren F. Kimball "'In Search of Monsters to Destroy': Roosevelt and Colonialism." In *The Juggler: Franklin Roosevelt As Wartime Statesman*. Princeton, N.J.: Princeton University Press, 1991, pp. 127–157; and William Roger Louis, *Imperialism at Bay: The United States and the Decolonization of the British Empire, 1941–1945*. Oxford: Oxford University Press, 1977.

31. For example, see LaFeber, "Roosevelt, Churchill, and Indochina."

32. My discussion of time as a critical element for the exercise of power is shaped by Johannes Fabian, *Time and the Other: How Anthropology Makes Its Object*. New York: Columbia University Press, 1983; Pierre Bourdieu, *Outline of a Theory of Practice*. Cambridge: Cambridge University Press, 1977, pp. 159–197; and Arjun Appadurai, *Modernity at Large: Cultural Dimensions of Globalization*. Minneapolis: University of Minnesota Press, 1996, pp. 66–85, 178–199.

33. My discussion on the interrelationship of modernity and the telescoping of time draws on David Harvey, *The Condition of Postmodernity*. Cambridge: Basil Blackwell, 1990, pp. 201–283; and more broadly, Karl Polanyi, *The Great Transformation*. Boston: Beacon, 1943.

34. The best-known proponent of modernization theory is Walt Rostow, from whose work these commonalties are drawn. See Walt W. Rostow, *The Stages of Economic Growth: A Non-Communist Manifesto*. Cambridge: Cambridge University Press, 1960. For a thoughtful discussion of modernization theory and its relationship to John F. Kennedy's policy toward Latin America, see Michael E. Latham, "Ideology, Social Science, and Destiny: Modernization and the Kennedy-Era Alliance for Progress." *Diplomatic History* 22, no. 3 (Spring 1998): 199–229.

35. David Halberstam, *The Best and the Brightest*. New York: Random House, 1972, pp. 512, 564.

36. Lyndon B. Johnson, speech of 7 April 1965, reprinted in U.S. Senate, Committee on Foreign Relations, *Background Information Relating to Southeast Asia and Vietnam*. 90th Cong., 2nd sess. Washington: D.C.: U.S. Government Printing Office, 1968, pp. 148–153.

37. My reading of the Johns Hopkins speech and the notion of internal colonization relies on a wonderful essay by Lloyd C. Gardner, "From the Colorado to the Mekong." In *Vietnam: The Early Decisions*, ed. Lloyd C. Gardner and Ted Gittinger. Austin: University of Texas Press, 1997, pp. 37–57; and Lloyd C. Gardner, *Pay Any Price: Lyndon Johnson and the Wars for Vietnam*. Chicago: Ivan R. Dee, 1995.

38. Doris Kearns Goodwin, *Lyndon Johnson and the American Dream*. New York: Harper and Row, 1976, p. 267; and Stanley Karnow, *Vietnam: A History*. New York: Viking, 1983, p. 416, cited in Gardner, "From the Colorado to the Mekong," p. 53.

## Chapter 13

1. Memorandum by Nitze, 5 March 1952, *Foreign Relations of the United States (FRUS), 1952–1954*. Vol. 22. Pt. 1, *East Asia and the Pacific*. Washington, D.C.: U.S. Government Printing Office, 1981, p. 68.

2. Memorandum of discussion at State Department–Joint Chiefs of Staff meeting, 16 January 1952, *FRUS, 1952–1954*. Vol. 22. Pt. 1, p. 32.

3. Memorandum of discussion between Acheson, Eden, and others, 26 May 1952, *FRUS, 1952–1954*. Vol. 22. Pt. 1, pp. 96–97.

4. For a fuller discussion of these points, see Robert J. McMahon, *Limits of Em-*

*pire: The United States and Southeast Asia since World War II.* New York: Columbia University Press, 1999.

5. Critical works include: William Borden, *The Pacific Alliance: United States Foreign Economic Policy and Japanese Trade Recovery, 1947–1955.* Madison: University of Wisconsin Press, 1984; Michael Schaller, *The American Occupation of Japan: The Origins of the Cold War in Asia.* New York: Oxford University Press, 1985; Andrew J. Rotter, *The Path to Vietnam: Origins of the American Commitment to Southeast·Asia.* Ithaca, N.Y.: Cornell University Press, 1987; Melvyn P. Leffler, *A Preponderance of Power: National Security, the Truman Administration, and the Cold War.* Stanford, Calif.: Stanford University Press, 1992; and Steven Hugh Lee, *Outposts of Empire: Korea, Vietnam, the Origins of the Cold War in Asia.* Montreal: McGill-Queens University Press, 1995.

6. For example, see Robert Blum, *Drawing the Line: The Origin of the American Containment Policy in East Asia.* New York: Norton, 1982.

7. Quoted in Thomas G. Paterson, "A Introduction: John F. Kennedy's Quest for Victory and Global Crisis." In *Kennedy's Quest for Victory: American Foreign Policy, 1961–1963,* ed. Thomas G. Paterson. New York: Oxford University Press, 1989, p. 10.

8. Quoted in Ted Gittinger, ed., *The Johnson Years: A Vietnam Roundtable.* Austin, Tex.: Lyndon B. Johnson Library, 1993, p. 101.

9. Robert J. McMahon, "Credibility and World Power: Exploring the Psychological Dimension of Postwar American Foreign Policy." *Diplomatic History* 15 (Fall 1991): 455–471.

10. Memorandum of conversation between Dulles, Eisenhower, and others, 28 May 1954, *FRUS, 1952–1954.* Vol. 21, *The Geneva Conference.* Washington, D.C.: U.S. Government Printing Office, 1981, pp. 521–522. For the broader context, see McMahon, *Limits of Empire,* pp. 64–68.

11. U.S. Department of State, *The Situation in Laos.* Washington, D.C.: U.S. Government Printing Office, 1959, p. i.

12. Brief prepared by the Joint Chiefs of Staff, *FRUS, 1961–1963.* Vol. 23, *Southeast Asia.* Washington, D.C.: U.S. Government Printing Office, 1994, pp. 2–4.

13. McMahon, "Credibility and World Power."

14. On the divergence of allied views, see especially Fredrik Logevall, *Choosing War: The Lost Chance for Peace and the Escalation of the War in Vietnam.* Berkeley: University of California Press, 1999.

15. Memorandum of conversation between Rusk, Alphand, and others, 2 July 1964, *FRUS, 1964–1968.* Vol. 1, *Vietnam 1964.* Washington, D.C.: U.S. Government Printing Office, 1992, 533–537.

16. Odd Arne Westad, "Introduction: Reviewing the Cold War." In *Reviewing the Cold War: Approaches, Interpretations, Theory,* ed. Odd Arne Westad. London: Frank Cass, 2000, p. 18.

17. Melvyn P. Leffler, "Bringing It Together: The Parts and the Whole." In *Reviewing the Cold War: Approaches, Interpretations, Theory,* ed. Odd Arne Westad. London: Frank Cass, 2000, p. 45.

18. Anders Stephanson, "Liberty or Death: The Cold War As US Ideology." In *Reviewing the Cold War: Approaches, Interpretations, Theory,* ed. Odd Arne Westad. London: Frank Cass, 2000, p. 95.

19. Michael H. Hunt, *Ideology and U.S. Foreign Policy.* New Haven, Conn.: Yale University Press, 1987; see also Douglas J. Macdonald, "Formal Ideologies in the

Cold War: Toward a Framework for Empirical Analysis." In *Reviewing the Cold War: Approaches, Interpretations, Theory,* ed. Odd Arne Westad. London: Frank Cass, 2000, pp. 180–204.

20. Michael H. Hunt, "Conclusions: The Decolonization Puzzle in US Policy: Promise versus Performance." In *The United States and Decolonization: Power and Freedom,* ed. David Ryan and Victor Pun gong. London: Macmillan, 2000, pp. 212–218; and Hunt, *Ideology and U.S. Foreign Policy,* pp. 19–45.

21. Quoted in Leffler, "Bringing It Together," p. 44.

22. Quoted in Melvyn P. Leffler, *The Specter of Communism: The United States and the Origins of the Cold War, 1917–1953.* New York: Hill and Wang, 1994, p. 63.

23. Quoted in Leffler, *Specter of Communism,* p. 62.

24. Hunt, "Decolonization Puzzle," p. 216.

25. Hunt, "Decolonization Puzzle," p. 217.

26. Hunt, "Decolonization Puzzle," p. 216.

27. Mark Philip Bradley, *Imagining Vietnam and America: The Making of Postcolonial Vietnam, 1919–1950.* Chapel Hill: University of North Carolina Press, 2000, p. 109; see also Mark Philip Bradley, chapter 12, in this volume.

28. Quoted in Bradley, *Imagining Vietnam and America,* pp. 135–136.

29. Foote to MacArthur, 29 January 1944, 856D.00/166, Department of State Central Files, U.S. National Archives, Washington, D.C.

30. Quoted in Nick Cullather, *Illusions of Influence: The Political Economy of United States–Philippines Relations, 1942–1960.* Stanford, Calif.: Stanford University Press, 1994, p. 83.

31. Hunt, *Ideology and U.S. Foreign Policy,* pp. 160–162; see also Michael E. Latham, *Modernization As Ideology: American Social Science and Nation Building in the Kennedy Era.* Chapel Hill: University of North Carolina Press, 2000; and Andrew Rotter, *Comrades at Odds: The United States and India, 1947–1964.* Ithaca, N.Y.: Cornell University Press, 2000, pp. 158–160.

32. For example, see George C. Herring, "Peoples Quite Apart: Americans, South Vietnamese, and the War in Vietnam." *Diplomatic History* 14 (Winter 1990): 1–23; Sandra C. Taylor, "Lyndon Johnson and the Vietnamese." In *Shadow on the White House: Presidents and the Vietnam War, 1945–1975,* ed. David L. Anderson. Lawrence: University Press of Kansas, 1993, pp. 113–129.

## Chapter 14

1. Minutes of discussion, July 14, 1953, PREM (Prime Minister's files)11/425–79695, Public Record Office, Kew, United Kingdom, pp. 58–59.

2. Dulles testimony to Senate Foreign Relations Committee, May 12, 1954, *Executive Sessions of the Senate Foreign Relations Committee* (Historical Series). Vol. 6. 83rd Cong., 2nd sess., 1954. Washington, D.C.: U.S. Government Printing Office, 1977, pp. 279–280.

3. Dulles's World War I experiences and Wilsonian views are discussed in Ronald W. Pruessen, *John Foster Dulles: The Road to Power, 1888–1952.* New York: The Free Press, 1982, pp. 19–57.

4. The evolution of Dulles's depression-era thoughts is discussed in Pruessen, *John Foster Dulles,* pp. 133–177. The remarks concerning the mandate system are found on p. 167.

5. Pruessen, *John Foster Dulles,* 178–217. His statement to Eden and Lord Cranborne is quoted on p. 211.

6. A useful overview of the New Look can be found in John Lewis Gaddis, *Strategies of Containment: A Critical Appraisal of Postwar American National Security Policy.* New York: Oxford University Press, 1982, chapters 5–6.

7. Dulles Speech, January 9, 1950, The Personal Papers of John Foster Dulles, Princeton University Library, Princeton, New Jersey

8. United States Minutes of the Second Meeting between President Rhee and the Secretary of State, August 6, 1953, *Foreign Relations of the United States (FRUS), 1952–1954.* Vol. 14, *China and Japan.* Washington, D.C.: U.S. Government Printing Office, 1985, p. 1475.

9. For example, see Ronald W. Pruessen, "Over the Volcano: The United States and the Taiwan Strait Crisis, 1954–1955," and Robert Accinelli, "'A Thorn in the Side of Peace': The Eisenhower Administration and the 1958 Offshore Islands Crisis." In *Re-examining the Cold War: U.S.-China Diplomacy, 1954–1973,* ed. Robert S. Ross and Jiang Changbin. Cambridge, Mass.: Harvard University Asia Center, 2001, pp. 77–140.

10. Dulles's remarks to the House Foreign Affairs Committee are quoted in Audrey R. Kahin and George McTurnan Kahin, *Subversion As Foreign Policy: The Secret Eisenhower and Dulles Debacle in Indonesia.* New York: The New Press, 1995, pp. 150–151. Kahin and Kahin's study offers numerous additional examples of the anticommunist tilt of American analysis and policy.

11. For example, see George C. Herring, *America's Longest War: The United States and Vietnam, 1950–1975.* New York: Knopf, 1986, chapter 1.

12. For example, see Pruessen, *John Foster Dulles,* pp. 178–217.

13. Pruessen, *John Foster Dulles,* pp. 259–261.

14. Michael Schaller provides an excellent overview of evolving American thinking concerning Southeast Asia and the global economy in *The American Occupation of Japan: The Origins of the Cold War in Asia.* New York: Oxford University Press, 1985. Quotations from Truman-era policy makers are taken from pp. 157–161.

15. Pruessen, *John Foster Dulles,* chapters 12, 13, 16, 17.

16. Dulles interview, September 12, 1951, The Personal Papers of John Foster Dulles, Princeton University Library, Princeton, New Jersey.

17. United States Summary Minutes of Meeting, November 9, 1954, *FRUS, 1952–1954.* Vol. 14, pp. 1779–1782.

18. Quoted in William S. Borden, *The Pacific Alliance: United States Foreign Economic Policy and Japanese Trade Recovery, 1947–1955.* Madison: University of Wisconsin Press, 1984, p. 215.

19. Dulles address, September 5, 1951, The Personal Papers of John Foster Dulles, Princeton University Library, Princeton, New Jersey.

20. United States Minutes of the Second Meeting between President Rhee and the Secretary of State, August 6, 1953, *FRUS, 1952–1954.* Vol. 14, p. 1475.

21. *Executive Sessions of the Senate Foreign Relations Committee* (Historical Series). Vol. 6. 83rd Cong., 2nd sess., 1954. Washington, D.C.: U.S. Government Printing Office, 1977, p. 23.

22. *Executive Sessions of the Senate Foreign Relations Committee* (Historical Series). Vol. 7. 84th Cong., 1st sess., 1955. Washington, D.C.: U.S. Government Printing Office, 1978, p. 395.

23. Memorandum of Conversation, October 8, 1958, *FRUS, 1958–1960.* Vol. X,

*Eastern Europe Region; Soviet Union; Cyprus.* Washington, D.C.: U.S. Government Printing Office, 1992, pp. 251–252.

24. Dulles testimony to Senate Foreign Relations Committee, May 12, 1954, *Executive Sessions of the Senate Foreign Relations Committee* (Historical Series). Vol. 6. 83rd Cong., 2nd sess., 1954 (Washington, D.C.: United States Government Printing Office, 1977), p. 258.

25. Memorandum of Conversation with the President, May 19, 1954, *FRUS, 1952–1954.* Vol. 13, *Indochina.* Washington, D.C.: U.S. Government Printing Office, 1982, p. 1584.

26. Dulles's lunchtime rage is described by Eden's private secretary in Evelyn Shuckburgh, *Descent to Suez.* London: Weidenfeld and Nicolson, 1986, pp. 183–185.

27. Memorandum of Conversation, by the Secretary of State, May 11, 1954, *FRUS, 1952–1954.* Vol. 13, p. 1522.

28. Pruessen, "Over the Volcano"; and Accinelli, "'Thorn in the Side of Peace.'"

29. For example, see Kahin and Kahin, *Subversion As Foreign Policy,* chapters 6–9.

30. Conference in the President's Office, June 2, 1954, memorandum in the Files of the National Security Adviser, Dwight D. Eisenhower Library, Abilene, Kansas.

31. Memorandum of Conversation with the President, March 24, 1954, *FRUS, 1952–1954.* Vol. 13, p. 1150.

32. Shuckburgh, *Descent to Suez,* p. 187.

33. Memorandum of Conversation with the President, December 3, 1956, Meetings with the President File, Dwight D. Eisenhower Library, Abilene, Kansas.

## Chapter 15

1. Joseph S. Nye, introduction to *International Regionalism: Readings,* ed. Joseph S. Nye. Boston: Little, Brown, 1968, p. vii.

2. For a discussion of the concepts of "regionalism" and "regional cooperation," see Andrew Hurrell, "Regionalism in Theoretical Perspective." In *Regionalism in World Politics: Regional Organization and International Order,* ed. Louise Fawcett and Andrew Hurrell. Oxford: Oxford University Press, 1995, pp. 37–73; Bruce M. Russett, *International Regions and the International System: A Study in Political Ecology.* Chicago: Rand McNally, 1969; and Walter Isard, *Introduction to Regional Science.* Englewood Cliffs, N.J.: Prentice-Hall, 1975.

3. "United States Policy toward Southeast Asia," Policy Planning Staff Paper (PPS/51), 29. March 1949, cited in Anna Kasten Nelson, ed., *The State Department Policy Planning Staff Papers, 1949.* Vol. 3. New York: Garland, 1983, p. 33.

4. For a discussion of the communist takeover in China and its implications for American Southeast Asian policy, see Melvyn P. Leffler, *The Preponderance of Power.* Stanford, Calif.: Stanford University Press, pp. 291–304, 333–341; and Andrew J. Rotter, *The Path to Vietnam: Origins of the American Commitment to Southeast Asia.* Ithaca, N.Y.: Cornell University Press, 1987, chapter 5. For U.S. post–World War II policy toward the Third World in general, see John Lewis Gaddis, *We Now Know: Rethinking Cold War History.* Oxford: Oxford University Press, 1997, chapter 3; and David S. Painter, "Explaining U.S. Relations with the Third World." *Diplomatic History* 19, no. 3 (Summer 1995): 529–535.

5. The Ambassador in China (Stuart) to the Secretary of State, 15 February 1949, *Foreign Relations of the United States (FRUS), 1949.* Vol. 7, *The Far East and Australasia.* Washington, D.C.: U.S. Government Printing Office, 1976, p. 1117.

6. "United States Policy toward Southeast Asia," Policy Planning Staff Paper, 29 March 1949, *FRUS, 1949*. Vol. 7, p. 1129.

7. U.S. Department of Defense, *United States–Vietnam Relations: Study Prepared by the Department of Defense*. Vol. 1. Washington, D.C.: U.S. Government Printing Office, 1971, p. 47.

8. "United States Policy toward Southeast Asia," p. 1130.

9. ECAFE was a regional organization of the United Nations, which was founded in Shanghai in 1947 with the purpose of trying to solve the postwar economic and social problems of Asia. ECAFE's headquarters moved to Bangkok in 1949; in 1974 the organization's name was changed to Economic and Social Commission for Asia and the Pacific.

10. Memorandum of Conversation, by the Director of the Office of Far Eastern Affairs (Butterworth), 12 September 1949, *FRUS, 1949*. Vol. 7, p. 1200.

11. Memorandum of Conversation, by the Director of the Office of Far Eastern Affairs (Butterworth), 12 September 1949, *FRUS, 1949*. Vol. 7, 1199.

12. The Asian Relations Conference, which had taken place in New Delhi from March 23 to April 2, 1947, was held on the initiative of Indian prime minister Jawaharlal Nehru, who had invited representatives from all the Asian states and liberation movements to discuss the creation of a regional organization. Western, and especially American, observers had feared the emergence of an anti-Western and pan-Asiatic movement. But the participants' objectives and interests were too diverse to find a common ground for any binding resolution. So the conference ended with a condemnation of colonialism and a call for national self-rule and independence. Its significance consisted in the fact that it took place at all. See Russell H. Fifield, *The Diplomacy of Southeast Asia, 1945–1958*. Hamden, Conn.: Archon, 1968, pp. 449–451. In January 1949, Nehru organized the so-called New Delhi Conference. But his proposal to create an organizational structure for regional cooperation in Asia was rejected by most of his fellow heads of state, who suspected an Indian bid for leadership in Asia. On the other hand, the United States saw the danger of the creation of an anti-Western bloc under Indian leadership and applied pressure on its Philippine allies to prevent the passing of an anti-Western resolution. See The Chargé in the Philippines (Lockett) to the Acting Secretary of State, 15 January 1949, *FRUS, 1949*. Vol. 7, p. 1115.

13. Fifield, *Diplomacy of Southeast Asia*, pp. 454–455.

14. U.S. Department of State, Office of Intelligence Research, "Prospects for Regional Cooperation in South and Southeast Asia," OIR Report 5206, 17 January 1951, cited in Paul Kesaris, ed., *OSS/State Department Intelligence and Research Reports*. Pt. 8, *Japan, Korea, Southeast Asia and the Far East Generally, 1950–1961 Supplement, reel 7*. Washington, D.C.: University Publications of America, 1977, p. 33.

15. Report to the President by the National Security Council, "The Position of the United States with Respect to Asia," NSC 48/2, 30 December 1949, *FRUS, 1949*. Vol. 7, p. 1216.

16. For a detailed account of the creation of ANZUS, see the memories of the former Australian foreign minister Percy Spender, *Exercises in Diplomacy: The ANZUS Treaty and the Colombo Plan*. Sydney: Sydney University Press, 1969.

17. The Secretary of Defense (Marshall) to the Secretary of State, 13 April 1951, *FRUS, 1951*. Vol. 6, *Asia and the Pacific*. Washington, D.C.: U.S. Government Printing Office, 1977, p. 202. Therefore, in August 1951 the United States and the Philippines signed a separate agreement, the Mutual Defense Treaty. But the government in

Manila was still angered by the American decision to exclude it from ANZUS and threatened to revive the idea of the Pacific Pact. See The Ambassador in the Philippines (Cowen) to the Secretary of State, 17 July 1951, *FRUS, 1951.* Vol. 6, p. 223.

18. See K. Suter, *ANZUS: The Empty Treaty.* Sydney: UN Association for Australia, Disarmament Committee, n.d., p. 2; and Michael McKinley, *ANZUS, New Zealand and the Meaning of Life.* Canberra: The Parliament of the Commonwealth of Australia, Legislative Research Service (Discussion Paper 6), 1985–1986, p. 8.

19. Chintamani Mahapatra, *American Role in the Origin and Growth of ASEAN.* New Delhi: ABC Publishing House, 1990, p. 55.

20. See Memorandum by the Joint Chiefs of Staff for the Secretary of Defense (Lovett), 28 December 1951, *FRUS, 1951.* Vol. 6, pp. 263–264; and Position Paper Prepared in the Department of State, "A Pacific Security Pact," 2 January 1952, *FRUS, 1951.* Vol. 6, pp. 264–265.

21. Ben C. Limp, "The Pacific Pact: Looking Forward or Backward." *Foreign Affairs* 29, no. 4 (July 1951): 540–541. The State Department was alarmed by the implications of an exclusion of Asian states from any future regional security alliance, "We have now come full circle. It is no longer the free nations against the Communist bloc. It is white men against Asians." See also Ogburn to Johnson, "U.S. Alliance with 'White' Powers in Asia," 13 February 1953, Bureau of Far Eastern Affairs—Miscellaneous Subject Files 1953, Entry 1198, Lot File 55 D 388, Box 5, Record Group 59, U.S. National Archives, Washington, D.C.

22. Report by the Secretary of State, Statement of John Foster Dulles, 12 May 1954, *Executive Sessions of the Senate Foreign Relations Committee.* Vol. 6. 83rd Cong., 2nd sess. Washington, D.C.: U.S. Government Printing Office, 1954, p. 263.

23. Russell H. Fifield, *Southeast Asia in United States Policy.* New York: Council on Foreign Relations, 1963, p. 39.

24. NSC 5405, "United States Objectives and Courses of Action with Respect to Southeast Asia," *FRUS, 1952–1954.* Vol. 12, *East Asia and the Pacific.* Washington, D.C.: U.S. Government Printing Office, 1987, p. 371.

25. "Special Committee Report on Southeast Asia, Part II," Draft (SC-P2–3), 5 April 1954, in U.S. Department of Defense, *United States–Vietnam Relations: Study Prepared by the Department of Defense.* Vol. 9. Washington, D.C.: U.S. Government Printing Office, 1971, pp. 351–352.

26. John Foster Dulles, "Security in the Pacific." *Foreign Affairs* 30 (January 1952): 183.

27. Cited in Evelyn Colbert, *Southeast Asia in International Politics, 1941–1956.* Ithaca, N.Y.: Cornell University Press, 1977, p. 293.

28. Anthony Short, "British Policy in Southeast Asia: The Eisenhower Era." In *The Great Powers in East Asia, 1953–1960,* ed. Warren I. Cohen and Akira Iriye. New York: Columbia University Press, 1990, p. 255.

29. *New York Times,* 20 May 1954.

30. Memorandum, Baldwin to Drumright, 11 May 1954, Division of Far Eastern Affairs—Office of the Assistant Secretary for Far Eastern Affairs 1954–56, Entry 1202, Lot File 56 D 206, Box 3, Record Group 59.

31. See Memorandum of Discussion at the 214th Meeting of the National Security Council, 12 September 1954, *FRUS, 1952–1954.* Vol. 12, p. 904. For a detailed account of the negotiations at Manila, see Leszek Buszynski, *SEATO: The Failure of an Alliance Strategy.* Singapore: Singapore University Press, 1983, pp. 37–43.

32. For the text of the treaty, see U.S. Department of State, *American Foreign*

*Policy, 1950–1955: Basic Documents.* Washington, D.C.: Government Printing Office, 1956, pp. 912–917.

33. For the significance of the Manila Treaty for U.S. policy toward Indochina, see George C. Herring, "'A Good Stout Effort': John Foster Dulles and the Indochina Crisis, 1954–1955." In *John Foster Dulles and the Diplomacy of the Cold War*, ed. Richard H. Immerman. Princeton, N.J.: Princeton University Press, 1990.

34. "Address by the Secretary of State," 15 September 1954, *American Foreign Policy, 1950–1955: Basic Documents,* p. 921.

35. The *New Republic* commented on the foundation of SEATO by saying, "Signing of SEATO is a warning to the communists to push no further. But the nations in agreement were not those which in reality will determine the future of Southeast Asia: they were either Western powers, who know but one evil, communism, or small Asian non-powers who long have depended on the West." See *New Republic,* 20 September 1954.

36. Indonesia in particular followed a policy of nonalignment. In April 1955, the government in Jakarta hosted the Bandung Conference, where representatives of twenty-nine Asian and African nations discussed international policy concepts. The conference ended with a formal condemnation of colonialism. Although it did not produce any further results, the conference is regarded as a significant step toward the development of the nonalignment movement. The U.S. government had been concerned about a possible anti-Western resolution, but in the end Secretary of State Dulles expressed his satisfaction with the outcome of the conference. Dulles claimed that even the United States could have signed the final communiqué. See H. W. Brands, *The Specter of Neutralism: The United States and the Emergence of the Third World, 1947–1960.* New York: Columbia University Press, 1989, pp. 115–116.

37. For a detailed analysis of SEATO, see Buszynski, *SEATO;* George Modelski, ed., *SEATO: Six Studies.* Melbourne: F. W. Cheshire, 1962; and Justus M. van der Kroef, *The Lives of SEATO.* Singapore: ISEAS (Occasional Paper 45), December 1976.

38. "Asian Economic Program: Its Proposed Character and Method of Operation," Annex Two to a Memorandum by the Economic Coordinator of the Bureau of Far Eastern Affairs (Baldwin) to the Director of the Political Planning Staff (Bowie), 30 August 1954, *FRUS, 1952–1954.* Vol. 12, p. 812.

39. "Asian Economic Aid Program Developments," Memorandum by the Economic Coordinator in the Bureau of Far Eastern Affairs (Baldwin) to the Deputy Assistant Secretary of State for Far Eastern Affairs (Sebald), 2 November 1954, *FRUS, 1952–1954.* Vol. 12, p. 960.

40. "Recommendations Relative to a Mutual Security Program," Message from the President of the United States Referred to the House Committee on Foreign Affairs, April 20, 1955, in *Executive Sessions of the Senate Foreign Relations Committee.* Vol. 7. 84th Cong., 1st sess., 1955. Washington, D.C.: U.S. Government Printing Office, 1978, p. 821.

41. See "The Fiscal Year 1956 Mutual Security Program," Memorandum by the Director of the Foreign Operations Administration (Stassen) to the Deputy Assistant to the President (Persons), 27 July 1955, *FRUS, 1955–1957.* Vol. 10, *Foreign Aid and Economic Defense Policy.* Washington, D.C.: U.S. Government Printing Office, 1989, p. 12.

42. "Observations and Proposals," Report by the Chairman of the Council on Foreign Economic Policy (Randall), December 1956, *FRUS, 1955–1957.* Vol. 9, *Foreign*

*Economic Policy: Foreign Information Program.* Washington, D.C.: U.S. Government Printing Office, 1987, p. 38.

43. "Statement of Policy by the National Security Council on Current U.S. Policy in the Far East," Draft, 19 November 1954, *FRUS, 1952–1954.* Vol. 12, p. 977.

44. The OEEC, founded in 1948 for the economic reconstruction of Europe, was renamed Organization for Economic Cooperation and Development in 1961.

45. See "Report of the Asian Economic Working Group Concerning the Inauguration of Large-Scale, Long-Range Program of Economic Assistance," Attachment to a Memorandum by the Economic Coordinator of the Bureau of Far Eastern Affairs (Baldwin) to the Director of the Policy Planning Staff (Bowie), 30 August 1954, *FRUS, 1952–1954.* Vol. 12, pp. 811–812. The Colombo Plan was founded in 1950 on an initiative by Great Britain. The United States joined the plan in February 1951. The Colombo Plan was a multilateral agreement, which enabled seventeen Asian states to apply for bilateral economic assistance from the United States, Great Britain, Canada, Australia, New Zealand, and Japan. For a detailed account of the plan's origins, see Spender, *Exercises in Diplomacy.* For its objectives and working procedures, see *The Colombo Plan.* London: HMSO, 1964; Michael Haas, *The Asian Way to Peace: A Story of Regional Cooperation.* New York: Praeger, 1989, pp. 23–30; and the Colombo Plan's Web site at www.colombo-plan.org (March 5, 2003).

46. Memorandum by the Deputy Under Secretary of State (Murphy) to the Secretary of State, n.d., *FRUS, 1952–1954.* Vol. 12, p. 1019.

47. "Observations and Proposals," Report by the Chairman of the Council on Foreign Economic Policy (Randall), December 1956, *FRUS, 1955–1957.* Vol. 9, p. 39.

48. See "Report of the Asian Economic Working Group Concerning the Inauguration of Large-Scale, Long-Range Program of Economic Assistance," Attachment to a Memorandum by the Economic Coordinator of the Bureau of Far Eastern Affairs (Baldwin) to the Director of the Policy Planning Staff (Bowie), 30 August 1954, *FRUS, 1952–1954.* Vol. 12, p. 817.

49. Section 14 of the Mutual Security Act of 1956, cited in a Letter from the Acting Secretary of State to the Chairman of the Council on Foreign Economic Policy (Randall), 9 March 1957, *FRUS, 1955–1957.* Vol. 10, p. 140.

50. "Statement of Policy on U.S. Policy in Mainland Southeast Asia," Enclosure, NSC 6012, 25 July 1960, *FRUS, 1958–1960.* Vol. 16, *East Asia–Pacific Region, Cambodia, Laos.* Washington, D.C.: U.S. Government Printing Office, 1992, p. 214.

51. Interview with an anonymous government official, *Far Eastern Economic Review,* 14 July 1960, 51. A U.S. State Department intelligence report pessimistically commented on this effort, "Despite recurrent proposals for some new regional grouping in Asia, there is no prospect that any regional scheme for the area will supplant or even approach in importance the existing alliances including SEATO or the existing economic groupings such as the Colombo Plan." See U.S. Department of State, Bureau of Intelligence and Research, "The Mirage of Regionalism in Asia," Intelligence Report 8192, 8 January 1960, cited in Kesaris, *OSS/State Department Intelligence and Research Reports,* p.1.

52. *Far Eastern Economic Review,* 28 July 1960, p. 162.

53. *Far Eastern Economic Review,* 11 August 1960. Apparently, this name was chosen because SEAFET sounded much alike SEATO, the ill-regarded military alliance, and thus would not have been acceptable for the neutral states of the region. See *Far Eastern Economic Review,* 21 September 1961, p. 548.

54. *New York Times,* 7 August 1961.

55. For detailed information on ASA, see Vincent K. Pollard, "ASA and ASEAN, 1961–1967: Southeast Asian Regionalism." *Asian Survey* 10, no. 3 (March 1979); Arnfinn Jorgensen-Dahl, *Regional Organization and Order in South-East Asia.* New York: St. Martin's, 1982, pp. 21–44; and Haas, *Asian Way,* pp. 120–123.

56. Bernard K. Gordon, *Toward Disengagement in Asia: A Strategy for American Foreign Policy.* Englewood Cliffs, N.J.: Prentice-Hall, 1969, p. 98.

57. *Far Eastern Economic Review,* 21 September 1961, p. 552.

58. *New York Times,* 2 February 1961.

59. Timothy P. Maga, *John F. Kennedy and the New Pacific Community, 1961–63.* New York: St. Martin's, 1990, p. 6.

60. See Memorandum by the Deputy Under Secretary of State for Political Affairs (Johnson) to the Under Secretary of State (Bowles), "Southeast Asian Regional Planning and Coordination," 24 June 1961, *FRUS, 1961–1963.* Vol. 23, *Southeast Asia.* Washington, D.C.: U.S. Government Printing Office, 1994, p. 10.

61. See Department of State Policy Directive, "Future of SEATO," 5 April 1962, *FRUS, 1961–1963.* Vol. 23, p. 56.

62. See Memorandum from Michael V. Forrestal of the National Security Council Staff to the President's Special Assistant for National Security Affairs (Bundy), 10 April 1962, *FRUS, 1961–1963.* Vol. 23, p. 60. In March 1962, U.S.-Thai security relations had already been put on a bilateral basis. In the so-called Rusk-Thanat Communiqué, the United States ensured Thailand's defense in case of communist aggression.

63. For detailed information on Maphilindo, see Albert Ravenholt, *Maphilindo: Dream or Achievable Reality?* New York: American Universities Field Staff (Southeast Asia Series 12.1), February 1964; Arnold C. Brackman, *Southeast Asia's Second Front: The Power Struggle in the Malay Archipelago.* London: Pall Mall, 1966, in particular chapter 15; and Haas, *Asian Way,* pp. 123–126.

64. This explains why Thailand did not become a member of Maphilindo.

65. The idea of a Malayan Union had originally been a British project, but was officially propagated by Malayan prime minister Tunku in May 1961, who announced the merging of Malaya with Singapore and two British provinces in northern Borneo— North Borneo and Sarawak. Indonesia and the Philippines were both opposed to the concept of a Federation of Malaysia—Jakarta regarded it as neocolonial British plot while Manila claimed sovereignty over North Borneo. For a detailed account of the dispute around the launching of the Federation of Malaysia, see Brackman, *Southeast Asia's Second Front;* Willard A. Hanna, *The Formation of Malaysia: New Factor in World Politics.* New York: American Universities Field Staff, 1964; and Alastair M. Taylor, "Malaysia, Indonesia—and Maphilindo." *International Journal* 19, no. 2 (Spring 1964): 155–171.

66. Kennedy adviser Roger Hilsman, cited in Arnfinn Jorgensen-Dahl, "Extraregional Influences on Regional Cooperation in S.E. Asia." *Pacific Community* 8, no. 3 (April 1977): p. 413. For an account of the Kennedy administration's policy toward Indonesia, see Maga, *John F. Kennedy,* pp. 51–70.

67. For the Kennedy mission, see *Department of State Bulletin,* 17 February 1964, pp. 239–243. For the U.S. position on the conflict around the formation of Malaysia, see "United States Support of the Inclusion of Sabah and Sarawak in Malaysia, to Be Proclaimed on September 16," Statement Read to Correspondents by the Director of the Office of News (Phillips), Department of State, 14 September 1963, U.S. Department of State, *American Foreign Policy, 1963: Current Documents.* Washington, D.C.: Government Printing Office, 1964, p. 823; and "United States Interest in Negotiation

of the Indonesia-Malaysia Dispute," Statement Made by the U.S. Representative (Stevenson) in the U.N. Security Council, 10 September 1964, U.S. Department of State, *American Foreign Policy, 1964: Current Documents*. Washington, D.C.:Government Printing Office, 1965, p. 902.

68. "Mission to Southeast Asia, India and Pakistan," Memorandum by the Vice President to the President, 23 May 1961, in U.S. Department of Defense, *United States–Vietnam Relations: Study Prepared by the Department of Defense*. Vol. 11. Washington, D.C.: U.S. Government Printing Office, 1971, p. 163.

69. "Peace without Conquest," Speech at Johns Hopkins University. *Public Papers of the Presidents of the United States: Lyndon B. Johnson, 1965*. Washington, D.C.: U.S. Government Printing Office, 1966, pp. 396–397.

70. Memorandum from the Counselor of the Department of State and Chairman of the Policy Planning Staff (Rostow) to the President's Special Assistant for National Security Affairs (Bundy), 30 March 1965, *FRUS, 1964–1968*. Vol. 27, *Mainland Southeast Asia: Regional Affairs*. Washington, D.C.: U.S. Government Printing Office, 2000, pp. 143–145.

71. Paper Prepared by Chester L. Cooper of the National Security Council Staff for the President's Special Assistant for National Security Affairs (Bundy), 1 April 1965, *FRUS, 1964–1968*. Vol. 27, pp. 146–148.

72. Memorandum from the Administrator of the Agency for International Development (Bell) and the Under Secretary of State for Economic Affairs (Mann) to President Johnson, n.d., *FRUS, 1964–1968*. Vol. 27, pp. 152–157. The donor countries would have been the Western countries—primarily the United States, which would have paid for roughly half of the assets, Japan, and West European countries.

73. The Johnson administration calculated that the bank would have to have $1 billion in assets, $200 million of which would be contributed by the United States. See Memorandum from Francis M. Bator of the National Security Council Staff to President Johnson, 21 June 1965, *FRUS, 1964–1968*. Vol. 27, pp. 170–172.

74. See Letter from the President's Special Adviser on Southeast Asia (Black) to President Johnson, 8 April 1966, *FRUS,1964–1968*. Vol. 27, 179f.

75. For additional information on the origin, organizational structure, and further development of the ADB, see Dick Wilson, *A Bank for Half the World: The Story of the Asian Development Bank, 1966–1986*. Manila: Asian Development Bank, 1987; John White, "The Asian Development Bank: A Question of Style." *International Affairs* 44, no. 4 (October 1968): 677–690; and the ADB's online presentation at www.adb.org (March 5, 2003). For the American role within the ADB, see Nitish K. Dutt, "The United States and Asian Development Bank." *Journal of Contemporary Asia* 27, no. 1 (1997): 71–84. And for Eugene R. Black's role, see his memoirs, *Alternative in Southeast Asia*. London: Pall Mall, 1969.

76. Lyndon B. Johnson, *The Vantage Point: Perspectives of the Presidency, 1963–1969*. New York: Holt, Reinhart and Winston, 1971, p. 348. In his memoirs, he described the situation in 1966, "Early in 1966 I was heartened by the growing evidence that most Asians understood . . . our policy in Southeast Asia. . . . [T]hey realized that they would have to take on increasing responsibility for their future through cooperation with each other" (p. 357). Walt W. Rostow also contributed the ADB's success to Johnson's policy, "The ADB emerged from . . . Johnson's vision of what a total policy toward the region should be." See Walt W. Rostow, *United States and the Regional Organization of Asia and the Pacific, 1965–1985*. Austin: University of Texas Press, 1986, p. 9.

77. *Far Eastern Economic Review Yearbook* (1967): 67.

78. Malaysia, Australia, New Zealand, Japan, the Philippines, Thailand, Taiwan, and South Vietnam.

79. ASPAC was officially dissolved in 1973.

80. Cited in Mahapatra, *American Role*, p. 74.

81. "Vice President Reviews Asian Problems with the Premier." *Department of State Bulletin*, 14 March 1966, pp. 396–397.

82. "Secretary Rusk's News Conference of September 16." *Department of State Bulletin*, 3 October 1966, p. 480.

83. For Johnson's speeches during this trip, see *Public Papers of the Presidents of the United States: Lyndon B. Johnson, 1966*. Washington, D.C.: U.S. Government Printing Office, 1967, pp. 1239–1293.

84. *New York Times*, 3 June 1966; see also Gordon, *Toward Disengagement in Asia*, pp. 112–113.

85. For a detailed account of the negotiations and diplomatic initiatives leading to the formation of ASEAN, see Gordon, *Toward Disengagement in Asia*, pp. 111–119; Pollard, "ASA and ASEAN"; and *Far Eastern Economic Review*, 24 August 1967, pp. 378–381.

86. ASEAN Secretariat, www.asean.or.id/history/leader67.htm ((March 5, 2003).

87. For a side-by-side comparison of the documents, see Gordon, *Toward Disengagement in Asia*, pp. 114–119.

88. Michael Leifer, *Indonesia's Foreign Policy*. London: Allen and Unwin, 1983, p. 121. In early 1966, the Philippine foreign minister Narcisco Ramos, in a memorandum to President Marcos, outlined the Philippine posture toward regionalism. With reference to Indonesia, the foreign minister remarked, "While the Philippines is committed to all that the ASA stands for, it would not to be to its national interest to pronounce a sentence of doom for Maphilindo, which Indonesia might construe as a rebuff against her." See Memorandum from Secretary of Foreign Affairs, Narcisco Ramos, to President Ferdinand Marcos, "Proposed Organization of Asian States," 6 January 1966, cited in Gordon, *Toward Disengagement in Asia*, p. 117.

89. See ASEAN Secretariat, www.asean.org.id/history/leader67.htm (March 5, 2003); and *Far Eastern Economic Review*, 24 August 1967, p. 379.

90. See ASEAN Secretariat, www.asean.org.id/history/leader67.htm; and *Far Eastern Economic Review*, 24 August 1967, p. 379.

91. Jörn Dosch, *Die ASEAN: Bilanz eines Erfolges. Akteure, Interessenlägen, Kooperationsbeziehungen.* Hamburg: Abera, 1997, pp. 23–24.

92. The Soviet Union and China reacted much more negatively; Moscow called the formation of ASEAN "a cause for serious concern in Asia." See Jorgensen-Dahl, "Extra-regional Influences," p. 415. Meanwhile, Beijing characterized the new organization as "an important link in the chain of the U.S.-Soviet campaign against China" and as an attempt "to actively rig up an encirclement of China." See *Peking Review* 52 (December 1967): 41.

93. Cited in Jorgensen-Dahl, "Extra-regional Influences," p. 414.

94. *Department of State Bulletin*, 11 December 1967, p. 792.

95. See Pollard, "ASA and ASEAN," pp. 254–255.

96. In 1977, Richard N. Cooper, the U.S. undersecretary of state for economic affairs, met with his ASEAN counterparts in the first direct U.S.-ASEAN discussions since the founding of the association ten years earlier. Cooper emphasized the U.S. commitment to deal with ASEAN as a "collective institution." See the speech by

Under Secretary of State for Economic Affairs, Richard N. Cooper, Chairman of the American delegation at the first U.S.-ASEAN Dialogue Meeting, Manila, September 8–10, 1977, *Department of State Bulletin,* 31 October 1977, pp. 595–599.

## Chapter 16

1. Hubert Butler, "The British Israelites at Tara." In *The Sub Prefect Should Have Held His Tongue and Other Essays.* London: Allen Lane, 1990, p. 68.

2. For instance, see David Reynolds, *One World Divisible: A Global History since 1945.* New York: Norton, 2000, p. 139; Richard W. Bulliet, ed., *The Columbia History of the Twentieth Century.* New York: Columbia University Press, 1998, pp. 359–361; J. M. Roberts, *Twentieth Century: The History of the World, 1901–2000.* New York: Penguin, 1999, p. 118; Paul Kennedy, *The Rise and Fall of the Great Powers.* New York: Random House, 1987, p. 440; Eric Hobsbawm, *The Age of Extremes: A History of the World, 1914–1991.* New York: Pantheon, 1991, pp. 292, 366; J. R. McNeill, *Something New under the Sun: An Environmental History of the Twentieth Century World.* New York: Norton, 2000, pp. 219–227; and Nicholas Tarling, ed., *Cambridge History of Southeast Asia.* Vol. 2. Cambridge: Cambridge University Press, 1992, p. 531. In each of these accounts, the Green Revolution is depicted as forestalling an approaching population crisis.

3. House Subcommittee on National Security Policy and Scientific Developments, *The Green Revolution: Symposium on Science and Foreign Policy* (hereafter Zablocki hearings). 91st Cong., 1st sess., 5 December 1969. Washington, D.C.: U.S. Government Printing Office, 1970; and Bruce McAllister, *Dream Baby.* New York: T. Doherty Associates, 1989. A sample of the literature can be found in M. Bazlul Karim, *The Green Revolution: An International Bibliography.* Westport, Conn.: Greenwood, 1986; and Zablocki hearings.

4. "In This White House." *The West Wing.* Season 2. Episode 4. October 25, 2000. Teleplay by Aaron Sorkin.

5. Ronald Bailey, "Billions Served." *Reason* (April 2000): 31; and Gregg Easterbrook, "Forgotten Benefactor of Humanity." *The Atlantic Monthly* (January 1997): 82.

6. For instance, see Mark Strauss, "When Malthus Meets Mendel." *Foreign Policy* 119 (Summer 2000): 106–108.

7. William C. Paddock, "How Green Is the Green Revolution?" *BioScience* 20, no. 16 (August 15, 1970): 897–902.

8. CIA Directorate of Intelligence, "India's Foodgrain Situation: Progress and Problems," August 1972. *Declassified Documents Reference Service,* fiche 1978–14B.

9. CIA, "Intelligence Memorandum: Philippine Economic Problems," August 1968. *Declassified Documents Reference Service,* fiche 1987–164: 2690.

10. New Delhi Embassy, "NCAER Finds Green Revolution Real, Industrial Policy Deficient," 23 February 1973. AGR 2 INDIA, State Department Subject-Numeric File, 1970–73, Box 470, Record Group 59, U.S. National Archives, Washington, D.C.

11. Forrest F. Hill oral history, 20 April 1973, Ford Foundation Archives, New York, New York.

12. Vandana Shiva, *The Violence of the Green Revolution.* London: Zed, 1991, pp. 53–54.

13. Sundhir Sen, *A Richer Harvest.* New York: Orbis, 1974, p. 39. Borlaug's dwarf wheat was also derived from a Japanese variety.

14. There was, in fact, nothing uniquely American about the breakthrough. Chinese scientists had developed IR-8 in 1959, six years before the IRRI. By 1965, it was growing on three million hectares. See Gordon Conway, *The Doubly Green Revolution.* Ithaca, N.Y.: Cornell University Press, 1997, p. 52.

15. Ben Rogers, "Just Deserts." *New Statesman,* 15 November 1999, p. 56.

16. Amartya Sen and Jean Drèze, *Hunger and Public Action.* Oxford: Clarendon, 1989, p. 49; Amartya Sen, *Poverty and Famines: An Essay on Entitlement and Deprivation.* New York: Oxford University Press, 1981; and Amartya Sen, *Development As Freedom.* New York: Anchor, 1999, pp. 160–188.

17. Quoted in Arundhati Roy, *The Cost of Living.* New York: Modern Library, 1999, p. 82. In 1954, Nehru had exulted at the sight of the Bhakra-Nangal Dam, "Probably nowhere else in the world is there a dam as high as this. . . . As I walked round the site I thought that these days the biggest temple and mosque and gurdwara is the place where man works for the good of mankind. Which place can be greater than this, this Bhakra-Nangal?" Quoted in Sunil Khilnani, *The Idea of India.* New York: Farrar, Straus, and Giroux, 1997, p. 61.

18. Gelia Tagumpay-Castillo, "'Miracle Rice' As 'Produced' by the Press." Paper presented at the International Seminar on Communications Media and National Development, University of the Philippines, Diliman, November 13, 1967, p. 1.

19. Rolando B. Modina, *IRRI Rice: The Miracle that Never Was.* Quezon City: ACES Foundation, 1987, p. 6.

20. Robert Chandler oral history, International Rice Research Institute Archive, Los Baños, Philippines, 1967, p. 43.

21. With proper care, IR-8 could double productivity per hectare. IRRI officials complained that the press was promising yields beyond what was even theoretically possible, but without the demonstrated high yields on experimental plots, one journalist noted, miracle rice "could be dismissed as just another political gimmick for campaign purposes." See Quijano de Manila, "Challenge and Experiment in Rizal." *Philippines Free Press,* 26 November 1966, p. 87.

22. Napoleon G. Rama, "Miracle Rice-Instant Increase." *Philippines Free Press,* 6 August 1966, p. 5.

23. Wesley C. Haraldson, "The World Food Situation and Philippine Rice Production." *Journal of the American Chamber of Commerce* (February 1966): 59; and USAID Philippines, *The Philippine Story of IR-8 The Miracle Rice.* Manila: U.S. Agency for International Development, 1967.

24. Quijano de Manila, "New Rice Bowls?" *Philippines Free Press,* 29 April 1967, p. 47.

25. Quoted in Victoria Arcega, "Technocrats As Middlemen and Their Networks in the Philippine Rice Project: The Case of the Masagana 99." Ph.D. diss., Michigan State University, 1976, p. 237.

26. Philip Bowring, "Rice: Manila's Facts and Fantasy." *Far Eastern Economic Review* 87, no. 3 (March 1975): 43–45.

27. Col. Osmundo Mondoñedo, "The Rise of the Miracle Men." *The Sunday (Manila) Times Magazine,* 1 October 1967, p. 30.

28. Berger to Secretary of State, "Rice," 25 January 1969, INCO RICE 17 VIET US, State Department Alpha-Numeric File, Record Group 59, Box 1142, NARA.

29. Robert Chambers, "Beyond the Green Revolution." In *Understanding Green Revolutions,* ed. Tim P. Baylis-Smith and Sudhir Wanmali. Cambridge: Cambridge University Press, 1984, p. 363.

30. Robert S. Anderson et al., *Rice Science and Development Politics.* Oxford: Clarendon, 1991, p. 324.

31. The debunking of Marcos's self-sufficiency was a public scandal, but it had amazingly little effect on the Green Revolution literature. In 1997, a monograph could still report that "the Philippines became self-sufficient in rice production in 1968 and 1969 for the first time in decades . . . The re-election of President Marcos in 1969 owed much to the attainment of self-sufficiency in rice production." See Conway, *Doubly Green Revolution,* pp. 53–55.

32. Donald Worster, *Nature's Economy: A History of Ecological Ideas.* 2nd ed. New York: Cambridge University Press, 1994, pp. 352–353. Human ecology's respectable but marginal position in policy circles is demonstrated by the CIA's choice of names for the bogus philanthropies it set up during the 1950s: the Human Ecology Fund and the Society for the Investigation of Human Ecology. See John Marks, *The Search for the Manchurian Candidate: The CIA and Mind Control.* New York: Times, 1979, pp. 147–163.

33. "Eat Hearty." *Time,* 8 November 1948, p. 27; and William L. Laurence, "Scientists Promise More Food for All." *New York Times,* 28 December 1949, p. 27.

34. Frank N. Edgerton, "Changing Concepts of the Balance of Nature." *Quarterly Review of Biology* 48, no. 2 (June 1973): 322–347.

35. John R. Hicks, quoted in Allen C. Kelley, "Economic Consequences of Population Change in the Third World." *Journal of Economic Literature* 26 (December 1988): 1698.

36. Max F. Millikan and Walt W. Rostow, "Notes on Foreign Economic Policy," 21 May 1954. In *Universities and Empire,* ed. Christopher Simpson. New York: New Press, 1998, p. 39.

37. H. W. Arndt, *Economic Development: The History of an Idea.* Chicago: University of Chicago Press, 1987, pp. 64–65.

38. Ansley J. Coale and Edgar M. Hoover, *Population Growth and Economic Development in Low Income Countries.* Princeton, N.J.: Princeton University Press, 1958.

39. Kelley, "Economic Consequences," pp. 1685–1728.

40. Peter J. Donaldson, "On the Origins of the United States Government's International Population Policy." *Population Studies* 44, no. 3 (November 1990): 387–388.

41. William Draper to Anthony Calabrezze, 16 August 1962, State Department Policy Planning Staff Records, Lot 69D121, Box 210, Record Group 59.

42. Dean Rusk, "The Tragedy of Cuba." *Vital Speeches of the Day* 28, no. 9 (February 15, 1962): 259.

43. Bernard B. Fall, "A Grain of Rice Is Worth a Drop of Blood." *New York Times Magazine,* 12 July 1964, pp. 10–16.

44. Richard Critchfield, "Feeding the Hungry." *The New Republic,* 25 October 1969, p. 16.

45. B. R. Sen, *Towards a Newer World.* Dublin: Tycooly International, 1982, pp. 154–157.

46. Kennedy, "Statement at the Opening Ceremony of the World Food Congress," 4 June 1963. In *President John F. Kennedy's Office Files, 1961–63,* ed. William Leuchtenburg. Bethesda, Md.: University Publications of America, 1989 (microfilm), pt. 1, reel 11: 1018.

47. Chambers, "Beyond the Green Revolution," p. 365.

48. Walt W. Rostow, *Pre-invasion Bombing Strategy: General Eisenhower's Decision of March 25, 1944.* Austin: University of Texas Press, 1981, pp. 21–23.

49. Simon Kuznets, *Modern Economic Growth: Rate, Structure, and Spread.* New Haven, Conn.: Yale University Press, 1966, p. 2.

50. Albert O. Hirschman, *The Strategy of Economic Development.* New Haven, Conn.: Yale University Press, 1958, pp. 6, 24–28.

51. Zablocki hearings, p. 63.

52. Lester R. Brown, *Seeds of Change: The Green Revolution and Development in the 1970s.* New York: Praeger, 1970, p. 10.

53. Averell Harriman, U.S. chief negotiator in 1968 and 1969, believed North Vietnam would agree to a peace on U.S. terms in return for miracle rice. See Hedrick Smith, "Harriman Suggests a Way out of Vietnam." *New York Times Magazine,* 24 August 1969, pp. 24–25.

54. Dwarf wheats reversed decades of agricultural decline in Britain. Frank Engledow, who studied under Borlaug, won a knighthood for it, but not a Nobel Peace Prize. See John H. Perkins, *Geopolitics and Green Revolution.* Oxford: Oxford University Press, 1997, p. 191.

55. Al Gore, *Earth in the Balance.* London: Earthscan, 1992, pp. 138, 221, 321; and Charles Windsor, "A Royal View on Sustainable Development." *Reith Lecture* (April 2000), http://news.bbc.co.uk/hi/english/static/events/reith_2000/lecture6.stm (May 26, 2000).

56. Senate Subcommittee on Foreign Aid Expenditures, Population Crisis. 89th Cong., 2nd sess., 1966. Washington, D.C.: U.S. Government Printing Office, 1967, p. 301.

57. Wayne G. Broehl Jr., *Cargill: Going Global.* Hanover, N.H.: University Press of New England, 1998, p. 97.

58. Shivaji Ganguly, *U.S. Policy toward South Asia.* Boulder, Colo.: Westview, 1990, pp. 173–183.

59. White House Press Secretary, "Text of the Remarks of the President at Los Baños, the Philippines," 25 October 1966, Forrest F. Hill Papers, Box 14564, Ford Foundation Archives, New York.

60. Michael Ignatieff, *The Warrior's Honor: Ethnic War and the Modern Conscience.* New York: Henry Holt, 1997, p. 97.

# About the Contributors

**Mark Philip Bradley** is an associate professor of history at the University of Wisconsin, Milwaukee. He is the author of *Imagining Vietnam and American: The Making of Postcolonial Vietnam, 1919–1950* (2000) and is currently working on a history of the global human rights revolution of the twentieth century.

**Nick Cullather** is an associate professor of history at Indiana University. He is the author of *Illusions of Influence: The Political Economy of United States–Philippines Relations* (1994) and *Secret History: The CIA's Classified Account of Its Operations in Guatemala* (1999).

**Kai Dreisbach** is a consultant for political education and communication. He was previously attached to the Institute of Anglo-American History, University of Cologne, as a research fellow. He is a coeditor of *Celebrating Ethnicity and Nation: American Festive Culture from the Revolution to the Early Twentieth Century* (2001). His dissertation on American Foreign Policy and Regional Cooperation in Southeast Asia, 1977–2000 will be published in 2004.

**Jost Dülffer** is a professor at the University of Cologne, where he teaches international relations history, conflict resolution, and peace research. He has published widely in German, French, and English. Among his most recent publication is *Jalta, 4 Februar 1945: Der Zweite Weltkrieg und die Entstehung der bipolaren Welt* (Yalta, 4 February 1945: World War II and the Emergence of the Bipolar World) (1998). He is currently writing a history of Europe since 1945.

**Marc Frey** is an assistant professor at the Institute for Anglo-American History at the University of Cologne. He is the author of *Der Erste Weltkrieg und die Niederlande* (World War I and the Netherlands) (1998) and *Geschichte des Vietnamkriegs* (A History of the Vietnam War) (2002). He has also published articles on the role of the Netherlands in World War I, decolonization in Southeast Asia, and twentieth-century international history in journals and anthologies, among them *Vierteljahrshefte fuer Zeitgeschichte*, *International History Review*, and *Diplomatic History*.

**Karl Hack** is an associate professor at Singapore's Nanyang Technological University, where he teaches Asian and world history. He is the author of *Defence and Decolonisation: Britain, Malaya and Singapore, 1941–1968* (2001) and, with Kevin Blackburn, *Did Singapore Have to Fall? Churchill and the Impregnable Fortress* (2003). He has also published several articles on counterinsurgency and intelligence, and is currently working on war and memory, colonial armies, and Chin Peng, the Malayan Communist Party's long-serving secretary-general.

**Paul H. Kratoska** is an associate professor with the Department of History at the National University of Singapore and the publishing director for Singapore University Press. He does research on the Japanese occupation of Southeast Asia and on the history of nutrition and food supplies in Asia. He is the author of *The Japanese Occupation of Malaya* (1998), and editor of *Food Supplies and the Japanese Occupation in South-East Asia* (1998), *Southeast Asian Minorities in the Wartime Japanese Empire* (2002), and *Labor in the Wartime Japanese Empire* (forthcoming, 2004).

**Albert Lau** is an associate professor of Malayan and Singapore history at the National University of Singapore, where he has been teaching since 1986. He is the author of *The Malayan Union Controversy, 1942–1948* (1991) and *A Moment of Anguish: Singapore in Malaysia and the Politics of Disengagement* (1998).

**J. Thomas Lindblad** has been teaching economic history at the University of Leiden since 1975 and presently is a reader affiliated with the Departments of History and Southeast Asian Studies. His main research interest is the modern economic history of Indonesia. Recent publications include *Foreign Investment in Southeast Asia in the Twentieth Century* (1998) and the textbook *The Emergence of a National Economy: An Economic History of Indonesia, 1800–2000* (2002), written jointly with Howard Dick, Vincent Houben, and Thee Kian Wie.

**Bruce M. Lockhart** is an assistant professor of history at the National University of Singapore. He has published a study of Bảo Đại entitled *The End of the Vietnamese Monarchy* (1993). He has written several major articles on recent Lao and Vietnamese history, among them for the journal *Crossroads*.

**Robert J. McMahon** is a professor of history at the University of Florida, Gainesville. He is the author of *Colonialism and Cold War: The United States and the Struggle for Indonesian Independence, 1945–49* (1981), *Cold War on the Periphery: The United States, India and Pakistan* (1994), *Major Problems in the History of the Vietnam War* (1995), and *The Limits of Empire: The United States and Southeast Asia since World War II* (1999). He is a past president of the Society for the History of American Foreign Relations. His current research interests include the legacy of the Vietnam War in American politics and society.

**Ronald W. Pruessen** is head of the Department of History at the University of Toronto. Author of *John Foster Dulles: The Road to Power, 1888–1952* (1982), he has published widely on American foreign relations in the twentieth century. More recently, he has become interested in the historical roots of globalization and is currently writing the book *The Long Road: The United States and Globalization in the Twentieth Century.*

**Kumar Ramakrishna** is an assistant professor in the Institute of Defense and Strategic Studies, Nanyang Technological University, Singapore. His current research interests include British propaganda in the Malayan Emergency, propaganda theory and practice, history of strategic thought, and countering radical Islamic terrorism. His articles have been published in journals such as *Intelligence and National Security, Journal of Imperial and Commonwealth History, War in History, Journal of Southeast Asian Studies, Journal of the Malaysian Branch of the Royal Asiatic Society*, and *The Washington Quarterly*. He is the author of *Emergency Propaganda: The Winning of Malayan Hearts and Minds, 1948–1958* (2002).

**Tan Tai Yong** is head of the Department of History at the National University of Singapore. An expert on South Asian and Southeast Asian history, his more recent publications include *Beyond Degrees: The Making of the National University of Singapore* (1996) and *The Aftermath of Partition in South Asia* (2000). His current research interests include Southeast Asian maritime history as well as Indian history after 1947.

**Nicholas Tarling** was formerly a professor of history, dean of the faculty of arts, and deputy vice chancellor at the University of Auckland and is currently a fellow at the New Zealand Asia Institute at the same university. His more recent publications include *Britain, Southeast Asia and the Onset of the Pacific War* (1996), *Nations and States in Southeast Asia* (1998), *A Sudden Rampage: The Japanese Occupation of Southeast Asia, 1941–1945*

(2001), and *Imperialism in Southeast Asia: "A Fleeting, Passing Phase"* (2001). He is now working on *British Policy in Southeast Asia 1950–1955*.

**Hugues Tertrais** is a professor at the Centre d'histoire des relations internationales contemporaines (Institut Pierre Renouvin), Université de Paris I Panthéon-Sorbonne. He is the author of *La paistre et le fusil: Le coût de guerre d'Indochine, 1945–1954* (2002) and *Asie du Sud-Est: enjeu régional ou enjeu mondial?* (2002).

**Wang Gungwu** is the director of the East Asian Institute, faculty professor in the faculty of arts and social sciences at the National University of Singapore, and emeritus professor at the Australian National University, Canberra. He has taught at the University of Malaya (in Singapore and Kuala Lumpur) and was vice chancellor at the University of Hong Kong from 1986 to 1995. Among his recent books are *The Chinese Overseas: From Earthbound China to the Quest for Autonomy* (2000), *Don't Leave Home: Migration and the Chinese* (2001), *Bind Us in Time: Nation and Civilisation in Asia* (2002), and *Anglo-Chinese Encounters since 1800* (2003). He also edited *The Chinese Diaspora* (1998), with Wang Ling-chi, in two volumes, and *Reform, Legitimacy and Dilemmas: China's Politics and Society* (2000), with Zheng Yongnian.

# Index

Malaysia *(continued)*
  foreign investment in, 45–48, 49, 50, 51
  foreign labor in, 114
  formation of, xii, 118, 142–160, 251
  Grand Design concept, xii, 116,
    147–151, 155
  independence of, 115
  *See also* Malaya
Malays in Singapore, 158, 182–183,
  184–185, 190–191
Malay States, Federated (FMS), 108
Malik, Adam, 254
Malthus, Thomas, 259, 262, 263, 264
Mandate system, 5–6
Manila Treaty, 140, 246–247
Maphilindo, 250–251, 255
Marcos, Ferdinand, 254, 260, 261, 267
Marshall, David, 143–144, 192, 195–196
Marshall Plan, 100, 102, 231, 234, 243
"Massive retaliation" doctrine, 230
Melby, John, 224
Méline tariff, 8
Merdeka Amnesty, 177, 178
Metropolitan theory of decolonization,
  34, 84
Millikan, Max F., 263
Milner, Alfred, 6
Milner, Anthony C., 118
Min Yuen, 173
Monarchy, role in decolonization, x, 75
  in Cambodia, 58–59
  historical and cultural framework for,
    70–71
  in Laos, 59–62
  levels of success, 62–67
  in Vietnam, 54–57, 132
Monireth, Prince, 58
Monnet, Jean, 73
Mountbatten, Louis, 86, 87, 88, 128, 150,
  191
Moutet, Marius, 8
Munich syndrome, 218
Murray, Dalton, 139
Musso, 97–98
Mutual Security Act of 1955, 248
Myers, Ramon H., 26

Naicker, E.V. Ramasamy, 183
Nair, Devan, 153
Nasser, Gamal Abdel, 27, 120
Nationalism, viii–ix
  in Indochina, xi, 73, 74, 80
  in Indonesia, xi, 14, 33, 85
  in Singapore, xii, 180–196
  U.S. policy and, xiii, 241–242
National Salvation Movement, 186
National Security Council (NSC), 244
Nation-building, 114
Ne Win, 138
Nehru, Jawaharlal, 29, 133, 134, 183, 260
Neo Lao Itsala, 63
Netherlands. *See* Dutch colonialism;
    Dutch decolonization; Dutch foreign
    investment
Netherlands East Indies. *See* Indonesia;
    Indonesian revolution
New Zealand
  Malayan federation and, 150
  in regional cooperation initiatives,
    244–245, 246–247
Ngô Đình Diệm, 56, 57, 113
Nguyễn Phan Long, 56
Nguyễn Trung Vinh, 76
Nguyễn Văn Tâm, 56, 67
Nguyễn Văn Trinh, 74
Nguyễn Văn Xuân, 56, 62, 74
Nitze, Paul H., 214
North Atlantic Treaty Organization
    (NATO), 134, 136, 231, 243
North Borneo (Sabah)
  in Malayan federation, 116, 142, 143,
    144, 148, 149, 150, 157, 158
  Philippines claim to, 251
Nouhak Phoumsavane, 63, 69
Nye, A., 133
Nye, Joseph S., 241

Oil investment, in Indonesia, 40
Omar, Ariffin, 118
Ong Eng Die, 38
Ong Eng Guan, 156
Ong Yoke Lin, 165
Ord, Harry, 181